بسم الله الرحمن الرحيم

"The house of al-Arqam is the house of Islām"

Al-Ḥākim (d.403h.) in *al-Mustadrak 'ala al-Ṣaḥiḥayn* (6185)

Illuminating the Darkness

The Virtues of Blacks and Abyssinians

al-'Allāmah Abu 'l-Faraj Ibn al-Jawzī (d. 597/1200)

تنوير الغبش في فضل السودان والحبش

DAR AL-ARQAM

ISBN: 19164756 3 2

British Library Cataloguing in Publishing Data
A catalogue record for this book is available from the British Library

First edition, 2019

Prepared and published by Dar al-Arqam Publishing
Birmingham, United Kingdom

www.daralarqam.bigcartel.com
Email: daralarqam@hotmail.co.uk

Translated by Adnan Karim
Head of translation at Dar al-Arqam. He has translated and edited a number of works for Dar al-Arqam.

Edited by Ayman Khalid
He studied the Islamic sciences under scholars in his homeland of Jordan, and has translated and edited a number of works for Dar al-Arqam.

If you would like to support our work, donations can be made via:

- www.daralarqam.bigcartel.com/product/donate
- www.patreon.com/daralarqam
- www.paypal.me/daralarqam

Printed in Turkey by Mega | export@mega.com

ILLUMINATING THE DARKNESS

THE VIRTUES OF BLACKS AND ABYSSINIANS

Al-ʿAllāmah Abu 'l-Faraj Ibn al-Jawzī (d. 597/1200)

DAR AL-ARQAM

الفهرس

Contents

تقديم المترجم ١٣

Translator's Note 13

مقدمة المؤلف ١٩

Author's Introduction 19

فِي ذكر من تنْسب إِلَيْهِ السودَان ٢٣

In mention of the origin of black people 23

فِي سَبَب سَواد ألوانهم ٢٧

The cause of their darkness in colour 27

فِي ذكر إحْيَاء عِيسَى بن مَرْيَم عَلَيْهِ السَّلَام حام بن نوح ٢٩

In mention of ʿĪsā ibn Maryam bringing Ḥām ibn Nūḥ back to life 29

فِي ذكر ممالك السودَان من الأَرْض وسعتها ٣١

In mention of the kingdoms of black people and their vastness 31

فِي ذكر فَضَائِل اجْتمعت فِي طباع السودَان ٣٣

In mention of the virtues ingrained in black people 33

فَضَائِل أَشْيَاء خصت بسواد اللَّوْن من الْحَيَوَانَات والنبات والأحجار ٣٥

35 Virtues specific to things of black colour amongst animals, plants and stones

فِي بَيَان أَنه لَا فضل لأبيض على أسود باللون وَإِنَّمَا الْفضل بالتقوى ٤٩

49 In proclamation that the white person has no superiority over the black, and that superiority lies in piety

فِي ذكر من هَاجر من الصَّحَابَة إِلَى أَرض الْحَبَشَة وعددهم ٥٣

53 In mention of those from amongst the Companions who emigrated to Abyssinia and their number

فِي إنْفَاذ قُرَيْش إِلَى النَّجَاشِيّ ليسلم إِلَيْهِم أَصْحَاب رَسُول اللَّهِ - صَلَّى اللَّهُ عَلَيْهِ وَسَلَّم - ٥٩

59 The request of the Quraysh to al-Najāshī to hand over the Companions of the Prophet ﷺ to them

فِي ذكر مُكَاتبَة النَّبِي - صَلَّى اللَّهُ عَلَيْهِ وَسَلَّم - النَّجَاشِيّ [رَضِي اللَّهِ عَنهُ] يَدعُوهُ إِلَى الْإِسْلَام وإسلامه ٧١

71 In mention of that which the Prophet ﷺ wrote to al-Najāshī ؓ, inviting him to Islam, and of his conversion

فِي ذكر قدوم الْحَبَشَة على رَسُول اللَّهِ ولعبهم بالحراب فِي الْمَسْجِد وَرَسُول الله - صَلَّى اللَّهُ عَلَيْهِ وَسَلَّم - ينظر ٧٣

73 In mention of the coming of the Abyssinians to the Messenger of Allāh ﷺ and their war game in the *masjid* whilst the Prophet ﷺ watched

في ذكر مَا جَاءَ من الْقُرْآن مُوَافقا للغة الْحَبَشَة

٧٧ 77

In mention of words in the Qur'ān which conform with the Abyssinian language

في ذكر مَا سَمعه رَسُول اللَّهِ - صَلَّى اللَّهُ عَلَيْهِ وَسَلَّمَ - من كَلَام الْحَبَشَة فأعجبه

٨١ 81

In mention of what the Messenger of Allāh ﷺ heard of the Abyssinian language and how he was impressed

في ذكر تَخْصِيص الْحَبَشَة بِالْأَذَانِ

٨٣ 83

In mention of the Abyssinians being singled out for the call to the prayer

فِيمَن ذكر أَنه كَانَ نَبيا من السودَان

٨٥ 85

Those of whom it has been said that they were Prophets from amongst black people

في ذكر كبار مُلُوك الْحَبَشَة

١٠٩ 109

In mention of the major kings of the Ḥabash

في ذكر أَشْرَاف السودَان من الصَّحَابَة

١٢٩ 129

In mention of the esteemed blacks amongst the Companions

في ذكر أَشْرَاف السوداوات من الصحابيات

١٥٩ 159

In mention of the noble black women from the female Companions

في ذكر المبرزين في الْعلم من السودَان

١٦٥ 165

In mention of the illustrious scholars from amongst the black people

١٧٩ في ذكر شعرائهم وَمن تمثل مِنْهُم بِشعر 179
In mention of their poets and those amongst them who recited some poetry to express a meaning

٢٠٣ فِي ذكر طَائِفَة من فطناء السودَان والسوداوات وأذكيائهم وكرمائهم 203
In mention of a group of discerning, intelligent and generous black men and women

٢١٧ فِي ذكر المتعبدين مِنْهُم والزهاد 217
In mention of the worshippers and ascetics amongst the black people

٢٥٩ فِي ذكر المتعبدات من السوداوات فَمن المعروفات الْأَسْمَاء 259
In mention of the worshippers from amongst the women of the black people

٢٧٣ فِي ذكر من كَانَ يُؤثر الْجَوَارِي السود على الْبيض وَمن كَانَ يعشقهن وَمن مَاتَ من عشقهن 273
In mention of those who preferred black bondmaidens to white ones, those who loved them, and those who died due to their love

٢٩٣ فِي ذكر أَبنَاء الحبشيات من قُرَيْش 293
In mention of the sons of Ḥabashī women from Quraysh

٢٩٧ فِي مواعظ ووصايا 297
In exhortation and counsel

٣٠٣ فِيهِ أذكار وتسبيحات 303
Words of remembrance and glorification of Allāh

فِي الْأَدْعِيَة

Supplications

تقديم المترجم

Translator's Note

إِنَّ الْحَمْدَ لِلَّهِ نَحْمَدُهُ وَنَسْتَعِينُهُ ونستغفره ونعوذ بالله من شرور أنفسنا ومن سيئات أعمالنا مَنْ يَهْدِهِ اللَّهُ فَلَا مُضِلَّ لَهُ وَمَنْ يُضْلِلْ فَلَا هَادِيَ لَهُ وَأَشْهَدُ أَنْ لَا إِلَهَ إِلَّا اللَّهُ وَحْدَهُ لَا شَرِيكَ لَهُ وَأَنَّ مُحَمَّدًا عَبْدُهُ وَرَسُولُهُ. أَمَّا بَعْدُ:

Before you is a classical work from the twelfth century which sets out to display the equality of races within Islam. The aim of translating and publishing this book is to display the falsity of certain claims against Islam which have resurfaced recently, and which have been amplified due to social media.

About the author Ibn al-Jawzī [extracts from *Siyar Aʿlām al-Nubalā*[1] by al-Dhahabī]:

He is the *shaykh*, the *imām*, the *ʿallāmah*, the *ḥāfiẓ*, the *mufassir*, *shaykh al-Islām*, the pride of Baghdād: Jamāl al-Dīn Abu al-Faraj ʿAbd al-Rahman ibn ʿAlī ibn Muḥammad ibn ʿAlī ibn ʿUbaydullāh ibn ʿAbdullāh ibn Ḥammādī ibn Aḥmad ibn Muḥammad ibn Jaʿfar ibn ʿAbdullāh ibn al-Qāsim ibn al-Naḍr ibn al-Qāsim ibn Muḥammad ibn ʿAbdullāh ibn al-Faqīh ʿAbd al-Raḥman ibn al-Faqīh al-Qāsim ibn Muḥammad ibn Khalifat Rasūlullāh ﷺ Abī Bakr al-Siḍḍīq, al-Qurashī, al-Taymī, al-Bakrī, al-Baghdādī, al-Ḥanbalī, the illustrious preacher and prolific author.

He was born during the year 510 or 509 [Hijri] (corresponding to 1116 or 1115), and he first took knowledge during the year 516.

He learned the knowledge of ḥadīth mainly from Ibn Nāṣir, the knowledge of Qurʾān and literature from the son of al-Khayyāṭ and Ibn al-Jawālīqī, and the knowledge of *fiqh* from many scholars.

---

1 Volume 21, pp. 365-384.

He was the master of preaching and had the throne in exhortations; he would utter eloquent words and astonishing prose naturally, he would elaborate and flabbergast the minds. There was no one like him that preceded him in such skills nor will there be one comparable after him. He was the carrier of the flag of exhortation, the master of its sciences, and he had a pleasant look, good voice with a strong influence upon people. His character was good amongst the people, and he was an ocean in *tafsīr*, a scholar in *siyar* and history. He was known for his knowledge in ḥadīth and its sciences, and as a *faqīh* with excellent knowledge in matters of consensus and difference of opinion. He made good contributions in the field of medicine, and he was highly intellectual, with an excellent memory and propensity for prompt recallment.

His father died when he was three years old and his paternal aunt raised him. His relatives were in the business of copper; thus, it could be possible that he was referred to as 'Abd al-Raḥmān ibn 'Alī al-Ṣaffār (i.e. in reference to the colour of copper). After he grew up, his aunt sent him to Ibn Nāṣir from whom he heard ḥadīth. When he was a teenager, he admired preaching, so he delivered sermons whilst he was still a young boy and he became highly esteemed and an example for others preachers to follow until he became famous.

He authored many books in different fields, such as *al-Mughnī* in *tafsīr*, which he later abridged into four volumes and titled *Zād al-Masīr*; he also authored *Tadhkirat al-Arīb*, *al-Wujūh wa al-Naẓā'ir*, *Funūn al-Afnān*, *Jāmi' al-Masānīd*, *al-Ḥadā'iq*, and many others.

He was famous and well known; renowned scholars, kings, rulers, and some of the Caliphs would attend his lectures, and people would come in their thousands to hear them.

His grandson, Abu al-Muẓaffar said, "I heard my grandfather say on the *minbar*, 'I wrote with my hands two thousand books, and one hundred thousand people repented upon my hands, and twenty thousand embraced Islam upon them.' He would complete the Qur'ān once each week."

He also said, "He was ascetic in his life; sufficing with the bare minimum;

and it was said about him that he never made a joke with anyone or played with a young boy, or ate from a source that he was not certain of it being lawful."

Abu ʿAbdullāh ibn al-Dubaythī said in his *Tārīkh*, "Our *shaykh* Jamāl al-Dīn authored many works within the branches of the Islamic sciences, such as *tafsīr*, *fiqh*, *ḥadīth*, history and other than them. He had prowess in the knowledge of *ḥadīth* and its sciences, differentiating the authentic from the weak. He was the best of people in speech and eloquence. He learned *fiqh* from al-Dīnawarī and preaching from Abī Qāsim al-ʿAlawī. He was blessed in his life and knowledge."

Al-Muwaffaq ʿAbd al-Laṭīf said, "Ibn al-Jawzī was handsome, pleasant-natured, with a melodious voice and he was good company. A hundred thousand would attend his assemblies, and [sometimes] more than that. He would not waste anything from his time, writing four booklets a day. He had a share in every branch of knowledge, however in *tafsīr* he was from the most remarkable, in *ḥadīth* he was a *ḥāfiẓ*, and his grasp of history was vast. He was competent in *fiqh*, and he had an amazing gift for preaching. In medicine he had a book named *al-Luqaṭ*."

He also said, "He had a lot of mistakes within his works, for he would finish his books and not review them (as he authored a vast number of works)." Al-Dhahabī commented upon this, "This is the case, and his mistakes are due to leaving off revision and taking from manuscripts [with errors in them,] for he authored such an amount that doing such revision would have required more than a second life."

He fell ill for five days and subsequently passed away. This occurred between the two night prayers (i.e. *maghrib* and *ʿishā*) on the thirteenth of Ramadan during the year 597 (1200), which was a Friday night. [End]

This book falls under the *faḍāʾil* (virtues) genre of literature, wherein the author provides narrations he possesses regarding the virtues of a certain subject. It is important to note that not everything in the book is authentic, neither is it the case that the author necessarily views everything to be authentic, and we may not agree with everything herein. However, we have translated his work as it is, and the author has provided the chain of transmission for every narration (through which their authenticity can be ascertained).

Note: The book has been translated completely unabridged except for one poem on page 285, which was difficult to render into English. The remainder of the narration wherein it is cited has been translated, and the Arabic text of the poem has been retained. The footnotes are mainly based upon the edition of the Arabic text edited by Marzūq 'Alī Ibrāhīm. Any additions to the footnotes by the translator have been marked with [T], and additions of the editor have been marked with [E].

بِسْمِ اللَّهِ الرَّحْمَٰنِ الرَّحِيمِ

In the name of Allāh, the Most Merciful, the Most Beneficient, my Lord, I seek your assistance.

قَالَ الشَّيْخ الإِمَام الْعَالم الْحَافِظ جمال الدّين أَبُو الْفرج عبد الرَّحْمَن بن عَليّ بن مُحَمَّد بن الْجَوْزِيّ رَحمَه اللَّهِ:

The *shaykh*, the *imām*, the *ʿālim*, the *ḥafīẓ*, Jamāl al-Dīn Abū al-Faraj ʿAbd al-Raḥmān ibn ʿAlī ibn Muḥammad al-Jawzī ﷺ said:

الْحَمد لله الَّذِي اخْتَار من جَمِيع الْمَخْلُوقَات الْإِنْسَان، ثمَّ اصْطفى مِنْهُ أهل التقى وَالْإِيمَان، ثمَّ جعل مَحل نظره الْقُلُوب لَا الْأَبدَان؛ هُوَ ينظر إِلَى صفاء الْأَسْرَار، لَا إِلَى نقاء الألوان، فاوت بَين الْآدَمِيّين، فَمنهمْ ملك وَمِنْهُم شَيْطَان، يخرج الْحَيّ من الْمَيِّت؛ فالخليل من آزر ذِي الكفران، وَيخرج الْمَيِّت من الْحَيّ؛ فَمن نوح: كنعان، جرى قدره، فَكفر أَبُو طَالب وَأسلم عُثْمَان، وضل أَبُو لَهب، وَأذن لِبلَال فِي الْأَذَان، يفني ويبقي، ويسعد ويشقي، كل يَوْم هُوَ فِي شان.

Praise be to Allāh Who has favoured man over the rest of creation, and among them He has favoured the people of piety and faith. He then made the heart the point of His concern and not the physical figure. He looks to the serenity of the inner (i.e. sincerity), and not to the purity of one's colour. He brought about differences amongst the human race; amongst them are those who are like angels and those who are like devils. He brings forth the living from the dead, and thus [Ibrāhīm,] al-Khalīl emerged from Āzar, the disbeliever. Likewise, He brings forth the dead from the living, thus Kanʿān emerged from Nūḥ. In accordance with the decree of Allāh, Abū Ṭālib disbelieved and ʿUthmān accepted Islam, and Abū Lahab went astray and Bilāl was the one authorised to perform the call to prayer. He causes some to perish and others to remain. He makes some to be content and others wretched. Every day He has a matter to bring forth.

أَحْمَده - إِذْ أنعم وصان - عدد الأوراق والأغصان، وَأقر بوحدانيته إِقْرَارا يصدر عَن برهَان، وأصلي على رَسُوله مُحَمَّد أشرف مَخْلُوق وجد وَكَانَ، وعَلى صَاحبه أبي بكر الصّديق الَّذِي انْفَرد بنصره فِي الْغَار وأعانه، وعَلى عمر الْفَارُوق المتشدد فِي الدّين فمالان، وعَلى التقي النقي عُثْمَان بن عَفَّان، وعَلى عَليّ بن أبي طَالب مقدم الْعلمَاء وَسيد الشجعان، وعَلى عَمه الْعَبَّاس بن عبد الْمطلب الْمُسْتَسْقى بشيبته، فَأقبل السح الهتان، جد سيدنَا ومولان الإِمَام المستضيء بِأَمْر اللَّهِ أَمِير الْمُؤمنِينَ الَّذِي أشرق بولايته الزَّمَان، سقِي زرع الْعدْل مياه الْفضل، فالدنيا فِي أَيَّامه بُسْتَان، فَذكره فِي مسام مشام الصَّالِحين أزكي من ريح وَرَيْحَان، وَقُلُوبهمْ معتلقة بحبه وَحب الْخلق لحب الْخَالِق عنوان، قرن اللَّهِ نعْمَة دُنْيَاهُ بِنِعْمَة أخراه، وَإِن الدَّار الْآخِرَة لهي الْحَيَوَان، واستجاب فِي أَيَّامه دُعَاء كل دَاع ذاق فِيهَا طعم الْإِحْسَان.

I praise Him frequently like the leaves and twigs, for He protects and safeguards us. I affirm His oneness, and this is an affirmation emanating from clear proof. I send *ṣalāh* upon His messenger Muḥammad, the most noble of creation to be found or exist, and upon his companion Abī Bakr al-Ṣiddīq who alone supported him in the cave and aided him. I also send it upon 'Umar al-Fārūq who was firm in the religion and did not compromise in it, and upon 'Uthmān ibn 'Affān, the pious and the pure. I send it upon 'Alī ibn Abī Ṭālib, the foremost of the scholars and the leader of the brave, and upon his uncle al-'Abbās ibn 'Abd al-Muṭṭalib, who was used as a means to Allāh for rain, and upon this intercession rain started to fall heavily, the grandfather of our Caliph, al-Mustaḍi' Bi Amrillah–the Commander of the Faithful whose rulership enlightened the time and drank from the fountain of justice and virtue; life under his authority was a garden and the scent of his name among the pious smells better than basil and aroma; their hearts attached to him, and such love is a sign of Allāh's love to him; Allāh linked the pleasures of this life to the pleasures of his hereafter, but the hereafter is truly the real life; during his time, the prayers of the people were answered and they tasted from the plate of his kindness.

أما بعد ... فَإِنِّي رَأَيْت جمَاعَة من أخيار الحبشان تنكسر قُلُوبهم لأجل اسوداد الألوان، فأعلمتهم أَن الِاعْتِبَار بِالْإِحْسَانِ لَا بالصور الحسان، وَوضعت لَهُم هَذَا الْكتاب فِي ذكر فضل خلق كثير من الْحَبَش والسودان، وَقد قسمته ثَمَانِيَة وَعشْرين بَابا، وَالله الْمُسْتَعَان.

To proceed: I bore witness to a group of eminent Ḥabash (Abyssinian) who were disheartened due to the darkness of their skin colour. I thus clarified to them that the matter upon which consideration is placed is good deeds rather than one's appearance, and I wrote this book for them to mention the virtue of many from amongst the Abyssinian and black people. I have divided it into twenty-eight chapters, and with Allāh aid is sought.

الْبَاب الأول

Chapter One[2]

فِي ذكر من تنْسب إِلَيْهِ السودَان

In mention of the origin of black people

[١] أخبرنَا أَبُو الْفَتْح مُحَمَّد بن عبد الْبَاقِي قَالَ: أَنا جَعْفَر بن أَحْمد السراج قَالَ: أَنا أَبُو الْقَاسِم عبد الْعَزِيز بن عَليّ الطَّحَّان قَالَ: ثَنَا عمر بن مُحَمَّد أَبُو الْقَاسِم الْقَاضِي قَالَ: ثَنَا عبد اللَّهِ بن مُحَمَّد الْبَغَوِيّ قَالَ: ثَنَا حَاجِب بن الْوَلِيد قَالَ ثَنَا مُحَمَّد بن سَلمَة عَن الزُّهْرِيّ عَن سعيد بن الْمسيب عَن أبي هُرَيْرَة أَن النَّبِي - صَلَّى اللَّهُ عَلَيْهِ وَسَلَّمَ - قَالَ: ((ولد لنوح [عَلَيْهِ السَّلَام] سَام وَحَام وَيَافث، فَأَما سَام فَأَبُو الْعَرَب وَفَارِس وَالروم، وَأما يافث فَأَبُو يَأْجُوج وَمَأْجُوج والخزر، وَأما حام فَأَبُو هَذِه الْجلْدَة السَّوْدَاء.))

Saʿīd ibn al-Musayyib reported on the authority of Abū Hurayrah that the Prophet ﷺ said, "Nūḥ bore three sons: Sām, Ḥām and Yāfith. As for Sām, he is the father of the Arabs, the Persians and the Byzantines. As for Yāfith, he is the father of Yājūj and Mājūj. As for Ḥām, he is the father of the black-skinned people."[3]

---

2 [T] There is a section before this wherein the author lists the chapters of the book. This has been omitted as they are listed in the contents page.

3 A similar report was reported by al-Bazzār in his *Musnad*, Ibn Abī Ḥātim and Ibn Mardawīh in *al-Tafsīr*, and al-Khaṭīb al-Baghdādī in *Thanī al-Talkhīṣ*. It was also mentioned by al-Suyūṭī in *al-Azhār al-ʿUrūsh*. [T] Ibn Ḥajar stated in *Fatḥ al-Bārī* that it was reported by Ibn Abī Ḥātim on the authority of Abu Hurayrah as *marfū*, however there is weakness in its *isnād* (16/222).

[٢] وروى الْحسن الْبَصْرِيّ عَن سَمُرَة عَن النَّبِي - صَلَّى اللَّهُ عَلَيْهِ وَسَلَّمَ - أَنه قَالَ، ((ولد نوح ساما وحاما وَيَافث، فسام أَبُو الْعَرَب، وَحَام أَبُو الزنج، وَيَافث أَبُو الرّوم)).

Al-Ḥasan al-Baṣrī reported upon the authority of Samrah that the Prophet ﷺ said, "The sons of Nūḥ were Sām, Ḥām and Yāfith. Sam is the father of the Arabs, Ḥām is the father of the Zanj and Yāfith is the father of the Byzantines."[4]

وَقَالَ وهب بن مُنَبّه: سَام أَبُو الْعَرَب وَفَارِس وَالروم، وَحَام أَبُو السود، وَيَافث أَبُو التّرْك وَأَبُو يَأْجُوج وَمَأْجُوج، وهم بَنو عَم التّرْك.

Wahb ibn Munabbih said, "Sām is the father of the Arabs, the Persians, and Byzantines. Ḥām is the father of black people, Yāfith is the father of the Turks and the father of Gog and Magog—who are related to the Turks.

قَالَ الْمُصَنّف [رَحمَه اللَّهِ] : ولد لحام كوش ونيرس وموعع وبوان، وَولد لكوش نمْرُود، وَهُوَ أول النماردة، ملك بعد الطوفان بثلاثمائة عَام، وعَلى عَهده قسمت الأَرْض فتفرق النَّاس، وَاخْتلفت الألسنة، ونمرود إِبْرَاهِيم من أَوْلَاده، وَمن ولد نيرس التّرْك والخزر، وَمن ولد موعع يَأْجُوج وَمَأْجُوج، وَمن ولد بوان الصقالبة والنوبة والحبشة والهند والسند. وَلما اقتسم أَوْلَاد نوح الأَرْض نزل بَنو حام مجْرى الْجنُوب وَالدبور فَجعل اللَّهِ [تَعَالَى] فيهم أدمة وبياضا قَلِيلا، وَلَهُم أَكثر الأَرْض.

The author ﷺ said: The sons of Ḥām are: Kūsh, Nīras, Maw'agh and Buwān. Kūsh bore a son named Namrūd—the first of the Namāridah [kings], who ruled three hundred years after the flood. It was during his time that the earth was divided up, and so subsequently the people began to separate

4 This was mentioned by al-Suyūṭī in *Azhār al-'Urūsh* (3/a) and he stated after it, "It was reported by al-Tirmidhī—who graded it as *ḥasan*, and Ibn Jarīr, Ibn al-Mundhir, Ibn Abī Ḥātim and Ibn Mardawīh in their *tafsīrs*, and al-Ḥākim in *al-Mustadrak*—who graded it as *ṣaḥīḥ*."

and form into different tribes. The Namrūd whom encountered Ibrāhīm was from amongst his sons. Those whom descended from Nīras were the Turks and the Khazr. Those whom descended from Maw'agh were Gog and Magog. Those whom descended from Buwān were al-Ṣaqālibah, the Nubians, the Abyssinians, the people of Hind and Sind. And when the earth had been divided by the descendants of Nūḥ, Ḥām's children settled in the direction of the south and westerly winds, thus Allāh put into their complexion darkness and a little whiteness, and they occupied the majority of the earth.

الْبَاب الثَّانِي

Chapter Two

فِي سَبَب سَواد أَلوانهم

The cause of their darkness in colour

قَالَ المُصَنّف [رَحمَه الله] : الظَّاهِر فِي الألوان أَنَّهَا خلقت على مَا هِيَ عَلَيْهِ بِلَا سَبَب ظَاهر، إِلَّا أَنا قد روينَا أَن أَوْلَاد نوح عَلَيْهِ السَّلَام اقتسموا الأَرْض بعد موت نوح، وَكَانَ الَّذِي قسم بَينهم الأَرْض قالغ بن عَابِر، فَنزل بَنو سَام سرة الأَرْض وَكَانَ فيهم الأدمة وَالْبَيَاض، وَنزل بَنو يافث مجْرى الشمَال وَالصبَا، فَكَانَت فيهم الْحمرَة والشقرة، وَنزل بَنو حام مجْرى الْجنُوب وَالدبور فتغيرت أَلوانهم.

The author said: The apparent, in terms of their skin colour is that there is no obvious cause for it being so, except that which we have reported in regards to the descendants of Nuḥ ﷺ dividing [and spreading] amongst the earth after his death. The person who divided the earth amongst them was Qālagh ibn ʿĀbir. The descendants of Sām settled in the centre of the earth, and so they possessed darkness and whiteness. The descendants of Yāfith settled in the direction of the north and the easterly winds, and so they possessed redness and fairness. The descendants of Ḥām settled in the direction of the south and westerly winds and so there was an alteration in their colour.

فَأَما مَا يرْوى أَن نوحًا انكشفت عَوْرَته فَلم يغطها فاسود، فشيء لَا يثبت وَلَا يَصح.

As for that which has been narrated in relation to Nūḥ that his *ʿawrah* (private parts) showed and he did not cover it and so he became black, this is something not established and evidently not *ṣaḥīḥ* (authentic).

الْبَاب الثَّالِث

Chapter Three

فِي ذكر إحْيَاء عِيسَى بن مَرْيَم عَلَيْهِ السَّلَام حام بن نوح

In mention of ʿĪsā ibn Maryam bringing Ḥām ibn Nūḥ back to life

[٣] أنبأنَا مُحَمَّد بن عبد الْبَاقِي بن أَحْمد قَالَ أنبأنَا جَعْفَر بن أَحْمد السراج قَالَ أنا أَبُو مُحَمَّد الْحُسَيْن بن مُحَمَّد الْخلال قَالَ نَا يُوسُف بن عمر الزَّاهِد قَالَ قرئ على عبد اللَّهِ بن مُحَمَّد بن زِيَاد النَّيْسَابُورِي وَأَنا أسمع قيل لَهُ: أخْبركُم يُونُس بن عبد الْأَعْلَى قَالَ أنا ابْن وهب قَالَ أَخْبرنِي ابْن لَهِيعَة عَن ابْن الْهَاد عَن ابْن شهَاب قَالَ:

قيل لعيسى بن مَرْيَم [عَلَيْهِ السَّلَام] أَحَي حام بن نوح، فَقَالَ: أروني قَبره. فأروه، فَقَامَ فَقَالَ: يَا حام بن نوح، احي بِإِذن اللَّهِ [عز وَجل]، فَلم يخرج، ثمَّ قَالَهَا الثَّانِيَة، [فَخرج] فَإِذا شقّ رَأسه ولحيته أَبيض، قَالَ: مَا هَذَا [الْبيَاض]؟ قَالَ: سَمِعت الدُّعَاء [الأول] فَظَنَنْت أَنه من اللَّهِ عز وَجل [لِلْحسابِ] فشاب لَهُ شقي، ثمَّ سَمِعت [الدُّعَاء] الثَّانِي فَعلمت أَنه من الدُّنْيَا، فَخرجت، قَالَ: مُنْذُ كم [مت]. قَالَ: مُنْذُ أَرْبَعَة آلَاف سنة مَا ذهبت عني سكرة الْمَوْت.

Ibn Shihāb reported that it was requested from ʿĪsā ibn Maryam ﷺ that he bring Ḥām ibn Nūḥ back to life. ʿĪsā replied, "Show me his grave," and so they showed him. He stated, "O Ḥām ibn Nūḥ, come back to life by the permission of Allāh ﷻ," however he did not come out. He stated this again and Ḥām came forth, and his hair and beard were white. ʿĪsā asked, "What is this whiteness?" He replied, "I heard the first call and thought that it was [the call] from Allāh ﷻ for the reckoning, and so my hair turned white from fright. Then I heard the second call and knew that it was from the *dunyā* (worldly existence), and so I exited." He asked, "How long since you [tasted] death?" He replied, "For four thousand years the agony of death has not left me."[5]

قَالَ المُصَنِّف: هَكَذَا فِي هَذَا الرِّوَايَة، وَقد رُوِيَ لنا من طَرِيق آخر عَن مُعَاوِيَة بن قُرَّة أن الَّذِي أَحْيَاهُ عِيسَى بن مَرْيَم: سَام بن نوح [عَلَيْهِ السَّلَام] وَالله أعلم.

The author stated: This is how it is narrated in this report, however it has also been reported to us through a different route on the authority of Mu'āwiyah ibn Qurrah that the one whom 'Īsā brought back to life was Sām ibn Nūḥ. And Allāh knows best.

---

5 Reported by Ibn Abī al-Dunyā in *Man 'Āsha ba'da al-Mawt* (75-76), and it was mentioned by al-Suyūṭī in *al-Durr al-Manthūr* (2/216). The narrator in its *isnād* (chain of narration) named Ibn Lahiyah is considered to be *ḍa'īf* (weak).

الْبَاب الرَّابِع
Chapter Four

فِي ذِكْرِ ممالك السُّودَان من الأَرْضِ وسعتها
In mention of the kingdoms of black people and their vastness

[٤] أخبرنَا عبد الرَّحْمَن بن مُحَمَّد القَزاز قَالَ ثَنَا أَبُو بكر أَحْمد بن عَلِيّ [بن ثَابت] الْخَطِيب قَالَ أنا أَحْمد بن عبد اللَّهِ الْأَصْبَهَانِيّ قَالَ نا أَبِي قَالَ ثَنَا مُحَمَّد بن أَحْمد بن يزِيد قَالَ ثَنَا أَبُو صَالح يحيى بن وَاقد قَالَ ثَنَا الْأَصْمَعِي عَن النمر بن هِلَال قَالَ: الأَرْض أَرْبَعَة وَعِشْرُونَ أَلْف فَرسَخ فاثنا عشر ألفا للسودان وَثَمَانِية [آلَاف] وَثَلَاثَة [آلَاف] للرُّوم وَألف [فَرسَخ] للْعَرَب.

Al-Aṣmaʿī reported upon the authority of al-Namr ibn Hilāl that he said, "The earth consists of twenty-four thousand *farsakhs*. From these, twelve thousand belong to the blacks, eight thousand to the Romans, three thousand to the Persians, and one thousand to the Arabs."

قَالَ أَبُو الْحُسَيْن أَحْمد بن جَعْفَر الْمُنَادِي: بلغنَا أَن الْبَحْر الْمَعْرُوف بنطس من وَرَاء قسطنطينية يَجِيء من بَحر الخزر وَعرض فوهته سِتَّة أَمْيَال، وإقليم الدُّنْيَا الأول يَبْتَدِئ من الْمشرق من أقاصي بِلَاد الصين فيمر على بِلَاد الصين مِمَّا يَلِي الْجنُوب، وَفِيه مَدِينَة ملك الصين ثمَّ يمر فِي جنوب بِلَاد الْهِنْد ثمَّ بِلَاد السَّنْد ثمَّ يقطع الْبَحْر إِلَى جَزِيرَة الْعَرَب فِي أَرض الْيمن فَيكون فِيهِ من الْمَدَائِن المعروفات مَدِينَة أظفار، وعمان، وحضرموت، وعدن، وَصَنْعَاء، وتبالة، وجرش. ثمَّ يقطع الأقاليم بَحر القلزم فيمر فِي بِلَاد الْحَبَشَة وَيقطع نيل مصر، وَفِيه مَدِينَة مملكة

الْحَبَشَة، وَتسَمى جرمى، ودنقلة مَدِينَة النّوبَة، ثمَّ يمر الإقليم فِي أَرض الْمغرب على جنوب بِلَاد البربر إِلَى أَن يَنْتَهِي إِلَى بَحر الْمغرب.

Abū al-Ḥusayn Aḥmad ibn Jaʿfar al-Munādī said, "It reached us that the sea known as Bunṭas behind Constantinople flows from the Caspian Sea and that the width of its mouth is six miles. The first province of the world commences from the East, stretching from the remotest parts of China to its southern border wherein the city of its emperor is located. Then it passes through the South of Hind and the land of al-Sind, then it goes through the Arabian Peninsula and the land of Yemen wherein there are the famous cities such Aẓfār, 'Omān, Ḥaḍramawt, 'Aden, Ṣanʿā', Tabāla, and Jurash. Then the province passes over the Red Sea and extends into Abyssinia and it passes through the Nile of Egypt. Within it is the city of the Abyssinian king named Jarmā, and also the Nubian city of Danqalah. Then the province traverses the Maghrib to the south of the land of the Berbers, and it ends at the Western Sea."

[٥] أنبأَنَا عَليّ بن عبيد اللَّهِ عَن أبي الْحُسَيْن بن الْمُهْتَدي عَن أبي حَفْص بن سناهر قَالَ ثَنَا نصر بن الْقَاسِم قَالَ ثَنَا أَحْمد بن عمر ثَنَا أَبُو مُعَاوِيَة قَالَ ثَنَا الْأَعْمَش عَن مُجَاهِد قَالَ: ربع من لَا يلبس الثِّيَاب من السودَان مثل جَمِيع النَّاس.

Al-Aʿmash reported upon the authority of Mujāhid that he said, "A quarter of those who do not wear clothing from amongst the blacks are like the rest of the people (i.e. in number)."

الْبَاب الْخَامِس
Chapter Five

فِي ذكر فَضَائِل اجْتمعت فِي طباع السودَان
In mention of the virtues ingrained in black people

مِنْهَا: قُوَّة الْبدن، وَقُوَّة الْقلب، وَذَلِكَ يُثمر الشجَاعَة، وَيذكر الْحَبَشَة بِالْكَرمِ الوافر، وَحسن الْخلق، وَقلة الْأَذَى، وَضحك السن، وَطيب الأفواه، وسهولة الْعبارَة، وعذوبة الْكَلَام.

From them: Strength in body and heart—of which bravery bears fruit. There is mention of the Abyssinians' abundant generosity, good manners, rareness in offense, baring of teeth in smiles, excellent eloquence, ease in expression, and charm in speech.

[٦] أنبأَنَا مُحَمَّد بن عبد الْملك بن خيرون قَالَ أنبأَنَا أَحْمد ابْن عَليّ بن ثَابت قَالَ أَنبأَنَا أَبُو عَليّ الجاذري قَالَ ثَنَا الْمعَافى بن زَكَرِيَّا قَالَ ثَنَا الْحُسَيْن بن الْقَاسِم الكوكبي قَالَ ثَنَا أَبُو الْفضل الربعِي قَالَ قَالَ إِسْحَاق بن إِبْرَاهِيم الْموصِلِي قَالَ شبيب بن شيبَة: دخل خَالِد بن صَفْوَان على أبي الْعَبَّاس السفاح فَقَالَ: يَا أَمِير الْمُؤمنِينَ، قد حرمت نَفسك استظراف الْجَوَارِي، إِن مِنْهُنَّ، السمراء اللعساء، والصفراء العجزاء، ومولدات الْمَدِينَة والطائف واليمامة ذَوَات الألسن والعذبة، وَالْجَوَاب الْحَاضِر.

Isḥāq ibn Ibrāhīm ibn Mūṣilī said that Shabīb ibn Shaybah stated that Khālid ibn Ṣafwān entered upon Abī al-ʿAbbās al-Saffāḥ and said, "O Commander of the Faithful, you have prohibited yourself from finding pleasure in female slaves. Some are dark-lipped and dark-skinned and some are yellow with large buttocks, and those born in Madīnah, Ṭā'if and Yamāmah are sweet talkers and quick witted.

الْبَاب السَّادِس

Chapter Six

فَضَائِل أَشْيَاء خصت بسواد اللَّوْن من الْحَيَوَانَات والنبات والأحجار

Virtues specific to things of black colour amongst animals, plants and stones

فصل

Section

فَمن الْحَيَوَانَات:

From animals:

سَواد الْعين: وَقد ركبت الْعين [من] عشرَة أَجزَاء، وَهِي سبع طَبَقَات وَثَلَاث رطوبات، والطبقات كقشور البصل، وَمَوْضِع النّظر مِنْهَا الْأسود، وَهَذَا يدل على شرف هَذَا اللَّوْن حِين اختير لهَذَا الْعُضْو الشريف، وَقد جعلت أهداب أشغار الجفن سُودًا لِتجمع الضَّوْء.

Blackness of the eyes: The eye is constructed of ten parts of which there are seven layers and three are wet, and its layers are reminiscent of the peeling of an onion. From them the place of the vision is black (i.e. the pupil), which displays the prestige of the colour as it has been selected for this prestigious organ. Furthermore, the eyelashes were made black so as to absorb light.

وَمن ذَلِك الكبد: وَهِي الَّتِي تطبخ الطَّعَام وتوجهه إِلَى الْبدن بوساطة الْعرق الأجوف النَّابِت من محدودبها، ثمَّ توجه المائية إِلَى الكليتين، والرغوة الصفراوية

إِلَى المرارة والرسوب السوداوي إِلَى الطحال، وللكبد عروق تحذف الْغذَاء لَهَا وَيُسمى الْبَاب، وعرق يحمل الْغذَاء مِنْهَا إِلَى الْأَعْضَاء وَيُسمى الأجوف، والكبد هِيَ الَّتِي تُعْطِي الْأَعْضَاء غذاءها الَّذِي بِهِ سقِي، وَمَعَ هَذَا الشّرف هِيَ سَوْدَاء وَهَذَا يدل على شرف السوَاد حِين اختير لهَذَا الْعُضْو الْكَرِيم.

From these things is the liver: Which metabolises food and directs it to the body through the hollow vein which grows in a crooked manner. It directs the liquid to the kidneys and the foam of bile to the gallbladder, and the black deposit is directed to the spleen. The liver has a vein within which food enters that is named as *al-bāb* (the door) and another vein which carries food from it to the other organs that is named as *al-ajwaf* (the hollow). The liver provides the organs with the substance with which their health is sustained and they are quenched. Bearing in mind this prestige, it is black, and this displays the noble nature of this colour, for it was selected as the colour for this prestigious organ.

وَمن ذَلِك الْقلب: وَهُوَ أشرف مَا فِي الْبدن وسويداوه، فِي وسطة كالعلقة تتنزل منزلَة الدِّمَاغ من الرَّأْس.

From them is the heart: It is the most prestigious part of the body and the black part found within its middle—which is like a blood clot—is the similitude in importance to the brain within the head.

[٧] أخبرنَا هبة الله بن مُحَمَّد قَالَ أَنا الْحسن بن عَليّ التَّمِيمِي قَالَ أَنا أَبُو بكر بن مَالك قَالَ ثَنَا عبد اللَّهِ بن أَحْمد قَالَ حَدثنِي أبي قَالَ ثنَا يحيى بن سعيد عَن زَكَرِيَّا قَالَ ثَنَا عَامر قَالَ: سَمِعت النُّعْمَان بن بشير يَقُول، سَمِعت رَسُول اللَّهِ - صَلَّى اللَّهُ عَلَيْهِ وَسَلَّمَ - يَقُول: ((إِن فِي الْجَسَد مُضْغَة إِذا صلحت صلح الْجَسَد كُله، وَإِذا فَسدتْ فسد الْجَسَد كُله، أَلا وَهِي الْقلب)). أَخْرجَاهُ فِي الصَّحِيحَيْنِ.

Al-Nuʿmān ibn Bashīr reported, "I heard the Messenger of Allāh ﷺ state, "In the body there is a morsel of flesh: If it is sound, the entire body shall be sound, and if it is corrupt then the entire body shall be corrupt. This is non other than the heart." This has been reported by al-Bukhārī and Muslim.

وَمن ذَلِك الشّعْر: فَإِنَّهُ إِذا كَانَ أسود كَانَ جمال الْآدَمِيّ، فَإِن ابيض زَالَ جماله.

From them is the hair: If it is dark, it denotes human beauty, and when it becomes white, this beauty abates.

[٨] أخبرنَا مُحَمَّد بن عمر بن يُوسُف قَالَ أنبأ مُحَمَّد بن عَليّ بن الْمُهْتَدي قَالَ أنبا عَليّ بن مُحَمَّد بن بَشرَان قَالَ أَنا الْحُسَيْن بن صَفْوَان قَالَ ثنا عبيد اللَّهِ بن مُحَمَّد الْقرشِي قَالَ ثنا أَبُو خَيْثَمَة قَالَ ثَنَا عَليّ بن الْحسن بن شَقِيق قَالَ ثَنَا حُسَيْن بن وَاقد قَالَ نَا أَبُو نهيك الْأَزْدِيّ عَن عَمْرو بن أَخطب قَالَ: استسقى رَسُول اللَّهِ - صَلَّى اللَّهُ عَلَيْهِ وَسَلَّمَ - فَأَتَيْته بِإِنَاء فِيهِ شَعْرَة فرفعتها ثمَّ ناولته فَقَالَ: ((اللَّهُمَّ جمله)).

Abū Nahīk al-Azdī reported that ʿAmr ibn Akhṭab stated, "The Messenger of Allāh ﷺ sought water, so I brought for him a vessel within which was a hair, and I took it out and gave it to him. He said, 'O Allāh beautify it.'"[6]

قَالَ أَبُو نهيك: فرأيته بعد ثَلَاث [وَتِسْعين سنة] وَمَا فِي رَأسه ولحيته شَعْرَة بَيْضَاء.

Abū Nahīk stated, "I came across [ʿAmr] when he was ninety-three years old,[7] and there was no hint of whiteness upon his head or beard."

[٩] وَقد روينَا عَن أبي قَتَادَة أَن رَسُول اللَّهِ [- صَلَّى اللَّهُ عَلَيْهِ وَسَلَّمَ -] دَعَا لَهُ فَقَالَ: ((اللَّهُمَّ بَارك فِي شعره وبشره)). فتوفي وَهُوَ ابْن سبعين سنة وَكَأَنَّهُ ابْن خمس عشرَة سنة. وَمَا زَالَت الْعَرَب تبْكي على رحيل الشَّبَاب ونزول المشيب.

6 Al-Ḥāfiẓ Ibn Ḥajar said in *al-Iṣābah* (4/78), "This was reported by al-Tirmidhī in *al-Sunan* and *al-Shamā'il*, and Ibn Ḥibbān and al-Ḥākim—who both graded it as *ṣaḥīḥ*, and it was also reported by Muslim."

7 In *al-Iṣābah* it states "ninety-four". In *al-Musnad* (22932) it also states that he was ninety-four: (وهو بن أربع وتسعين ليس في لحيته شعرة بيضاء).

We have reported upon the authority of Abū Qatādah that the Messenger of Allāh ﷺ supplicated for him, "O Allāh, bless him in his hair and body."[8] He died when he was seventy[9] but it was as if he was fifteen years of age. The Arabs still weep over the departure of youth and the arrival of white hair.

قالَ عَمْرو بن الْوَلِيد:

أَمْسَى الشَّبَاب مودعا　　لما رأى نور المشيب

يَا لَيْت أَنا نشتري قرب　　الْبعيد بذا الْقَرِيب

لَا يبعدن عصر الشَّبَاب　　الرامح الْغُصْن العجيب

كَانَ الشَّبَاب حبيبنا　　كَيفَ السَّبِيل إِلَى الحبيب

'Amr ibn al-Walīd said:

Youth packed and left, once it saw the light of my grey hair.
I wish I could replace that which has arrived, with what has gone away.
May the age of youth never cease, for it is the age of strength and wonders.
Youth was my beloved one, so how can I come closer to my beloved?"

وَقَالَ دعبل:

لَا تعجبي يَا سلم من رجل　　ضحك المشيب بِرَأْسِهِ فبكا

قد كَانَ يضْحك فِي شبيبته　　فَمضى الشَّبَاب فَقل مَا ضحكا

أَيْن الشَّبَاب وأيه سلكا　　لَا أَيْن يطْلب ضل بل هلكا

Da'bal said:

8 Al-Ḥāfiẓ stated in *al-Iṣābah* (4/128), "This was reported by al-Wāqidī from the route of Yaḥyā ibn 'Abdullāh from the route of Abī Qatādah."
9 It has been said that his age was seventy-two. His biography is in *al-Iṣābah* (4/158-159).

O Salma, do not be surprised from a man, who cried once grey hair landed on his head,
He used to laugh when he was young, but once the youth had gone he rarely laughed,
Where is youthfulness and in which direction it went, and where to find it, nay it is gone and never to come back.

وَقَالَ أَبُو تَمام:

لَا تلم من يبكي شبيبته　　إِلَّا إِذا لم يبكها بِدَم
لسنا نرَاهَا حق رؤيتها　　إِلَّا زمَان الشيب والهرم
كَالشَّمْسِ لَا تبدو فضيلتها　　حَتَّى تغشى الأَرْض بالظلم
ولرب شَيْء لَا تبينه وجدا　　بِهِ إِلَّا مَعَ الْعَدَم

Abū Tammām said:

Blame not who cries over his lost youthfulness except if he does not cry blood over it,
We never appreciate it well enough until after we grow old and age with grey hair,
It is like the sun; its merit does not manifest until after darkness covers the earth,
Many things we take for granted, and only become fond of once they no longer exist.

وَقَالَ المتنبي:

وَقد أَرَانِي الشَّبَاب الرّوح فِي بدني　　وَقد أَرَانِي المشيب الرّوح فِي بدلي

Al-Muṭanabbī said:

Youth brought forth energy into my soul, while old age showed me such energy in others.

[١٠] أخبرنَا أَبُو مَنْصُور الْقَزاز قَالَ أَنا أَحْمد بن عَليّ بن ثَابت قَالَ أَنا الْحسن بن

أبي بكر قَالَ أنا أَبُو جَعْفَر أَحْمد بن يَعْقُوب قَالَ أنشدنا أَبُو طَالب الدعبلي قَالَ أنشدنا عَليّ ابْن الجهم:

لما رَأَتْ شيبا يلوح بمفرقي صدت صدود مفارق متجمل

فظلت أطلب وَصلهَا بتذلل والشيب يغمزها بِأَن لَا تفعلي

Abū Ṭālib al-Daʻbalī said, "Alī ibn al-Jaham composed the following for us:

When she saw the grey hear invading my head, she rejected me in a polite manner.
I keep asking for her love humbly, but my grey hair kept gesturing to say not to accept me."

[١١] أنبأَنَا زَاهِر بن طَاهِر قَالَ أنبأَنَا أَبُو بكر الْبَيْهَقِيّ قَالَ ثَنَا أَبُو عبد اللَّهِ الْحَاكِم قَالَ أَنْشدني نصر بن مُحَمَّد الطوسي قَالَ أَنْشدني أَبُو بكر الصنوبري:

مَلَأت وَجههَا عَليّ عبوسا واستثارت من المآقي الأروسا

ورأتني أسرح العاج بالعاج فظلت تستحسن الآبنوسا

Zāhir reported that Abū Bakr al-Ṣanwabrī composed:

She showed me nothing but a grumpy and frowning face, which prompted the tears in my eyes.
She saw me comb my ivory like hair with an ivory comb, but she still liked ebony like hair (i.e. youth).

وللرضى:

سَواد الرَّأْس سلم للغواني وَبَين الْبيض وَالْبيض الحروب

ودلال الشَّبَاب على الغواني فبادر قبل يعزلك المشيب

Al-Rāḍī composed:

The black hair attracts young women, but white hair entices the en-

mity of fair women,
Enjoy their pampering while you are young, for they will stop once you are old.

وَله أَيْضا:

من شَافِعِيّ وذنوبي عِنْدهَا الْكبر   إِن الْبيَاض لذنب لَيْسَ يغْتَفر
رَأَتْ بيَاضًا مسودا مطالعة   مَا فِي للحب لَا عين وَلَا أثر
وَلَيْسَ كل ظلام دَامَ غيهبه   يسر خابطه أَن يطلع الْقَمَر

And he also composed:

Who to intercede for me with her when she finds old age is my sin, and grey hair is a sin which may not be forgiven.
The whiteness of my hair was enough to remove all traces of love from her heart,
Indeed, it is not always a pleasure to see brightness (i.e. white hair) break the darkness (i.e. black hair).

ولمهيار:

وَلما توافقنا وَفِي الْوَصْل فضلَة   بِقدر الْوُقُوف سَاعَة ثمَّ تَنْقَضِي
رَأَتْ شيبَة مَا صرحت بعوارضي   فَصرحَ بالهجران كل معرض
وَقَالَت أشيخ قلت كهل فأطرقت   وَقَالَت أَمَام الْهم إنذار منبض
نبا عَنْك بعد الشيب قلبِي وناظري   وَمن أَيْن يصفو أسودان لأبيض

Mihyār composed:

After we came close and stood together, I was about to leave,
She noticed a few grey hairs hiding in my head, so her face changed in disapproval,
She exclaimed, you are an old man but I said, I am just middle aged,

so she said, this is a worrying sign and an alert,
Neither my heart nor my eyes like to see you, how could a black hair like its opposite!

وَله:

ذكرتها الْعَهْد على كاظمة قَالَت نسيت والفراق ينسي
وشعرا مبدلا بِشعر بدل فِيك بالنفار أنسي
هَل هُوَ إِلَّا الشيب أم مَالك لَابُد أَن يصبح ليل الممسي

And he also composed:

I reminded her of our pledge but she said I forgot as being away makes one forget.
And your hair seems to have changed, which replaced my affability with aversion.
[I replied] it is just grey hair but do you not know that dawn will follow night.

[قَالَ الْمُؤلف رَحمَه اللَّهِ:] وَقد كَانَت الْعَرَب تُؤثر ميل الشفتين فِي حق الْمَرْأَة إِلَى السوَاد لِأَنَّهُ أشهى عِنْدهم للتقبيل.

The author ﷺ said: Arabs at that time would prefer the lips of women to be nearly black, as it would make them desire to kiss them.

قَالَ ذُو الرمة:

لمياء فِي شفتيها حوة لعس وَفِي اللثاث وَفِي أنيابها شنب

Dhū al-Rummah said:

A mouth with lips that are black mixed with red, and a glowing outer tooth.

فصل
Section

[قَالَ الْمُصَنِّف] وَفِي النَّبَات أَشْيَاء كَثِيرَة لَا نطيل بذكرها وَمِنْهَا:

The author stated: Amongst plants there are many such things but [we do not wish] to lengthen their mention:

الشونيز: وَهُوَ الْمُسَمّى بِحَبَّة السَّوْدَاء، يحلل الرِّيَاح الْبَارِدَة، وَيقطع البلغم، وينقي الصَّدْر من الرطوبات اللزجة، ويقلع الثآليل والبهق، وَيقتل الديدان ويدر الطمث، ويسقى بالعسل وَالْمَاء الْحَار للحصاة فِي المثانة والكلية، ويجمد الحميات البلغمية والسوداوية، ويهرب الْهَوَام من دخانه.

From them is al-Shūnīz: It has been named as black seed. It resolves the cold wind, prevents [the build up of] phlegm, clears the chest of wet and sticky substances, removes warts and vitiligo, exterminates worms and regulates the menses, and is mixed with honey and hot water to treat bladder and kidney stones. It dries up feverish phlegm and melancholy (black bile) and removes vermin with its smoke.

[١٢] أخبرنَا عبد الْوَهَّاب الْأَنمَاطِي قَالَ أنبأ أَبُو الْحُسَيْن ابْن النقور قَالَ أنبأ عِيسَى بن عَليّ الْوَزير قَالَ أنبأ الْبَغَوِيّ قَالَ ثَنا كَامِل بن طَلْحَة قَالَ نَا لَيْث بن سعد عَن عقيل عَن الزُّهْرِيّ عَن أبي سَلمَة بن عبد الرَّحْمَن عَن أبي هُرَيْرَة عَن النَّبِي - صَلَّى اللَّهُ عَلَيْهِ وَسَلَّمَ - قَالَ: ((إِن فِي الْحبَّة السَّوْدَاء شِفَاء من كل دَاء إِلَّا السام)). قَالَ الزُّهْرِيّ: السام الْمَوْت، والحبة السَّوْدَاء: الشونيز. أَخْرجَاهُ فِي الصَّحِيحَيْنِ.

Abī Salamah ibn ʿAbd al-Raḥmān reported upon the authority of Abū Hurayrah that the Prophet ﷺ said, "There is healing within the black seed for all diseases except *al-sām*." Al-Zuhrī stated, "*Al-sām* refers to death, and black seed refers to *al-shūnīz*." This was reported in the two *Ṣaḥīḥs* [of al-Bukhārī and Muslim.]

وَمِنْهَا: ثَمَر الْأَرَاك:

From them is the fruit of *arāk*:

[١٣] روى الزُّهْرِيّ عَن أبي سَلمَة عَن جَابر قَالَ: كُنَّا مَعَ النَّبِي - صَلَّى اللَّهُ عَلَيْهِ وَسَلَّمَ - بمر الظهْرَان نجني الكباث، فَقَالَ: ((عَلَيْك بالأسود مِنْهُ فَإِنَّهُ أطيبه)).

Al-Zuhrī reported on the authority of Jābir that he said, "We were with the Messenger of Allāh ﷺ passing through al-Ẓahrān, and we were picking the *kabāth* (the ripe fruits of *arāk*). He ﷺ said, 'Take the blackest ones, for they are the nicest.'"[10]

قَالَ الْأَصْمَعِي: النضيج من ثَمَر الْأَرَاك هُوَ الكباث، وأسوده أَشد نضجا.

Al-Aṣma'ī said, "The ripe fruits from the *arāk* are called *al-kabāth* and the blackest of them are the most ripe."

وَمِنْهَا: الأبهل: وَهُوَ ثَمَر العرعر الْجبلي مختاره الْأسود، ينفع من القروح العفنة، والسدد، وأورام الأعصاب.

From them is the savin: This refers to the fruit of the mountain juniper plant, of which the best ones are the black. It is beneficial for septic injuries, blocked fallopian tubes and for swelling of the nerves.

وَمِنْهَا: الأهليلج الْأسود: فَإِنَّهُ يسهل السَّوْدَاء، وينشف البلغم من الْمعدة، وينفع الجذام.

From them is the black *ihlīlaj*:[11] This relieves blackheads and dries the phlegm within the stomach and it is beneficial for leprosy.

وَمِنْهَا: بزر قطونا: أجوده أشده سوادا يسكن الكرب والحرارة.

10 Reported by Imām Aḥmad in *al-Musnad* (3/326). It is also found in *Ṣaḥīḥ al-Bukhārī* and *Ṣaḥīḥ Muslim*.

11 A tree which grows in Hind, Kābul and China.

From them is the plantago seed: The best type is the black one, and it abates anxiety and high temperature.

وَمِنْهَا: الآبنوس: يفتت حَصى المثانة وينفع الْبيَاض الْحَادِث فِي الْعين والغشاوة إِذا سحق مِنْهُ وزن دِرْهَم مَعَ دِرْهَم من السكر، وكحل بِهِ مرَارًا ولونه مستحسن.

From them is ebony: It dissipates bladder stones and reduces the white covering which occurs in the eye and cataracts when a small quantity of it is crushed with a small amount of sugar and applied to the eye repeatedly, and its colour is pleasant.

فصل
Section

وَمن الْأَحْجَار، الْحجر الْأسود

From stones: The black stone [of the Ka'bah].

[١٤] أخبرنَا أَبُو الْقَاسِم [هبة اللَّهِ] بن الْحصين أَبُو بكر بن عبد الْبَاقِي قَالَ ثَنَا أَبُو الطّيب الطَّبَرِيّ قَالَ ثَنَا [أَبُو أَحْمد الغطريفي، قَالَ ثَنَا أَبُو خَلِيفَة قَالَ حَدثنَا] شَاذ بن فياض قَالَ ثَنَا عمر بن إِبْرَاهِيم الْعَبْدي عَن قَتَادَة عَن أنس قَالَ: قَالَ رَسُول اللَّهِ - صَلَّى اللَّهُ عَلَيْهِ وَسَلَّمَ -: ((الْحجر الْأسود من حِجَارَة الْجنَّة)).

Qatādah reported on the authority of Anas that the Messenger of Allāh ﷺ said, "The black stone is from the stones of Paradise."[12]

12 Reported by al-Fākihī in *Akhbār Makkah* (1/84) and al-Bazzār in *Kashf al-Astār* (2/23). Al-Haythamī mentioned it in *al-Majma'* (3/243) and said, "It was reported by al-Bazzār and al-Ṭabarānī in *al-Awsaṭ*, and there is a narrator in its *isnād* named 'Umar ibn Ibrāhīm al-'Abdī. He was adjudged to be *thiqah* (trustworthy) by Ibn Ma'īn and others, though he has some weakness."

[١٥] أخبرنَا أَبُو مَنْصُور القراز قَالَ أنبأ عبد الْعَزِيز بن عَليّ الْحَرْبِيّ قَالَ أنبأ أَبُو طَاهِر المخلص قَالَ ثَنَا أَبُو بكر النَّيْسَابُورِي قَالَ ثَنَا إِسْحَاق بن خلدون قَالَ حَدثنِي حَفْص بن عمر الْعَدنِي قَالَ ثَنَا الحكم بن أبان عَن عِكْرِمَة عَن ابْن عَبَّاس قَالَ: ((الْحجر يَمِين اللَّهِ، فَمن لم يدْرك بيعَة رَسُول اللَّهِ - صَلَّى اللَّهُ عَلَيْهِ وَسَلَّمَ - فَمسح الْحجر فقد بَايع الله وَرَسُوله)).

'Ikrimah reported on the authority of Ibn 'Abbās that he said, "The black stone is the right hand of Allāh. He who has not given the pledge of allegiance to the Messenger of Allāh ﷺ [directly], if he has touched this stone then he has given this pledge to Allāh and His Messenger."[13]

[١٦] أخبرنَا عَليّ بن عبيد اللَّهِ وَأحمد بن الْحُسَيْن وَعبد الرَّحْمَن ابْن مُحَمَّد قَالُوا ثَنَا عبد الصَّمد بن الْمَأْمُون قَالَ أنبأ عَليّ بن عمر السكرِي قَالَ ثَنَا أَحْمد بن الْحسن الصُّوفِي قَالَ ثَنَا عبد الرَّحْمَن بن صَالح الْأَزْدِيّ قَالَ ثَنَا عبد الرَّحِيم بن سُلَيْمَان قَالَ ثَنَا عبد الله بن عُثْمَان بن خُثَيْم عَن سعيد بن جُبَير قَالَ: سَمِعت ابْن عَبَّاس يَقُول: قَالَ رَسُول الله - صَلَّى اللَّهُ عَلَيْهِ وَسَلَّمَ -: ((ليبْعَثن هَذَا الْحجر يَوْم الْقِيَامَة لَهُ عينان يبصر بهما ولسان ينْطق بِهِ يشْهد على من استلمه بِحَق)).

Sa'īd ibn Jubayr reported upon the authority of Ibn 'Abbās, "The Messenger of Allāh ﷺ said, 'This stone will resurrect during the Day of Judgement, upon it will be two eyes with which it will see, and a tongue with which it will utter and testify in favour of those who touched it with sincerity.'"[14]

---

13 This was reported by al-Ṭabarānī in *al-Mu'jam* and Ibn Abī al-Fawāris in *Tāsi' al-Talkhīṣat*. It is *ḍa'īf* (weak). [T] Ibn al-Jawzī said in *al-'Ilal al-Mutanāhiyyah* (575/2), "This ḥadīth is not *ṣaḥīḥ*."

14 Reported by Imām Aḥmad in *al-Musnad* (1/291, 307 and 371), al-Azraqī in *Akhbār Makkah* (1/324) in a *mawqūf* form, Ibn Ḥibbān in his *Ṣaḥīḥ* (6/10), and al-Ḥākim in *al-Mustadrak* (1/457), who said, "This *ḥadīth* is *ṣaḥīḥ* and they (al-Bukhārī and Muslim) did not report it."

قَالَ الْمُصَنّف [رَحمَه اللَّهِ: قلت:] وَالْحجر الَّذِي يُسمى المغناطيس حجر أسود وَفِيه الخصيصة العجيبة وَهُوَ اجتذاب الْحَدِيد إِلَيْهِ من غير مس.

The author ﷺ said: The stone named *maghnāṭis* (magnet) is a black stone which has a unique and marvellous characteristic in that it pulls iron towards it without touching it.

وَالْحجر الَّذِي يحك عَلَيْهِ الذَّهَب فَيظْهر سر بَاطِنه. وَالْحِجَارَة الَّتِي ينقدح بهَا النَّار أَكْثَرهَا على لون الْحَبَشَة. وَمن الْحِجَارَة الَّتِى قد عَم نَفعهَا حِجَارَة الْكحل الْمُسَمّى: بالإثمد، وَهِي حِجَارَة شَدِيدَة السوَاد.

And the stone which—through rubbing against it—reveals the inner secret of gold, and the stones which kindle fire are mainly of the Abyssinian colour. From the stones of which their benefits are widespread are the *kohl* stones named *al-ithmid*, and they are extremely black in colour.

[١٧] أخبرنَا ابْن الْحصين قَالَ أنبأ ابْن الْمَذْهَب قَالَ أَنا أَحْمد بن جَعْفَر قَالَ ثَنَا عبد اللَّهِ بن أَحْمد قَالَ حَدثنِي أبي قَالَ ثَنَا يعلى بن عبيد قَالَ نَا سُفْيَان عَن عبد اللَّهِ بن عُثْمَان عَن سعيد بن جُبَير عَن ابْن عَبَّاس قَالَ: قَالَ رَسُول اللَّهِ - صَلَّى اللَّهُ عَلَيْهِ وَسَلَّمَ - ((خير أكحالكم الإثمد؛ يجلو الْبَصَر، وينبت الشّعْر)).

Sa'īd ibn Jubayr reported on authority of Ibn 'Abbās that the Messenger of Allāh ﷺ said, "The best of your *kohl* is *al-ithmid*; it brightens the sight and strengthens the growth of eye lashes."[15]

[قَالَ الْمُصَنّف رَحمَه اللَّهِ] : وَلَو تتبعنا مثل هَذِه الْأَشْيَاء طَال الْأَمر وَكُنَّا نذْكر الْمسك فَإِن النَّبِي - صَلَّى اللَّهُ عَلَيْهِ وَسَلَّمَ - قَالَ فِي الْمسك: ((هُوَ أطيب الطّيب)). وَكُنَّا نذْكر الْعود [العنبر] وَغير ذَلِك، لَكِن الْإِشَارَة تَنْبِيه على مَا ترك.

The author ﷺ stated: If we were to continue listing such things, the matter

15 Reported by Ibn Ḥibbān in *al-Ṣaḥīḥ* (8/624).

would be prolonged, and we would have mentioned musk, for the Prophet ﷺ said, "It is the best of scents."[16] And we would have mentioned *al-'ūd* and others, but what we have mentioned so far serves as an indication to give notice to that which has not been listed.

16 Reported by al-Ḥākim in *al-Mustadrak* on the authority of Abī Sa'īd al-Khudrī (361/1).

الْبَاب السَّابِع
Chapter Seven

فِي بَيَان أَنه لَا فضل لأبيض على أسود باللون وَإِنَّمَا الْفضل بالتقوى
In proclamation that the white person has no superiority over the black, and that superiority lies in piety

[١٨] أخبرنَا عبد الْوَهَّاب بن الْمُبَارك قَالَ ثَنَا أَبُو الْحسن بن عبد الْجَبَّار قَالَ ثنا أَبُو طَالب مُحَمَّد بن عَليّ العشاري قَالَ ثنا أَحْمد ابْن مُحَمَّد بن يُوسُف العلاف قَالَ ثَنَا الْحُسَيْن بن صَفْوَان قَالَ ثنَا أَبُو بكر الْقرشِي قَالَ ثنَا مُحَمَّد بن الرّبيع الْأَسدي قَالَ ثنَا عبد الرَّحِيم بن زيد الْعمي عَن أَبِيه عَن مُحَمَّد بن كَعْب عَن ابْن عَبَّاس قَالَ: قَالَ رَسُول اللَّهِ - صَلَّى اللَّهُ عَلَيْهِ وَسَلَّمَ -: ((من سره أَن يكون أكْرم النَّاس فليتق اللَّهِ [عز وَجل])).

Muḥammad ibn Kaʿb reported upon the authority of Ibn ʿAbbās that the Messenger of Allāh ﷺ said, "He who would be happy by being the most honourable of people should have *taqwā* (God-consciousness) of Allāh ﷻ."[17]

[١٩] قَالَ الْقرشِي، وحَدثني مُحَمَّد بن أبي معشر عَن سعيد المَقْبُري عَن أبي هُرَيْرَة قَالَ: جَاءَ رجل إِلَى النَّبِي - صَلَّى اللَّهُ عَلَيْهِ وَسَلَّمَ - فَقَالَ: يَا رَسُول اللَّهِ، من أكْرم النَّاس؟ قَالَ: ((أَتْقَاهُم لله عز وَجل)).

---

17 It is a part of the longer ḥadīth reported by al-Ḥākim in *al-Mustadrak*, al-Ṭabarānī in *al-Muʿjam* and *al-ʿUqaylī* in his book. It is considered to be defective due to the narrator Hishām ibn Ziyād. Al-Dhahabī said, "Hishām ibn Ziyād was said to be *ḍaʿīf* by al-Bukhārī, al-Nasāʾī, Aḥmad ibn Ḥanbal and Ibn Maʿīn." He agreed with them and said, "The weakness of his narrations is clear."

Saʿīd al-Maqburī reported on the authority of Abū Hurayrah, "A man came to the Prophet ﷺ and said, 'O Messenger of Allāh, who is the most honourable amongst men?' He replied, 'The one with the most *taqwā* of Allāh ﷻ.'"

[٢٠] أخبرنَا ابْن الْحصين قَالَ أَنا ابْن الْمَذْهَب قَالَ أَنا أَحْمد ابْن جَعْفَر قَالَ: ثَنَا عبد اللَّهِ بن أَحْمد قَالَ: حَدثنِي أبي قَالَ ثَنَا أَبُو الْمُغيرَة قَالَ: ثنَا صَفْوَان قَالَ: حَدثنِي رَاشد بن سعد عَن عَاصِم بن حميد عَن معَاذ بن جبل أَن النَّبِي - صَلَّى اللَّهُ عَلَيْهِ وَسَلَّمَ - لما بَعثه إِلَى الْيمن خرج مَعَه يوصيه، ومعاذ رَاكب، وَرَسُول اللَّهِ - صَلَّى اللَّهُ عَلَيْهِ وَسَلَّمَ - يمشي تَحت رَاحِلَته فَلَمَّا فرغ قَالَ: ((يَا معَاذ إِنَّك عَسى أَن لَا تلقانِي بعد عَامي هَذَا، ولعلك أَن تمر بمسجدي هَذَا وقبري)). فَبكى معَاذ جزعا لفراقه رَسُول اللَّهِ - صَلَّى اللَّهُ عَلَيْهِ وَسَلَّمَ -، ثمَّ الْتفت فَأقبل بِوَجْهِهِ نَحْو الْمَدِينَة فَقَالَ ((إِن أولى النَّاس بِي المتقون، من كَانُوا وَحَيْثُ كَانُوا)).

ʿĀṣim ibn Ḥumayd reported on the authority of Muʿādh ibn Jabal, "When the Prophet ﷺ sent him to Yemen [as an emissary], the Prophet accompanied him [for a short distance] to advise him—while Muʿadh rode and the Messenger of Allāh ﷺ walked next to his ride. When he finished, he stated, 'O Muʿadh, it may be that you will not meet me after this year. And it may be that when you pass by my *masjid* [you will find] my grave." Muʿādh wept due to the grief he felt at the fact that he would be separated from the Messenger of Allāh ﷺ. Then he ﷺ turned and faced towards al-Madīnah and said, 'The most worthy people to me are the pious, regardless whom they are or where they are from.'"[18]

وَقَالَ بعض الْعلمَاء لبَعض الْأَشْرَاف: شرفك يحْتَاج إِلَى تقوى، وَصَاحب التَّقْوَى لَا يحْتَاج إِلَى شرف.

One of the *ʿulamā* (scholars) said to a noble, "Your nobility is in need of piety, but the one with piety is not in need of nobility."

18 *Ṣaḥīḥ Ibn Ḥibbān* (2/20).

[٢١] وَفِي الصَّحِيحَيْنِ من حَدِيث أبي هُرَيْرَة عَن النَّبِي - صَلَّى اللَّهُ عَلَيْهِ وَسَلَّمَ - أنه قَالَ: ((للْعَبد المصلح الْمَمْلُوك أَجْرَانِ)).

It is reported in the two *ṣaḥīḥs* on the authority of Abū Hurayrah that the Prophet ﷺ said, "There are two rewards for the righteous slave."

[٢٢] وَفِي أَفْرَاد البُخَارِيّ من حَدِيث أبي مُوسَى عَن النَّبِي - صَلَّى اللَّهُ عَلَيْهِ وَسَلَّمَ - أنه قَالَ: ((الْمَمْلُوك الَّذِي يحسن عبَادَة ربه وَيُؤَدِّي إِلَى سَيّده الَّذِي عَلَيْهِ من الْحق والنصيحة وَالطَّاعَة لَهُ أَجْرَانِ)).

There is another *ḥadīth* reported only by al-Bukhārī on the authority of Abū Mūsā that the Prophet ﷺ said, "The reward is doubled for the slave who performs his *'ibādah* (worship) to Allāh well and also carries out his duties to his master well by being dutiful, sincere and obedient."

الْبَاب الثَّامِن
Chapter Eight

فِي ذكر من هَاجر من الصَّحَابَة إِلَى أَرض الْحَبَشَة وعددهم
In mention of those from amongst the Companions who emigrated to Abyssinia and their number

كَانَ السَّبَب فِي هِجْرَة من هَاجر إِلَى الْحَبَشَة أَن رَسُول اللَّهِ - صَلَّى اللَّهُ عَلَيْهِ وَسَلَّمَ - لما أظهر الْإِسْلَام نصب لَهُ الْمُشْركُونَ الْعَدَاوَة وبالغوا فِي أَذَاهُ وأذى الصَّحَابَة، فَمَنعه اللَّهِ تَعَالَى بِعَمِّهِ أبي طَالب، فَأمر أَصْحَابه بِالْخرُوجِ إِلَى أَرض الْحَبَشَة وَقَالَ لَهُم: ((إِن بهَا ملكا لَا يظلم النَّاس ببلاده فتحرزوا عِنْده حَتَّى يأتيكم اللَّهِ بفرج مِنْهُ)).

The reason for the emigration of the emigrants to Abyssinia is that when the Messenger of Allāh ﷺ displayed Islam openly, the Polytheists became hostile to him and strove to cause harm to him and his Companions. However, Allāh ﷻ protected him through the means of his uncle Abī Ṭālib. [Then in light of this hostility] he ordered his Companions to set forth to the land of Abyssinia, and he stated to them, "There is a king therein who does not oppress the people within his land, so stay with him until Allāh provides you with relief."

وَهَاجر جمَاعَة، واستخفى جمَاعَة، ثمَّ بلغ أهل الْحَبَشَة أَن الْمُشْركين قد لانوا لرَسُول اللَّهِ - صَلَّى اللَّهُ عَلَيْهِ وَسَلَّمَ - فَرَجَعُوا إِلَى مَكَّة فَبَلغهُمْ أَنهم قد عَادوا لَهُ بِالشَّرِّ، فَرَجَعُوا إِلَى الْحَبَشَة وَلم يدْخل أحد [مِنْهُم] مَكَّة إِلَّا ابْن مَسْعُود فَإِنَّهُ دخل

بجوار، وَخرج مَعَهم عدد كَبِير من الْمُسلمين.

[Of the Companions,] one group emigrated and one group went into hiding. Then the news reached those in Abyssinia that the Polytheists had softened towards the Messenger of Allāh ﷺ and so they returned to Makkah. However, when it came to their attention that they had resumed persecuting him they returned to Abyssinia and not one from amongst them entered Makkah except Ibn Mas'ūd who entered with protection. A large number from the Muslims went with them.[19]

وَهَذِه تَسْمِيَة الْمُهَاجِرين من الصَّحَابَة إِلَى الْحَبَشَة على حُرُوف المعجم:

الْأسود بن نَوْفَل، أَسمَاء بنت عُمَيْس، بركَة بنت يسَار، تَمِيم بن الْحَارِث، جَابر بن سُفْيَان، جَعْفَر بن أبي طَالب، جُنَادَة بن سُفْيَان، جهم ابْن قيس، الْحَارِث بن حَاطِب، الْحَارِث بن خَالِد، الْحَارِث بن عبد قيس. حَاطِب بن الْحَارِث، حَاطِب بن عَمْرو، الْحجَّاج بن الْحَارِث، خُزَيْمَة بنت عبد الْأسود، الْحَارِث بن عَمْرو، حَسَنَة أم شُرَحْبِيل، خَالِد بن سُفْيَان، خَالِد بن سعيد، خَالِد بن حزَام، خُزَيْمَة بن جهم، خُنَيْس بن حذافة، ربيعَة بن هِلَال، رقية بنت رَسُول اللَّهِ - صَلَّى اللَّهُ عَلَيْهِ وَسَلَّمَ -، رَملَة بنت أبي عَوْف، ريطة بنت الْحَارِث، الزبير بن الْعَوام، السَّائِب بن الْحَارِث، السَّائِب بن عُثْمَان ابْن مَظْعُون، سعد بن خَوْلَة، سعيد بن الْحَارِث، سعيد بن عبد قيس، سعيد بن عَمْرو، سُفْيَان بن معمر، السَّكْرَان بن عَمْرو، سَلمَة بن هِشَام، سليط بن عَمْرو، سويط [بن سعد] ، سَوْدَة زوج رَسُول اللَّهِ - صَلَّى اللَّهُ عَلَيْهِ وَسَلَّم-، سهلة بنت سُهَيْل، شُرَحْبِيل بن عبد اللَّهِ، شماس بن عُثْمَان، طليب بن أَزْهَر، طليب بن عُمَيْر، عَامر بن ربيعَة، عَامر بن أبي وَقاص، عَامر، أَبُو عُبَيْدَة بن الْجراح، عبد اللَّهِ بن جحش، عبد اللَّهِ ابْن الْحَارِث، عبد اللَّهِ بن سُفْيَان، عبد اللَّهِ بن سُهَيْل، عبد اللَّهِ بن شهَاب، عبد اللَّهِ ابْن عبد

19 See *Sīrat Ibn Hishām* (1/321 onwards) and *Ṭabaqāt Ibn Sa'd* (1/161-162).

الْأسد، عبد اللَّهِ أَبُو مُوسَى، عبد اللَّهِ بن مخرمَة، عبد اللَّهِ بن مَسْعُود، عبد اللَّهِ بن مَظْعُون، عبد الرَّحْمَن بن عَوْف، عتبَة بن غزوَان، عتبَة بن مَسْعُود، عُثْمَان بن عَفَّان، عُثْمَان بن مَظْعُون، عُثْمَان بن ربيعَة، عُثْمَان بن عبد غنم، عدي بن نَضْلَة، عُرْوَة بن أبانة، عمار بن يَاسر، عمرَان بن رِئَاب، عَمْرو بن أُميَّة، عَمْرو بن جهم، عَمْرو بن الْحَارِث، عَمْرو بن سعيد، عَمْرو بن عُثْمَان، عَمْرو بن أبي سرح، عُمَيْر بن رِئَاب، عميرَة بنت السَّعْدِيّ، عَيَّاش بن أبي ربيعَة، عِيَاض بن زُهَيْر بن أبي شَدَّاد، فَاطِمَة بنت صَفْوَان، فَاطِمَة بنت عَلْقَمَة، فَاطِمَة بنت الْمُحَلّل، فراس بن النَّضر، فكيهة بنت سِنَان، قدامَة بن مَظْعُون، قيس بن حذافة، قيس بن عبد الله، ليلى بنت أبي حثْمَة، مَالك بن زَمعَة، مُحَمَّد بن حَاطِب، محمية بن جُزْء، مُصعب بن عُمَيْر، الْمطلب بن أَزْهَر، معبد بن الْحَارِث، معتب بن عَوْف، معمر بن عبد اللَّهِ، معيقيب، الْمِقْدَاد، نبيه بن عُثْمَان، هَاشم بن أبي حُذَيْفَة، هَبَّار بن سُفْيَان، هِشَام بن العَاصِي، هِشَام بن عتبَة، همينة، هِنْد زوج رَسُول اللَّهِ - صَلَّى اللَّهُ عَلَيْهِ وَسَلَّمَ -، يزِيد بن زَمعَة، الرّوم بن عُمَيْر، أَبُو سُبْرَة بن أبي رهم، أَبُو فكيهة، أَبُو قيس بن الْحَارِث، أم كُلْثُوم بنت سُهَيْل.

Below are the names of the Companions who emigrated to Abyssinia, according to the order of the letters of *al-muʿjam* (the dictionary): Al-Aswad ibn Nawfal, Asmāʾ bint ʿUmays, Barkah bint Yasār, Tamīm ibn al-Ḥarīth, Jābir ibn Sufyān, Jaʿfar ibn Abī Ṭālib, Junādah ibn Sufyān, Jaham ibn Qays, Al-Ḥarīth ibn Ḥāṭib, al-Ḥarīth ibn Khālid, al-Ḥarīth ibn ʿAbd Qays, Ḥāṭib ibn ʿAmr, al-Ḥajjāj ibn al-Ḥarīth, Khuzaymah bint ʿAbd al-Aswad, al-Ḥārith ibn ʿAmr, Ḥasanah Umm Shuraḥbīl, Khālid ibn Sufyān, Khālid ibn Saʿīd, Khālid ibn Ḥizām, Khuzaymah ibn Jaham, Khunays ibn Ḥuzāfah, Rabīʿah ibn Hilāl, Ruqayyah—daughter of the Messenger of Allāh ﷺ, Ramlah bint Abī ʿAwf, Rayṭah bint al-Ḥarīth, al-Zubayr ibn al-ʿAwwām, al-Sāʾib ibn al-Ḥarīth, al-Sāʾib ibn ʿUthmān ibn Maẓʿūn, Saʿd ibn Khawlah, Saʿīd ibn Ḥarīth, Saʿīd ibn ʿAbd Qays, Saʿīd ibn ʿAmr, Sufyān ibn Maʿmar, al-Sakrān ibn ʿAmr, Salamah ibn Hishām, Sulayṭ ibn ʿAmr, Suwayṭ ibn Saʿd,

Sawda'—wife of the Messenger of Allāh ﷺ, Sahlah bint Suhayl, Shuraḥbīl ibn 'Abdullāh, Shamās ibn 'Uthmān, Ṭulayb ibn Azhar, Ṭulayb ibn 'Amīr, 'Āmir ibn Rabī'ah, 'Āmir ibn Abī Waqqāṣ, 'Āmir: Abū 'Ubaydah ibn al-Jarrāḥ, 'Abdullāh ibn Jaḥsh, 'Abdullāh ibn al-Ḥarīth, 'Abdullāh ibn Sufyān, 'Abdullāh ibn Shihāb, 'Abdullāh ibn 'Abd al-Asad, 'Abdullāh Abū Mūsā, 'Abdullāh ibn Makhzamah, 'Abdullāh ibn Mas'ūd, 'Abdullah ibn Maẓ'ūn, 'Abd al-Raḥmān ibn 'Awf, 'Utbah ibn Ghazwān, 'Utbah ibn Mas'ūd, 'Uthmān ibn 'Affān, 'Uthmān ibn Maẓ'ūn, 'Uthmān ibn Rabī'a, 'Uthmān ibn 'Abd Ghanam, 'Adī ibn Naḍlah, 'Urwa ibn Abānah, 'Ammār ibn Yāsir, 'Imrān ibn Ri'āb, 'Amr ibn Ummayah, 'Amr ibn Jahm, 'Amr ibn al-Ḥārith, 'Amr ibn Sa'īd, 'Amr ibn 'Uthmān, 'Amr ibn Abī Sarḥ, 'Umayr ibn Ri'āb, 'Umayrah bint al-Sa'dī, 'Ayyāsh ibn Abī Rabī'ah, 'Iyāḍ ibn Zuhayr ibn Abī Shaddād, Fāṭimah bint Ṣafwān, Fāṭimah bint 'Alqamah, Fāṭimah bint al-Muḥallal, Firās ibn al-Naḍr, Fukayhah ibn Sinān, Qudāmah ibn Maẓ'ūn, Qays ibn Ḥudhāfah, Qays ibn 'Abdullāh, Laylā bint Abī Ḥathmah, Mālik ibn Zam'ah, Muḥammad ibn Ḥāṭib, Maḥmiyah ibn Jaz', Muṣ'ab ibn 'Umayr, Al-Muṭṭalib ibn Azhar, Ma'bad ibn al-Ḥarīth, Mu'attib ibn 'Awf, Ma'mar ibn 'Abdullāh, Mu'ayqīb, al-Miqdād, Nabīh ibn 'Uthmān, Hāshim ibn Abī Ḥudhayfah, Hubār ibn Sufyān, Hishām ibn al-'Āṣī, Hīshām ibn 'Utbah, Humaynah, Hind—the wife of the Messenger of Allāh ﷺ, Yazīd ibn Zam'ah, al-Rūm ibn 'Umayr, Abū Sabrah ibn Abī Ruhm, Abū Fukayhah, Abū Qays ibn al- Ḥārith and Umm Kulthūm bint Suhayl.

ذكر من ولد بِالْحَبَشَةِ لِلْمُسلمين

In mention of the Muslims who were born in Abyssinia

عبد اللَّهِ وَعون وَمُحَمّد أَوْلَاد جَعْفَر بن أبي طَالب، سعيد وَأمة ابْنا خَالِد بن سعيد، عبد اللَّهِ بن الْمطلب، مُحَمَّد بن أبي حُذَيْفَة، مُحَمَّد بن حَاطِب، زَيْنَب بنت أبي سَلمَة، مُوسَى وَعَائِشَة وَزَيْنَب أَوْلَاد الْحَارِث بن خَالِد.

'Abd Allāh, 'Awn, and Muḥammad—the sons of Ja'far ibn Abī Ṭālib, Sa'īd and Ummah—the offspring of Khālid ibn Sa'īd, 'Abdullāh ibn al- Muṭṭalib;

Muḥammad ibn Abī Ḥudhayfah; Muḥammad ibn Ḥāṭib, Zaynab bint Abī Salamah; Mūsā, 'Ā'ishah and Zaynab, the children of al-Ḥarīth ibn Khālid.

الْبَاب التَّاسِع

Chapter Nine

فِي إِنْفَاذ قُرَيْش إِلَى النَّجَاشِيّ ليسلم إِلَيْهِم أَصْحَاب رَسُول اللَّهِ - صَلَّى اللَّهُ عَلَيْهِ وَسَلَّم -

The request of the Quraysh to al-Najāshī to hand over the Companions of the Prophet ﷺ to them

[٢٣] أخبرنَا ابْن الْحصين قَالَ أنبأ أَبُو عَلِيّ الْحسن بن عَلِيّ بن الْمَذْهَب قَالَ أَنا أَبُو بكر أَحْمد بن جَعْفَر قَالَ ثَنا عبد الله بن أَحْمد قَالَ نَا أبي قَالَ نَا يَعْقُوب قَالَ ثَنا أبي عَن ابْن إِسْحَاق قَالَ حَدثنِي مُحَمَّد ابْن مُسلم بن شهَاب عَن أبي بكر بن عبد الرَّحْمَن بن الْحَارِث عَن أم سَلمَة زوج النَّبِي - صَلَّى اللَّهُ عَلَيْهِ وَسَلَّمَ - قَالَت:

لما نزلنَا الْحَبَشَة جاورنا بهَا خير جَار النَّجَاشِيّ؛ أمننا على ديننَا، وعبدنا اللَّهِ [عز وَجل] لَا نؤذى، وَلَا نسمع شَيْئا نكرهه، فَلَمَّا بلغ ذَلِك قُرَيْشًا ائْتَمرُوا أَن يبعثوا إِلَى النَّجَاشِيّ منا رجلَيْنِ جلدين وَأَن يهدى إِلَى النَّجَاشِيّ هَدَايَا مِمَّا يستطرف من مَتَاع مَكَّة، وَكَانَ من أعجب مَا يَأْتِين مِنْهَا الْأدم، فَجمعُوا لَهُ أدما كثيرا، ، وَلم يتْركُوا من بطارقته بطريقا إِلَّا أهدوا لَهُ هَدِيَّة، ثمَّ بعثوا بذلك عبد الله بن أبي ربيعَة المَخْزُومِي وَعَمْرو بن الْعَاصِي، وأمروهما [أمرهم] وَقَالُوا لَهما: ادفعا إِلَى كل بطرِيق هديته قبل أَن تكلمُوا النَّجَاشِيّ فيهم، ثمَّ قدمُوا إِلَى النَّجَاشِيّ هداياه، ثمَّ سلوه أَن يسلمهم إِلَيْكُم قبل أَن يكلمهم.

Abī Bakr ibn ʿAbd al-Raḥmān ibn al-Ḥārith reported upon the authority of Umm Salamah—the wife of the Prophet ﷺ—that she said, "When we arrived in Abyssinia we were received by the best of hosts, al-Najāshī. We were safe in our religion, we worshipped Allāh and were not harmed, nor did we hear anything offensive said to us. When information regarding this reached the Quraysh, they resolved to send two firm envoys regarding us to al-Najāshī, and to gift him with some choice items of Makkah. From the nicest items they brought was tanned leather, and so they gathered a large amount for him, and they did not leave one from his generals except that a gift was set for him. This was then despatched with 'Abdullāh ibn Abī Rabī'ah al-Makhzūmī and 'Amr ibn al-'Āṣ with the following instructions, 'Provide each general with his gift before you talk to al-Najāshī regarding them. Then present al-Najāshī's gift to him, following this, ask him to hand them over to you before he can speak to them.'"

قَالَت: فخرجنا فقدمنا على النَّجَاشِيّ، وَنحن عِنْده بِخَير دَار، وَعند خير جوَار، فَلم يبْق من بطارقته بطرِيق إِلَّا دفعا إِلَيْهِ هديته قبل أَن يكلما النَّجَاشِيّ، ثمَّ قَالَا لكل بطرِيق مِنْهُم: إِنَّه قد صبا إِلَى بلد الْملك منا غلْمَان سُفَهَاء فارقوا دين قَومهمْ، وَلم يدخلُوا فِي دينكُمْ، وَجَاءُوا بدين مُبْتَدع لَا نعرفه نَحن وَلَا أَنْتُم، وَقد بعثنَا إِلَى الْملك فيهم أَشْرَاف قَومهمْ ليردهم إِلَيْهِم، فَإِذا كلمنا الْملك فيهم فأشيروا عَلَيْهِ أَن يسلمهم إِلَيْنَا وَلَا يكلمهم، فَإِن قَومهمْ أَعلَى بهم عينا، وَأعلم بِمَا عابوا عَلَيْهِم، فَقَالُوا لَهما: نعم.

She continued, "So we were with al-Najāshī, enjoying our stay and the hospitality we were being shown. There was not a general from the generals except that they presented him his gift before they went to speak to al-Najāshī. Then they confided to each of the generals, 'Indeed, there have defected to the king's land some ignorant young people from our tribe who have renounced the religion of their forefathers and have not embraced your religion, but have brought forth a new religion that neither of us recognise. The noblemen of their tribe have sent us to the king seeking their extradition, so when we speak with the king about this, counsel him to deliver them to us without talking with them, for their own people are more cognisant of them and better acquainted with their beliefs and wrongdoing.' They (the generals) agreed with this.

ثمَّ إِنَّهُمَا قربا هداياهم إِلَى النَّجَاشِيّ فقبلها مِنْهُم ثمَّ كلماه فَقَالَا لَهُ: أَيهَا الْملك، إِنَّه قد حبا إِلَى بلدك منا غلْمَان سُفَهَاء فارقوا دين قَومهمْ، وَلم يدخلُوا فِي دينك، وَجَاءُوا بدين مُبْتَدع لَا نعرفه نَحن وَلَا أَنْت، وَقد بعثنَا إِلَيْك فيهم أَشْرَاف قَومهمْ من آبَائِهِم وأعمامهم وعشائرهم لتردهم إِلَيْهِم، فهم أَعلَى بهم عينا، وَأعلم بِمَا عابوا عَلَيْهِم وعاتبوهم فِيهِ.

Then they presented their gifts to al-Najāshī, and they were accepted by him. Then they stated to him, 'O king, indeed there have defected to your land some ignorant young people from our tribe, who have renounced the religion of their forefathers and have not embraced your religion, but have come up with a new religion that neither of us recognise. The noblemen of their tribe including their parents, uncles, and clansmen have sent us to you seeking their extradition, for their own people are more cognisant of them and better acquainted with their beliefs and wrongdoing.'"

قَالَت: وَلم يكن شَيْء أبْغض إِلَى عبد اللَّهِ بن أبي ربيعَة وَعَمْرو بن العَاصِي من أَن يسمع النَّجَاشِيّ كَلَامهم، فَقَالَت بطارقته حوله: صدقُوا أَيهَا الْملك، قَومهمْ أَعلَى بهم، وَأعلم بِمَا عابوا عَلَيْهِم، فأسلمهم إِلَيْهِمَا فليردا هما إِلَى بِلَادهمْ وقومهم.

She continued, "Nothing could have been more disliked to ʿAbdullāh ibn Abī Rabīʿ and ʿAmr ibn al-Āṣ than al-Najāshī giving his ear to them (i.e. the Companions). The generals around him stated, 'This is the truth O king. Their people are most cognisant regarding them and better acquainted with their faults. So hand them over to these two and permit them to return them to their country and their people.'"

قَالَت: فَغَضب النجاشي ثمَّ قَالَ: لَا هَا اللَّهِ إِذا لَا أسلمهم إِلَيْهِمَا، وَلَا أكاد قوما جاوروني ونزلوا بلادي، واختاروني على من سواي حَتَّى أدعوهم، وأسألهم مَا يَقُول

هَذَانِ فِي أَمرهم، فَإِن كَانُوا كَمَا يَقُولُونَ سلمتهم إِلَيْهِمَا، ورددتهم إِلَى قَومهمْ، وَإِن كَانُوا على غير ذَلِك منعتهم مِنْهُم؛ وَأمنت جوارهم مَا جاوروني.

She said, "Al-Najāshī became angry and then said, 'I will not turn them over to these two men and will not dishonor a group of people who are my guests and who have chosen my protection over all others, until I call them and ask them about whatever these two men accuse them of. If they are like what these two men have stated, then I will hand them over to them, and permit their return to their people. But if they are not so, then I shall offer them my protection and hospitality as long as they wish to remain with me.'"

قَالَت: ثمَّ أرسل إِلَى أَصْحَاب رَسُول اللَّهِ - صَلَّى اللَّهُ عَلَيْهِ وَسَلَّمَ - فَدَعَاهُمْ، فَلَمَّا أَن جَاءَهُم رَسُوله اجْتَمعُوا ثمَّ قَالَ بَعضهم لبَعض: مَا تَقولُونَ للرجل إِذا جئتموه؟ قَالُوا: نقُول وَالله مَا علمناه وَمَا أمرنَا رَسُول اللَّهِ - صَلَّى اللَّهُ عَلَيْهِ وَسَلَّمَ - كَائِن فِي ذَلِك مَا هُوَ كَائِن. فَلَمَّا جَاءُوهُ وَقد دَعَا النَّجَاشِيّ أساقفته فنشروا مصاحفتهم حوله سَأَلَهُمْ فَقَالَ: مَا هَذَا الدّين الَّذِي فارقتم فِيهِ قومكم وَلم تدْخلُوا فِي ديني وَلَا فِي دين أحد من هَذِه الْأُمَم؟

She said, "Then he sent for the Companions of the Messenger of Allāh ﷺ. When his messenger arrived to them, they gathered and consulted each other, 'What will you say to this man when you stand before him?' They said, 'By Allāh, we shall say what we know of the truth and of the commandments of our Prophet ﷺ, no matter what.' When they arrived at the court of al-Najāshī, they found that he had called his bishops who were seated around him with their scriptures open to ask the Muslims about their beliefs. He said, 'What is this religion with which you have renounced the religion of your people, and have turned away from my religion and the religion of other nations?'"

قَالَت: وَكَانَ الَّذِي كَلمه جَعْفَر بن أبي طَالب فَقَالَ لَهُ: أَيهَا الْملك، كُنَّا قوما أهل جَاهِلِيَّة نعْبد الْأَصْنَام، وَنَأْكُل الْميتَة، ونأتي الْفَوَاحِش، ونقطع الْأَرْحَام،

ونسيء الْجوَار، فيأكل الْقوي منا الضَّعِيف، وَكُنَّا على ذَلِك حَتَّى بعث اللَّهِ عز وَجل إِلَيْنَا رَسُولا منا نَعْرِف نسبه وَصدقه وأمانته وَشرف عفافه فَدَعَانَا إِلَى الله عز وَجل، لنوحده ونعبده، ونخلع مَا كُنَّا نعْبد نَحن وآباؤنا من دونه من الْحِجَارَة والأوثان، وأمرنا بِصدق الحَدِيث، وَأَدَاء الْأَمَانَة، وصلَة الرَّحِم، وَحسن الْجوَار [وكف الْأَذَى] والكف عَن الْمَحَارِمِ والدماء، ونهانا عَن الْفَوَاحِش، وَقَول الزُّور، وَأكل مَال الْيَتِيم، وَقذف المحصنة، وأمرنا أَن نعْبد اللَّهِ لَا نشْرك بِهِ شَيْئا، وأمرنا بِالصَّلَاةِ وَالزَّكَاة وَالصِّيَام.

She said, "The one who served as the spokesperson was Jaʿfar ibn Abī Ṭālib, he said, 'O king, we were a group of people living in ignorance and immorality; we used to worship idols, eat the flesh of dead animals, engage in debauchery, sever the ties of kinship, break the rights of neighbors, and the strong amongst us would take the rights of the weak. We remained in this manner until Allāh ﷻ sent to us a messenger [from amongst us,] whose lineage, truthfulness, honesty, and chastity were already well-known to us. He invited us to Allāh ﷻ—to single him out and worship Him—and to renounce the stones and idols which we and our forefathers worshipped besides Him. He commanded us to speak the truth, keep our promises, keep good ties with relatives, show kindness to neighbors and avoid harming them, to avoid all forbidden acts and bloodshed. He prohibited and warned us against performing debauchery, false testimony, taking the property of the orphan, and against falsely accusing chaste women. He ordered us to worship Allāh alone and not to associate anything with Him, to establish the prayer, to give *zakāt* and to fast.'"

قَالَت: فعدد عَلَيْهِ أُمُور الْإِسْلَام فصدقنا وآمنا بِهِ واتبعناه على مَا جَاءَ بِهِ فعبدنا اللَّهِ وَحده فَلم نشْرك بِهِ شَيْئا، وحرمنا مَا حرم علينا، وأحللنا مَا أحل لنا، فَعدا علينا قَومنَا فعذبونا وفتنونا عَن ديننَا، ليردونا إِلَى عبَادَة الْأَوْثَان من عبَادَة الله عز وَجل، وَأَن نستحل مَا كُنَّا نستحل من الْخَبَائِث، فَلَمَّا قهرونا وظلمونا وشقوا علينا وحالوا

بَيْننَا وَبَين ديننَا، خرجنَا إِلَى بلدك فاخترناك على من سواك، ورغبنا فِي جوارك، ورجونا أَن لَا نظلم عنْدك أَيهَا الْملك.

She said, "So he enumerated for him the key principles of Islām. [He then said,] 'So we affirmed [his message,] believed in him and followed him in that which he brought forth, and we worshipped Allāh alone without associating anything with Him. We prohibited ourselves from that which he made prohibited and we viewed lawful to us that which he made so. Our people thus persecuted us and abused us in order to turn us from our religion, and return to the worship of idols instead of the worship of Allāh ﷻ and for us to make lawful that which we previously deemed as such from the immoral matters. So, when they subdued and oppressed us, made miserable our lives, and prevented us from practicing our religion, we sought refuge in your land, choosing you over others, desiring your protection and hoping to live in justice and peace under your rule, O king.'"

قَالَت: فَقَالَ [لَهُ] النَّجَاشِيّ: هَل مَعَك مِمَّا جَاءَ بِهِ عَن الله عز وَجل من شَيْء؟ فَقَالَ [لَهُ] جَعْفَر: نعم، فَقَالَ لَهُ النَّجَاشِيّ: فاقرأه عَليّ:

She said, "Al-Najāshī said to him, 'Do you have with you anything which was revealed from Allāh ﷻ? Ja'far replied to him, 'Yes.' So, al-Najāshī said, 'Then recite it for me.'"

قَالَت: فَقَرَأَ عَلَيْهِ صَدرا من ﴿**كهيعص**﴾. قَالَت: فَبكى وَالله النَّجَاشِيّ حَتَّى اخضلت لحيته، وبكت أساقفته حَتَّى اخضلت مصاحفهم حِين سمعُوا مَا تلِي عَلَيْهِم، ثمَّ قَالَ النَّجَاشِيّ: إِن هَذَا وَالَّذِي جَاءَ بِهِ عِيسَى ليخرج من مشكاة وَاحِدَة، انْطَلقَا فوَاللَّه لَا أسلمهم إِلَيْكُمَا أبدا وَلَا أكاد.

She said, "So he recited for him a passage from the opening of **{Kāf-Ha-Ya-'Ayn-Ṣād}** (Sūrah Maryam)." She continued, "By Allāh, al-Najāshī wept until his tears moistened his beard, and his bishops wept until their tears moistened their scriptures when they heard his recital. Then al-Najāshī stated, 'Verily, this and that which came from Mūsā are from the same *mishkāt* (niche). You two must leave, for—by Allāh—I will not hand them over to you and would never do so.'"

قَالَت أم سَلمَة: فَلَمَّا خرجنَا من عِنْده قَالَ عَمْرو بن العَاصِي: وَالله لَآتِيَنه غدا أعيبهم عِنْده بِمَا أستأصل بِهِ غضراءهم، فَقَالَ لَهُ عبد اللَّهِ بن أبي ربيعَة - وَكَانَ أتقى الرجلَيْن - فِينَا: لَا تفعل، فَإِن لَهُم أرحاما، وَإِن كَانُوا قد خالفونا. قَالَ: وَالله لأخبرنه أَنهم يَزْعمُونَ أَن عِيسَى ابْن مَرْيَم [عَلَيْهِ السَّلَام] عبد.

Umm Salamah said, "When we left them, 'Amr ibn al-'Āṣ said, 'By Allāh, tomorrow I will tell him a defect of theirs which will remove their prosperity.' 'Abdullāh ibn Abī Rabī'ah—who was the more pious of them—said to him regarding us, 'Do not do so, for they are bonded to us through the womb despite their differing with us.' He replied, 'By Allāh, I will inform him that they view that 'Īsā ibn Maryam is a slave.'"

قَالَت: ثمَّ غدا عَلَيْهِ الْغد، فَقَالَ: أَيهَا الْملك، أنهم يَقُولُونَ فِي عِيسَى بن مَرْيَم قولا عَظِيما، فَأرْسل إِلَيْهِم فَسَأَلْهُمْ عَمَّا يَقُولُونَ فِيهِ.

She said, "The next morning he went and said, 'O king, these people state a grave thing about 'Īsā ibn Maryam. Send for them and ask them in regards to what they state.'"

قَالَت: فَأرْسل إِلَيْهِم يسألهم عَنهُ، قَالَت: وَلم ينزل بِنَا مثلهَا، فَاجْتمع الْقَوْم، فَقَالَ بَعضهم لبَعض: مَاذَا تَقولُونَ فِي عِيسَى إِذا سألكم عَنهُ؟ قَالُوا: نقُول وَالله فِيهِ مَا قَالَ اللَّهِ عز وَجل وَمَا جَاءَ بِهِ نَبينَا كَائِنا فِي ذَلِك مَا هُوَ كَائِن.

She said, "So he sent for them and enquired in regards to 'Īsā." She continued, "We had not experienced such a thing before, and so the party consulted, asking one another, 'What shall you say if you are asked regarding 'Īsā?' And they said, 'By Allāh we shall say that which Allāh ﷻ said and which our Prophet stated, no matter what may arise.'

فَلَمَّا دخلُوا عَلَيْهِ قَالَ لَهُم: مَا تَقولُونَ فِي عِيسَى بن مَرْيَم؟ فَقَالَ لَهُ جَعْفَر بن أبي طَالب: نقُول فِيهِ الَّذِي جَاءَ بِهِ نَبينَا - صَلَّى اللَّهُ عَلَيْهِ وَسَلَّمَ - هُوَ عبد اللَّهِ وكلمته أَلْقَاهَا إِلَى مَرْيَم الْعَذْرَاء البتول.

When they entered the court of al-Najāshī, he asked them, 'What do you say about 'Īsā ibn Maryam?' Ja'far ibn Abī Ṭālib replied to him, 'We say regarding him that which our Prophet ﷺ brought forth: He is a slave of Allāh, a prophet from Him cast into the womb of Mary, the virgin maiden.'"

قَالَت: فَضرب النَّجَاشِيّ يَده على الأَرْض فَأخذ مِنْهَا عودا ثمَّ قَالَ: مَا عدا عِيسَى بن مَرْيَم مَا قلت هَذَا الْعود، فتناخرت بطارقته حوله حِين قَالَ مَا قَالَ، فَقَالَ: وَإِن نخرتم وَالله اذْهَبُوا فَأَنْتم سيوم بأرضي، والشيوم الآمنون من سبكم غرم، من سبكم غرم، مَا أحب أَن لي دبرا [من] ذهب، وَأَنِّي آذيت رجلا مِنْكُم - والدبر بِلِسَان الْحَبَشَة: الْجَبَل - ردوا عَلَيْهِمَا هداياهما فَلَا حَاجَة لنا بهَا فوَاللَّه مَا أَخذ اللَّهِ مني الرِّشْوَة حِين رد عَليّ ملكي فآخذ الرِّشْوَة فِيهِ، وَمَا أطَاع النَّاس فِي فأطعهم فِيهِ.

She continued, "Then al-Najāshī struck the ground with his hand and picked up a small stick from the ground and stated, "'Īsā ibn Maryam is no different to what you have said as much as the length of this stick.' His generals surrounding him snorted when he said this. So he said, 'By Allāh, even if you snort. [Speaking to the Companions:] Go, for you are safe and secure in my land, the one who curses you will be punished, [indeed] the one who curses you will be punished. I would not like to have a mountain of gold while anyone of you should come to any harm.'—The word *al-dabr* in the language of the Abyssinians means 'mountain'—'Return their gifts for we are not in need of them, for—by Allāh—Allāh did not take a bribe from me when he returned to me my kingdom so [how could I] take a bribe in regards to this. And he [did not] make me obeyed by the people so that I obey them in this.'"

قَالَت: فَخَرَجَا من عِنْده مقبوحين مردودا عَلَيْهِمَا مَا جَاءَا بِهِ، وأقمنا عِنْده بِخَير

دَار مَعَ خير جَار.

She said, "They left his court dejected and that which they came with was rejected, while we remained residing with him in a peaceful location with a hospitable host."

قَالَت: فوَاللَّه إِنَّا على ذَلِك إِذْ نزل بِهِ من ينازعه فِي ملكه، قَالَت: فوَاللَّه مَا علمنَا حزنا قطّ كَانَ أَشد من حزن حزناه عِنْد ذَلِك تخوفا أَن يظْهر ذَلِك على النَّجَاشِيّ، فَيَأْتِي رجل لَا يعرف من حَقنا مَا كَانَ النَّجَاشِيّ يعرف مِنْهُ.

She said, "By Allāh, during this time an opposer arose to take his kingdom." She said, "By Allāh, we did not ever know a sadness stronger than the sadness we felt at the thought that the opposition should overpower al-Najāshī, and that a leader should come who does not understand our case how al-Najāshī did."

قَالَت: وَسَار النَّجَاشِيّ وَبَينهمَا عرض النّيل.

She said, "Al-Najāshī went [to meet the enemy] and the breadth of the Nile was between the two parties."

قَالَت: فَقَالَ أَصْحَاب رَسُول الله - صَلَّى اللَّهُ عَلَيْهِ وَسَلَّمَ -[هَل] من رجل يخرج حَتَّى يحضر وقيعة الْقَوْم، ثمَّ يأتينا بالْخبر؟

She said, "The Companions of the Messenger of Allāh ﷺ stated, 'Who will go to the scene of the battle between the people and then bring us news of the event?'

فَقَالَ الزبير بن الْعَوام: أَنا.

Al-Zubayr ibn al-'Awwām said, 'I will do so.'"

قَالَت: وَكَانَ من أحدث الْقَوْم سنا، قَالَت: فنفخوا لَهُ قربَة فَجَعلهَا فِي صَدره،

ثمَّ سبح عَلَيْهَا حَتَّى خرج إِلَى بَاب النّيل الَّتِي بهَا ملتقى الْقَوْم، ثمَّ انْطلق حَتَّى حضرهم.

She continued, "He was from the youngest of the group." She said, "We blew into a water-skin for him and he placed it on his chest and swam on it until he reached the part of the Nile where the armies were gathered. He then rushed until he reached them.

قَالَت: ودعونا اللَّهِ للنجاشي بالظهور على عدوه والتمكين لَهُ فِي بِلَاده. واستوسق عَلَيْهِ أَمر الْحَبَشَة، وَكُنَّا عِنْده فِي خير منزل حَتَّى قدمنَا على رَسُول اللَّهِ - صَلَّى اللَّهُ عَلَيْهِ وَسَلَّمَ - وَهُوَ بِمَكَّة.

She said, "We supplicated to Allāh to make al-Najāshī overcome his adversary and to establish his power in his land. The matter in Abyssinia ended in al-Najāshi's favour, and we lived pleasantly with him until we returned to the Messenger of Allāh ﷺ in Makkah."

[٢٤] أَنبأَنَا الْحُسَيْن بن مُحَمَّد بن عبد الْوَهَّاب قَالَ أَنا أَبُو جَعْفَر بن الْمسلمَة قَالَ أَنا أَبُو طَاهِر المخلص قَالَ أَنا أَحْمد بن سُلَيْمَان بن دَاوُد قَالَ أَنا الزبير بن بكار قَالَ: حَدثنِي عمي مُصعب بن عبد اللَّهِ قَالَ: بعثت قُرَيْش عمَارَة بن الْوَلِيد مَعَ عَمْرو بن العَاصِ إِلَى النَّجَاشِيّ يكلمانه فِيمَن قدم عَلَيْهِ من الْمُهَاجِرين، فراسل عمَارَة بن الْوَلِيد جَارِيَة للنجاشي لعَمْرو بن العَاصِ وَكَانَت مَعَه حَتَّى مَضَت إِلَيْهِ فَأطلع على ذَلِك عَمْرو بن العَاصِ فَقَالَ:

Zubayr ibn Bakkār reported on the authority of Musʿab ibn ʿAbdullāh, "The Quraysh despatched ʿUmārah ibn al-Walīd and ʿAmr ibn al-ʿĀṣ to al-Najāshī to discuss with him in regards to those who emigrated to him. ʿUmārah ibn al-Walīd corresponded with a female servant of al-Najāshi about ʿAmr ibn al-ʿĀṣ, and she was with him until she passed by ʿAmr and he became aware of this and said,

تعلم عمَارَة أَن من شرشيمة　　لمثلك أَن تدعى ابْن عم لَهُ ابْن أما

فَإِن كنت ذَا بردين أحوى مرجلا　　فلست برَاء لِابْنِ عمك محرما

إِذا الْمَرْء لم يتْرك طَعَاما يُحِبهُ　　وَلم ينه قلبا هاويا حَيْثُ يمما

قضى وطرا مِنْهُ وغادر سبة　　إِذا ذكرت أَمْثَالهَا تملأ الفما

ʿUmārah, know that the worst trait for your like who calls his cousin a brother.[20]

If you are a person with two garments, yet you are not innocent of trespassing upon that which your cousin viewed sacred.

If a man does not leave food he likes, and does not forbid his desiring heart from landing wherever it wants.

It will fulfil what it wants and then leave him alone, the examples of which when mentioned would fill the mouth.

وَقد كَانَ عمَارَة أخبر عمرا أَن زَوْجَة الْملك النَّجَاشِيّ علقته وأدخلته، فَلَمَّا يئس عَمْرو بن العَاصِي من أمر الْمُهَاجِرين عِنْد النَّجَاشِيّ مَحل بعمارة عِنْده، فَأخْبرهُ خَبره وَخبر زَوجته. فَقَالَ لَهُ النَّجَاشِيّ: ائْتِنِي بعلامة أستدل بهَا على مَا قلت، فَعَاد عمَارَة وَأخْبر عمرا بِأَمْرِهِ وَأمر زَوْجَة النَّجَاشِيّ فَقَالَ لَهُ عَمْرو: لَا أقبل هَذَا مِنْك، إِلَّا بِأَن لَا ترْضى مِنْهَا إِلَّا بِأَن تعطيك [شَيْئا] من دهن الْملك الَّذِي لَا يدهن بِهِ غَيره. فكلمها عمَارَة فِي الدّهن، فَقَالَت: أَخَاف من الْملك. فَأبى أَن يرضى مِنْهَا حَتَّى تعطيه ذَلِك الدّهن فَأَعْطَتْهُ مِنْهُ فَأعْطَاهُ عمرا، فجَاء بِهِ إِلَى النَّجَاشِيّ، فَنفخ سحرًا فِي إحليله، فَذهب مَعَ الْوَحْش فِيمَا يَقُوله قُرَيْش، فَلم يزل مستوحشا يرد مَاء فِي جَزِيرَة بِأَرْض الْحَبَش، حَتَّى خرج إِلَيْهِ عبد اللَّهِ بن أبي ربيعَة فِي جمَاعَة من أَصْحَابه، فرصده على المَاء فَأَخذه فَجعل يَصِيح بِهِ: أَرْسلنِي فَإِنِّي أَمُوت إِن

20 [T] The context behind this and what follows is that ʿUmārah oppressed ʿAmr in regards to ʿAmr's wife on the ship journey en route to Abyssinia, as cited in historical sources such as *Siyar Aʿlām al-Nubala* (1/439, in the biography of al-Najāshi).

أمسكتني، فأمسكه فَمَاتَ فِي يَده.

'Umārah confided in 'Amr that the woman of al-Najāshī had performed intercourse with him. When 'Amr ibn al-'Āṣ became despondent in regards to the affair of the emigrants who were with al-Najāshī, he attempted to harm 'Umārah by informing al-Najāshī about the incident between him and his woman. Al-Najāshī stated to him, 'Bring me a sign proving what you have said.' Later 'Umārah mentioned again what took place between him and the woman of al-Najashī and so 'Amr said to him, 'I will not accept your account except if [you say to her] that you are not pleased with her until she brings for you something from amongst the king's oils which no one uses except him. 'Umārah spoke to her regarding the oil but she replied, 'I am afraid of the king." He pressed her regarding the matter and stated that he would not be pleased with her until she brought him this oil, and so she brought the oil, which he subsequently passed to 'Amr. This was then brought before al-Najāshī, [and as punishment] he blew a magic substance in his private part and he went away whilst behaving feral, according to what the Quraysh stated, and he remained in this state, roaming by the water of the peninsula of the Abyssinian land until 'Abdullāh ibn Abī Rabī'ah alongside some of his companions came for him and laid in wait for him before catching him. This caused him to begin shouting at him, 'Release me for I will die if you touch me.' He took hold of him, and he passed away in his hands.'"

الْبَاب الْعَاشِر
Chapter Ten

فِي ذكر مُكَاتبَة النَّبِي - صَلَّى اللَّهُ عَلَيْهِ وَسَلَّم - النَّجَاشِيّ [رَضِي اللَّهِ عَنهُ] يَدعُوهُ إِلَى الْإِسْلَام وإسلامه
In mention of that which the Prophet ﷺ wrote to al-Najāshī ؓ, inviting him to Islam, and of his conversion

[قَالَ مُؤَلفه رَحمَه اللَّهِ] : كتب رَسُول اللَّهِ - صَلَّى اللَّهُ عَلَيْهِ وَسَلَّمَ - إِلَى النَّجَاشِيّ يَدعُوهُ إِلَى الْإِسْلَام، فَأسلم وآمن مَعَه جمَاعَة من أَصْحَابه، وأجابه عَن كِتَابه وَبعث إِلَيْهِ وَلَده فِي سِتِّينَ من الْحَبَشَة فغرقُوا فِي الْبَحْر، وَسَيَأْتِي ذكر قصَّته فِي بَاب ذكر مُلُوك الْحَبَشَة إِن شَاءَ اللَّهِ تَعَالَى.

The author stated: The Messenger of Allāh ﷺ wrote to al-Najāshī inviting him to Islam. Subsequently, al-Najāshī accepted Islam and a group of his companions believed also. Then he responded to the letter and sent his son to him with sixty Abyssinians, and all of them drowned in the sea. The story of this incident will follow in the chapter mentioning the kings of Abyssinia, by the will of Allāh ﷻ.

الْبَاب الْحَادِي عشر
Chapter Eleven

فِي ذكر قدوم الْحَبَشَة على رَسُول اللَّهِ ولعبهم بالحراب فِي الْمَسْجِد وَرَسُول الله - صَلَّى اللَّهُ عَلَيْهِ وَسَلَّمَ - ينظر

In mention of the coming of the Abyssinians to the Messenger of Allāh ﷺ and their war game in the *masjid* whilst the Prophet ﷺ watched

[٢٥] أخبرنَا ابْن الْحصين قَالَ أَنا ابْن الْمَذْهَب قَالَ أَنا أَحْمد بن جَعْفَر قَالَ ثنَا عبد اللَّهِ بن أَحْمد قَالَ حَدثنِي أبي قَالَ ثنَا أَبُو الْمُغيرَة قَالَ ثنَا الْأَوْزَاعِيّ قَالَ ثنَا الزُّهْرِيّ عَن عُرْوَة بن الزبير عَن عَائِشَة [رَضِي اللَّهِ عَنْهَا] قَالَت: رَأَيْت رَسُول اللَّهِ - صَلَّى اللَّهُ عَلَيْهِ وَسَلَّمَ - يسترني بردائه وَأَنا أنظر إِلَى الْحَبَشَة يَلْعَبُونَ فِي الْمَسْجِد حَتَّى أكون أَنا أسأم، فاقدروا قدر الْجَارِيَة الحديثة السن الحريصة على اللَّهْو.

'Urwah ibn al-Zubayr reported that 'Āishah ﷺ said, "I recall the Messenger of Allāh ﷺ covering me with his upper garment whilst I was watching the Abyssinians performing in the *masjid* until I grew weary—and you know the length with which a young girl remains interested in entertainment (i.e. displaying the length of their performance)."[21]

[٢٦] قَالَ أَحْمد وثنا عبد الرَّزَّاق قَالَ ثنَا معمر عَن ثَابت عَن أنس قَالَ: لما قدم رَسُول اللَّهِ الْمَدِينَة لعبت الْحَبَشَة لقدومه بِحِرَابِهِمْ فَرحا بذلك.

Thābit reported that Anas said, "When the Messenger of Allāh arrived at

21 Reported by Imām Aḥmad in *al-Musnad* (6/84-85, 166 and 273) and al-Nasā'ī.

Madīnah the Abyssinians joyfully performed with their weapons in happiness at his coming."[22]

[٢٧] أنبأنَا مُحَمَّد بن أبي طَاهِر الْبَزَّار قَالَ أنبأنَا إِبْرَاهِيم بن عمر الْبَرْمَكِي أَن أَبَا بكر أَحْمد بن جَعْفَر بن مُحَمَّد بن سلم أخبرهُ إجَازَة قَالَ ثَنَا أَبُو بكر بن دَاوُد قَالَ ثَنَا أَحْمد بن صَالح قَالَ ثَنَا عبد اللَّهِ ابْن وهب قَالَ أَخْبرنِي عَمْرو ابْن الْحَارِث قَالَ حَدثنِي أَبُو الْأسود عَن عُرْوَة بن الزبير عَن عَائِشَة [رَضِي اللَّهِ عَنْهَا] قَالَت: كَانَ عِنْدِي رَسُول اللَّهِ يَوْم لعب السودَان بالدرق والحراب. فإمَّا سَأَلت رَسُول اللَّهِ، ، وَإِمَّا قَالَ لي: ((تشتهين تنظرين؟)) فَقلت: نعم، فأقامني من وَرَائه خدي على خَدّه وَهُوَ يَقُول: ((دونكم يَا بني أرفدة)). حَتَّى إِذا مللت قَالَ: ((حَسبك؟)). قلت: نعم. قَالَ: ((فاذهبي)).

'Urwah ibn al-Zubayr reported that 'Āishah ﵂ said, "The Messenger of Allāh was with me on the day that the black people performed with their shields and weapons. So, either I requested from the Messenger of Allāh ﷺ or he asked me, 'Do you wish to see?' I replied affirmatively and so he stood me behind him—my cheek touching his, and he was saying, 'Carry on, O Banī Arfadah.'[23] When I grew weary, he asked me, 'Are you satiated?' I replied that I was and so he said, 'Then leave.'"[24]

[٢٨] قَالَ ابْن مُسلم: وَحدثنَا أَبُو عبد اللَّهِ الْحُسَيْن بن مُحَمَّد بن سعيد قَالَ ثَنَا مُحَمَّد بن مَنْصُور الطوسي قَالَ: ثنَا زيد بن الْحباب قَالَ: حَدثنِي خَارِجَة بن عبد اللَّهِ قَالَ ثَنَا يزِيد بن رُومَان عَن عُرْوَة عَن عَائِشَة قَالَت: كَانَ النَّبِي - صَلَّى اللَّهُ

22 This was mentioned by al-Suyūṭī in *Raf' Shàn al-Ḥubshān* (48/a), "This ḥadīth is *ṣaḥīḥ*, and it was reported by Abū Dāwūd and Aḥmad on the authority of 'Abd al-Razzāq."

23 Al-Suyūṭī reported in *Raf' Shàn al-Ḥubshān* (48/a) that al-Zarkashī said, "This refers to an ancestor of the Ethiopians." He also quoted Abū 'Amr as saying, "Banū Arfadah refers to a group from the Ethiopians who were known for this type of dancing."

24 Reported in *Ṣaḥīḥ al-Bukhārī* (443 and 944) and by Muslim (892).

عَلَيْهِ وَسَلَّمَ - جَالِسا فَسمع لَغطا وَصَوت صبيان فَقَامَ فَإِذا حبشية تزفن وَالصبيان حولهَا، فَقَالَ رَسُول اللَّهِ - صَلَّى اللَّهُ عَلَيْهِ وَسَلَّمَ -: ((يَا عَائِشَة تعالي وانظري)). فَجئْت فَوضعت ذقني على منْكب رَسُول اللَّهِ - صَلَّى اللَّهُ عَلَيْهِ وَسَلَّمَ -، فَجعلت أنظر إِلَيْهَا مَا بَين مَنْكِبَيْه إِلَى رَأسه فَقَالَ لي: ((أما شعبت؟)). فَقلت: لَا؛ لأنظر منزلتي عِنْده.

'Urwah reported that 'Āishah said, "The Messenger of Allāh ﷺ was sitting and he heard some commotion and the voices of children, so he stood and there was an Abyssinian woman prancing for some children around her. The Messenger of Allāh ﷺ said, 'O 'Āishah, get up and look.' So I got up and placed my chin on the shoulder of the Messenger of Allāh ﷺ watching her from between his shoulders and his head. Then he said to me, 'Are you satisfied?' I said, 'No,' so as to see my station with him (i.e. to see how he ﷺ would respond to her)."[25]

[٢٩] أَنبأَنَا مُحَمَّد بن عبد الْبَاقِي بن أَحْمد قَالَ أَنبأَنَا جَعْفَر بن أَحْمد السراج قَالَ أَنا عبيد اللَّهِ بن عَمْرو بن أَحْمد المروروذي قَالَ ثَنَا أبي قَالَ: ثَنَا نصر بن الْقَاسِم قَالَ ثَنَا لوين قَالَ ثَنَا أَبُو عوَانَة عَن أبي بشر أَن النَّبِي - صَلَّى اللَّهُ عَلَيْهِ وَسَلَّمَ - وَأَبا بكر مرا بِالْحَبَشَةِ وهم يَلْعَبُونَ وَيَقُولُونَ:

يَا أَيهَا الطيف المعرج طَارِقًا   لَوْلَا مَرَرْت بآل عبد الدَّار
لَوْلَا مَرَرْت بهم تُرِيدُ قراهم   مفعول من جهد وَمن إقتار

Abū 'Awānah reported on the authority of Abī Bishr that the Messenger of Allāh ﷺ and Abū Bakr passed by some Abyssinians who were playing while saying:

25 Reported by al-Tirmidhī in *al-Sunan* (3691), and he graded it as *ḥasan ṣaḥīḥ gharīb min hadha al-wajh* (*ḥaṣan ṣaḥīḥ* which is *gharīb* (singular) in this way). [T] In *Tuḥfat al-Ahwadhī* (10/170), al-Mubarakfūrī states that it was also reported by Ibn 'Adī in *al-Kāmil* (3/51).

O you guest knocking [on the door], you should have visited the house of 'Abd al-Dār,
Had you asked for their hospitality, they would have saved you the hardship and hunger.

الْبَاب الثَّانِي عشر

Chapter Twelve

فِي ذكر مَا جَاءَ من الْقُرْآن مُوَافقا للغة الْحَبَشَة

In mention of words in the Qur'ān which conform with the Abyssinian language

[٣٠] أَنبأَنَا مُحَمَّد بن أبي طَاهِر الْبَزَّاز قَالَ أَنا أَبُو مُحَمَّد الْحسن بن عَليّ الْجَوْهَرِي قَالَ أَنا مُحَمَّد بن المظفر الْحَافِظ قَالَ أَنا عَليّ بن إِسْمَاعِيل بن حَمَّاد قَالَ ثنا أَبُو حَفْص عَمْرو بن عَليّ قَالَ ثنا عبد الرَّحْمَن بن مهْدي قَالَ ثنا إِسْرَائِيل عَن أبي إِسْحَاق عَن أبي الْأَحْوَص عَن أبي مُوسَى: **﴿يُؤْتكُم كِفْلَيْنِ من رَحمته﴾**، قَالَ: ضعفين وَهُوَ بِلِسَان الْحَبَشَة: كِفْلَيْنِ.

Abū al-Aḥwaṣ reported on the authority of Abū Mūsā [in regards to the word "*kiflayn*" in the *āyah*,] **{He will [then] give you a double portion of His mercy}**: This word means "*ḍi'fayn* (two-fold)" and this is "*kiflayn*" according to the Abyssinian language.

قَالَ ابْن قُتَيْبَة: والمشكاة: الكوة بِلِسَان الْحَبَشَة.

Ibn Qutaybah said, "'*Al-mishkāt*' is a word in the Abyssinian language which refers to a small window.

[٣١] أَنبأَنَا مُحَمَّد بن عبد الْبَاقِي بن أَحْمد قَالَ ثَنَا جَعْفَر بن أَحْمد السراج قَالَ أَنبأَنَا أَبُو الْحسن عَليّ بن عمر قَالَ أَنا أَحْمد بن إِبْرَاهِيم الْبَزَّاز عَن شيخ لَهُ قَالَ ثنا مُحَمَّد بن إِسْمَاعِيل الحساني قَالَ نَا وَكِيع قَالَ نَا إِسْرَائِيل عَن سعيد بن عِيَاض

قَالَ: الْمشكاة: الكوة بِلِسَان الْحَبَشَة.

Sa'īd ibn 'Iyād said, "'*Al-mishkāt*' in the Abyssinian language refers to a small window."

قَالَ وَكِيع: وَحدثنَا عمر بن أبي زَائِدَة قَالَ: سَمِعت عِكْرِمَة يَقُول ﴿طه﴾ بِلِسَان الْحَبَشَة: قل يَا رجل.

Wakī' said that 'Umar ibn Abī Zā'idah said, "I heard 'Ikrimah say that **{Ṭāha}** in the Abyssinian language means: 'Say, O man.'" [26]

قَالَ وَكِيع: وَحدثنَا أَبُو إِسْرَائِيل عَن أبي إِسْحَاق عَن سعيد بن جُبَير عَن ابْن عَبَّاس: ﴿إِن ناشئة اللَّيْل﴾ قَالَ بِلِسَان الْحَبَشَة إِذا شَاءَ قَامَ.

Wakī' said that Sa'īd ibn Jubayr reported upon the authority of Ibn 'Abbās that he said [in regards to the *āyah*] **{Verily, the rising by night}**, "According to the Abyssinian language this means, 'If he wills, he stands.'"[27]

وَقَالَ ابْن مَسْعُود: هِيَ قيام اللَّيْل بِلِسَان الْحَبَشَة.

Ibn Mas'ūd said, "It means 'standing during the night [in prayer]' in the language of the Abyssinians."

وَقَالَ الزّجاج: ناشئة اللَّيْل: ساعاته كل مَا تشَاء مِنْهُ.

Al-Zajāj said, "'Rising by night' means any part of the night."

[٣٢] أخبرنَا عبد الْوَهَّاب بن الْمُبَارك قَالَ أَنا أَبُو الْفضل ابْن خيرون قَالَ أَنا ابْن

26 Al-Suyūṭī said in *Azhār al-'Urūsh* (11/b), "This was reported by Ibn Abī Shaybah in *al-Muṣannaf* and Ibn Abī Ḥātim on the authority of 'Ikrimah, and al-Ḥākim in *al-Mustadrak* on the authority of Ibn 'Abbās—who graded it as *ṣaḥīḥ*."

27 See *Raf' Shān al-Ḥubshān* (p. 62/b) and al-Suyūṭī said in *Azhār al-'Urūsh* (12/b), "This was reported from Ibn 'Abbās by Wakī', Sa'īd ibn Manṣūr, Ibn Jarīr, Ibn Mundhir and al-Bayhaqī in *al-Sunan*."

شاذان قَالَ أَنا أَحْمد بن كَامِل قَالَ أَنا مُحَمَّد بن سعيد قَالَ حَدثنِي أبي قَالَ حَدثنِي عمر عَن أَبِيه عَن جده عَن ابْن عَبَّاس ﴿إِن إِبْرَاهِيم لأواه حَلِيم﴾ قَالَ: الأواه: الْمُؤمن وَهُوَ بالحبشية.

Ibn ʿAbbās said, "**{Indeed Ibrāhīm was *awāhun* and forbearing}**[28]: '*Al-awāhun*' means 'believer' according to the Abyssinian language."[29]

28 Al-Tawbah: 114

29 The author of *al-Ṭirāz al-Manqūsh* (21/b and 22/a) said, "[In relation to the matter of exegetes citing words being found in other languages:] This does not mean that these words are not Arabic i.e. that they are Ḥabashih or Zanjīh, rather it is merely to highlight that the words are present in those languages as well [...] This is because Allāh did not speak to the Prophet except in the tongue of the Quraysh, as explicitly stated by Ibn al-Anbārī."

الْبَاب الثَّالِث عشر
Chapter Thirteen

فِي ذكر مَا سَمعه رَسُول اللَّهِ - صَلَّى اللَّهُ عَلَيْهِ وَسَلَّمَ - من كَلَام الْحَبَشَة فأعجبه
In mention of what the Messenger of Allāh ﷺ heard of the Abyssinian language and how he was impressed

[٣٣] أنبأنَا مُحَمَّد بن نَاصِر الْحَافِظ قَالَ أنا جَعْفَر بن أَحْمد قَالَ أنا عبيد اللَّهِ بن عمر الْوَاعِظ قَالَ حَدثنِي أبي قَالَ نَا عَليّ بن مُحَمَّد ابْن أَيُّوب الرقي وَعبد اللَّهِ بن مُحَمَّد بن زِيَاد النَّيْسَابُورِي قَالَا ثَنَا يُونُس بن عبد الْأَعْلَى قَالَ ثَنَا ابْن وهب قَالَ أَخْبرنِي مُسلم بن خَالِد عَن ابْن خثيم عَن أبي الزبير عَن جَابر قَالَ: لما رجعت مهاجرة الْحَبَشَة إِلَى رَسُول اللَّهِ قَالَ: ((أَلا تحدثوني بِأَعْجَب شَيْء رَأَيْتُمْ بِأَرْض الْحَبَشَة)).

Abī al-Zubayr reported upon the authority of Jābir, "When the emigrants of Abyssinia returned to the Messenger of Allāh ﷺ, he said, 'Would you inform me of the most remarkable thing you witnessed in the land of Abyssinia?'

قَالَ فتية مِنْهُم: يَا رَسُول اللَّهِ، بَينا نَحن جُلُوس إِذْ مرت علينا عَجُوز من عجائزهم، تحمل على رَأسهَا قلَّة من مَاء، فمرت بفتى مِنْهُم، فَجعل إِحْدَى يَدَيْهِ بَين كتفيها، ثمَّ رَفعهَا [فخرت] على ركبتيها فانْكَسَرت قلتهَا فَلَمَّا ارْتَفَعت التفتت إِلَيْهِ فَقَالَت: سَوف تعلم يَا غدر إِذا وضع اللَّهِ عز وَجل الْكُرْسِيّ، وَجمع الْأَوَّلين

والآخرين، وتكلمت الْأَيْدِي والأرجل بِمَا كَانُوا يَكْسِبُونَ، تعلم أَمْرِي وأمرك عِنْده غَدا.

A youngster from amongst them stated, 'O Messenger of Allāh, whilst we were sitting, an elderly woman from them passed by us and upon her head was a *qullah* (container) of water which she was carrying. She passed by a youngster from them, and he placed one of his hands between her two shoulders and pushed her, thus she fell to her knees and the container broke. When she stood back up she turned to him and stated, 'You will know O conniver when Allāh ﷻ establishes the *kursī* and gathers the first of mankind and the last, when the hands and feet will unveil what they used to earn, you will come to know my case and yours then.'

فَقَالَ رَسُول الله - صَلَّى اللَّهُ عَلَيْهِ وَسَلَّمَ -: ((صدقت: كَيفَ يقدس اللَّهِ قوما، لَا يُؤْخَذ لضعيفهم من قويهم؟)).

Then the Messenger of Allāh ﷺ said, 'She spoke the truth. Why would Allāh sanctify a people when they do not make their weak safe from their strong?'"[30]

30 Reported by Ibn Mājah (2/1329). It states in *al-Zawā'id*, "Its *isnād* (chain of narration) is *ḥasan*."

الْبَاب الرَّابِع عشر
Chapter Fourteen

فِي ذكر تَخْصِيص الْحَبَشَة بِالْأَذَانِ
In mention of the Abyssinians being singled out for the call to the prayer

[٣٤] أخبرنَا الكروخي قَالَ: أَنا أَبُو عَامر الْأَزْدِيّ قَالَ: أَنا الجراحي قَالَ ثَنَا المحبوبي قَالَ ثَنَا التِّرْمِذِيّ قَالَ ثَنَا أَحْمد بن منيع قَالَ ثَنَا زيد بن حباب قَالَ ثَنَا مُعَاوِيَة بن صَالح قَالَ ثَنَا أَبُو مَرْيَم الْأَنْصَارِيّ عَن أبي هُرَيْرَة [رَضِي اللَّهِ عَنهُ] قَالَ: قَالَ رَسُول اللَّهِ - صَلَّى اللَّهُ عَلَيْهِ وَسَلَّمَ -: ((الْملك فِي قُرَيْش، وَالْقَضَاء فِي الْأَنْصَار، وَالْأَذَان فِي الْحَبَشَة، وَالْأَمَانَة فِي الأزد)) يَعْنِي: الْيمن.

Abū Maryam al-Anṣārī reported on the authority of Abī Hurayrah that he said, "The Messenger of Allāh ﷺ said, 'Leadership is for the Quraysh, the judiciary is for the Anṣār, the call to prayer is for the Abyssinians and the trust is amongst the Azd (i.e. the Yemenis).'"[31]

31 Reported by al-Tirmidhī in *al-Sunan*, within the Chapter of Virtues, section of the virtues of Yemen (9/421).

الْبَاب الْخَامِس عشر
Chapter Fifteen

فِيمَن ذكر أَنه كَانَ نَبيا من السودَان
Those of whom it has been said that they were Prophets from amongst black people

فَمِمَّنْ رُوِيَ أَنه كَانَ من الْأَنْبِيَاء أسود نَبِي أَصْحَاب الْأُخْدُود.

From those whom it has been narrated that they were black and from the Prophets is the prophet of Aṣḥāb al-'Ukhdūd (the people of al-'Ukhdūd).

[٣٥] فروى جَعْفَر بن مُحَمَّد بن الْفضل الرَّسْعَنِي فِي تَارِيخه بِإِسْنَادِهِ عَن عَليّ بن أبي طَالب قَالَ: كَانَ نَبِي أَصْحَاب الْأُخْدُود حَبَشِيًّا.

Ja'far ibn Muḥammad ibn al-Faḍl al-Ras'anī narrated in his *Tārīkh* (book of history) with his *isnād* (chain of narration) on the authority of 'Alī ibn Abī Ṭālib, "The Prophet of Aṣḥāb al-'Ukhdūd[32] was an Abyssinian."[33]

[وَذكر أهل التَّفْسِير: أَن الَّذين أحرقوا كَانُوا من الْحَبَشَة].

The scholars of *tafsīr* have stated that the ones who burned were from the Abyssinians.

قَالَ وهب بن مُنَبّه: كَانُوا اثْنَي عشر ألفا.

Wahb ibn al-Munabbih said, "They were twelve thousand in number."

---

32 People of the Ditch, see Sūrah al-Burūj.

33 Al-Suyūṭī said in *Azhār al-'Urūsh* (6/a), "This was reported by Ibn Abī Ḥātim on the authority of 'Alī ﷺ.

وَقَالَ ابْن السَّائِب: سبعين ألفا.

Ibn al-Sā'ib said, "They were seventy thousand in number."

وَكَانَ السَّبَب فِي إحراقهم مَا روينَا عَن عَليّ بن أبي طَالب رَضِي اللَّهِ عَنهُ أنه قَالَ: كَانَ ملك من الْمُلُوك قد سكر فَوَقع على أُخْته، فَلَمَّا أَفَاق قَالَ لَهَا: وَيحك، كَيفَ الْمخْرج؟ فَقَالَت لَهُ: اجْمَعْ أهل مملكتك فَأخْبرهُم أَن اللَّهِ قد أحل نِكَاح الْأَخَوَات، فَإِذا ذهب هَذَا فِي النَّاس وتناسوه، خطبتهم تحرمه، فَفعل ذَلِك، فَأَبَوا أَن يقبلُوا ذَلِك مِنْهُ، فَبسط فيهم السَّوْط، ثمَّ جرد السَّيْف فَأَبَوا، فَخدَّ لَهُم أُخْدُودًا وأوقد فِيهِ النَّار، وَقذف من أبى قبُول ذَلِك.

The reason for their burning is found within that which we have reported from 'Alī ibn Abī Ṭālib ﵁, "One of the kings became intoxicated and approached his sister intimately. When he became sober, he said to her, 'Woe to you, what should we do to get out of this trouble?' She replied, 'Gather your people and inform them that Allāh has permitted marriage between siblings, and then when this leaves the minds of the people and they forget, address them regarding its forbiddance.' He did this and the people rejected this from him, so he lashed his whip at them and uncovered his sword but they still rejected him. Then he prepared a ditch for them and ignited a fire within it, and those who opposed were thrown in it.'"

فصل
Section

وَقد اخْتلفُوا فِي ذِي القرنين

There is a difference of opinion in regards to Dhū al-Qarnayn.

فَقَالَ عبد اللَّهِ بن عَمْرو بن سعيد بن الْمسيب وَالضَّحَّاك بن مُزَاحم: كَانَ نَبيا.

ʿAbd Allāh ibn ʿAmr ibn Saʿīd ibn al-Musayyib and al-Ḍaḥḥāk ibn Muzāhim said, "He was a Prophet."

[٣٦] وروينا عَن عَليّ بن أبي طَالب رَضِي اللَّهِ عَنهُ أَنه قَالَ: كَانَ عبدا صَالحا من الْقُرُون الأول من ولد يافث بن نوح.

We have reported on the authority of ʿAlī ibn Abī Ṭālib ﷺ that he said, "He was a righteous servant from the early centuries from the descendants of Yāfith ibn Nūḥ."[34]

[٣٧] وَذكر جَعْفَر بن مُحَمَّد الرَّسْعَني فِي تَارِيخه عَن إِبْرَاهِيم عَن عَليّ ابْن أبي طَالب رَضِي اللَّهِ عَنهُ قَالَ: كَانَ ذُو القرنين أسود.

Jaʿfar ibn Muḥammad al-Rasʾanī mentioned in his *Tārīkh* upon the authority of Ibrāhīm that ʿAlī ibn Abī Ṭālib ﷺ said, "Dhū al-Qarnayn was black."

وَقَالَ أَبُو الْحُسَيْن بن الْمُنَادِي: كَانَ ذُو القرنين فِي زمن [إِبْرَاهِيم] الْخَلِيل [عَلَيْهِ السَّلَام] وَمَات فِي ذَلِك الزَّمن.

Abū al-Ḥusayn al-Munādī said, "Dhū al-Qarnayn lived during Ibrāhīm al-Khalīl's era and he passed away during that period."[35]

وَفِي عِلّة تَسْمِيَته بِذِي القرنين عشرَة أَقْوَال:

In terms of him being called Dhū al-Qarnayn there are ten opinions regarding why:

الأول: أَنه دَعَا قومه إِلَى اللَّهِ تَعَالَى فضربوه على قرنه فَهَلَك، فغبر زَمَانا ثمَّ بَعثه اللَّه تَعَالَى فَدَعَاهُمْ إِلَى اللَّهِ [تَعَالَى] فضربوه على قرنه الآخر فَهَلَك، فَذَلِك قرناه، قَالَه عَليّ [بن أبي طَالب] .

34 See *al-Bidāyat wa al-Nihāyat* of Ibn Kathīr (2/103).

35 This view was deemed as preponderant by Ibn Kathīr. See *al-Bidāyat wa al-Nihāyat* (2/103).

One. He called his people to Allāh ﷻ and they struck him upon his horn, causing him to die. This time period passed and Allāh ﷻ resurrected him [in another time period] and so he again called them to Allāh and they struck him on another horn, causing him to die. These are his two horns, and this was stated by 'Alī ibn Abī Ṭālib.

الثَّانِي: أَنه سمي بذلك لِأَنَّهُ سَار إِلَى مغرب الشَّمْس وَإِلَى مطْلعهَا. رَوَاهُ أَبُو صَالح عَن ابْن عَبَّاس.

Two. He travelled to where the sun sets and to where it rises. This was reported by Abū Ṣāliḥ on the authority of Ibn 'Abbās.[36]

وَالثَّالِث: لِأَن صفحتي رَأسه كَانَتَا من نُحَاس.

Three. The sides of his head [had horns] made from copper.

الرَّابِع: لِأَنَّهُ رأى فِي النّوم كَأَنَّهُ امْتَدَّ من السَّمَاء إِلَى الأَرْض فَأخذ بقرني الشَّمْس فقص ذَلِك على قومه فَسُمي بِذِي القرنين.

Four. He saw himself in a dream and it was as if he extended (i.e. fell) from the sky to the earth and so he held onto the sun by its two horns. He subsequently informed his people about this and so he was named Dhū al-Qarnayn.

الْخَامِس: لِأَنَّهُ ملك فَارس وَالروم.

Five. He was king of both the Persians and Romans.

السَّادِس: لِأَنَّهُ كَانَ فِي رَأسه شبه القرنين.

Six. There was something on his head which resembled two horns.

رويت هَذِه الْأَقْوَال الْأَرْبَعَة عَن وهب بن مُنَبّه.

36 This view was deemed as preponderant by Ibn Kathīr. See *al-Bidāyat wa al-Nihāyat* (2/103-104).

The latter four opinions were reported upon the authority of Wahb ibn Munabbih.

السَّابِع: لِأَنَّهُ كَانَت لَهُ غديرتان من شعر. قَالَه الْحسن. قَالَ ابْن الْأَنْبَارِي: وَالْعرب تسمى ضفيرتي الشّعْر غديرتين وقرنين.

Seven. He had two braids of hair. This was stated by al-Ḥasan. Ibn al-Anbārī said, "The Arabs intend through '*ḍafīratay al-sha'r*': 'two braids' and 'two horns'.

الثَّامِن: أنه كَانَ كريم الطَّرفَيْنِ من أهل بَيت ذَوي شرف.

Eight. He was from a noble and eminent family on both sides.

التَّاسِع: لِأَنَّهُ انقرض فِي زَمَانه قرنان من النَّاس وَهُوَ حَيّ.

Nine. The people of two centuries during his time passed whilst he remained living.

الْعَاشِر: لِأَنَّهُ سلك الظلمَة والنور.

Ten. He would travel during the darkness and the light.

ذكر هَذِه الْأَقْوَال الثَّلَاثَة أَبُو إِسْحَاق الثَّعْلَبِيّ.

These latter three views were mentioned by Abū Isḥāq al-Tha'labī.

قَالَ مُجَاهِد: ملك الأَرْض أَرْبَعَة: مُؤْمِنَانِ وَكَافِرَانِ، فالمؤمنان: سُلَيْمَان بن دَاوُد [نَبِي اللَّهِ] وَذُو القرنين، والكافران: نمْرُود، وبخت نصر.

Mujāhid said, "The rulers of the earth were four, two of them were believers and two of them were disbelievers. The believers were Sulaymān ibn Dāwūd (the Prophet of Allāh) and Dhū al-Qarnayn. The disbelievers were Namrūd and Bukhtu Naṣṣar.

[٣٨] أخبرنَا مُحَمَّد بن عمر الأرموي قَالَ أنا أَبُو الْحُسَيْن بن الْمُهْتَدي قَالَ نَا أَبُو حَفْص بن شاهين قَالَ نَا مُحَمَّد بن مُحَمَّد الباغندي قَالَ ثنَا عُثْمَان بن أبي شيبَة قَالَ ثنَا أَبُو أُسَامَة قَالَ حَدثنِي زَائِدَة عَن سماك بن حَرْب عَن حبيب بن حَازِم قَالَ: قَالَ رجل لعَلي [رَضِي اللَّهِ عَنهُ] كَيفَ بلغ ذُو القرنين الْمشرق وَالْمغْرب؟

Samāk ibn Ḥarb reported upon the authority of Ḥabīb ibn Ḥāzim, "A man stated to 'Alī ﷺ, 'How did Dhū al-Qarnayn reach the east and the west?'

فَقَالَ عَليّ: سخر لَهُ السَّحَاب، ومدت لَهُ الْأَسْبَاب، وَبسط لَهُ النُّور.

'Alī replied, 'The clouds were subjected to him, the means were laid out for him and the light accompanied him at all times (i.e. the day and the night were the same for him).'"

قَالَ الْحسن الْبَصْرِيّ: كَانَ ذُو القرنين يركب فِي ألف ألف، وعَلى مقدمته سِتّمائَة ألف، وعَلى ساقته مائَة ألف. [فسبحان الْحَيّ الْبَاقِي] .

Al-Ḥasan al-Baṣrī said, "Dhū al-Qarnayn rode amongst a million, he was preceded by six hundred thousand, and he was followed by one hundred thousand."[37] And exalted is al-Ḥayy (the Everlasting), al-Bāqī (the Ever Remaining).

ذكر صفة بنائه السد

In mention of how he built the barrier

[٣٩] روى أَبُو الْحُسَيْن بن الْمُنَادِي: أَنه لما عزم ذُو القرنين على الْمسير إِلَى مطلع الشَّمْس أَخذ على طَرِيق كابل والهند وتبت فتَلَقَّتْهُ الْمُلُوك بالتحف وَالْأَمْوَال، وانتهى إِلَى الْحُصُون المعطلة، وَقد بقيت فِيهِ بقايا فَسَأَلُوهُ أَن يسد الرَّدْم، فَنزل مَعَه

37 See *al-Bidāyat wa al-Nihāyat* of Ibn Kathīr (2/106).

الصناع، فَاتخذ قدور [النّحاس و] الْحَدِيد الْكِبَار، والمغارف الْحَدِيد.

It was reported by Abū al-Ḥusayn ibn al-Munādī, "When Dhū al-Qarnayn resolved to travel to the place where the sun rises he took the route through Kabul, Hind and Tibet, and the kings greeted him with ornaments and wealth. He reached a place where there were ruined fortresses of which some remained, and he was asked to help rebuild the ruins. So he went to do this alongside some craftsmen, taking copper cauldrons, large pieces of iron and iron trowels.

وَأمر أَن يَجْعَل كل أَرْبَعَة من تِلْكَ الْقُدُور على حِدة، كَانَ طول كل وَاحِد خَمْسُونَ ذِرَاعا، وَأمر الصناع أَن يضْربُوا لبن الْحَدِيد فضربوها طول كل لبنة ذِرَاع وَنصف، وسمكها شبر، وبنوا السد، وَجعلُوا فِي وَسطه بَابا عَظِيما عَلَيْهِ مصراعان، كل مصراع خَمْسُونَ ذِرَاعا وَعَلِيهِ قفل نَحْو عشرَة أَذْرع، فَلَمَّا فرغ من بِنَاء السد أضرم عَلَيْهِ النَّار فَصَارَ معجونا كَأَنَّهُ حجر وَاحِد.

He ordered his subjects to place each four pots upon a base the measurement of which its length was fifty cubits. Then he ordered the craftsmen to smite the iron to produce iron bricks, and the length of each brick was one and a half cubits, and the thickness was a hand-span. Thus, they built the barrier and placed in the middle of it a great door of which there were two panels—of which each was fifty cubits—and upon it was a lock which was approximately ten cubits. When the building of the barrier was completed, fire was kindled upon it and so it set together as if it was a single stone.

[٤٠] قَالَ أَبُو الْحُسَيْن بن الْمُنَادِي: وَبَلغنِي عَن ابْن خرداذبة قَالَ: حَدثنِي سَلام الترجمان أَن الواثق لما رأى فِي الْمَنَام أَن السد الَّذِي سَده ذُو القرنين قد انْفَتح وجهني فَقَالَ: عاينه وائتني بِخَبَرِهِ. وَضم إِلَيّ خمسين رجلا، ووصلني بِخَمْسَة آلَاف دِينَار وَأَعْطَانِي ديتي عشرَة آلَاف دِرْهَم، [وَأمر بِإِعْطَاء كل رجل معي ألف دِرْهَم] ، ورزق سِتَّة أشهر، وَأَعْطَانِي مِائَتي بغل تحمل الزَّاد وَالْمَاء، فشخصنا من

سر من رأى بِكِتَاب من الواثق إِلَى أبي إِسْحَاق بن إِسْمَاعِيل صَاحب أرمينية فِي إنفاذها فَكتب لنا إِسْحَاق إِلَى صَاحب السرر، فَكتب لنا ذَلِك إِلَى اللاب وَكتب لنا إِلَى فيلا نشاه، فَكتب لنا إِلَى الخزر، فَأَقَمْنَا عِنْد ملك الخزر يَوْمًا وَلَيْلَة، ثمَّ وَجه مَعنا خمسين رجلا أدلاء، فسرنا من عِنْده خمْسا وَعشْرين يَوْمًا ثمَّ صرنا إِلَى أَرض سَوْدَاء منتنه الرّيح، وَقد كُنَّا تزودنا قبل دُخُولهَا طيبا نشمه للرائحة الْمَكْرُوهَة فسرنا فِيهَا عشرَة أَيَّام، ثمَّ صرنا إِلَى مدن خراب، فسرنا فِيهَا سَبْعَة وَعشْرين يَوْمًا، فسألنا عَن تِلْكَ المدن فخبرنا أَنَّهَا المدن الَّتِي كَانَ يَأْجُوج وَمَأْجُوج يطرقونها، فخربوها، ثمَّ صرنا إِلَى حصون بِالْقربِ من الْجَبَل الَّذِي السد فِي شعب مِنْهُ، وَفِي تِلْكَ الْحُصُون قوم يَتَكَلَّمُونَ بِالْعَرَبِيَّةِ والفارسية، مُسلمُونَ يقرؤون الْقُرْآن لَهُم كتاتيب ومساجد، فَسَأَلُونَا من أَيْن أقبلتم؟ فأخبرناهم أَنا رسل أَمِير الْمُؤمنِينَ فَأَقْبَلُوا يتعجبون وَيَقُولُونَ: أَمِير الْمُؤمنِينَ! قُلْنَا: نعم، فَقَالُوا: شيخ هُوَ أم شَاب؟ فَقُلْنَا: شَاب، فَقَالُوا: أَيْن يكون؟ قُلْنَا: بالعراق فِي مَدِينَة يُقَال لَهَا: سر من رأى، فَقَالُوا: مَا سمعنَا بِهَذَا قطّ.

Abū Ḥusayn ibn al-Munādī said that it reached him from Ibn Khurdādbīh upon the authority of Sallām al-Tarjamān, "When al-Wāthiq saw in a dream that the barrier which Dhū al-Qarnayn had built opened, he dispatched a message to me, 'Observe this and bring me news regarding it.' He provided me with fifty men, five thousand dinars, and gave me my blood money should I die in this journey, which was ten thousand dirhams, he ordered me to give each man with me one thousand dirhams, and six months' provisions. He also provided me with two hundred mules to carry the provisions and water. We embarked from [a town called] Surra Man Ra'ā (it has been said that this refers to a city in Irāq) with a letter from al-Wāthiq to Abī Isḥāq ibn Ismā'īl from Armenia which detailed our duty. Īsḥāq then wrote a letter for us to [the leader known as] Ṣāḥib al-Sarīr (holder of the throne), he wrote for us to Lāb, who wrote for us to Fīlā Nashāh, who wrote for us to Khazr, and we spent a day and a night with the king of Khazr. He then sent with us fifty guides and we embarked from him for twenty-five days, then we reached the Black Land where there was a putrid smell. We had prepared ourselves before entering it with perfume to smell, so as to combat the bad smell. We marched ten days within there and then we reached ruined towns. We marched for twenty-seven days there and we enquired about the towns, and we were informed that they were the towns which Yā'jūj and Ma'jūj use to descend into during the night and lay ruin to. Then we travelled to some fortresses close to the mountain within which the barrier was present in one of its passes. In these fortresses were a group of people who spoke Arabic and Persian and they were Muslims who recited the Qur'ān and they had *kuttāb* (schools for learning to read and write, and to learn the Qur'ān) and *masājid*. They inquired from us, 'From where did you come from?' We informed them that we were envoys sent by the Commander of the Faithful and they became surprised at this, saying, 'The Commander of the Faithful?' We replied affirmatively and they said, 'Is he a *shaykh* (i.e. mature in age) or is he a youth?' We replied, 'He is a youth.' They stated, 'Where is he situated?' We replied, 'He is in Iraq in a town known as Surra Man Rāā.' They said, 'We have never heard of this before.'

ثمَّ صرنا إِلَى جبل أملس لَيْسَ عَلَيْهِ خضراء، وَإِذا جبل مَقْطُوع بواد عرض مائَة وَخَمْسُونَ ذِرَاعا، وَإِذا عضادتان مبنيتان مِمَّا يَلِي الْجَبَل من جنبتي الْوَادي عرض كل عضادة خمس وَعِشْرُونَ ذِرَاعا، الظَّاهِر من تحتهَا عشرَة أَذْرع خَارج الْبَاب، وَعَلِيهِ بِنَاء بِلَبن من حَدِيد مغيب فِي نُحَاس فِي سمك خمسين ذِرَاعا، وَإِذا دروند حَدِيد طرفاه على العضادتين طوله مائَة وَعِشْرُونَ ذِرَاعا، قد ركب على العضادتين على وَاحِد بِمِقْدَار عشرَة أَذْرع فِي عرض خَمْسَة أَذْرع، وَفَوق الدروند بِنَاء بذلك الْحَدِيد المغيب فِي النّحاس إِلَى رَأس الْجَبَل فِي ارتفاعه مد الْبَصَر، وَفَوق ذَلِك شرف حَدِيد فِي كل شرفة قرنان، ينثني كل وَاحِد مِنْهُمَا إِلَى صَاحبه، وَإِذا بَاب حَدِيد عَلَيْهِ مصراعان مغلقان عرض كل مصراع خَمْسُونَ ذِرَاعا، فِي ارْتِفَاع خمسين فِي نَحْو خَمْسَة أَذْرع وقائمتاهما فِي دوارة فِي قدر الدروند وعَلى

الْبَاب قفل طوله تِسْعَة أَذْرع فِي غلظ ذِرَاع فِي الاستدارة وارتفاع القفل من الأَرْض خمس وَعِشْرُونَ ذِرَاعا، وَفَوق القفل بِقدر خَمْسَة أَذْرع غلق طوله أَكثر من طول القفل، وقفيز كل وَاحِد مِنْهُمَا ذراعان، وعَلى الغلق مِفْتَاح مُعَلّق طوله ذِرَاع وَنصف، وَله اثْنَتَا عشرَة دريجة، كل وَاحِدَة قدر فَرسَخ أكبر مَا يكون من هاون مُعَلّق فِي سلسلة طولهَا ثَمَان أَذْرع فِي استدارة أَرْبَعَة أشبار، وَالْحَلقَة الَّتِي فِيهَا السلسلة مثل حَلقَة المنجنيق، وَعتبَة الْبَاب عشرَة أَذْرع بسط مائَة ذِرَاع سوى مَا تَحت العضادتين، وَالظَّاهِر مِنْهَا خَمْسَة أَذْرع، وَهَذَا الذِّرَاع كُله بالذراع السرداء.

After this, we embarked to a mountain which was smooth and bereft of plantation. There was a mountain cut with a valley which was one hundred and fifty cubits wide, there were two posts built following the mount, one on each side of the valley and the width of each post was twenty-five cubits—from underneath it ten cubits were visible outside the door. There was building work upon it constructed from bricks of iron which was covered by copper, the depth of which was fifty cubits. Between the posts there was an iron hinged flat section—the length of which was one hundred and twenty cubits—which was built over the two posts, the measurement of each side on each post was ten cubits in length by five cubits in width. Above the hinged flat section was a construction made from the iron which was covered by the copper, and it ascended to the highest point of the mountain—going as far as the eye could see. Above this was a balcony constructed of iron, and upon each balcony were two horns—each bent towards its counterpart. There was a door made of iron upon which there were two closed panels, each being fifty cubits wide and fifty cubits high. Their supports were round and similar in size to the hinged flat section and upon the door was a lock—the length of which was nine cubits and its thickness was one cubit. The height of the lock from the ground was twenty-five cubits. Five cubits above this lock there was a fastening which was longer than the lock, and the measurement of each was two cubits. Upon the fastening there was a hanging key which was one and a half cubits long and which had twelve small slots,[38] the size of each being equal to a *farsakh*,

38 This is a Farsi word.

the largest of all mortars hinged in a chain that was eight cubits in length and the distance around a circle-shaped pot was four hand spans. The ring through which the chain was placed was similar to the ring of the catapult, and the doorstep was ten cubits by one hundred cubits excluding the area underneath the two posts, but only five cubits of it was visible. All of these measurements are based upon the black cubit measurement (i.e. one black cubit equals 26.33 finger lengths).

وَرَئِيس تِلْكَ الْحُصُون يركب فِي كل جُمُعَة فِي عشرَة فوارس مَعَ كل فَارس مرزبة حَدِيد، فِي كل وَاحِدَة خَمْسُونَ وَمِائَة منا، فَيضْرب القفل بِتِلْكَ المرزبات فِي كل يَوْم مَرَّات ليسمع من وَرَاء الْبَاب الصَّوْت، فيعلموا أَن هُنَالك حفظَة، وَيعلم هَؤُلَاءِ أَنه أُولَئِكَ لم يحدثوا فِي الْبَاب حَدثا، وَإِذا ضرب أَصْحَابنَا القفل وضعُوا آذانهم فيسمعون لمن هُوَ دَاخل دويا، وبالقرب من هَذَا الْموضع حصن كَبِير يكون عشرَة فراسخ فِي عشرَة فراسخ تكسير مائَة فَرسَخ، وَمَعَ الْبَاب حصنان يكون كل وَاحِد مِنْهُمَا مِائَتي ذِرَاع فِي مِائَتي ذِرَاع، وعَلى بَاب هذَيْن الحصنين شجرتان، وَبَين الحصنين عين عذبة، فِي أحد الحصنين آلَة الْبناء الَّذِي بني بِهِ السد من الْقُدُور الْحَدِيد والمغارف الْحَدِيد.

Every Friday, the head of this fortress would ride with ten horsemen and every horseman would carry an iron hammer—each one being one hundred and fifty *mannan* (an old measurement). The lock was hit with these hammers on a number of occasions during each day so that those behind the door would hear the sound, and so that they would know that it was being guarded, and so that the ones [on this side] would know that the door had not been tampered by them. When our companions would strike the lock, they would place their ears against it so as to hear the echoing voices. Close to this location there was a large fortress which was ten *farsakhs* by ten *farsakhs*, divided into one hundred *farsakhs*. Next to the door there were two fortresses, each of which was two hundred cubits by two hundred cubits, and in front of their doors there were two trees, and there was a spring of fresh water between the two fortresses. In one of the fortresses were the tools used to construct the barrier, including the iron cauldrons and the trowels.

على كل أثفية أَربع قدور مثل قدور الصابون، وَهُنَاكَ بَقِيَّة من اللَّبن قد التزق بَعْضهَا بِبَعْض من الصدأ، واللبنة ذِرَاع وَنصف فِي سمك شبر، وسألوا من هُنَالك؟ هَل رَأَوْا أحدا من يَأْجُوج وَمَأْجُوج فَذكرُوا أنهم رَأَوْا مرّة عددا فَوق الشّرف فهبت ريح سَوْدَاء، فألقتهم إِلَى جانبهم، وَكَانَ مِقْدَار الرجل مِنْهُم فِي رَأْي الْعين شبْرًا وَنصفا.

[There were stones to hold up the cauldrons] and upon each stone there were four cauldrons, similar to soap pots. In this location we found the remainder of the bricks and they had conjoined together due to rust. Each of them was one and a half cubits with the thickness of a hand-span. We asked those present if they had seen anyone from Ya'jūj and Ma'jūj. They mentioned that they had seen them on a few occasions on the roof but they were blown back by the black wind. The size of each individual from them from the distance they viewed them was one and a half hand-spans."

قَالَ سَلام الترجمان: فَلَمَّا انصرفنا أخذتنا الأدلاء إِلَى نَاحيَة خُرَاسَان فسرنا إِلَيْهَا حَتَّى خرجنَا خلف سَمَرْقَنْد بِسبع فراسخ، وَقد كَانَ أَصْحَاب الْحُصُون زودونا مَا كفانا، ثمَّ صرنا إِلَى عبد اللَّهِ بن طَاهِر، قَالَ سَلام: فوصلني بِمِائَة ألف دِرْهَم، وَوصل كل رجل معي بِخَمْسِمِائَة دِرْهَم، وأجرى للفراس خَمْسَة دَرَاهِم، وللراجل ثَلَاثَة دَرَاهِم فِي كل يَوْم إِلَى الرّى، فرجعنا إِلَى سر من رأى بعد خروجنا بِثمَانِيَة وَعشْرين شهرا.

Sallām al-Tarjamān continued, "When we exited from there, the guides took us towards the direction of Khurāsān and we marched towards it until we were seven *farsakhs* behind Samarqand. The inhabitants of the fortresses had provided us with sufficient provisions. Then we went to 'Abdullāh ibn Ṭāhir." Sallām said, "He gave me ten thousand dirhams, and he provided each of the men accompanying me with five hundred dirhams. He allocated each horseman with five dirhams and three dirhams to those on foot for each day until we reached the city of al-Ray. We returned to Surra Man Rāā twenty-eight months after we left."

قَالَ ابْن خرداذبة: فَحَدثني سَلام الترجمان بجملة هَذَا الْخَيْر، ثمَّ أمله عَليّ من كتاب كتبه للواثق.

Ibn Khurdādhbih said, "Sallām al-Tarjamān narrated this story to me in a general manner, and then he dictated to me that which he wrote for al-Wāthiq."

وَقد روى عَطاء عَن ابْن عَبَّاس أَن ذَا القرنين لَقِي إِبْرَاهِيم الْخَلِيل [عَلَيْهِ السَّلَام] بِمَكَّة فَسلم عَلَيْهِ واعتنقه.

'Aṭā narrated on the authority of Ibn 'Abbās that Dhū al-Qarnayn met Ibrāhīm al-Khalīl ﷺ in Makkah, and he greeted him and embraced him.

وَفِي حَدِيث آخر أَنه سمع بإبراهيم فَنزل فَمشى إِلَيْهِ، وَقَالَ: مَا كنت لأركب فِي بلد فِيهِ إِبْرَاهِيم.

Another narration states that he heard about Ibrāhīm and so he dismounted and walked to him. He said, "Indeed I would not ride a mount within a city wherein Ibrāhīm is located."[39]

وروى أَرْبَاب السّير: أَن ذَا القرنين أَمر بِبِنَاء مدن كَثِيرَة مِنْهَا، الدهرسية، وجهدان، وسيرل، وبرج الْحِجَارَة، وَلما بلغ الْهِنْد بنى مَدِينَة: سرنديب، وَأَن أَرْبَاب الْحساب قَالُوا لَهُ: إِنَّك لَا تَمُوت إِلَّا على أَرض [من] حَدِيد وسماء من خشب. وَكَانَ يدْفن كنوز كل أَرض بهَا، وَيكْتب ذَلِك بمقداره وموضعه فَبلغ بابل فرعف فَسقط عَن دَابَّته فبسطت لَهُ درع، فَنَامَ عَلَيْهِ، فآذته الشَّمْس فأظلوه بترس فَنظر فَقَالَ:

---

39 This narration and the one before it were mentioned by Ibn Kathīr in *al-Bidāyat wa al-Nihāyah* (2/103).

هَذِه أَرض من حَدِيد وسماء من خشب، فأيقن بِالْمَوْتِ فَمَاتَ وَهُوَ ابْن ألف وسِتمِائَة سنة.

It was reported by the great fable-tellers that Dhū al-Qarnayn ordered the construction of many cities. Amongst them were al-Dahrasiyyah, Juhudān, Sayral, Burj al-Hijārah and then when he reached al-Hind he constructed the city Sarandīb, and a great soothsayer stated to him, "You will not die except upon a ground made of iron and [under] a sky made of wood." Dhū al-Qarnayn would bury treasure in every land [he visited], and he would record it alongside the amount. When he reached Babylon, he suffered from a nose bleed and subsequently fell from the animal he was riding. His armour was opened for him and he slept upon it. He became annoyed by the sun and so those around him provided him with shade with a shield. It was after seeing this that he noted, "This is the ground made of iron and the sky made of wood," and he ascertained that he was to die. So, he died and he was one thousand six hundred years old.

فصل
Section

[قَالَ الْمُصَنّف رَحمَه الله] وَقد اخْتلفُوا فِي لُقْمَان: فَقَالَ الْأَكْثَرُونَ: إِنَّه كَانَ حكيما وَلم يكن نَبيا.

The author said: They differed in regards to Luqmān, however the majority are of the view that he was a wise man and not a prophet.[40]

وَقَالَ سعيد بن الْمسيب: بل كَانَ نَبيا.

Sa'īd ibn al-Musayyib asserted, "He was a prophet."

قَالَ ابْن إِسْحَاق: كَانَ لُقْمَان أسود، وَقَالَ غَيره: كَانَ حَبَشِيًّا لرجل قصار من بني

40 See *al-Bidāyat wa al-Nihāyah* (2/123).

إِسْرَائِيل اشْتَرَاهُ بِثَلَاثِينَ دِينَارا، وَإِن مَوْلَاهُ أمره يَوْمًا بِذبح شَاة وأوصاه أَن يخرج مِنْهَا أطيب مضغتين فِيهَا فَأخْرج اللِّسَان وَالْقلب، ثمَّ إِن مَوْلَاهُ قَالَ لَهُ بعد مُدَّة: اذْبَحْ لنا شَاة، وَأخرج أَخبث مضغتين فِيهَا، فَأخْرج مِنْهَا اللِّسَان وَالْقلب، فَقَالَ لَهُ مَوْلَاهُ: مَا هَذَا؟ فَقَالَ: مَا فِي الشَّاة أطيب من قلبهَا ولسانها [إِذا طابا] ، وَلَا أَخبث مِنْهُمَا - إِذا خبثا -[وَكَذَلِكَ ابْن آدم لَيْسَ شَيْء أحسن من قلبه وَلسَانه وَلَا أَخبث مِنْهُمَا إِذا خبثا] .

Ibn Isḥāq said, "Luqmān was black." Others said, "He was an Abyssinian and he was the slave of a bleacher from the tribe of Israel who purchased him for thirty dinars." [And they said,] "One day his master ordered him to slaughter a sheep with the instruction to remove its best two parts, and so he removed its tongue and heart. After some time, his master said, 'Slaughter a sheep for us and take out the vilest of its parts.' So, he removed its tongue and heart from it. Upon this his master said, 'Explain this.' He replied, 'There is nothing in the sheep better than its heart and tongue (if they are sound), and there is nothing viler than them (if they are vile). Likewise, is the case for the descendants of Ādam, there is nothing better than his heart and tongue, and nothing worse than them if they are vile.'"

وَقَالَ الْحسن: اعتزل لُقْمَان النَّاس فنزل فِيمَا بَين الرملة وَبَيت الْمُقَدّس لَا يخالطهم.

Al-Ḥasan said, "Luqmān detached himself from the people and he resided between al-Ramlah and Bayt al-Maqdis, not mixing with their people."

[٤١] حَدثنَا الْمُبَارك بن عَليّ الصَّيْرَفِي لفظا قَالَ أَنا أَحْمد بن الْحُسَيْن بن قُرَيْش قَالَ أَنا إِبْرَاهِيم بن عمر الْبَرْمَكِي قَالَ أَنا أَبُو بكر مُحَمَّد بن زَكَرِيَّا الدقاق قَالَ ثَنَا عبد اللَّهِ بن سُلَيْمَان قَالَ ثَنَا عبد الْملك بن مُحَمَّد بن عبد اللَّهِ قَالَ نَا ابْن عَائِشَة قَالَ ثَنَا سعيد بن عَامر قَالَ حَدثنِي حسن أَبُو جَعْفَر قَالَ: كَانَ لُقْمَان الحبشي عبدا لرجل جَاءَ بِهِ إِلَى السُّوق ليَبِيعهُ قَالَ: فَكَانَ كلما جَاءَ إِنْسَان يَشْتَرِيه، قَالَ

لَهُ لُقْمَان: مَا تصنع بِي؟ قَالَ: أصنع بك كَذَا وَكَذَا، قَالَ: حَاجَتي إِلَيْك أَن لَا تشتريني حَتَّى جَاءَ رجل فَقَالَ: مَا تصنع بِي؟ قَالَ: أصيرك بوابا على بَابي، قَالَ: أَنْت اشترني، فَاشْتَرَاهُ، وَجَاء بِهِ إِلَى دَاره، [قَالَ: قَالَ:] وَكَانَ لمَوْلَاهُ ثَلَاث بَنَات يبغين فِي الْقرْيَة، وَأَرَادَ أَن يخرج إِلَى ضَيْعَة لَهُ فَقَالَ: إِنِّي قد أدخلت إِلَيْهِنَّ طعامهن وَمَا يحتجن إِلَيْهِ فَإِذا خرجت فأغلق الْبَاب واقعد من وَرَائه وَلَا تفتحه حَتَّى أجيء. قَالَ: فخرجن إِلَيْهِ كَمَا كن يخرجن، فَقُلْنَ لَهُ: افْتَحْ الْبَاب، فَأبى عَلَيْهِنَّ فشججنه، فَغسل الدَّم وَجلسَ فَلَمَّا قدم لم يُخبرهُ، ثمَّ عَاد مَوْلَاهُ بعد الْخُرُوج فَقَالَ: إِنِّي قد أدخلت إِلَيْهِنَّ مَا يحتجن إِلَيْهِ فَلَا تفتحن الْبَاب، فَلَمَّا خرج خرجن إِلَيْهِ فَقُلْنَ لَهُ: افْتَحْ فَأبى فشججن ورجعن فَجَلَسَ [يبكي] فَلَمَّا جَاءَ الْمولى لم يُخبرهُ بِشَيْء. قَالَ: فَقَالَت الْكَبِيرَة: وَمَا بَال هَذَا العَبْد الحبشي أولى بِطَاعَة اللَّهِ [عز وَجل] مني! وَالله لأتوبن، فتابت. فَقَالَت الصُّغْرَى: وَمَا بَال هَذَا العَبْد الحبشي وَهَذِه الْكُبْرَى أولى بِطَاعَة الله مني! وَالله لأتوبن، فتابت: فَقَالَت الْوُسْطَى: مَا بَال هَاتَانِ وَهَذَا العَبْد الحبشي أولى بِطَاعَة اللَّهِ عز وَجل مني! وَالله لأتوبن. قَالَ: فَقُلْنَ غواة الْقرْيَة: مَا بَال هَذَا العَبْد الحبشي وَبَنَات فلَان أولى بِطَاعَة اللَّهِ عز وَجل منا فتبن إِلَى اللَّهِ عز وَجل، فَكُن عوابد الْقرْيَة.

Saʿīd ibn ʿAmir reported upon the authority of Ḥasan ibn Jaʿfar, "Luqmān al-Ḥabashī was the slave of a man who took him to the marketplace so as to sell him." He continued, "Whenever someone came to purchase him, Luqmān would say to him, 'What would you make me do?' The reply would be, 'I would make you do such and such.' Luqmān would thus say, 'I request that you do not purchase.' This was the case until a man came and was asked, 'What would you make me do?' His reply was, 'I would utilise you as a gatekeeper of my door.' So, he said, 'Purchase me,' and the man took him to his home." He said, "His master had three daughters who were promiscuous in the village. Once when the master desired to go to his farm, he said, 'I have provided them with their food and that which they need, so when I leave, lock the door and sit behind it. Do not open it until I return.'" He continued, "The daughters came out to the door as they would normally do so and they said to him, 'Open the door.' He refused and so they caused him injury. He washed the blood and sat in his place until his master returned. He did not inform him of what took place. His master left again and said to him, 'I have provided them with their needs so do not open the door for them.' When he left, they again went to him and demanded the door to be opened. He resisted and so they caused him injury and returned back. He sat in his place whilst crying. However, when his master returned, he did not inform him of anything." He continued, "The eldest of them said, 'How is it that this Abyssinian slave is superior in obedience to Allāh than me? By Allāh I will repent.' And so she repented. The youngest of them stated, 'How is it that this Abyssinian slave and [my] elder [sister] can be superior in obedience to Allāh than me? By Allāh I will repent.' And so she repented. The middle one said, 'How is it that these two and this Abyssinian slave can be superior in obedience to Allāh than me? By Allāh I will repent.' He continued, "The sinful of the village [saw this] and stated, 'How is it that this Abyssinian and the daughters of this individual can be superior in obedience to Allāh ﷻ than us. We will repent to Allāh, and become the devout worshippers in the village.'"

[٤٢] أنبأَنَا يحيى بن ثَابت بن بنْدَار قَالَ أَنا أبي قَالَ أَنا الْحسن ابْن الْحُسَيْن بن دَوْمًا قَالَ أَنا مُحَمَّد بن جَعْفَر الباقرجي قَالَ أَنا الْحسن بن عَليّ الْقطَّان قَالَ أَنا إِسْمَاعِيل بن عِيسَى الْعَطَّار قَالَ ثَنَا إِسْحَاق بن بشر الْقرشِي قَالَ أَنا عبد اللَّهِ بن زِيَاد عَن مَكْحُول: أَن لُقْمَان كَانَ عبدا أسود، وَكَانَ قد أعطَاهُ اللَّهِ الْحِكْمَة وَكَانَ لرجل من بني إِسْرَائِيل اشْتَرَاهُ بِثَلَاثِينَ مِثْقَالا وَنصف وَكَانَ مَوْلَاهُ يلْعَب بالنرد يخاطر عَلَيْهِ، وَكَانَ لَهُ على بَابه نهر جَار، فلعب يَوْمًا بالنرد على أَن من قمر صَاحبه شرب المَاء الَّذِي فِي النَّهر كُله أَو افتدى مِنْهُ، فقهر سيد لُقْمَان فَقَالَ لَهُ سيد لُقْمَان: اشرب مَا فِي النَّهر وَإِلَّا فافتد مِنْهُ، فَقَالَ: سلني الْفِدَاء، فَقَالَ: عَيْنَيْك أفقؤهما وَجَمِيع مَا تملك، قَالَ: أمهلني يَوْمًا، قَالَ: لَك ذَلِك. فأمسى

كئيبا حَزينًا إِذْ جَاءَ لُقْمَان وَقد حمل حزمة من حطب على ظَهره فَسلم وَوضع مَا مَعَه، وَقَالَ لسَيِّده: مَالِي أَرَاك كئيبا حَزينًا؟ فَأَعْرض عَنهُ، فَأَعَادَ القَوْل فَأَعْرض عَنهُ، فَأَعَادَ فَأَعْرض، فَقَالَ لَهُ: أَخْبرنِي فَلَعَلَّ لَك عِنْدِي فرج [فَأخْبرهُ] قَالَ: وَمَا هُوَ؟ قَالَ: إِذا قَالَ الرجل لَك: اشرب مَا فِي النَّهر، فَقل لَهُ: أَشْرب مَا بَين ضفتي النَّهر أَو الْمَدّ فَإِنَّهُ سَيَقُولُ لَك: مَا بَين الضفتين، فَقل لَهُ: احْبِسْ عني الْمَدّ حَتَّى أَشْرب مَا بَين الضفتين، فَإِنَّهُ لَا يَسْتَطِيع [ذَلِك] وَتَكون قد خرجت مِمَّا ضمنت لَهُ، فَعرف الرجل أَنه قد صدقه، فطابت نَفسه، فَلَمَّا أصبح الرجل جَاءَ فَقَالَ لَهُ: فِ لي بشرطي، فَقَالَ لَهُ: نعم، أَشْرب مَا بَين الضفتين أَو الْمَدّ؟ فَقَالَ: لَا، مَا بَين الضفتين، قَالَ: فاحبس عني الْمَدّ، قَالَ كَيفَ أستطع! فخصمه. قَالَ: فَأعْتقهُ مَوْلَاهُ، فَأكْرمه اللَّهِ.

'Abdullāh ibn Ziyād reported upon the authority of Makhūl, "Luqmān was a black slave, and Allāh bestowed him with wisdom. He was owned by a man from Banī Isrā'īl who brought him with thirty *mithqāl* and a half. His master would play backgammon and place wagers upon it, and there was a river that flowed near his door. One day he was playing backgammon with a wager set that the loser drinks all of the water in the river or he pays a ransom. Luqmān's master was defeated and it was said to him, 'Drink that which is in the river or pay a ransom.' He replied, 'Inform me of the ransom.' The man said, 'I will remove your eyes and take everything you own.' His master stated, 'Give me a respite of a day [to think]' and he agreed to this. He thus became despondent and sad. Luqmān entered upon him whilst carrying a bundle of firewood upon his back. He greeted him and put down the load he was carrying, then he said to his master, 'Why is it that I see you so, despondent and sad? His master turned away from him. He repeated his question and his master turned away again. This took place a third time and so Luqmān stated to him, 'Inform me and maybe I can find for you a positive outcome.' His master then said to him, 'What is your solution?' He replied, 'If the man tells you to drink the water in the river, say, 'I will drink the water which is between the river banks or its length.' If

Illuminating the Darkness: The Virtues of Blacks and Abyssinians

he tells you to drink the water between the banks, say to him, 'Confine the water of the length until I drink what is between the banks.' The man will not be able to do this so you will free yourself from your liability to him.' The master realised he was right and so he became pleased. When the man [who won the backgammon game] arrived on the next morning he said, 'Now, fulfil the terms we have agreed on.' The master of Luqmān replied, 'Yes, shall I drink that which is between the banks or the length?' The man replied, 'That which is between the banks.' So he said, 'So confine the length for me.' The man replied, 'How will I be able to do this?' And the master gained respite through this." He continued, "Thus his master emancipated him and Allāh blessed him."

وَكَانَ يَخْتَلِفُ إِلَى دَاوُد يقتبس مِنْهُ [الْحِكْمَة] فَاخْتَلَفَ إِلَيْهِ سنة. وَدَاوُد يتَّخذ درعا وَلَا يسْأَله مَا هَذَا؟ وَلَا يُخبرهُ دَاوُد حَتَّى فرغ مِنْهَا، فصبها دَاوُد على نَفسه فَقَالَ حِين رَأى ذَلِك: الصمت حكم.

He used to visit Dāwūd, taking wisdom from him and he did this for a year. [On one occasion] Dāwūd was crafting armour and Luqmān did not ask regarding this until he had completed it, and neither did Dāwūd inform him until he had finished. Then Dāwūd put it on, and when he saw this he said, "Silence is wisdom."

قَالَ الْقرشِي: وَأَخْبرنَا خَالِد بن النَّضر عَن مَكْحُول: إِن أول مَا سمع دَاوُد [عَلَيْهِ السَّلَام] من حِكْمَة لُقْمَان أَنه رأى النَّاس يَخُوضُونَ وَهُوَ سَاكِت، فَقَالَ دَاوُد: أَلَا تَقول يَا لُقْمَان كَمَا يَقُول النَّاس؟ فَقَالَ: لَا خير فِي الْكَلَام إِلَّا بِذكر اللَّهِ عز وَجل وَلَا فِي السُّكُوت إِلَّا فِي الفكرة فِي الْمعَاد، وَإِن صَاحب الدّين قد فكر، فعلته السكينَة، وشكر فتواضع، وقنع، فاستغنى، وَرَضي فَلم يهتم، وخلع الدُّنْيَا فنجا من الشرور، ورفض الشَّهَوَات فَصَارَ حرا، وَانْفَرَدَ، فَكفى الأحزان، وَطرح الْحَسَد، فظهرت الْمحبَّة، واستكمل الْعقل وَأبْصر الْعَاقِبَة، فَأمن الندامة، فَالنَّاس مِنْهُ فِي رَاحَة، وَهُوَ من نَفسه فِي تَعب، فَقَالَ دَاوُد: صدقت يَا لُقْمَان، وأعجب

بِهِ وشاع ذكره بالحكمة، وَاجْتمعَ بعد ذَلِك النَّاس إِلَيْهِ يقتبسون مِنْهُ ويسمعون مِنْهُ الْحِكْمَة.

Al-Qurashī said: We were informed by Khālid ibn al-Naḍr upon the authority of Makḥūl, "The first occasion upon which Dāwūd ﷺ heard a wise statement from Luqmān was when he witnessed people debating whilst Luqmān remained silent. So Dāwūd said to him, 'Why do you not speak like the rest?' He replied, 'There is no good in speech except the mention of Allāh and neither is there good in silence except in pondering about the resurrection. A religious person contemplates [about his hereafter] and thus he becomes overwhelmed with serenity. He is thankful and so he has humility, he is content, so he is sufficed, and he is pleased [with his affair] so he does not live in a state of distress. He is detached from this world and so he escapes from its evil, denying his desires and so he becomes free. He secludes himself, and so he is protected from worries, and he drives off envy, so love is displayed [for him.] He is of excellent mind and adept at foreseeing consequences, so he is safe from regret thereafter. The people are at ease with him whilst he is tirelessly focusing on himself (i.e. he keeps pushing himself to do better every day as he does not find a limit to improvement).' Dāwūd said, 'You have spoke the truth O Luqmān.' He admired Luqmān and his reputation for wisdom became widespread. After this the people would congregate around him to take knowledge from him and to hear his wisdom."

قَالَ الْقرشِي: وَحدثنَا ابْن سمْعَان عَن زيد بن أسلم أَن لُقْمَان لما ظَهرت حكمته للنَّاس جَاءَهُ رجل من عُظَمَاء بني إِسْرَائِيل فَقَالَ لَهُ: يَا لُقْمَان، ألم تكن عبدا نوبيا لفُلَان؟ قَالَ: بلَى، قَالَ: فَمن أَيْن بلغت هَذِه الْمنزلَة؟ قَالَ: صدق الحَدِيث، وتركي مَالا يعنيني.

Al-Qurashī said: It was reported to us by Ibn Samʿān upon the authority of Zayd ibn Aslam, "When Luqmān's wisdom became apparent to the people, one of the great men from Banī Isrā'īl came to him and said, 'O Luqmān, were you not a Nubian slave?' He replied affirmatively. So, the man said, 'So how did you attain this level?' He replied, 'Through truthfulness in speech and leaving that which does not benefit me.'"

قَالَ الْقرشِي: وَحدثنَا ابْن سمْعَان عَن مَكْحُول عَن كَعْب أَن لُقْمَان قَالَ لِابْنِهِ: يَا بني، إِن الدُّنْيَا بَحر عريض، وَقد هلك فِيهِ عَالم كثير، فَإِن اسْتَطَعْت أَن تجْعَل سفينتك فِيهَا الْإِيمَان بِاللَّه، وشراعها التَّوَكُّل على اللَّهِ، وزادك فِيهَا التَّقْوَى، فَإِن نجوت فبرحمة اللَّهِ، وَإِن هَلَكت فبذنوبك.

Al-Qurashī said: Ibn Samʿān reported upon the authority of Makḥūl, upon the authority of Kaʿb. "Luqmān stated to his son, 'O my son, this world is like a wide sea within which many people have drowned. If you make your ship within it *īmān* (faith) in Allāh, *tawakkul* (reliance) on Allāh as its sail, *taqwā* (God-consciousness) as your provision, then your success will be through the mercy of Allāh and your destruction will be through your sins.'"

قَالَ: وَحدثنَا عُثْمَان بن عَطاء عَن أَبِيه قَالَ: قَالَ لُقْمَان لِابْنِهِ: يَا بني، رح من الدُّنْيَا باليسير، وَلَا تنافس فِي نعيمها؛ فَإِن الْقَلِيل يَكْفِيك مِنْهَا، إِن خير الْعلم مَا نفع، يَا بني، أعلم النَّاس أَشَّدهم خشيَة.

He said: ʿUthmān ibn ʿAṭā' reported upon the authority of his father that Luqmān stated to his son, "O my son, take little from this world, and do not jostle for its delights. For indeed a little from them will suffice you. The best of knowledge is the beneficial. O my son, know that the most knowledgeable of people are those from them with the most humility."

قَالَ الْقرشِي: وَقَالَ إِبْرَاهِيم بن أدهم: بَلغنِي أَن لُقْمَان لما حَضرته الْوَفَاة بَكَى، فَقَالَ لَهُ ابْنه: يَا أَبه، مَا يبكيك؟ قَالَ: يَا بني، لَيْسَ على الدُّنْيَا أبْكِي، وأنما أبْكِي على مَا أَمَامِي: شقة بعيدَة، ومفازة سحيقة، وَعقبَة كئود، وَزَاد قَلِيل، وَحمل ثقيل، فَمَا أَدْرِي أيحط ذَلِك الْحمل حَتَّى أبلغ الْغَايَة، أَو يبْقى عَليّ، فأساق مَعَه إِلَى نَار جَهَنَّم؟ ثمَّ مَاتَ.

Al-Qurashī said: Ibrāhīm ibn Adham said, "It reached me that Luqmān, when he was close to death, began to cry. His son asked him, 'O father, what causes you to cry?' He replied, 'O my son, it is not for the world that I cry, rather I am crying because of the journey I will have to embark upon. It is a lengthy toil, [akin to an] endless wilderness, an insurmountable obstacle, with little provisions and a burdensome load. I do not know whether this load will be lifted when I reach my destination, or whether it will remain upon me whilst I am driven to hell with it.' Then he died."

قَالَ: وَبَلغنِي أَن قبر لُقْمَان مَا بَين مَسْجِد الرملة وَمَوْضِع سوقها الْيَوْم، وفيهَا قُبُور سبعين نَبيا مَاتُوا بعد لُقْمَان كلهم فِي يَوْم وَاحِد من الْجُوع؛ أخرجهم بَنو إِسْرَائِيل فألجأوهم إِلَى الرملة، ثمَّ أحاطوا بهم فماتوا كلهم جوعا [عَلَيْهِم السَّلَام] .

Al-Qurashī said, "It reached me that the grave of Luqmān was between the *masjid* of Ramlah and where the market stands today. The graves of seventy prophets are there,[41] all of them died after Luqmān and they all died during a single day due to starvation. They had been driven to Ramlah by Banū Isrā'īl and were barricaded [within the city] by them. Thus, they all passed away ﷺ."

فصل
Section

[قَالَ الْمُصَنّف] : وكما ضرب النَّاس الْمثل بحكمة لُقْمَان ضربوا الْمثل بنومة عبود وَكَانَ عبود أسود حطابا فَبَقى فِي محطبه أسبوعا لم ينم، ثمَّ انْصَرف فَنَامَ أسبوعا، فَضرب بِهِ الْمثل لمن ثقل نَومه.

The author said: Just as people utilise Luqmān as a paragon of wisdom, they utilise 'Abūd as a paragon of [heavy] sleeping. 'Abūd was a black man and

41 There is no established location for a grave of a prophet except our Prophet ﷺ. This was stated by Ibn al-Jawzī and al-Qārī in *al-Asrār al-Marfū'ah*.

a gatherer of firewood. On one occasion he spent an entire week gathering firewood without sleeping, then he left and slept for a week. Thus he was used as an example of a heavy sleeper.

قَالَ الشَّرْقِي بن قطامي: تماوت عبود على أَهله، وَقَالَ: اندبوني لأَعْلم كَيفَ تندبوني إِذا مت، فسجينه وندبته فَإِذا هُوَ قد مَاتَ.

Al-Sharqī ibn Qaṭāmī said, "'Abūd feigned death to his people. He said, 'Mourn me so that I can see how you would do so if I passed.' Thus, they covered him with a sheet and started to mourn him, but then noticed that death had subsequently struck him."

الْبَاب السَّادِس عشر
Chapter Sixteen

فِي ذكر كبار مُلُوك الْحَبَشَة
In mention of the major kings of the Ḥabash

سيدهم النَّجَاشِيّ الَّذِي هَاجَرت إِلَى بَلَده الصَّحَابَة، وَكتب إِلَيْهِ رَسُول اللَّهِ - صَلَّى اللَّهُ عَلَيْهِ وَسَلَّمَ – فَأسلم.

Their master was the Najāshī to whom the Companions emigrated to his land, to whom the Messenger of Allāh ﷺ wrote to and that accepted Islām.

وملوك الْحَبَشَة كلهم يتسمى بالنجاشي كَمَا يتسمى مُلُوك فَارس بكسرى.

The kings of Abysinnia were all named as the Najāshī (Negus), just as the kings of Persia were all named as the Kisrā (Khosrow).

قَالَ ابْن إِسْحَاق: اسْم النَّجَاشِيّ: أَصْحَمَة، وَهُوَ بِالْعَرَبِيَّةِ: عَطِيَّة.

Ibn Isḥāq said, "The name of al-Najāshī is Aṣḥamah. This corresponds to 'Atiyyah (gift) in Arabic."[42]

---

42 [T] The following quote has been paraphrased. Al-Suyūṭī said in *Raf' Shàn al-Ḥubshān* (p. 88), "There are eight different views on his name. [The above] أصحمه is the famous view and which is found in the *Ṣaḥīḥ*. The other variations are: (ii) صحمة, as narrated by al-Qāḍī 'Iyyād, (iii) صمحة, as narrated by Ibn Abī Shaybah in his *Musnad*, (iv) أصمة, as narrated by al-Rāfi'ī in *Sharḥ al-Musnad*, (v) مصحمة, as narrated by al-Ḥākim in *al-Mustadrak* upon the authority of Ibn Shihāb, (vi) أضحمة, as narrated by al-Ismā'īlī, (vii) أصحبة, as narrated by al-Kirmānī in *Sharḥ al-Bukhārī*, and (viii) مكحول بن صعصعة, as narrated by al-Zarkashī upon the authority of Muqātil."

وَقَالَ ابْن قُتَيْبَة: إِنَّمَا النَّجَاشِيّ اسْم الْملك كَقَوْلِك: هِرقل وَقَيْصَر، قَالَ: وَلست أَدْرِي أَبَا الْعَرَبيَّة أم وفَاق وَقع بَين الْعَرَبيَّة وَغَيرهَا؟ والناجشي هُوَ الناجش، والنجش استثارة الشَّيْء، وَمِنْه قيل للزائد فِي ثمن السّلْعَة: ناجش ونجاش.

Ibn Qutaybah said, "Al-Najāshī is a name designated for a king, similar to the terms Hirqil and Qayṣar." He continued, "I am not aware whether this word is an Arabic word or whether it is a word between which there is concordance in the Arabic language with another language. [Analysis of the word linguistically:] *al-najāshī* means *al-nājish*, and *al-najsh* means to incite something, e.g. the person who [incites a potential buyer during the course of pre-sale negotiations or who builds hype] through insincere bidding is called a *nājish* or a *najjāsh*."[43]

قَالَ ابْن إِسْحَاق: بعث رَسُول اللَّهِ - صَلَّى اللَّهُ عَلَيْهِ وَسَلَّمَ - عَمْرو بن أُميَّة إِلَى النَّجَاشِيّ، وَكتب مَعَه:

Ibn Isḥāq said, "The Messenger of Allāh ﷺ sent 'Amr ibn Umayyah to al-Najāshī. With him was sent the following letter:

((بِسم اللَّهِ الرَّحْمَن الرَّحِيم. من مُحَمَّد رَسُول الله إِلَى النَّجَاشِيّ ملك الْحَبَشَة: إِنِّي أَحْمد إِلَيْك اللَّهِ الْملك القدوس السَّلَام الْمُؤمن الْمُهَيْمِن، وَأشْهد أَن عِيسَى بن مَرْيَم روح اللَّهِ وكلمته أَلْقَاهَا إِلَى مَرْيَم البتول الطّيبَة، فَحملت بِعِيسَى، وَإِنِّي أَدْعُوك إِلَى اللَّهِ وَحده لَا شريك لَهُ وَأَن تتبعني فتؤمن بِالَّذِي جَاءَنِي؛ فَإِنِّي رَسُول اللَّهِ، وَقد بعثت إِلَيْكُم ابْن عمي جَعْفَر، وَمَعَهُ نفر من الْمُسلمين، وَالسَّلَام على

43 Al-Suyūṭī quotes al-Muḥib al-Ṭabarī in *Raf' Shản al-Ḥubshān* (pp. 88-89/a), "[Al-Najāshī] is a title used for every king of the Abysinnians, just as the Khalīfah of the Muslims is termed as Amīr al-Mu'minīn, the king of the Romans is termed as Qayṣar, the king of the Turks is termed as Khāqān, the king of the Persians is termed as Kisrā, the king of the Coptics is termed as Fir'awn, the king of the Egyptians is termed as al-'Azīz, the king of the Yemenis is termed as Tubba', the king of the Ḥimyarite Kingdom is termed as al-Qayl, the king of al-Hind is termed as Yas'ūd, the king of the Sabeans is termed as al-Nimrūd and the king of the Berbers is Jaloot."

من اتبع الْهدى)).

'In the name of Allāh, al-Raḥmān, al-Raḥīm. From Muḥammad, the Messenger of Allāh, to al-Najāshī, king of Abyssinia. I praise Allāh, the King, the Pure, the Perfect, the Bestower of Faith, the Overseer. I bear witness that 'Īsā ibn Maryam is the spirit of Allāh and His word which He placed into Maryam, the virgin maiden, thus she bore 'Īsā. I call you to Allāh alone without any partner [to Him,] and to follow me and believe in that which has been revealed to me, for I am the Messenger of Allāh. I have sent my cousin Ja'far to you with a party of Muslims. Peace be upon those who follow the [true] guidance.'

فكتب النَّجَاشِيّ إِلَى رَسُول اللَّهِ - صَلَّى اللَّهُ عَلَيْهِ وَسَلَّمَ -:

Al-Najāshī wrote back to the Messenger of Allāh ﷺ stating:

بِسم اللَّهِ الرَّحْمَن. إِلَى مُحَمَّد رَسُول اللَّهِ - صَلَّى اللَّهُ عَلَيْهِ وَسَلَّمَ - من النَّجَاشِيّ: سَلام عَلَيْك يَا نَبِي اللَّهِ وَرَحْمَة اللَّهِ وَبَرَكَاته الَّذِي لَا إِلَه إِلَّا هُوَ الَّذِي هَدَانِي إِلَى الْإِسْلَام. أما بعد، فقد بَلغنِي كتابك يَا رَسُول اللَّهِ، فَمَا ذكرت من أَمر عِيسَى فورَبِّ السَّمَاء وَالْأَرْض إِن عِيسَى بن مَرْيَم [عَلَيْهِ السَّلَام] مَا يزِيد على مَا ذكرت ثفروقا إِنَّه كَمَا قلت، وَقد عرفنَا مَا بعثت بِهِ إِلَيْنَا، وَقد قدم ابْن عمك وَأَصْحَابه، وَأشْهد أَنَّك رَسُول اللَّهِ، وَقد بَايَعْتُك وبايعت ابْن عمك، وَأسْلمت على يَدَيْهِ لله رب الْعَالمين، وَقد بعثت إِلَيْك ابْنِي، وَإِن شِئْت أَن آتِيك فعلت يَا رَسُول اللَّهِ، فَإِنِّي أشهد أَن مَا تَقول حق، وَالسَّلَام عَلَيْك وَرَحْمَة اللَّهِ وَبَرَكَاته؟

'In the name of Allāh, al-Raḥmān, al-Raḥīm, to Muḥammad ﷺ from al-Najāshī. Peace be upon you O Prophet, and [upon you] be the mercy and blessings of Allāh, the one Whom besides there is no deity worthy of being worshipped and Whom guided me towards Islam. To proceed: Your letter reached me O Messenger of Allāh, and that which you mentioned in regards to 'Īsā—by the Lord of the heavens and the earth—'Īsā ibn Maryam ﵇ is not more than what you stated by a cupule. Indeed, he is as you have stated.

We were already aware of that which you have presented to us, and your cousin and his companions have reached us. I bear witness that you are the Messenger of Allāh, I have given *bay'ah* (the pledge of allegiance) to you and to your cousin, and I have accepted Islam, submitting to Allāh, the Lord of the worlds. I have despatched my son to you, and if you wish me to come to you then I will do so, O Messenger of Allāh. I testify that what you state is the truth. May peace be upon you and the mercy and blessing of Allāh.'"

قَالَ ابْن إِسْحَاق: فَذكر لي [أَنه] بعث ابْنه فِي سِتِّينَ من الْحَبَشَة [فِي سفينة] فَغَرقُوا.

Ibn Isḥāq said, "It was mentioned to me that he despatched his son with sixty Abyssinians in a vessel and they drowned."

وَقَالَ الْوَاقِدِيّ عَن أشياخه: كَانَ أول رَسُول بَعثه رَسُول اللَّهِ - صَلَّى اللَّهُ عَلَيْهِ وَسَلَّمَ - عَمْرو بن أُميَّة إِلَى النَّجَاشِيّ، وَكتب إِلَيْهِ كتابين يَدعُوهُ فِي أَحدهمَا إِلَى الْإِسْلَام وَيَتْلُو عَلَيْهِ الْقُرْآن، وَأخذ كتاب رَسُول اللَّهِ فَوَضعه على عَيْنَيْهِ، وَنزل عَن سَرِيره فَجَلَسَ على الأَرْض تواضعا، ثمَّ أسلم وَشهد شَهَادَة الْحق، وَقَالَ: لَو كنت أَسْتَطِيع أَن آتيه لأتيته، وَكتب إِلَى رَسُول اللَّهِ [- صَلَّى اللَّهُ عَلَيْهِ وَسَلَّمَ -] بإجابته وتصديقه وإسلامه.

Al-Wāqidī stated upon the authority of his *shaykhs*, "The first messenger sent by the Messenger of Allāh ﷺ to al-Najāshī was 'Amr ibn Umayyah. He wrote two letters to al-Najāshī, calling to him in one of them towards Islam and citing the Qur'ān. Al-Najāshī took the letter and placed it before his eyes, descended from his chair and sat upon the ground in modesty. Then he accepted Islam and testified the testification of truth. He said, 'If it was possible for me to go to him then I would do so.' Then he wrote to the Messenger of Allāh with his response and to attest his Islam.

وَفِي الْكتاب الآخر يَأْمُرهُ أَن يُزَوجهُ أم حَبِيبَة بنت أبي سُفْيَان، وَكَانَت قد هَاجَرت

إِلَى الْحَبَشَة مَعَ زَوجهَا، وَأمره فِي الْكتاب أَن يبْعَث إِلَيْهِ بِمن قبله من أَصْحَابه ويحملهم، فَفعل ذَلِك.

In the other letter, he ordered him to conduct his marriage to Umm Ḥabībah bint Abī Sufyān—who had emigrated to Abyssinia with her husband (ʿUbaydallāh ibn Jaḥsh, who became a Christian there)—and he also ordered him in this letter to return his companions who were with him and provide them with what they needed for the trip. And he actioned this."

ذكر أَمر رَسُول اللَّهِ - صَلَّى اللَّهُ عَلَيْهِ وَسَلَّمَ - النَّجَاشِيّ أَن يُزَوجهُ أم حَبِيبَة بنت أبي سُفْيَان بن حَرْب:

In mention of the request of the Messenger of Allāh ﷺ to al-Najāshī to give his marriage proposal to Umm Ḥabibah bint Abī Sufyān ibn Ḥarb:

كَانَت أم حَبِيبَة قد خرجت إِلَى أَرض الْحَبَشَة مَعَ زَوجهَا عبيد اللَّهِ بن جحش فَتَنَصَّرَ هُوَ هُنَاكَ وَثبتت [هِيَ] على الْإِسْلَام.

Umm Ḥabibah had emigrated to the land of Abyssinia with her husband ʿAbdullāh ibn Jaḥsh, he had became a Christian there, whilst she remained a Muslim.

[٤٣] فأنبأنا مُحَمَّد بن عبد الْبَاقِي عَن الْحسن بن عَليّ الْجَوْهَرِي قَالَ ثَنَا أَبُو عمر بن حيوية قَالَ أَنا ابْن مَعْرُوف قَالَ نَا ابْن الْفَهم قَالَ ثَنَا مُحَمَّد بن سعد قَالَ أَنا مُحَمَّد بن عمر قَالَ ثَنَا عبد اللَّهِ بن عَمْرو بن زُهَيْر عَن إِسْمَاعِيل بن عَمْرو بن سعيد بن الْعَاصِ قَالَ: قَالَت أم حَبِيبَة: رَأَيْت فِي الْمَنَام كَأَن عبيد اللَّهِ ابْن جحش زَوجي بأسوء صُورَة وأشوهها فَفَزِعت، فَقلت: تَغَيَّرت وَالله حَاله، فَإِذا هُوَ يَقُول حِين أصبح: يَا أم حَبِيبَة، إِنِّي نظرت فِي الدّين فَلم أر دينا خيرا من النَّصْرَانِيَّة، وَكنت قد دنت بهَا ثمَّ دخلت فِي دين مُحَمَّد، ثمَّ قد رجعت إِلَى النَّصْرَانِيَّة،

فَقلت: وَالله مَا خير لَك، وأخبرته بالرؤيا الَّتِي رَأَيْت فَلم يحفل بهَا، وأكب على الْخمر حَتَّى مَاتَ. فَأرى فِي الْمَنَام كَأَن آتِيَا يَقُول: يَا أم الْمُؤمنِينَ، فَفَزِعت فَأَوَّلتهَا أَن رَسُول الله - صَلَّى اللَّهُ عَلَيْهِ وَسَلَّمَ - يَتَزَوَّجنِي.

Ismāʿīl ibn ʿAmr ibn Saʿīd ibn al- ʿĀṣ reported upon the authority of Umm Ḥabibah, "I saw in my sleep as if my husband ʿAbdullāh ibn Jaḥsh had the vilest and most deformed form. Thus, I became frightened and said, 'Allāh has altered his *ḥāl* (state).' Then in the morning he stated to me, 'O Umm Ḥabībah, I pondered in regards to religion and did not see a religion better than Christianity, thus I took it as my religion and then I entered the religion of Muḥammad. Now I have returned back to Christianity.' I said, 'By Allāh there is no good for you [in it.]' Then I informed him of what I saw during my sleep but he did not pay heed to it. He took to alcohol until [the time] he died. Then I saw him during my sleep as if he came to me whilst saying, 'O Umm al-Mu'minīn (Mother of the Believers).' I became frightened and interpreted it to mean that the Messenger of Allāh ﷺ would marry me."

قَالَت: فَمَا هُوَ إِلَّا أَن انْقَضتْ عدتي فَمَا شَعرت إِلَّا برَسُول النَّجَاشِيّ على أتان يسْتَأْذن، فَإِذا جَارِيَة لَهُ يُقَال لَهَا: أَبْرَهَة كَانَت تقوم على ثِيَابه ودهنه، فَدخلت عَليّ فَقَالَت: إِن الْملك يَقُول [لَك] : إِن رَسُول اللَّهِ - صَلَّى اللَّهُ عَلَيْهِ وَسَلَّمَ - كتب إِلَيّ أَن أزَوجك، فَقلت: بشرك اللَّهِ بِخَير يَقُول لَك الْملك: وكلي من يزوجك، فَأرْسلت إِلَى خَالِد بن سعيد ابْن العَاصِي فَوَكَّلْتهُ، وَأَعْطيت أَبْرَهَة سِوَارَيْنِ من فضَّة، وخدمتين كَانَتَا فِي رجْلي، وخواتيم فضَّة كَانَت فِي أَصَابِع رجْلي سُرُورًا بِمَا بشرت، فَلَمَّا كَانَ الْعشي أَمر النَّجَاشِيّ جَعْفَر بن أبي طَالب وَمن هُنَاكَ من الْمُسلمين فَحَضَرُوا، فَخَطب النَّجَاشِيّ [رَضِي اللَّهِ عَنهُ] وَقَالَ: الْحَمد لله الْملك القدوس السَّلَام الْمُؤمن الْمُهَيْمِن الْعَزِيز الْجَبَّار، أشهد أَن لَا إِلَه إِلَّا اللَّهِ وَأَن مُحَمَّدًا عَبده وَرَسُوله، وَأَن الَّذِي بشر بِهِ عِيسَى بن مَرْيَم صلى اللَّهِ عَلَيْهِ وَسلم، أما بعد:

She continued, "Once my *iddah* (waiting) period had finished, an envoy of al-Najāshī had come and was seeking permission to enter. It was a slave girl of his named Abrahah, who was charged with his oiling and clothing. She entered [my room] and stated, 'The king states to you that the Messenger of Allāh wrote to him to propose marriage to you.' I said, 'May Allāh cause you happiness through this good [news.]' The king said, 'Appoint a representative for your marriage.' So I sent a message to Saʿīd ibn al-ʿĀṣ and he was appointed as my representative. I gifted Abrahah two bracelets made from silver, and two anklets I wore, and silver rings worn upon my toes due to the happiness I felt due to this good news. When evening fell, al-Najāshī ordered [the presence of] Jaʿfar ibn Abī Ṭālib and the Muslims who remained there and so they attended. Al-Najāshī ﷺ delivered a speech stating, 'All praise be to Allāh, the King, the Most Holy, the Provider of Peace, the Guardian of Faith, the Preserver, the Almighty, the Compeller. I testify that there is no deity worthy of being worshipped except Allāh and that Muḥammad is His slave and messenger, and that he is the one whom ʿĪsā ibn Maryam gave glad tidings of ﷺ. To proceed:

فَإن رَسُول الله - صَلَّى اللَّهُ عَلَيْهِ وَسَلَّمَ - كتب إِلَيّ أَن أزوجهُ أم حَبِيبَة بنت أبي سُفْيَان، فأجبت إِلَى مَا دَعَا إِلَيْهِ رَسُول اللَّهِ، وَقد أصدقهَا أَربع مائَة دِينَار، ثمَّ سكب الدَّنَانِير بَين يَدي الْقَوْم.

The Messenger of Allāh ﷺ wrote to me [requesting] that I conduct his marriage to Umm Ḥabībah bint Abī Sufyān. Thus, I have acceded to the request of the Messenger of Allāh and he gave her a dowry of four hundred dinars.' Then he poured forth the dinars in front of the people.

فَتكلم خَالِد بن سعيد فَقَالَ: الْحَمد للَّهِ، أَحْمَده وَأَسْتَعِينهُ وأستغفره، وَأشْهد أَن لَا إِلَه إِلَّا اللَّهِ وَأَن مُحَمَّدًا عَبده وَرَسُوله أرْسلهُ بِالْهدى وَدين الْحق لِيظْهرهُ على الدّين كُله وَلَو كره الْمُشْركُونَ، أما بعد: فقد أجبْت إِلَى مَا دَعَا إِلَيْهِ رَسُول اللَّهِ وَزَوجته أم حَبِيبَة بنت أبي سُفْيَان، فَبَارك الله لرَسُول اللَّهِ - صَلَّى اللَّهُ عَلَيْهِ وَسَلَّمَ -، وَدفع الدَّنَانِير لخَالِد بن سعيد فقبضها، ثمَّ أَرَادوا أَن يقومُوا فَقَالَ: اجلسوا فَإِن سنة

الْأَنْبِيَاء إِذا تزوجوا أَن يُؤْكَل طَعَام على التَّزْوِيج، فدعي بِطَعَام فَأَكَلُوا، ثمَّ تفرقُوا.

Khālid ibn Sa'īd said, 'All praise be to Allāh, I praise Him, seek His aid and forgiveness. I bear witness that there is no deity worthy of being worshipped except Allāh and that Muḥammad is His slave and messenger, He sent him with the guidance and the true religion for him to make it prevail over all other religions, even if the polytheists detest it. To proceed: I accede to that which the Messenger of Allāh has requested and I marry him to Umm Ḥabībah bint Abī Sufyān. May Allāh bless the Messenger of Allāh ﷺ.' Then al-Najāshī gave the dinars to Khālid ibn Sa'īd who accepted them. Then the attendants wished to stand up [so as to leave,] but al-Najāshī stated to them, 'Sit, for the Sunnah of the Prophets is that when they get married, food is eaten [in celebration of the marriage.]' So, he called for some food to be served and they ate and then dispersed."

قَالَت أم حَبِيبَة: فَلَمَّا وصل إِلَيّ المَال أرسلت إِلَى أَبْرَهَة الَّتِي بشرتني فَقلت لَهَا: إِنِّي كنت أَعطيتك مَا أعطيتك يَوْمئِذ وَلَا مَال بيدي، فَهَذِهِ خَمْسُونَ دِينَارا فخذيها واستعيني بهَا، فَأَبت وأخرجت حقًّا فِيهِ كل مَا كنت أعطيتهَا فردته عَليّ وَقَالَت: عزم عَليّ الْملك أَن لَا أرزأك شَيْئا، وَأَنا الَّتِي أقوم على ثِيَابه ودهنه، وَقد اتبعت دين مُحَمَّد رَسُول اللَّهِ، وَأسلمت لله رب الْعَالمين، وَقد أَمر الْملك نِسَاءَهُ يبْعَثْنَ إِلَيْك بِكُل مَا عِنْدهن من الْعطر قَالَت: فَلَمَّا كَانَ الْغَد جَاءَتْنِي بِعُود وورس وَعَنْبَر وَزِبَاد كثير، فَقدمت بذلك كُله على رَسُول اللَّهِ - صَلَّى اللَّهُ عَلَيْهِ وَسَلَّمَ -، وَكَانَ يرَاهُ عَليّ وَعِنْدِي فَلَا يُنكره، ثمَّ قَالَت أَبْرَهَة: حَاجَتي إِلَيْك أَن تقرئي على رَسُول الله - صَلَّى اللَّهُ عَلَيْهِ وَسَلَّمَ - مني السَّلَام، وتعلميه أنني اتبعت دينه. قَالَت: وَكَانَت الَّتِي جهزتني، وَكَانَت كلما دخلت عَليّ تَقول: لَا تنسي حَاجَتي إِلَيْك، فَلَمَّا قدمت على رَسُول اللَّهِ - صَلَّى اللَّهُ عَلَيْهِ وَسَلَّمَ - أخبرته كَيفَ كَانَت الْخطْبَة، وَمَا فعلت بِي أَبْرَهَة فتبسم وَأَقْرَأته السَّلَام مِنْهَا فَقَالَ ((وَعَلَيْهَا السَّلَام وَرَحْمَة اللَّهِ وَبَرَكَاته)).

Umm Ḥabībah said, "When the money reached me I requested the presence of Abrahah who brought be the good news. I said to her, 'Indeed I gave you what I had on a day upon wherein there was no money in my possession. Here are fifty dinars, take them and utilise them. She refused and took out a bag in which there was all that I gave to her. She returned everything to me and said, 'I have been strictly ordered by the king that I do not take anything, and I am the one charged with his clothing and oiling. I have come to follow the religion of Muḥammd the Messenger of Allāh, and have submitted to Allāh the Lord of the worlds. Furthermore, the king has ordered the women to send to you everything they possess from perfume.'" She continued, "During the next day she came to me with *'ūd*, wars, 'anbar and an abundance of fragrance. I brought all of this when I came to the Messenger of Allāh ﷺ. He used to see them upon me and with me but he did not rebuke this. Then Abrahah stated, 'My requirement from you is that you convey my *salām* to the Messenger of Allāh ﷺ and that you inform him that I am a follower of his religion.'" She said, "She was the one who prepared me [for the journey back,] and each time she entered my presence she would say, 'Do not forget my need.' Thus when I came to the Messenger of Allāh ﷺ I informed him in regards to the speech and also regarding how Abrahah treated me. He became happy at this, and I conveyed her *salām* to him, to which he replied, 'And peace be upon her, and the mercy and blessing of Allāh.'"[44]

قَالَ عبد اللَّهِ بن أبي بكر بن حزم: وَكَانَ ذَلِك [فِي] سنة سبع.

'Abdullāh ibn Abī Bakr ibn Ḥazm said, "This occurred during the seventh year."

قَالَ الزُّهْرِيّ: وجهزها النَّجَاشِيّ وَبعث مَعهَا شُرَحْبِيل بن حَسَنَة. وَلما بلغ أَبُو سُفْيَان تَزْوِيج رَسُول اللَّهِ أم حَبِيبَة قَالَ: ذَلِك الْفَحْل لَا يقرع أَنفه.

Al-Zuhrī said, "Al-Najāshī provided her with provisions and sent with her Shurḥabīl ibn Ḥasanhah. When Abū Sufyān came to know of the Messenger of Allāh's marriage to Umm Ḥabībah he said, 'He is indeed an honour-

44 Reported by Ibn Sa'd in *Tabaqāt al-Kubrā* (77).

able man who is highly esteemed and generous.'"

قَالَ الزُّهْرِيّ: فَلَمَّا قدم أَبُو سُفْيَان بن حَرْب الْمَدِينَة جَاءَ إِلَى رَسُول اللَّهِ - صَلَّى اللَّهُ عَلَيْهِ وَسَلَّمَ - فَكَلمهُ أَن يزِيد فِي هدنة الْحُدَيْبِيَة، فَلم يقبل عَلَيْهِ رَسُول اللَّهِ فَقَامَ فَدخل على ابْنَته أم حَبِيبَة، فَلَمَّا ذهب ليجلس على فرَاش النَّبِي - صَلَّى اللَّهُ عَلَيْهِ وَسَلَّمَ - طوته دونه، فَقَالَ: يَا بنية أرغبت بِهَذَا الْفراش عني أم بِي عَنهُ، فَقَالَت: بل هُوَ فرَاش رَسُول اللَّهِ - صَلَّى اللَّهُ عَلَيْهِ وَسَلَّمَ -، وَأَنت امْرُؤ نجس مُشْرك. فَقَالَ: يَا بنية لقد أَصَابَك بعدِي شَرّ.

Al-Zuhrī said, "When Abū Sufyān ibn Ḥarb entered Madīnah, he went to the Messenger of Allāh ﷺ and addressed him in regards to an extension of the Treaty of Ḥudaybīyah. However, the Messenger of Allāh ﷺ did not accept this. So, he went to his daughter Umm Ḥabībah. When he was about to sit upon the carpet of the Prophet ﷺ she took it and folded it. He stated, 'O daughter, do you covet this carpet over me, or vice versa?' She replied, 'Indeed this is the carpet of the Messenger of Allāh ﷺ. You are a person who is impure [spiritually] and a polytheist.' He stated, 'O daughter, verily you have been stricken with evil after you left me.'"

قَالَت عَائِشَة [رَضِي اللَّهِ عَنْهَا]: دعتني أم حَبِيبَة عِنْد مَوتهَا فَقَالَت: قد كَانَ يكون بَيْننَا مَا بَين الضرائر، فغفر اللَّهِ لي وَلَك، فَقلت: غفر اللَّهِ لَك ذَلِك كُله وَتجَاوز، وحللك من ذَلِك، فَقَالَت: سررتيني، سرك اللَّهِ، وَأرْسلت إِلَى أم سَلمَة فَقَالَت لَهَا مثل ذَلِك. وَتوفيت سنة أَربع وَأَرْبَعين فِي خلَافَة مُعَاوِيَة.

'Āʾishah رضي الله عنها said, "Umm Ḥabībah called for me when she was in the throes of death and she said, 'We both had [frictions which often] occur between co-wives, so I ask Allāh to forgive me and you.'" She ('Āʾishah) said, "May Allāh forgive you for everything therein and overlook [your sins] and absolve you from that." "She said, 'You have brought me happiness, may Allāh reciprocate for you happiness.' She then sent for Umm Salamah and stated something similar to her. She passed away in the year forty-four during

Muʿāwiyah's caliphate."

ذكر إِعْلَام رَسُول اللَّهِ - صَلَّى اللَّهُ عَلَيْهِ وَسَلَّمَ - النَّاس بِمَوْت النَّجَاشِيّ وَصلَاته عَلَيْهِ:

In mention of the Messenger of Allāh ﷺ informing the people of the death of al-Najāshī and his performance of the funeral prayer for him:

توفّي النَّجَاشِيّ فِي رَجَب سنة تسع من الْهِجْرَة.

Al-Najāshī passed away during the month of Rajab in the ninth year after the *hijrah*.

[٤٤] وَأخْبرنَا ابْن الْحصين قَالَ أَنا ابْن الْمَذْهَب قَالَ أَنا أَبُو بكر ابْن مَالك قَالَ ثَنَا عبد اللَّهِ بن أَحْمد قَالَ حَدثنِي أبي قَالَ ثَنَا يحيى عَن مَالك قَالَ حَدثنِي الزُّهْرِيّ عَن سعيد بن الْمسيب عَن أبي هُرَيْرَة قَالَ: نعى لنا رَسُول الله - صَلَّى اللَّهُ عَلَيْهِ وَسَلَّمَ - النَّجَاشِيّ الْيَوْم الَّذِي مَاتَ فِيهِ، فَخرج إِلَى الْمصلى، فَصف أَصْحَابه خَلفه، فَكبر عَلَيْهِ أَرْبعا.

Saʿīd ibn al-Musayyib reported upon the authority of Abī Hurayrah, "The Messenger of Allāh ﷺ announced the passing of al-Najāshī on the day wherein he died. Thus, he went out to the *muṣallā* (a place of the prayer besides the *masjid*) and ordered his Companions to stand in rows behind him. He [performed the funeral prayer for him,] making the *takbīr* (*Allāhu akbar*) on him four times."[45]

قَالَت عَائِشَة [رَضِي اللَّهِ عَنْهَا] : لما مَاتَ النَّجَاشِيّ كُنَّا نتحدث أَنه لَا يزَال يرى على قَبره نور.

ʿĀʾishah ﷺ said, "When al-Najāshī passed away, we were told that a light

45 Al-Suyūṭī stated in *Azhār al-ʿUrūsh* (p. 17/a), "This was reported by Mālik, al-Shāfiʿī, al-Bukhārī, Muslim, Abū Dāwūd and al-Nasāʾī."

remained showing upon his grave."[46]

ذكر ملك كَبِير من مُلُوك الْحَبَشَة

In mention of one of the major Abyssinian kings

[٤٥] أخبرنَا مُحَمَّد بن نَاصِر الْحَافِظ قَالَ أَنا مَحْفُوظ بن أَحْمد قَالَ أَنا مُحَمَّد بن الْحُسَيْن الجازري قَالَ ثَنَا الْمعَافِي بن زَكَرِيَّا قَالَ ثَنَا الْحُسَيْن بن الْقَاسِم الكوكبي قَالَ ثَنَا الْفضل بن الْعَبَّاس الربعِي قَالَ حَدثنِي إِبْرَاهِيم بن عِيسَى بن أبي جَعْفَر الْمَنْصُور قَالَ سَمِعت عمي سُلَيْمَان بن أبي جَعْفَر يَقُول: كنت وَاقِفًا على رَأس الْمَنْصُور لَيْلَة وَعِنْده إِسْمَاعِيل بن عَليّ وَصَالح بن عَليّ وَسليمَان بن عَليّ وَعِيسَى بن عَليّ فتذاكروا زَوَال ملك بني أُميَّة، وَمَا صنع بهم عبد اللَّهِ، وَقتل مَن مِنْهُم بنهر أبي فطرس.

Ibrāhīm ibn 'Isā ibn Abī Ja'far al-Manṣūr said, "I heard my uncle, Sulaymān ibn Abī Ja'far say, 'I was standing with al-Manṣūr one night when Ismā'īl ibn 'Alī, Ṣāliḥ ibn 'Alī Ṣulaymān ibn 'Alī and 'Isā ibn 'Alī were with him. They were recalling the collapse of the kingdom of the Umayyads, what 'Abdullāh did to them, and how he fought some from them in the river of Abī Fuṭrus.

فَقَالَ الْمَنْصُور: أَلا من عَلَيْهِم ليروا من دولتنا مَا رَأينَا من دولتهم وَيرغبُوا إِلَيْنَا كَمَا رغبنا إِلَيْهِم، فقد لعمري عاشوا سعداء وماتوا فُقَرَاء.

Al-Manṣūr stated, 'Is it not possible that we can be considerate with them so that they see from our reign what we saw from theirs, and that they ask from

46 Al-Suyūṭī said in *Azhār al-'Urūsh* (p. 17/b), "This was reported by Abū Dāwūd." [T] Shaykh 'Abd al-Muḥsin al-'Abbād said in his commentary upon this report (255/11) that it is a *mawquf* narration of 'Ā'ishah and not *marfū'* (raised) to the Prophet ﷺ. Her statement indicates that this news reached them or its occurrence was a rumour. Proof supporting it has not been established and al-Albānī graded it as *ḍa'īf*. [End]

us what we used to ask from them. For—indeed—they lived in fortunate circumstances and died in poverty.'

فَقَالَ لَهُ إِسْمَاعِيل بن عَليّ: يَا أَمِير الْمُؤمنِينَ إِن فِي حَبسك عبد اللَّهِ بن مَرْوَان بن مُحَمَّد، وَقد كَانَت لَهُ قصَّة عَجِيبَة مَعَ ملك النّوبَة، فَابْعَثْ إِلَيْهِ فسله عَنْهَا.

Then Ismā'il ibn 'Alī stated to him, 'O Commander of the Faithful, 'Ubaydullāh ibn Marwān ibn Muḥammad is currently incarcerated by you, and he had a strange story [concerning his interaction] with the Nubian king. So, send for him and ask him.'

قَالَ: يَا مسيب، عَليّ بِهِ.

He stated, 'O Musayyib, bring him before me.'

فَأخْرج فَتى مُقَيّدا بِقَيْد ثقيل وغل ثقيل، فَمثل بَين يَدَيْهِ، وَقَالَ: السَّلَام عَلَيْك يَا أَمِير الْمُؤمنِينَ وَرَحْمَة اللَّهِ وَبَرَكَاته.

Then a youthful man was brought forth, he was constricted by heavy chains and heavy shackles on his feet, and the like upon his hands. He said, 'Peace be upon you O Commander of the Faithful, and Allāh's mercy and blessings.'

فَقَالَ: يَا عبيد اللَّهِ، رد السَّلَام أَمن. وَلم تسمح لَك نَفسِي بذلك بعد، وَلَكِن اقعد.

He (i.e. al-Manṣūr) said, 'O 'Ubaydullāh, replying to your greeting of peace shall assure your safety and I do not find myself yet inclined towards giving you protection, but you may sit.'

فجاؤوا بوسادة فثنيت فَقعدَ عَلَيْهَا، فَقَالَ لَهُ: قد بَلغنِي أَنه كَانَت لَك قصَّة عَجِيبَة مَعَ ملك النّوبَة، فَمَا هِيَ؟

So, they brought a cushion, it was folded and he sat upon it. Then he said to him, 'I have come to know that you have a strange story concerning the Nubian king. What is it?'

قَالَ: يَا أَمِير الْمُؤمنِينَ: لَا وَالَّذِي أكرمك بالخلافة مَا أقدر على النَّفس من ثقل الْحَدِيد، وَلَقَد صديء قيدي مِمَّا أرشش عَلَيْهِ من الْبَوْل، وأصب عَلَيْهِ المَاء فِي أَوْقَات الصَّلَاة.

He replied, 'O Commander of the Faithful, I am not—and I swear on this by the One who honoured you with the Caliphate—capable of breathing due to the heaviness of the iron. My chain has become rusty due to me urinating upon it, and due to water being poured upon it during the times of prayer.'

فَقَالَ: يَا مسيب، أطلق عَنهُ حديده.

He said, 'O Musayyib, remove the iron from him.'

ثمَّ قَالَ: نعم يَا أَمِير الْمُؤمنِينَ، وَلما قصد عبد اللَّهِ بن عَليّ إِلَيْنَا كنت [أَنا] الْمَطْلُوب من بَين الْجَمَاعَة، لِأَنِّي كنت ولي عهد أبي من بعده فَدخلت إِلَى خزانَة فاستخرجت مِنْهَا عشرَة آلَاف دِينَار، ثمَّ دَعَوْت عشرَة من غلماني وحملت كل وَاحِد على دَابَّة، وَدفعت إِلَى كل غُلَام ألف دِينَار وأوقرت خَمْسَة أبغل، وشددت فِي وسطي جوهرا لَهُ قيمَة مَعَ ألف دِينَار، وَخرجت هَارِبا إِلَى بلد النّوبَة، فسرت فِيهَا ثَلَاثًا، فَوَقَعت إِلَى مَدِينَة خراب فَأَمرت الغلمان فعدلوا إِلَيْهَا فكسحوا مِنْهَا مَا كَانَ قذرا، ثمَّ فرشوا بعض تِلْكَ الْفرش، ودعوت غُلَاما لي كنت أَثِق بعقله فَقلت: انْطلق إِلَى الْملك فأقرئه مني السَّلَام، وَخذ مِنْهُ الْأمان، وابتع لي ميرة. قَالَ: فَمضى فَأَبْطَأَ حَتَّى سُؤْت ظنا، ثمَّ أقبل وَمَعَهُ رجل آخر، فَلَمَّا أَن دخل كفر لي، ثمَّ قعد بَين يَدي فَقَالَ لي: الْملك يقْرَأ عَلَيْك السَّلَام، وَيَقُول لَك: من أَنْت؟ وَمَا جَاءَ بك إِلَى بلادي؟ أمحارب لي، أم رَاغِب إِلَيّ، أم مستجير بِي؟

He then said, 'That is right O Commander of the Faithful, when 'Abdullāh ibn 'Alī headed towards us, I was the one sought within the group as I was to have the rule after my father. So I entered his treasury and took ten thousand dinars. Then I called ten individuals from my young slaves and gave them each a ride, and to each of them I gave one thousand dinars. I also loaded five mules and tied to my waist some valuable jewels and one thousand dinars. I then fled to the land of Nubia. I proceeded through it for three days, and then I reached a town called Kharāb. I ordered my slaves to stop there and clean the area and so they went to it, and they swept the dirt from it, then they laid some carpets down. I then called one of the slaves in whom I could put trust in his intelligence, and I said to him, 'Go to the king, convey to him my greetings and take from him a guarantee of safety. Also purchase provisions for me.' He continued, 'So he went and he was delayed [to the extent that] I started to have bad thoughts. Then he returned and he was accompanied by another man. When he entered, he bowed to me, then he sat before me and said, 'The king sent his greetings to you and asks you, 'Who are you? What brings you to my land? Are you antagonistic to me, seeking to change your religion to the religion I am upon or seeking asylum with me?"

قلت: ترد على الْملك السَّلَام، وَتقول: أما محَارب لَك فمعاذ اللَّهِ، وَأما رَاغِب فِي دينك فَمَا كنت لأبغي بديني بَدَلا، وَأما مستجير بك فلعمري، قَالَ: فَذهب ثمَّ رَجَعَ إِلَيّ فَقَالَ: إِن الْملك يقْرَأ عَلَيْك السَّلَام، وَيقُول لَك: أَنا صائر إِلَيْك غَدا، فَلَا تحدثن فِي نَفسك حَدثا وَلَا تتَّخذ شَيْئا من ميرة، فَإِنَّهَا تَأْتِيك وَمَا تحْتَاج إِلَيْهِ.

I said, 'Reciprocate my greetings to him, and say: As for me being antagonistic to you then I seek refuge in Allāh. As for me wishing to change to your religion then I do not seek a substitute for my religion. As for seeking refuge with you, then yes [I do so]." He continued, 'He left and then returned to me, stating, 'The king sends his greetings to you and says, 'I am coming to you tomorrow, so do not do anything and do not take any provisions as they will be sent to you and your needs will be provided."

فَأَقْبَلت الْميرَة، فَأَمرت غلماني فرشوا ذَلِك الْفرشة كُله، وَأمرت بفرشة ففرش لَهُ ولي مثله، [وَأَقْبَلت] من غَد أرقب مَجِيئه، فَبَيْنَمَا أَنا كَذَلِك أقبل غلماني يحْضرُون وَقَالُوا: إِن الْملك قد أقبل، فَقُمْت بَين شرفتين من شرف الْقصر أنظر إِلَيْهِ فَإِذا أَنا بِرَجُل قد لبس بردين ائتزر بِأَحَدِهِمَا وارتدى بِالْآخرِ حاف راجل، وَإِذا عشرَة مَعَهم الحراب، ثَلَاثَة يقدمونه وَسَبْعَة خَلفه، وَإِذا الرجل الموجه إِلَى جنبه، فاستصغرت أمره، وَهَان عَليّ لما رَأَيْته فِي تِلْكَ الْحَال، وسولت لي نَفسِي قتله، فَلَمَّا قرب من الدَّار إِذا أَنا بسواد عَظِيم.

I received the provisions and I ordered my slaves to lay all the carpets, and I ordered them to lay one carpet for him and the like for me. On the next day I awaited his arrival when one of my slaves came and stated that the king had come. I stood between two balconies of the palace to see him. I saw a man wearing two garments, wearing one as a lower garment and the other as an upper garment. He was walking barefoot with ten companions who were armed, three preceded him and seven followed him, and I viewed him disparagingly, when I saw his lowly state it was to the extent that I thought to kill him. When he began to draw close to the abode, I saw a great crowd.

فَقلت: مَا هَذَا السوَاد؟ فَقيل: الْخَيل توافي يَا أَمِير الْمُؤمنِينَ زهاء عشرَة آلَاف عنان.

So, I asked what this was, and it was said, 'It is horses drawing close O Commander of the Faithful, approximately ten thousand horses with their riders.'

فَكَانَت موافاة الْخَيل إِلَى الدَّار وَقت دُخُوله، فأحدقوا بهَا فَدخل إِلَيّ، فَلَمَّا نظر إِلَيّ قَالَ لِترْجُمَانِهِ: أَيْن الرجل؟ فَأَوْمأ الترجمان إِلَيّ فَلَمَّا نظر إِلَيّ وَثَبت إِلَيْهِ فأعظم ذَلِك، وَأخذ بيَدي فقبلها ووضعها على صَدره، وَجعل يدْفع مَا على الْفسْطَاط بِرجلِهِ، فتشوش الْفرش، فَظَنَنْت أَن ذَلِك يجلونه أَن يطأوا على مثله، حَتَّى انْتهى

إِلَى الْفرش، فَقلت لِترْجُمَانِهِ: سُبْحَانَ اللَّهِ! لم لم يقْعد على الْموضع الَّذِي وطئ لَهُ؟

The horses arrived at the abode at the time that the man entered, and as he entered, they had encircled it. When he looked at me, he said to his translator, 'Where is this man?' The translator beckoned with his head towards me. Then he looked at me again and so I rushed to embrace him, but he was too humble to accept it so he took my hand, kissed it and placed it against his chest. He began to remove the carpets with his foot, rolling up the carpet—I thought that they considered this too luxurious to walk upon—until he reached the cushions where he and I were supposed to sit. Then I stated to his translator, '*Subḥānallāh*, why does he not sit upon the place specially prepared for him [to sit upon.]'

فَقَالَ: قل لَهُ: إِنِّي ملك، وكل ملك حَقه أَن يكون متواضعا لِعَظَمَة اللَّهِ سُبْحَانَهُ إِذْ رَفعه اللَّهِ تَعَالَى ثمَّ أقبل ينكت بِأُصْبُعِهِ فِي الأَرْض طَويلا، ثمَّ رفع رَأسه فَقَالَ لي: كَيفَ سلبتم هَذَا الْملك وَأخذ مِنْكُم وَأَنْتُم أقرب النَّاس إِلَى نبيكم؟

He replied, 'I am a king, and it is incumbent upon every king to show humility to Allāh ﷻ who raised him in rank.' Then he stuck his finger in the sand for quite some time, and he then raised his head and stated to me, 'How is it that your people were deprived of leadership when you are the closest people to your Prophet?'

فَقلت: جَاءَ من هُوَ أقرب قرَابَة إِلَى نَبينَا - صَلَّى اللَّهُ عَلَيْهِ وَسَلَّمَ - فسلبنا وقتلنا وطردنا، فَخرجت إِلَيْك مستجيرا بِاللَّه عز وَجل ثمَّ بك.

I replied, 'A group of people arose who were closer in proximity to the Prophet ﷺ than us, they robbed us, slaughtered us and expelled us. Thus, I fled to you, seeking aid firstly with Allāh ﷻ and then with you.'

قَالَ: فَلم كُنْتُم تشربون الْخمر وَهِي مُحرمَة عَلَيْكُم فِي كتابكُم؟

He said, 'Did you people drink alcohol though it is prohibited in your book?'

فَقلت: فعل ذَلِك عبيد وَأَتْبَاع وأعاجم دخلُوا فِي ملكنا من غير رَأينَا.

I replied, 'This was done by the slaves, followers and foreigners who entered our lands and they did it without our permission.'

قَالَ: [فلم] كُنْتُم تَرْكَبُونَ على الديباج وعَلى دوابكم الذَّهَب وَالْفِضَّة، وَقد حرم ذَلِك عَلَيْكُم؟

He said, 'Do you not sit on silk cloth when you mount your rides, and have your horses decorated with gold and silver though this is forbidden for you?'

قلت: عبيد وَأَتْبَاع وأعاجم دخلُوا فِي مملكتنا.

I replied, 'This was done by the slaves, followers and foreigners who entered our kingdom.'

قَالَ: فَلم كُنْتُم إِذا خَرجْتُمْ إِلَى صيد تقحمتم على الْقرى وكلفتم أَهلهَا مَا لَا طَاقَة لَهُم بِهِ بِالضَّرْبِ الوجيع، ثمَّ لَا يقنعكم ذَلِك حَتَّى تموشوا زُرُوعهمْ فتفسدوها فِي طلب دراج قِيمَته نصف دِرْهَم، أَو فِي عُصْفُور قِيمَته لَا شَيْء، وَالْفساد محرم عَلَيْكُم فِي دينكُمْ؟

He said, 'Why is it that when you would go hunting you would place force upon the villages, imposing upon their people that which they could not bear with severe beatings? Furthermore, you would not be satisfied until you walked over their crops and damaged them in seeking a *durāj* (a type of bird)—worth half a dirham—or a bird of no value, and this is despite damaging [property] being prohibited in your religion.'

قلت: عبيد وَأَتْبَاع.

I said, 'This was done by the slaves and followers.'

قَالَ: لَا، وَلَكِنَّكُمْ استحللتم مَا حرم اللَّهِ وأتيتم مَا نهاكم عَنهُ فسلبكم اللَّهِ [تعَالَى] الْعِزّ، وألبسكم الذل، وَللَّه فِيكُم نقمة لم تبلغ غايتها بعد، وَإِنِّي أَتَخَوَّف أَن تنزل النقمَة بك إِذا كنت من الظلمَة فتشملني مَعَك، فَإِن النقمَة إِذا نزلت عَمت وشملت، فَاخْرُج بعد ثَلَاث، فإنني إِن أخذتك بعْدهَا أخذت جَمِيع مَا مَعَك وقتلتك وَقتلت جَمِيع من مَعَك.

He said, 'Nay, rather you made lawful that which Allāh made unlawful, and you performed that which He prohibited. Thus, He took your honour from you and adorned you with abjectness. And [it may be that] Allāh's course for you has not yet reached its end point, and I fear that a punishment is to befall you if you were among the transgressors, and it will consequently fall upon me as well. This is because when punishment descends it is wide and encompassing. I order you to leave after three [days,] and if I find you here after [this time limit] indeed I will take all of your possessions and kill you alongside your entire party.'

ثمَّ وثب فَخرج فأقمت ثَلَاثًا وَخرجت إِلَى مصر، فأخذني وليك فَبعث بِي إِلَيْك وَهَا أَنا إِذا وَالْمَوْت أحب إِلَيّ من الْحَيَاة.

He then leapt up and left. I remained there for three days and then exited towards Egypt. Your vassal apprehended me there and sent me to you. So here I am, and death is more beloved to me than living [in this state.]'

فهم أَبُو جَعْفَر بِإِطْلَاقِهِ، فَقَالَ لَهُ إِسْمَاعِيل بن عَليّ: فِي عنقِي بيعَة لَهُ قَالَ: فَمَا ترى؟ قَالَ: ينزل فِي دَار من دُورنَا وَيخرج عَلَيْهِ مَا يخرج على مثله. قَالَ: فَفعل ذَلِك بِهِ، فوَاللَّه مَا أَدْرِي أمات فِي حَبسه أم أطلقهُ الْمهْدي.

Abū Ja'far intended to release him then Ismā'īl ibn 'Alī said to him (i.e. Abū Ja'far), 'I have given a pledge to him.' He said, 'What is your view?' He (i.e. Ismā'īl ibn 'Alī) replied, 'He will stay in one of our prisons and his fate will be that of his likes.'' Sulaymān ibn Abī Ja'far said, 'And this is what happened to him, and by Allāh I do not know if he died in his prison or whether al-Mahdī released him.'"

ملك آخر

Another King

[٤٦] روى أَبُو الْقَاسِم النَّخعِيّ قَالَ حَدثنِي مُحَمَّد بن يُوسُف قَاضِي صنعاء قَالَ: كتب إِلَيّ ملك الزنج فَكَانَ فِي آخر كِتَابه:

Abū al-Qāsim al-Nakhaʿī reported on the authority of Muḥammad ibn Yūsuf, the judge of Ṣanʿā', "A king of the Zanj wrote to me. At the end of his letter it was written:

لَا أسأَل النَّاس عَن مَا فِي نُفُوسهم   مَا فِي ضميري لَهُم من ذَاك يَكْفِينِي
وَلَا أَقُول لعرس الْجَار فِي لطف   فِي غَفلَة من عُيُون الْحَيّ أرويني
لَا أَبْتَغِي وصل من يَبْغِي مفارقي   وَلَا أَلين لمن لَا يَبْتَغِي ليني
وَالله لَو كرهت كفي مصاحبتي يَوْمًا   لَقلت لَهَا من ساعدي بيني
ثمَّ الْتفت إِلَى الْأُخْرَى وَقلت لَهَا   مهلا عَلَيْك وَإِلَّا مثلهَا كوني

I do not ask people about what they think of me, I suffice with what I think of them.

I do not ask my neighbour in his wedding, away from the eyes of the people to let me in.

I do not go after who does not wish to be with me, and I do not show kindness to who does not want my kindness.

By Allāh, if my hand disliked being with me, I would ask it to leave my arm.

And I would look at my other hand and say to it, be at ease or you can leave like my other hand.

الْبَاب السَّابِع عشر

Chapter Seventeen

فِي ذكر أَشْرَاف السودَان من الصَّحَابَة

In mention of the esteemed blacks amongst the Companions

سَالم مولى أبي حُذَيْفَة

Sālim, the *mawlā* (freedman) of Abī Ḥudhayfah

كَانَ يؤم الْمُهَاجِرين من مَكَّة حَتَّى قدم الْمَدِينَة لِأَنَّهُ كَانَ أقرأهم وَصلى خَلفه أَبُو بكر وَعمر [رَضِي اللَّهِ عَنْهُمَا وأرضاهما] .

He used to lead the Muhājirīn in prayer from Makkah until they reached Madīnah because he was the most competent with the Qur'ān. Those who prayed behind him included Abū Bakr and 'Umar.

[٤٧] أخبرنَا مُحَمَّد بن عبد الْبَاقِي بن أَحْمد قَالَ أَنا حمد بن أَحْمد قَالَ أَنا أَبُو نعيم أَحْمد بن عبد اللَّهِ الْحَافِظ قَالَ: نَا أَبُو حَامِد بن جبلة قَالَ نَا مُحَمَّد بن إِسْحَاق السراج قَالَ نَا مَحْمُود بن خِدَاش قَالَ ثَنَا مَرْوَان بن مُعَاوِيَة قَالَ نَا سعيد قَالَ سَمِعت شهر بن حَوْشَب يَقُول: قَالَ عمر بن الْخطاب [رَضِي اللَّهِ عَنهُ] : لَو اسْتخْلفت سالما مولى أبي حُذَيْفَة فَسَأَلَنِي عَنهُ رَبِّي عز وَجل: مَا حملك على ذَلِك لَقلت: رب سَمِعت نبيك - صَلَّى اللَّهُ عَلَيْهِ وَسَلَّمَ - وَهُوَ يَقُول: ((يحب اللَّهِ [عز وَجل] حَقًا من قلبه)).

Shahr ibn Ḥawshab reported upon the authority of 'Umār ibn al-Khaṭṭāb, 'If I were to anoint Sālim, the *mawlā* of Hudhayfah, as the Caliph, and my

Lord ﷻ asked regarding it, I would reply, 'My Lord, I heard your Prophet ﷺ state, 'He loves Allāh ﷻ truly from his heart.'"[47]

قَالَ أَبُو نعيم: أَخذ سَالم يَوْم الْيَمَامَة لِوَاء الْمُسلمين بِيَدِهِ فَقطعت، فَأَخذهَا بِشمَالِهِ فَقطعت، ثمَّ اعتنق اللِّوَاء، وَجعل يقْرَأ: **﴿وَمَا مُحَمَّد إِلَّا رَسُول قد خلت من قبله الرُّسُل﴾** [فقتل رَضِي اللَّهِ عَنهُ] .

Abū Nu'aym said, "On the Day of al-Yamāmah Sālim took hold of the banner of the Muslims with his hand, and then it was cut off. He thus took hold of it with his left hand and it was also cut off. Then he embraced the banner with his arms and recited, **{Muhammad is not but a messenger. [Other] messengers have passed on before him}**[48] And then he was killed."[49]

بِلَال بن رَبَاح
Bilāl ibn Rabāḥ

وينسب إِلَى أمه فَيُقَال: بِلَال بن حمامة، وَفِي الصَّحَابَة جمَاعَة نسبوا إِلَى أمهاتهم، واشتهر ذَلِك، مِنْهُم: معَاذ ومعوذ ابْنا عفراء، وَهِي أمهما، وأبوهما الْحَارِث بن رِفَاعَة، وَسُهيْل وَصَفوَان ابْنا بَيْضَاء وَهِي أمهما، وَاسم أَبِيهِمَا وهب، وَمَالك بن نميلَة وَهِي أمه، وَاسم أَبِيه ثَابت الْمُزَكي، وشرحبيل بن حَسَنَة وَهِي أمه، أَبوهُ عبد اللَّهِ بن المطاع، وَبشر بن الخصاصية وَهِي أمه، وَأَبوهُ معبد بن شرَاحِيل، وَابْن أم مَكْتُوم، وَأَبُو عَمْرو بن قيس، وَعبد اللَّهِ بن بُحَيْنَة، وَهِي أمه، وَاسم أَبِيه مَالك الأَزْدِيّ، والْحَارث بن البرصاء وَهِي أمه وَاسم أَبِيه مَالك بن قيس، ويعلى بن منية، وَهِي أمه، وَاسم أَبِيه أُميَّة، ويعلى بن سيابة وَهِي أمه، وَاسم

47 *Jamu' al-Jawāmi'* (11/301).
48 Ālī 'Imrān: 144
49 See *Ḥilyat al-Awliyā* of Abī Nu'aym (1/370-371).

أَبِيه مرّة، وَسعد بن حبتة، وَهِي أمه، وَأَبوهُ بحير بن مُعَاوِيَة وَمن وَلَده أَبُو يُوسُف الْقَاضِي، وَبُدَيْل بن أم أَصْرَم [وَهِي أمه] وَاسم أَبِيه سَلمَة وخفاف بَين ندبة، وَهِي أمه، وَاسم أَبِيه عُمَيْر، وَهَؤُلَاء كلهم صحابة.

He was named after his mother i.e. Bilāl ibn Ḥamāmah, and there were numerous individuals amongst the Companions who were attributed to their mothers, and this was widely known. They include: Muʿādh and Muʿwidh ibnā (the two sons of) ʿAfrā'—i.e. their mother—and their father was al-Ḥārith ibn Rifāʿah; Suhayl and Ṣafwān ibnā Bayḍā'—i.e. their mother—and their father was Wahb; Mālik ibn Numīlah—i.e. his mother—and his father was Thābit al-Muznī; Sḥurabīl ibn al-Ḥaṣanah—i.e. his mother—and his father was ʿAbdullāh ibn al-Mutāʿ; Bishr ibn al-Ḥaṣāṣīyah—i.e. his mother—and his father was Maʿbad ibn Shurāḥabīl; Ibn Umm Maktūm, and his father was ʿAmr ibn Qays; ʿAbdullāh ibn Buḥaynah—i.e. his mother—and his father was Mālik al-Azarī; al-Hārith ibn al-Barsā'—i.e. his mother—and his father was Mālik ibn Qays; Yaʿlā ibn Munabbah—i.e. his mother—and his father was Umayyah; Yaʿlā ibn Siyyābah—i.e. his mother—and his father was Murrah; Saʿd ibn Ḥatbah—i.e. his mother—and his father was Buḥayr ibn Muʿāwiyyah and amongst his sons was Abū Yūsuf al-Qādī; Badīl ibn Umm Aṣram—i.e. his mother—and whose father was Salamah; and Khaffāf ibn Nudbah—i.e. his mother—and his father was ʿUmayr. All of those mentioned are Companions.

وَفِي التَّابِعين وَمن بعدهمْ خلق اشتهروا بأسماء أمهاتهم كإسماعيل بن علية وَاسم أَبِيه إِبْرَاهِيم، وَمُحَمّد بن عتمة [وَهِي أمه] وَاسم أَبِيه خَالِد، وَسليمَان بن قتَّة، وَمَنْصُور بن صَفِيَّة وَغَيرهم.

And amongst the Tābiʿīn (the generation after the Companions) and those after them were many individuals who were famously referred to with the names of their mothers. Examples are Ismāʿīl ibn ʿUlyah, and his father's name was Ibrāhīm; Muḥammad ibn ʿUtmah—i.e. his mother—and his father's name was Khālid; Sulaymān ibn Qattah; Manṣūr ibn Ṣafīyyah, and other than them.

فَأَما حَدِيث بِلَال

As for Bilāl's story:

فَإِنَّهُ أسلم قَدِيما وَكَانَ قومه يعذبونه وَيَقُولُونَ لَهُ: رَبك اللات والعزى، وَهُوَ يَقُول: أحد أحد، فَأتى عَلَيْهِ أَبُو بكر [الصّديق رَضِي اللَّهِ عَنهُ] وَاشْتَرَاهُ بِسبع أَوَاقٍ، فَأَعْتقهُ، فَشهد بَدْرًا وأحدا والمشاهد كلهَا، وَهُوَ أول من أذن لرَسُول اللَّهِ - صَلَّى اللَّهُ عَلَيْهِ وَسَلَّمَ - كَانَ يُؤذن لَهُ حضرا وسفرا، وَكَانَ خازنه على بَيت مَاله، وَكَانَ آدم شَدِيد الأدمة نحيفا طوَالًا أقنى لَهُ شعر كثير، خَفِيف العارضين بِهِ شمط.

He was one of the earliest people to embrace Islam and his people would abuse him and say, "Your lords are al-Lāt and al-'Uzzā." To which he would reply, "*Aḥadun, aḥad* (One [Lord], One)." Then Abū Bakr al-Ṣiddīq ﵁ came to him, purchased him for seven *awāq* and emancipated him. He witnessed the Battle of Badr, 'Uḥud and all the other battles. He was the first one to perform the *adhān* (call to prayer) for the Messenger of Allāh ﷺ, and he would perform it at home and whilst travelling. He was also [appointed by him] as the treasurer of the Bayt al-Māl. In appearance he was extremely dark, thin, tall, with a curved nose and a full head of hair, and a little dark and grey hair on his cheeks.

[٤٨] أخبرنَا مُحَمَّد بن أبي طَاهِر الْبَزَّاز قَالَ أَنا الْجَوْهَرِي قَالَ أَنا ابْن حيويه قَالَ أَنا أَحْمد بن مَعْرُوف قَالَ ثَنَا الْحُسَيْن ابْن الْفَهم قَالَ ثَنَا مُحَمَّد بن سعد قَالَ أَنا جرير بن عبد الحميد عَن مَنْصُور عَن مُجَاهِد قَالَ: أول من أظهر الْإِسْلَام سَبْعَة: رَسُول اللَّهِ، وَأَبُو بكر، وبلال، وخباب، وصهيب، وعمار، وَسُمَيَّة أم عمار. فَأَما رَسُول اللَّهِ فَمَنعه عَمه، وَأما أَبُو بكر فَمَنعه قومه، وَأخذ الْآخرُونَ فَأَلْبَسُوهُمْ أَدْرَاع الْحَدِيد، ثمَّ صهروهم فِي الشَّمْس، حَتَّى بلغ الْجهد مِنْهُم كل مبلغ، فأعطوهم مَا سَأَلُوا فجَاء إِلَى كل [رجل] مِنْهُم بأنطاع الْأدم فِيهَا المَاء وألقوهم فِيهِ، وحملوا بجوانبه، إِلَّا بِلَال، فَإِنَّهُ هَانَتْ عَلَيْهِ نَفسه فِي اللَّهِ حَتَّى جعلُوا فِي عُنُقه حبلا، ثمَّ

أمروا صبيانهم يشدونه بَين أخشبي مَكَّة، فَجعل بِلَال يَقُول: أحد أحد.

Muḥammad ibn Abī Ṭāhir al-Bazzāz reported upon the authority of Mujāhid, "The first to openly display Islam were seven: the Messenger of Allāh, Abū Bakr, Bilāl, Khabbāb, Ṣuhayb, 'Ammār, and Sumayah Umm 'Ammār. [In terms of protection:] As for the Messenger of Allāh, he was protected by his uncle. As for Abū Bakr, he was protected by his tribe. As for the rest [of the seven,] they were made to wear iron armour and then they were exposed to the sun until their wills were broken and they succumbed to what they were asked of. Then they came to each man from them with a human sized leather skin filled with water, then threw them in it and carried them alongside it. The only one not to succumb was Bilāl as he did not value his life [over faith] in Allāh. They went to the extent of placing a rope around his neck and ordering their children to drag him between the two mountains of Makkah. However Bilāl kept proclaiming, '*Aḥadun, aḥad.*'"

[٤٩] أخبرنَا مُحَمَّد بن أبي الْقَاسِم الْبَغْدَادِيّ قَالَ أَنا حمد ابْن أَحْمد قَالَ أَنا أَحْمد بن عبد اللَّهِ الْحَافِظ قَالَ ثَنَا جُنْدُب بن الْحسن قَالَ نَا مُحَمَّد بن يحيى قَالَ ثَنَا أَحْمد بن مُحَمَّد بن أَيُّوب قَالَ ثَنَا إِبْرَاهِيم بن سعد عَن مُحَمَّد بن إِسْحَاق قَالَ حَدثنِي هِشَام بن عُرْوَة بن الزبير عَن أَبِيه: كَانَ ورقة بن نَوْفَل يمر ببلال وَهُوَ يعذب وَهُوَ يَقُول: أحد أحد، ثمَّ أقبل ورقة على أُميَّة بن خلف فَقَالَ: أَحْلف بِاللَّه عز وَجل لأتخذنه حنانا، حَتَّى مر بِهِ أَبُو بكر الصّديق يَوْمًا وهم يصنعون ذَلِك بِهِ، فَقَالَ لأمية: أَلا تتقي اللَّهِ عز وَجل فِي هَذَا الْمِسْكِين، حَتَّى مَتى؟ قَالَ: أَنْت أفسدته، فأنقذه مِمَّا ترى، فَقَالَ أَبُو بكر: أفعل، عِنْدِي غُلَام أسود أجلد مِنْهُ وَأقوى على دينك أعطيكه بِهِ. قَالَ: قد قبلت. قَالَ: هُوَ لَك. فَأعْطَاهُ أَبُو بكر غُلَامه ذَلِك وَأخذ بِلَالًا.

Muḥammad ibn Abī al-Qāsim al-Baghdādī informed us upon the authority of Hishām ibn 'Urwah ibn al-Zubayr's father, "Waraqah ibn Nawfal passed by Bilāl whilst he was being tortured and whilst he was stating, '*Aḥadun, aḥad.*' Then Waraqah approached Umayyah ibn Khalaf and said to him, 'I swear by Allāh ﷻ that you should show him compassion.' Until Abū Bakr passed by him one day whilst he was being tortured and stated to Umayyah, 'Are you not fearful of Allāh in treating this poor man in such a manner? How long will you continue?' He replied. 'You corrupted him so rescue him from what you see.' So Abū Bakr said, 'I have a young black slave who is stronger and sturdier than him, and more steadfast in your religion, so I will exchange him for Bilāl.' He replied, 'I accept.' Abū Bakr then said, 'Here he is for you.' Thus Abū Bakr exchanged his slave with Bilāl."

قَالَ مُحَمَّد بن إِسْحَاق: وَكَانَ أُميَّة يُخرجهُ إِذا حميت الظهيرة فيطرحه على ظَهره فِي بطحاء مَكَّة، ثمَّ يَأْمر بالصخرة الْعَظِيمَة فتوضع على صَدره، ثمَّ يَقُول لَهُ: لَا تزَال هَكَذَا حَتَّى تَمُوت أَو تكفر بِمُحَمد وَتعبد اللات والعزى فَيَقُول - وَهُوَ فِي ذَلِك الْبلَاء - أحد أحد.

Muḥammad ibn Isḥāq said: Umayyah would take him out when the heat of the afternoon sun became scorching and make him lie down upon his back in the valley of Makkah. Then he would order a large rock to be collected and placed upon his chest, and he would say to him, "This state of yours will not cease until you die or you reject Muḥammad and worship al-Lāt and al-'Uzzā." Bilāl would respond in the face of this anguish. "*Aḥadun, aḥad.*"

[٥٠] أخبرنَا يحيى بن ثَابت بن بنْدَار قَالَ: أَنا أبي، قَالَ: أَنا أَبُو بكر البرقاني قَالَ أَنا أَحْمد بن إِبْرَاهِيم الْإِسْمَاعِيلِيّ قَالَ: أَخْبرنِي أَبُو يعلى قَالَ نَا صَالح بن مَالك قَالَ نَا عبد الْعَزِيز بن الْمَاجشون قَالَ نَا مُحَمَّد بن الْمُنْكَدر قَالَ سَمِعت جَابر بن عبد اللَّهِ يَقُول: قَالَ عمر: كَانَ أَبُو بكر سيدنَا وَأعْتق سيدنَا، يَعْنِي بِلَالًا.

Jābir ibn 'Abdullāh reported upon the authority of 'Umār, "Abū Bakr was our master, and he emancipated our master (i.e. Bilāl)."[50]

---

50 Reported by al-Ḥākim in *al-Mustadrak* (3/285) and he said, "It is *ṣaḥīḥ* but Muslim and al-Bukhārī did not report it." Al-Dhahabī concurred with him. It was also reported by Ibn Sa'd in *al-Ṭabaqāt* (3/175).

[٥١] أَخْبَرَنَا مُحَمَّد بن أَبِي الْقَاسِم قَالَ أَنا حمد بن أَحْمَد قَالَ أَنا أَبُو نعيم أَحْمَد بن عبد اللَّهِ قَالَ نَا سُلَيْمَان بن أَحْمَد قَالَ نَا عَلِيّ بن عبد الْعَزِيز قَالَ نَا أَبُو حُذَيْفَة قَالَ نَا عمَارَة بن زَاذَان عَن ثَابت عَن أنس قَالَ: قَالَ رَسُول اللَّهِ - صَلَّى اللَّهُ عَلَيْهِ وَسَلَّمَ -: ((بِلَال سَابق الْحَبَشَة)).

Thābit reported on the authority of Anas that the Messenger of Allāh ﷺ said, "Bilāl preceded the Abyssinians [to Jannah]."[51]

[٥٢] قَالَ سُلَيْمَان: وَحدثنَا أَحْمَد بن حَامِد قَالَ ثَنَا أَبُو تَوْبَة قَالَ ثَنَا مُعَاوِيَة بن سَلام عَن زيد سَلام يَقُول: [حَدثنِي عبد اللَّهِ الْهَوْزَنِي قَالَ: لقِيت بِلَالًا فَقلت يَا بِلَال:] حَدثنِي كَيفَ كَانَت نَفَقَة رَسُول اللَّهِ - صَلَّى اللَّهُ عَلَيْهِ وَسَلَّمَ -؟ فَقَالَ: مَا كَانَ لَهُ شَيْء، كنت أَنا الَّذِي آتِي لَهُ بعد ذَلِك مذ بَعثه اللَّه عز وَجل حَتَّى توفّي وَكَانَ إِذا أَتَاهُ الرجل الْمُسلم فَرَآهُ عَارِيا فيأمرني فأنطلق فأستقرض لَهُ الْبردَة فأكسوه وأطعمه.

Zayd ibn Salām reported upon the authority 'Abdullāh al-Hawzanī that he met Bilāl and stated to him, "O Bilāl, inform me of the finances of the Messenger of Allāh." He replied, "He did not have anything, I was the one who would inform him about his finances from the time he was despatched by Allāh ﷻ until he passed away, and whenever he would see a Muslim come bereft of clothing he would order me [to handle the affair] and I would go and borrow some money to buy a garment for him, cover him and feed him."

[٥٣] أَخْبَرَنَا ابْن الْحصين قَالَ أَنا ابْن الْمَذْهَب قَالَ أَنا أَبُو بكر بن مَالك قَالَ

---

[51] Reported by al-Ḥākim in *al-Mustadrak* (3/284-285 and 402). Al-Ḥākim did not mention anything further, however al-Dhahabī stated, "I say: The narrator 'Amārah is very weak, and he was declared to be *ḍaʿīf* by al-Dāraquṭnī." And Ibn Abī Ḥātim mentioned it in *al-'Ilal* from the route Muḥammad ibn Ziyād—Abī Amāmah and said, "I heard my father and Abu Zur'ah state, "This ḥadīth is *bāṭil* (baseless), there is no basis for it with this *isnād*." It was also reported by Ibn Saʿd in *al-Ṭabaqāt* (3/175).

نَا عبد اللَّهِ بن أَحْمد قَالَ حَدثنِي أبي قَالَ حَدثنِي زيد بن الْحباب قَالَ حَدثنِي حُسَيْن بن وَاقد قَالَ أَخْبرنِي عبد اللَّهِ بن بُرَيْدَة قَالَ سَمِعت أبي يَقُول: أصبح النَّبِي فَدَعَا بِلَالًا، فَقَالَ: ((يَا بِلَال بِمَ سبقتني إِلَى الْجنَّة؟ مَا دخلت الْجنَّة قطّ إِلَّا سَمِعت خشخشتك أَمَامِي، إِنِّي دخلت البارحة الْجنَّة فَسمِعت خشخشتك)). قَالَ: مَا أحدثت إِلَّا تَوَضَّأت وَصليت رَكْعَتَيْنِ، فَقَالَ رَسُول اللَّهِ - صَلَّى اللَّهُ عَلَيْهِ وَسَلَّمَ -: ((بِهَذَا)).

'Abdullāh ibn Buraydah reported upon the authority of his father that the Prophet ﷺ arose one day and called Bilāl, stating, "O Bilāl, with what have you preceded me into Jannah? For I have never entered it except that I hear your footsteps in front of me. Indeed, I entered Jannah yesterday and heard your footsteps." He replied, "I do not do anything [particular] except that when I perform ablution, I pray two units." The Messenger of Allāh ﷺ thus stated, "It is due to this."[52]

[٥٤] قَالَ أَحْمد وثنا يُونُس قَالَ ثَنَا حَمَّاد - يَعْنِي بن زيد - عَن هِشَام ابْن عُرْوَة عَن أَبِيه عَن عَائِشَة [رَضِي اللَّهِ عَنْهَا] قَالَت: قدم رَسُول اللَّهِ الْمَدِينَة وَهِي وبيئة، فَكَانَ بِلَال إِذا أَخَذته الْحمى يَقُول:

Hishām ibn 'Urwah reported upon the authority of his father that 'Ā'ishah ﵂ said, "The Messenger of Allāh entered Madīnah during an epidemic, and whenever Bilāl would suffer from a fever he would say:

أَلا لَيْت شعري هَل أبيتن لَيْلَة بواد وحولي إذخر وجليل
وَهل أردن يَوْمًا مياه مجنة وَهل يبدون لي شامة وطفيل

I wish I could know if I would live a night, in the valley [of Makkah]
surrounded with its scented grass and plants.

52 Reported by Imām Aḥmad in *al-Musnad* (5/354 and 360) and al-Ḥākim in *al-Mustadrak* (3/285). Al-Ḥākim said, "It is *ṣaḥīḥ* upon the conditions of the two *shaykhs* and they did not report it." Al-Dhahabī concurred with him.

And whether I will be to drink from the waters of Majannah, and see
the two mountains of Shamah and Tafīl.

اللَّهُمَّ الْعَنِ عتبَة بن ربيعَة وَشَيْبَة بن ربيعَة وَأُمَيَّة بن خلف كَمَا أخرجونا من مَكَّة.

[Continued...] O Allāh curse ʿUtbah ibn Rabīʿah, Shaybah ibn Rabīʿah, and Umayyah ibn Khalaf, as they expelled us from Makkah."[53]

قَالَ مُحَمَّد بن إِبْرَاهِيم التَّيْمِيّ: لما توفّي رَسُول اللَّهِ - صَلَّى اللَّهُ عَلَيْهِ وَسَلَّمَ - أذن بِلَال وَرَسُول اللَّهِ لم يقبر، وَكَانَ إِذا قَالَ أشهد أَن مُحَمَّدًا رَسُول الله، انتحب النَّاس فِي الْمَسْجِد، فَلَمَّا دفن رَسُول اللَّهِ قَالَ لَهُ أَبُو بكر: أذن، فَقَالَ: إِن كنت إِنَّمَا أعتقتني لِأَن أكون مَعَك فسبيل ذَلِك، وَإِن كنت أعتقتني لله [عز وَجل] فخلني وَمن أعتقتني لَهُ، فَقَالَ: مَا أَعتقتك إِلَّا للَّهِ [عز وَجل]. قَالَ: فَإِنِّي لَا أُؤذن لأحد بعد رَسُول اللَّهِ - صَلَّى اللَّهُ عَلَيْهِ وَسَلَّمَ - قَالَ: فَذَاك إِلَيْك. قَالَ: فَأَقَامَ حَتَّى خرج بعوث الشَّام فَسَار مَعَهم.

Muḥammad ibn Ibrāhīm al-Tamūmī said, "When the Messenger of Allāh ﷺ passed away, Bilāl called the *adhān* whilst he had not yet been buried. Whenever he would say, 'I bear witness that Muḥammad is the Messenger of Allāh,' the people would begin to weep. When the Messenger of Allāh had been buried, Abū Bakr stated to Bilāl, 'Perform the *adhān*.' He replied, 'If you emancipated me so as to make me subservient to you then I will do so, however if you emancipated me for Allāh ﷻ then leave me [to serve] the one you emancipated me for.' Abū Bakr said, 'I did not emancipate you except for Allāh ﷻ.' Thus, he said, 'I will not perform the *adhān* for anyone after the Messenger of Allāh ﷺ.' [Abū Bakr] replied, 'It is as you wish.'" He said, "He remained there until the expedition set off to al-Shām and he travelled with them."

53 This was reported by the author in *Muthīr al-ʿAzm*, and he attributed it to al-Bukhārī and Muslim (1/103-104). It was also reported by Imām Aḥmad in *al-Musnad* (6/56 and 65).

قَالَ الْمُصَنِّف: توفّي بِلَال بِدِمَشْق سنة ثَمَانِي عشرَة وَهُوَ ابْن بضع وَسِتِّينَ وَسنة.

The author said, "Bilāl passed away in Damascus in the year eighteen when he was over sixty-three years of age."

مهجع مولى عمر بن الْخطاب

Mahja', the *Mawlā* (freed slave) of 'Umar ibn al-Khaṭṭāb

كَانَ من الْمُهَاجِرين الْأَوَّلين، وَهُوَ أول من قتل من الْمُسلمين يَوْم بدر، قَتله عَامر بن الْحَضْرَمِيّ.

He was amongst the first of the Muhājirīn, and he was the first of the Muslims to be killed during the Battle of Badr. He was killed by 'Āmir ibn al-Ḥaḍramī.

[٥٥] أَنبأَنَا هبة اللَّهِ بن أَحْمد الحريري قَالَ أَنبأَنَا مُحَمَّد بن عَليّ ابْن الْفَتْح قَالَ نَا ابْن سمعون قَالَ نا أَحْمد بن سُلَيْمَان الدِّمَشْقِي قَالَ نَا هِشَام بن عمار قَالَ ثنَا صَدَقَة بن خَالِد قَالَ نَا عبد الرَّحْمَن ابْن يزِيد بن جَابر قَالَ: بَلغنِي أَن رَسُول اللَّهِ - صَلَّى اللَّهُ عَلَيْهِ وَسَلَّمَ - قَالَ: ((سادة السودَان أَرْبَعَة: لُقْمَان وَمهجع وبلال وَالنَّجَاشِي)).

Ṣadaqah ibn Khālid reported upon the authority of 'Abdul Raḥmān ibn Yazīd ibn Jābir, "It reached me that the Messenger of Allāh ﷺ said, 'The masters of the black people are four, Luqmān, Mahja', Bilāl and al-Najāshī.'"[54]

أسامة بن زيد بن حارثة بن شراحيل

54 Reported by Ibn 'Asākir in his *Tārīkh*. This was stated by al-Suyūṭī in *Raf' Shān al-Ḥubshān* (p. 79/b) and *Azhār al-'Urūsh* (p. 5/a).

Usāmah ibn Zayd ibn Ḥārithah ibn Sharāḥīl

كَانَت خيل لبني الْقَيْن فِي الْجَاهِلِيَّة قد أغارت على أَبْيَات بني معن فاحتملوا زيدا وَهُوَ يومئذ غُلَام، فوافوا بِهِ سوق عكاظ. فَعَرَضُوهُ للْبيع، فَاشْتَرَاهُ حَكِيم بن حزَام لِعَمَّتِهِ خَدِيجَة بأربعمائة دِرْهَم، فَلَمَّا تزَوجهَا رَسُول اللَّهِ - صَلَّى اللَّهُ عَلَيْهِ وَسَلَّمَ - وهبته لَهُ، فتَبَنَّاهُ قبل الْإِسْلَام، وَكَانَ زيد قَصِيرا آدم شَدِيد الأدمة، فِي أَنفه فطس، فَأَعْتقهُ رَسُول اللَّهِ وزوجه مولاته أم أَيمن وَكَانَت حاضنة رَسُول اللَّهِ فَولدت لَهُ أُسَامَة ويكنى أُسَامَة أَبَا مُحَمَّد، وَكَانَ يُقَال لَهُ: الْحبّ بن الْحبّ وَكَانَ أسود.

During the era of Jāhiliyyah (i.e. pre-Islam) the horsemen of Banī al-Qayn raided the dwellings of the Banī Maʿn, and they took Zayd—who at that time was a young boy—and brought him to the marketplace of ʿUkāẓ so as to present him for sale. He was purchased by Ḥakīm ibn Ḥizām on behalf of his aunt Khadījah for four hundred dirhams. When the Messenger of Allāh ﷺ married her, she gifted Zayd to him and he adopted him as a son before the advent of Islam. Zayd was a short man, extremely dark and he had a flat nose. The Messenger of Allāh then emancipated him and married him to his *mawlāh* (freed woman) Umm Ayman, the nurse of the Messenger of Allāh. She bore a child for him named Usāmah, who was given the *kunyā* (nick-name) Usāmah Abā Muḥammad. He was also called, al-Ḥibb ibn al-Ḥibb (the beloved, son of the beloved). He was dark skinned.

[٥٦] أخبرنَا أَبُو بكر بن أبي طَاهِر الْبَزَّاز قَالَ أَنبأَنَا أَبُو إِسْحَاق الْبَرْمَكِي قَالَ أَنا ابْن حيويه قَالَ: أَنا ابْن مَعْرُوف قَالَ أَنا ابْن الْقَاسِم قَالَ ثَنا مُحَمَّد بن سعد قَالَ ثَنا يزِيد بن هَارُون قَالَ نَا حَمَّاد بن سَلمَة عَن هِشَام بن عُرْوَة عَن أَبِيه أَن رَسُول اللَّهِ - صَلَّى اللَّهُ عَلَيْهِ وَسَلَّمَ - أخر الْإِفَاضَة من عَرَفَة من أجل أُسَامَة بن زيد ينتظره، فجَاء غُلَام أفطس أسود، فَقَالَ أهل الْيمن: إِنَّمَا حبسنا من أجل هَذَا، قَالَ: فَلذَلِك كفر أهل الْيمن من أجل ذَا، قلت ليزِيد بن هَارُون: وَمَا يَعْنِي بقوله: كفر أهل الْيمن؟ قَالَ:

ردتهم حِين ارْتَدُّوا فِي زمن أبي بكر، إِنَّمَا كَانَت لاستخفافهم بِأَمْر النَّبِي - صَلَّى اللَّهُ عَلَيْهِ وَسَلَّمَ -.

Ḥishām ibn 'Urwah reported upon the authority of his father, "The Messenger of Allāh ﷺ delayed his descent from 'Arafah due to waiting for Usāmah ibn Zayd. Then a dark-skinned young man with a flat nose came. The people of Yemen said, 'You delayed us due to him?' He (i.e. the father of Ḥishām) said, 'It is due to this that the people of Yemen disbelieved.' I asked Yazīd ibn Hārūn (he is one of the narrators in the chain, i.e. he was asked by the one who reported it from him), 'What did he mean by 'the people of Yemen disbelieved'?' He replied, 'Their apostasy when they apostatised during the time of Abī Bakr. This was due to their belittlement of the Prophet ﷺ.'"

[٥٧] قَالَ ابْن سعد: وَأخبرنَا عبد الْوَهَّاب بن عَطاء قَالَ ثَنَا الْعمريّ عَن نَافِع عَن ابْن عمر أَن النَّبِي - صَلَّى اللَّهُ عَلَيْهِ وَسَلَّمَ - بعث سَرِيَّة فيهم أَبُو بكر وَعمر وَاسْتعْمل عَلَيْهِم أُسَامَة بن زيد فَكَأَن النَّاس طعنوا فِيهِ - أَي فِي صغرة - فَبلغ رَسُول اللَّهِ فَصعدَ الْمِنبَر فَحَمدَ اللَّهِ وَأثنى عَلَيْهِ، وَقَالَ: ((إِن النَّاس قد طعنوا فِي إِمَارَة أُسَامَة ابْن زيد، وَقد كَانُوا طعنوا فِي إِمَارَة أَبِيه من قبله، وإنهما الخليقان لَهَا، وَكَانَا خليقين لذَلِك، وَإِنَّهُ لمن أحب النَّاس إِلَيّ، وَكَانَ أَبوهُ من أحب النَّاس إِلَيّ، أَلا فأوصيكم بأسامة خيرا)).

Nāfi' reported upon the authority of Ibn 'Umar, "The Prophet ﷺ sent out a detachment within which was Abū Bakr and 'Umar, and he placed the detachment under the command of Usāmah ibn Zayd. And it was as if the people were contesting this [decision] due to his young age. This reached the Messenger of Allāh ﷺ and so he ascended upon his pulpit, glorified Allāh and praised Him. Then he said, 'The people have contested the leadership of Usamah ibn Zayd and they contested that of his father before him. However, both befit leadership and they were befitting for the roles. Indeed he (Usāmah) is from the most beloved of people to me, and likewise his father was from the most beloved of people to me. Thus, I exhort you to treat Usāmah well.'"[55]

[٥٨] قَالَ ابْن سعد: وَحدثنَا الْفضل بن دُكَيْن قَالَ نَا حَنش قَالَ: سَمِعت أبي يَقُول: اسْتعْمل النَّبِي - صَلَّى اللَّهُ عَلَيْهِ وَسَلَّمَ - أُسَامَة وَهُوَ ابْن ثَمَانِي عشرَة سنة.

Ibn Sa'd said: Al-Faḍl ibn Dukayn reported upon the authority of Ḥanash [ibn 'Abdullāh al-San'anī], "I heard my father stating that the Messenger of Allāh ﷺ appointed Usāmah as a leader when he was eighteen years of age."

[٥٩] قَالَ ابْن سعد: وَأخبرنَا مُسلم بن إِبْرَاهِيم قَالَ ثَنَا قُرَّة بن خَالِد قَالَ ثَنَا مُحَمَّد بن سِيرِين قَالَ: بلغت النَّخْلَة على عهد عُثْمَان بن عَفَّان [رَضِي اللَّهِ عَنهُ] ألف دِرْهَم، قَالَ: فَعمد أُسَامَة إِلَى نَخْلَة فنقرها، فَأخْرج جمارها فأطعمه أمه، فَقَالُوا لَهُ: مَا يحملك على هَذَا وَأَنت ترى النَّخْلَة قد بلغت ألف دِرْهَم؟ قَالَ: إِن أُمِّي سألتنيه وَلَا تَسْأَلنِي شَيْئا أقدر عَلَيْهِ إِلَّا أعطيتهَا.

Ibn Sa'd said: Muslim ibn Ibrāhīm [...] reported upon the authority of Muḥammad ibn Sirīn, "The price of date palms during the rule of 'Uthmān ibn 'Affān ﷺ reached one thousand dirhams." He continued, "[During this time,] Usāmah went to his date palm, pierced it and took out palm pith—feeding his mother with it. He was asked, 'Why do you do this when you can see that the price of the date palm has reached one thousand dirhams?' He replied, 'My mother asked me for it, and whenever I am asked by her do something which I am capable of, I fulfil her request.'[56]

قَالَ الْوَاقِدِيّ: قبض النَّبِي - صَلَّى اللَّهُ عَلَيْهِ وَسَلَّمَ - وَأُسَامَة ابْن عشْرين سنة، وَكَانَ قد سكن بعد النَّبِي - صَلَّى اللَّهُ عَلَيْهِ وَسَلَّمَ - وَادي الْقرى ثمَّ نزل الْمَدِينَة، فَمَات بالجرف فِي آخر خلَافَة مُعَاوِيَة.

Al-Wāqidī said, "Usāmah was twenty years old when the Prophet ﷺ passed

55 Reported by Ibn Sa'd in *al-Ṭabaqāt* (4/49 and 2/192).
56 Reported by Ibn Sa'd in *al-Ṭabaqāt* (4/49) and the second report (4/52).

away. He resided in Wādī al-Qurrā after the Prophet's death ﷺ. He passed away in al-Jurf during the end of Mu'āwiyah's caliphate."

قَالَ الزُّهْرِيّ: حمل أُسَامَة حِين مَاتَ من الجرف إِلَى الْمَدِينَة.

Al-Zuhrī said, "Usāmah's body was transferred from al-Jurf to Madīnah."

أبُو بكرَة واسْمه: نفيع

Abū Bakrah, whose name was Nufay'

لما حاصر رَسُول اللَّهِ - صَلَّى اللَّهُ عَلَيْهِ وَسَلَّمَ - الطَّائِف نَادَى مناديه: أَيّمَا عبد نزل من الْحصن وَخرج إِلَيْنَا فَهُوَ حر، فَخرج جمَاعَة مِنْهُم أَبُو بكرَة، نزل فِي بكرَة، فَقيل: أَبُو بكرَة. فَهُوَ يعد من موَالِي رَسُول اللَّهِ - صَلَّى اللَّهُ عَلَيْهِ وَسَلَّم -.

When the Messenger of Allāh ﷺ besieged the city of al-Ṭā'if, his herald called out, "Any slave who leaves the stronghold and joins us will be set free. A group came to them, within which was Abū Bakrah. He descended within a pulley (*bakrah*) and so was named Abū Bakrah. He was considered as one of the *mawālī* (pl. of *mawla*, freedman) of the Messenger of Allāh ﷺ.

أسلم الْأسود

Aslam al-Aswad

كَانَ غُلَاما لرجل من بني نَبهَان من طَيئ، بَعثه طَيئ ربية، فَلَمَّا ورد عَليّ بن أبي طَالب بِلَادهمْ أَخذ أَصْحَابه هَذَا العَبْد وأوثقوه وخوفوه الْقَتْل، فَأسلم وَشهد مَعَ خَالِد الْيَمَامَة.

He was a slave belonging to a man from Banī Nabhān of Ṭay—who was assigned to monitor the movement of the Muslims as they arrive. When 'Alī ibn Abī Ṭālib arrived in their land, his comrades detained this slave, binded him and made him fear that he was going to be killed. He embraced Islam and witnessed al-Yamāmah alongside Khālid.

مغيث زوج بَرِيرة
Mughīth, the husband of Barīrah

[٦٠] روى البُخَارِيّ فِي صَحِيحه من حَدِيث عِكْرِمَة عَن ابْن عَبَّاس قَالَ: كَانَ زوج بَرِيرَة عبدا أسود يُقَال لَهُ: مغيث عبدا لبني فلَان كَأَنِّي أنظر إِلَيْهِ يطوف وَرَاءَهَا فِي سِكَك الْمَدِينَة، ودموعه تسيل على لحيته، فَقَالَ النَّبِي - صَلَّى اللَّهُ عَلَيْهِ وَسَلَّمَ - للْعَبَّاس: ((يَا عَبَّاس، أَلا تعجب من حب مغيث بَرِيرَة وَمن بغض بَرِيرَة مغيثا)).

Al-Bukhārī reported in his *Ṣaḥīḥ* upon the authority of 'Ikrimah from Ibn 'Abbās, "The husband of Barīrah (the freed slave of 'Āishah) was a black slave named Mughīth the slave of such-and-such a tribe. It is as if I can [still] see him now pacing behind her in the pathways of Madīnah and his tears would stream down into his beard. The Prophet ﷺ said to 'Abbās, 'O 'Abbās, is it not amazing the extent of Mughīth's love for Barīrah and her hate of him?'

فَقَالَ النَّبِي - صَلَّى اللَّهُ عَلَيْهِ وَسَلَّمَ -: ((أَو راجعتيه)). فَقَالَت: يَا رَسُول اللَّهِ، تَأْمُرنِي؟

The Prophet ﷺ said to Barīrah, 'Will you not go back to him (as she had terminated the marriage upon being freed)?" She said, 'O Messenger of Allāh, are you ordering me?'

قَالَ: ((إِنَّمَا أشفع)). قَالَت: فَلَا حَاجَة لي فِيهِ.

He said, 'I am merely mediating.' She said, 'Then I have no need for him.'"

[٦١] أخبرنَا مُحَمَّد بن نَاصِر قَالَ أنا أَبُو الْحُسَيْن بن عبد الْجَبَّار قَالَ أنا أَبُو مُحَمَّد الْجَوْهَرِي قَالَ أَنا أَبُو عمر بن حيوية قَالَ أنبأ أَبُو بكر مُحَمَّد بن خلف بن الْمَرْزُبَان قَالَ نَا مُحَمَّد بن الْهَيْثَم قَالَ ثَنَا يُوسُف بن عدي عَن سعيد وَأَيوب عَن قتَادَة عَن عِكْرِمَة عَن ابْن عَبَّاس: أَن زوج بَرِيرَة كَانَ عبدا أسود [مولى] لبني الْمُغيرَة، وَالله لكَأَنِّي بِهِ فِي أَطْرَاف الْمَدِينَة ونواحيها وَإِن دُمُوعه لتجري على لحيته يتبعهَا يَتَرَضَّاهَا لتختاره، فَلم تفعل.

ʿIkrimah reported upon the authority of Ibn ʿAbbas, "The husband of Barīrah was a black slave, the *mawlā* of Banī Mughīrah. By Allāh it is as if I am with him now in the outer part of Madīnah and its suburbs, with his tears streaming into his beard. He would pursue her, attempting to persuade her to choose him. However, she would not do so."

سعد الْأسود

Saʿd al-Aswad

[٦٢] أخبرنَا أَبُو مَنْصُور مُحَمَّد بن عبد الْملك قَالَ أَنا إِسْمَاعِيل ابْن مسْعدَة قَالَ أَنا حَمْزَة بن يُوسُف قَالَ أَنا أَبُو أَحْمد بن عدي قَالَ أَنا بهْلُول بن إِسْحَاق عَن بهْلُول الْأَنْبَارِي وَعبد اللهِ بن مُحَمَّد بن عبد الْعَزِيز قَالَا ثَنَا سُوَيْد بن سعيد (ح) وأنبأنا أَبُو بكر مُحَمَّد بن أبي طَاهِر الْبَزَّاز قَالَ أَنبأَنَا أَبُو الْقَاسِم عَليّ بن المحسن التنوخي قَالَ أَنا أَبُو طَاهِر مُحَمَّد بن عبد الرَّحْمَن بن الْعَبَّاس قَالَ نَا عبد اللهِ بن مُحَمَّد بن عبد الْعَزِيز قَالَ نَا سُوَيْد بن سعيد قَالَ نَا مُحَمَّد بن عمر بن صَالح بن مَسْعُود الكلَاعِي قَالَ حَدثنِي الْحسن وَقَتَادَة عَن أنس بن مَالك قَالَ: جَاءَ رجل إِلَى رَسُول الله - صَلَّى اللَّهُ عَلَيْهِ وَسَلَّمَ - فَقَالَ: يمْنَع سوَادِي ودمامتي دُخُول الْجنَّة؟

Al-Ḥasan and Qatādah reported upon the authority of Anas ibn Mālik, "A man came to the Messenger of Allāh ﷺ and said, 'Does my darkness and ugliness prevent me from entering Jannah?'

قَالَ: ((لَا وَالَّذِي نَفسِي بِيَدِهِ مَا اتَّقَيْت اللَّهِ عز وَجل وَآمَنت بِمَا جَاءَ بِهِ رَسُوله)).

He answered, 'Nay, by the One in whose hand is my soul, [you will not be prevented from entering it] if you fear Allāh and believe in that which came with his Messenger.'

قَالَ: فوالذي أكرمك بِالنُّبُوَّةِ لقد شهِدت أَن لَا إِلَه إِلَّا اللَّهِ وَحده لَا شريك لَهُ وَأَن مُحَمَّدًا عَبده وَرَسُوله وَالْإِقْرَار بِمَا جَاءَ بِهِ من قبل أَن أَجْلِس مِنْك هَذَا الْمجْلس بِثَمَانِيَة أشهر، فَمَا لي يَا رَسُول اللَّهِ؟

He replied, 'By the one whom honoured you with prophethood, I have testified that there is no deity worthy of being worshipped besides Allāh, alone and without partner, and that Muḥammad is his slave and Messenger, and I affirmed [my belief] in that which he came with eight months before this meeting. So, what will come to me O Messenger of Allāh?'

قَالَ: ((لَك مَا للْقَوْم وَعَلَيْك مَا عَلَيْهِم، وَأَنت أخوهم)).

He replied, 'You have the same responsibilities of the people and the same rights as them, you are their brother.'

قَالَ: فَلَقَد خطبت إِلَى عَامَّة من بحضرتك وَمن لَيْسَ مَعَك فردوني لسوادي ودمامة وَجْهي، وَإِنِّي لفي حسب من قومِي من بني سليم مَعْرُوف الْآبَاء، وَلَكِن غلب عَليّ سَواد أخوالي.

He said, 'Indeed I have asked everyone present with you and those absent [for a woman to marry] but they have rejected me due to my darkness and the poor appearance of my face. However, I am a nobleman amongst my people from Banī Salīm, and my father and grandfathers are well-known, but the dark skin of my maternal uncles prevailed over me.'

قَالَ رَسُول اللَّهِ - صَلَّى اللَّهُ عَلَيْهِ وَسَلَّمَ -: ((هَل شهد الْمجْلس الْيَوْم عَمْرو بن وهيب؟))

The Messenger of Allāh ﷺ said, 'Is ʿAmr ibn Wuhayb present in this gathering?'

وَكَانَ رجلا من ثَقِيف قريب الْعَهْد بِالْإِسْلَامِ - قَالُوا: لَا.

[ʿAmr] was a man from Thaqīf who had embraced Islam close to the time [of this narration.] Those present replied, 'No.'

قَالَ: ((تعرف منزله؟))

He said, 'Do you know where he lives?'

قَالَ: نعم.

He replied positively.

قَالَ: ((فَاذْهَبْ واقرع الْبَاب قرعا رَفِيقًا، ثمَّ سلم، فَإِذا دخلت عَلَيْهِ فَقل: زَوجنِي رَسُول الله - صَلَّى اللَّهُ عَلَيْهِ وَسَلَّمَ – فتاتكم)).

He said, 'Go to his abode and knock softly upon his door and then greet him. When you enter it, say, 'The Messenger of Allāh ﷺ has given me your daughter's hand in marriage.'

وَكَانَت لَهُ ابْنة عاتق، وَكَانَ لَهَا حَظّ من جمال وعقل، فَلَمَّا أَتَى الْبَاب قرع وَسلم، فرحبوا بِهِ وسمعوا لُغَة عَرَبِيَّة ففتحوا الْبَاب، فَلَمَّا رَأَوْا سَوَاده ودمامة وَجهه انقبضوا عَنهُ، قَالَ: إِن رَسُول اللَّهِ - صَلَّى اللَّهُ عَلَيْهِ وَسَلَّمَ - زَوجنِي فتاتكم، فردُّوا عَلَيْهِ ردا قبيحا، فَخرج الرجل، وَخرجت الْجَارِيَة من خدرها، وَقَالَت: يَا عبد اللَّهِ، ارْجع، فَإِن يَك رَسُول اللَّهِ - صَلَّى اللَّهُ عَلَيْهِ وَسَلَّمَ - زوجنيك، فقد رضيت لنَفْسي مَا رَضِي اللَّه عز وَجل لي وَرَسُوله. فَأتى رَسُول اللَّهِ - صَلَّى اللَّهُ عَلَيْهِ وَسَلَّمَ - فَأخْبرهُ،

وَقَالَت لأَبِيهَا: يَا أبتاه، النجا النجا قبل أَن يفضحك الْوَحْي، فَإِن يَك رَسُول الله - صَلَّى اللَّهُ عَلَيْهِ وَسَلَّمَ - زوجنيه فقد رضيت مَا رَضِي لي رَسُول اللَّهِ.

He had a freeborn daughter who possessed a great amount of beauty and intelligence. And when the man reached the door, he knocked and gave the greeting. They welcomed him as they heard him speaking Arabic so they opened the door. However, when they saw how dark the man was and the bad appearance of his face, they drew back from him. He said, 'The Messenger of Allāh ﷺ has betrothed me to your daughter.' In response to this they turned him away in a rough manner, so the man left. The girl then exited the area within which she was concealed and stated, 'O 'Abdullāh return, for if the Messenger of Allāh has betrothed me to you then I am pleased deep within myself with what Allāh ﷻ and His Messenger have approved for me.' He went to the Messenger of Allāh and informed him of what took place, and the girl said to her father, 'O father, save yourself, save yourself before the revelation exposes you. If the Messenger of Allāh has betrothed me to him then I am pleased with what he has assented.'

فَخرج الشَّيْخ حَتَّى أَتَى رَسُول اللَّهِ - صَلَّى اللَّهُ عَلَيْهِ وَسَلَّمَ - وَهُوَ فِي أدنى الْقَوْم مَجْلِسا، فَقَالَ النَّبِي - صَلَّى اللَّهُ عَلَيْهِ وَسَلَّمَ -: ((أَنْت الَّذِي رددت على رَسُول اللَّهِ مَا رددت؟))

The *shaykh* (old man) then left to see the Messenger of Allāh, he came to him and found him sitting in his assembly, so he sat at the furthest point in the sitting, and then he said, 'Are you the one who rejected that which the Messenger of Allāh has approved?'

قَالَ: قد فعلت ذَلِك، وَأَسْتَغْفِر اللَّهِ، فظننا أَنه كَاذِب، فقد زوجناها إِيَّاه، فنعوذ بِاللَّه من سخط اللَّهِ وَسخط رَسُول اللَّهِ.

He said, 'Yes I did so, and so I seek forgiveness from Allāh. I thought that he was lying, [otherwise] I would have married her to him. Thus, I seek refuge with Allāh from His anger, and that of His Messenger.'

فَقَالَ رَسُولُ اللَّهِ - صَلَّى اللَّهُ عَلَيْهِ وَسَلَّمَ -: ((اذْهَبْ إِلَى صَاحِبَتِكَ فَادْخُلْ بِهَا)).

The Messenger of Allāh ﷺ then said [to the man,] 'Go to your wife and settle down with her.'

قَالَ: وَالَّذِي بَعَثَكَ بِالْحَقِّ مَا آخذ شَيْئًا حَتَّى أَسْأَل إِخْوَانِي.

He replied, 'By the One who despatched you with the truth, I will not take anything until I ask my brothers [to the pay the dowry.]'

فَقَالَ لَهُ رَسُولُ اللَّهِ - صَلَّى اللَّهُ عَلَيْهِ وَسَلَّمَ -: ((مهر امْرَأَتك على ثَلَاثَة من الْمُؤمنِينَ، اذْهَبْ إِلَى عُثْمَان بن عَفَّان فَخذ مِنْهُ مِائَتي دِرْهَم))، فَأَعْطَاهُ وزاده، ((واذهب إِلَى عَليّ بن أَبِي طَالب فَخذ مِنْهُ مائَة دِرْهَم))، فَأَعْطَاهُ وزاده، ((واذهب إِلَى عبد الرَّحْمَن بن عَوْف فَخذ مائَة دِرْهَم))، فَأَعْطَاهُ وزاده.

The Messenger of Allāh ﷺ said to him, 'The dowry of your woman [will be paid] by three from the believers. Go to 'Uthmān ibn 'Affān and take from him two hundred dirhams.' He was given this amount and more. 'Go to 'Alī ibn Abī Ṭālib and take from him one hundred dirhams.' He was given this amount and more. 'And go to 'Abd al-Raḥmān ibn 'Awf and take from him one hundred dirhams.' He was given this amount and more.

وَاعْلَم أَنَّهَا لَيست بِسنة جَارِيَة وَلَا بفريضة فَمن شَاءَ فليتزوج على الْقَلِيل وَالْكثير.

However, one should know that this amount is not a prescribed Sunnah and it is not mandatory, so one could marry with a small dowry or a large one.

فَبَيْنَمَا هُوَ فِي السُّوق مَعَه مَا يَشْتَرِي لزوجته ينظر مَا يجهزها بِهِ إِذْ سمع صَوتا يُنَادِي: يَا خيل اللَّهِ ارْكَبِي وَأَبْشِرِي، فَنظر نظرة إِلَى السَّمَاء ثُمَّ قَالَ: اللَّهُمَّ إِلَه السَّمَاء وإله الأرْض وَرب مُحَمَّد لأجعلن هَذِه الدَّرَاهِم الْيَوْم فِيمَا يحب اللَّهُ وَرَسُوله والمؤمنون، وانتفض انتفاضة الْفرس الْعرق فَاشْترى سَيْفا ورمحا وفرسا، وَاشْترى جُبَّة

وَشد عمَامَته على بَطْنه، واعتجر بِالْأُخْرَى، فَلم تَر مِنْهُ إِلَّا حماليق عَيْنَيْهِ حَتَّى وقف على الْمُهَاجِرين فَقَالُوا: من هَذَا الْفَارِس الَّذِي لَا نعرفه؟

When the man was in the market with the money looking to purchase for his wife what she needed for the wedding, he heard a voice calling, 'O steed[s] of Allāh, ride and rejoice.' Thus he placed his vision upon the sky and said, 'O Allāh, the God of the heavens and the earth, the Lord of Muḥammad, I will not use this money today except in that which Allāh, His Messenger and the believers love.' Upon this he sought for a well-bred horse, and so he purchased a sword, spear and a horse. He also purchased a *jubbah* and tied his turban around his abdomen, veiling himself with the other garment so that nothing could be seen of him except his eyes. He was veiled to an extent that when he came amongst the Muhājirīn they said, 'Who is this unknown horseman?'

فَقَالَ لَهُم عَليّ بن أبي طَالب: كفوا عَن الرجل فَلَعَلَّهُ مِمَّن طَرَأَ عَلَيْكُم من قبل الْبَحْرين أَو من قبل الشَّام حَتَّى يسألكم عَن معالم دينه فَأحب أَن يواسيكم الْيَوْم بِنَفسِهِ، إِذْ رَآهُ رَسُول اللَّهِ فَقَالَ: ((من هَذَا الْفَارِس الَّذِي لم يأتنا؟)) فرغبن فِي الْجِهَاد إِذا اقتحمت الكتيبتان فَجعل يضْرب بِسَيْفِهِ، ويطعن برمحه قدما قدما، إِذْ قَامَ بِهِ فرسه، فَنزل عَنهُ وحسر عَن ذِرَاعَيْهِ، فَلَمَّا رأى رَسُول اللَّهِ سَواد ذِرَاعَيْهِ عرفه، فَقَالَ: ((أسعد؟)) قَالَ: سعد: فدَاك أبي وَأمي يَا رَسُول اللَّهِ. قَالَ: ((سعد جدك))، فَمَا زَالَ يضْرب بِسَيْفِهِ ويطعن برمحه، إِذْ قَالُوا: صرع سعد، فَخرج رَسُول اللَّهِ نَحوه، فَرفع رَأسه فَوَضعه فِي حجره فَأخذ يمسح عَن وَجهه التُّرَاب بِثَوْبِهِ، وَقَالَ: ((مَا أطيب رِيحك، وَأحسن وَجهك، وَأَحَبَّك إِلَى اللَّهِ [عز وَجل] وَإِلَى رَسُوله)).

'Alī ibn Abī Ṭālib said to them, 'Leave this man for he may have been from those who recently arrived from the direction of al-Baḥrayn or al-Shām so as to inquire from you about matters of his religion, and he wishes to support you in battle today.' Then he was seen by the Messenger of Allāh who said, 'Who is this horseman who did not present himself to us?' He was ardent in participating in *jihad*, so when the two sides clashed he fought with his sword and spear, advancing forward fiercely. His horse could no longer move (i.e. it was exhausted due to the intensity of the battle) so he dismounted the horse, baring his arms. When the Messenger of Allāh saw the darkness of his arms he realised who it was and stated, 'O Sa'd!' Sa'd replied, 'I sacrifice my parents for you O Messenger of Allāh.' He said, 'Sa'd exert yourself.'He did not cease striking with his sword and stabbing with his spear until it was said, 'Sa'd has been struck down.' The Messenger of Allāh went to him, raised his head and placed it within his lap. He then wiped the dust from his face with his garment and said, 'How a good a smell is your scent, how beautiful is your face and how beloved you are to Allāh ﷻ and his Messenger.'

وَبكى رَسُول اللَّهِ - صَلَّى اللَّهُ عَلَيْهِ وَسَلَّمَ - ثمَّ ضحك، ثمَّ أعرض عَنهُ بِوَجْهِهِ، ثمَّ قَالَ: ((ورد الْحَوْض وَرب الْكَعْبَة)) فَقَالَ أَبُو لبَابَة: بِأبي أَنْت وَأمي، مَا الْحَوْض؟ قَالَ: ((حَوْض أعطانيه رَبِّي [عز وَجل] مَا بَين صنعاء إِلَى بصرى، حافتاه مكلل بالدر والياقوت، آنيته كعدد نُجُوم السَّمَاء مَاؤُهُ أَشد بَيَاضًا من اللَّبن وَأحلى من الْعَسَل، من شرب مِنْهُ شربة لم يظمأ بعْدهَا أبدا)). قَالُوا: يَا رَسُول اللَّهِ، رَأَيْنَاك بَكَيْت وضحكت ورأيناك أَعرَضت بِوَجْهِك، فَقَالَ: ((أما بُكَائِي فشوقا إِلَى سعد، وَأما ضحكي فَفَرِحت لَهُ بِمَنْزِلَتِهِ من اللَّهِ عز وَجل وكرامته عَلَيْهِ. وَأما إعراضي فَإِنِّي رَأَيْت أَزوَاجه من الْحور الْعين يتبادرون كاشفات سوقهن بارزات خلاخيلهن، فَأَعْرَضت حَيَاء مِنْهُنَّ)).

The Messenger of Allāh cried, then he laughed, turned his face from him and said, 'He has reached the *Ḥawḍ*, by the Lord of the Ka'bah.' Abū Lubābah said, 'My father and mother be sacrificed for you, what is the *Ḥawḍ*?' He replied, 'The *Ḥawḍ* [is the pond] given to me by my Lord ﷻ, [its size is] the distance between Ṣan'a' and Baṣrah. Its edges are encased with pearls and rubies, and its vessels are numerous like the stars in the sky. Its water is whiter than milk and sweeter than honey. The one who drinks from it will not suffer thirst again.' They said, 'O Messenger of Allāh, we saw you crying and smiling, then we saw you turning your face.' He replied, 'As for my weeping, it was due to my longing for Saʿd. As for my laughter, it was due to my happiness at his station from Allāh ﷻ and His generosity to him. As for my turning away, I saw his wives from *al-Ḥūr al-ʿĪn* hastening towards him, displaying their legs and exposing their anklets, thus I turned due to modesty towards them.'"

قَالَ: وَأمر بسلاحه وَمَا كَانَ لَهُ فَقَالَ: ((اذْهَبُوا بِهِ إِلَى زَوجته وَقُولُوا لَهَا: إِن اللَّهِ عز وَجل قد زوجه خيرا من فتاتكم، وَهَذَا مِيرَاثه، وَالَّذِي نفس مُحَمَّد بِيَدِهِ إِنِّي لأذب عَن الْحَوْض كَمَا يذب الْبَعِير الأجرب عَن الْإِبِل أَن تخالطها، إِنَّه لَا يرد على حَوْضِي إِلَّا التقي)).

He said, "He ordered [the gathering of] Saʿd's weapons and belongings and then said, 'Take them to his wife and state to her, 'Verily Allāh ﷻ has married him to maidens better than yours. Here are his possessions (i.e. his estate).' By the One who holds Muḥammad's soul in His hand, I will separate [the bad] from the *Ḥawḍ* as the mangy camel is pushed away from mixing with the [healthy] camels. Verily none will be present at my *Ḥawḍ* except the pious.'"[57]

قَالَ أَبُو عبد اللَّهِ الصُّورِي: هَذَا حَدِيث غَرِيب من حَدِيث الْحسن وَقَتَادَة، وَلَا أعلم حدث بِهِ عَنْهُمَا غير مُحَمَّد بن عمر الكَلَاعِي وَلَا رَأَيْته عَنهُ إِلَّا من حَدِيث

---

57 This was reported by Ibn ʿAdī, Ibn Ḥibbān and al-Mukhaliṣ in chapter two of his *Fawāʾid*. All of them report it from the route of Suwayd ibn Saʿīd—Muḥammad ibn ʿUmar ibn Ṣāliḥ—Qatādah—Anas. Al-Ḥāfiẓ Ibn Ḥajar said this in *al-Iṣābah* (2/39). As for the narrator named Suwayd ibn Saʿīd: Al-Bukhārī said that he had issues. He was blind and so he would dictate ḥadīth which were not his. Al-Nasāʾī said that he was *ḍaʿīf*. Ibn ʿAdī said, "He is closer to being weak." See *Mukhtasar al-Kāmil fī al-Ḍuʿafā* (399) and *al-Taqrīb* (26). As for the narrator named Muḥammad ibn ʿUmar ibn Ṣāliḥ al-Kalāʿī: Ibn ʿAdī said, "His ḥadīth are rejected (*munkar*) [even though they are] reported from the *thiqāt* (trustworthy) of the people, and he is not well-known." See *Mukhtaṣar al-Kāmil* (p. 675).

سُوَيْد بن سعيد.

Abū ʿAbdullāh al-Ṣūrī said, "This ḥadīth is *gharīb* (strange) as it is reported by both al-Ḥasan and Qatādah. I am not aware of a ḥadīth reported by both of them except from Muḥammad ibn 'Umar al-Kalāʿī, and I have not seen it reported from him except from the ḥadīth of Suwayd ibn Saʿīd."

يسار الأسود

Yasār al-Aswad[58]

[٦٣] أنبأَنَا مُحَمَّد بن نَاصِر قَالَ أنبأَنَا جَعْفَر بن أَحْمد قَالَ أنا الْحسن ابْن مُحَمَّد الْخلال قَالَ: كتب إِلَيّ أَحْمد بن عَليّ بن هِشَام يذكر أَن عبد اللَّهِ بن زَيْدَانَ حَدثهمْ قَالَ نَا أَحْمد بن حَازِم قَالَ نَا الحكم بن سُلَيْمَان الْجبلي قَالَ ثَنَا سيف بن عمر عَن مُوسَى بن عقيل الْبَصْرِيّ عَن ثَابت الْبنانِيّ عَن أبي هُرَيْرَة قَالَ: دخلت على النَّبِي - صَلَّى اللَّهُ عَلَيْهِ وَسَلَّمَ - فَقَالَ لي: ((يَا أَبَا هُرَيْرَة، يدْخل عَليّ من هَذَا الْبَاب السَّاعَة رجل من أحد السَّبْعَة الَّذين يدْفع اللَّهِ [عز وَجل] عَن أهل الأَرْض بهم)).

Thābit al-Bunānī reported upon the authority of Abū Hurayrah, "I entered into the presence of the Prophet ﷺ. He said to me, 'O Abā Hurayrah, a man will enter my presence through this door in a moment whom is one of the seven people that Allāh ﷻ protects the people of the earth with [due to their virtue and high rank.]'

فَإِذا حبشِي قد طلع من ذَلِك الْبَاب، أجدع على رَأسه جرة من مَاء فَقَالَ رَسُول الله: ((هُوَ هَذَا)).

58 He is the *mawlā* of al-Mughīrah ibn Shuʿbah. Ibn al-Athīr said, "He passed away during the time of the Prophet." See *Rafʿ Shȧn al-Ḥubshān* (120/a).

Thereafter an Abyssinian man came through the door. He was carrying a container of water upon his head. The Messenger of Allāh ﷺ said, 'This is him'"

قَالَ: وَقَالَ رَسُول الله - ثَلَاث مَرَّات -: ((مرْحَبًا بيسار)).

He said, "The Messenger of Allāh ﷺ said thrice, 'Welcome Yasār.'"

قَالَ: وَكَانَ يرش الْمَسْجِد ويكنسه.

He said, "He would sprinkle water in the *masjid* and sweep it."[59]

جُلَيْبِيب

Julaybīb

قَالَ الْمُصَنّف: ذكر أَنه كَانَ أسود.

The author said: It has been mentioned that he was black.

[٦٤] أخبرنَا أَبُو بكر بن أبي طَاهِر الْبَزَّار قَالَ أنا أَبُو مُحَمَّد الْجَوْهَرِي قَالَ أنا أَبُو عَمْرو بن حيوية قَالَ أنا أَحْمد بن مَعْرُوف قَالَ نَا الْحُسَيْن بن الْفَهم قَالَ نَا مُحَمَّد بن سعد قَالَ أَنا عَارِم قَالَ ثَنَا حَمَّاد بن سَلمَة قَالَ نَا ثَابت عَن كنَانَة بن نعيم الْعَدوي عَن أبي بَرزَة الْأَسْلَمِيّ أَن جليبيبا كان امْرأ من الْأَنْصَار، وَكَانَ أَصْحَاب النَّبِي - صَلَّى اللَّهُ عَلَيْهِ وَسَلَّمَ - إِذا كَانَ لأَحَدهم أيم لم يُزَوّجهَا حَتَّى يعلم أَلرسول اللَّهِ فِيهَا حَاجَة أم لَا، فَقَالَ رَسُول اللَّهِ ذَات يَوْم لرجل من الْأَنْصَار: ((يَا فلَان، زوجنِي ابْنَتك)). قَالَ: نعَم ونعُم عين، قَالَ: ((إِنِّي لست لنَفْسي أريدها)). قَالَ: فلِمَنْ؟ قَالَ: ((لجليبيب)). قَالَ: يَا رَسُول اللَّهِ، حَتَّى أَستَأْمر أمهَا، فَأَتَاهَا فَقَالَ:

59 Reported by al-Khalāl in *Karāmāt al-Awliyah*. Al-Suyūṭī said this in *Azhār al-'Urūsh* (p. 20), and he mentioned it with this *isnād* in *Raf' Shān al-Ḥubshān* (p. 80).

إن رَسُول اللَّهِ - صَلَّى اللَّهُ عَلَيْهِ وَسَلَّمَ - يخْطب ابْنَتك، قَالَت: نعَم ونعُم عين، زوج رَسُول اللَّهِ - صَلَّى اللَّهُ عَلَيْهِ وَسَلَّمَ -، قَالَ: إِنَّه لَيْسَ لنَفسِهِ يريدها، قَالَت: فلِمَنْ؟ قَالَ: لجليبيب، قَالَت: حلقي ألجليبيب! لَا، لعمر اللَّهِ لَا أزوج جليبيبا.

Kinānah ibn Nu'aym al-'Adawī reported upon the authority of Abū Barzah al-Aslamī, "He was a man from the Anṣār. The Companions of the Prophet would not marry the women under their guardianship until they knew if the Messenger of Allāh ﷺ had a requirement for her or not. So, one day the Messenger of Allāh said to a man from the Anṣār ﷺ, 'O so-and-so, give me your daughter to marry.' He said, 'Yes, I agree for your sake.' He replied, 'It is not for myself that I request her.' He said, 'Then for whom?' He said, 'Julaybīb.' He replied, 'O Messenger of Allāh, allow me to consult with her mother.' He went to her and said, 'The Messenger of Allāh ﷺ seeks your daughter.' She replied, 'Yes, we will not object for the sake of Allāh's Messenger, marry her to the Messenger of Allāh ﷺ.' He said to her, 'He does not seek her for himself.' She asked, 'Then for whom?' He said, 'For Julaybīb.' She replied, 'What! For Julaybīb? Never, by Allāh, I will not marry her to Julaybīb.'

فَلَمَّا قَامَ أَبوهَا ليَأْتِي النَّبِي - صَلَّى اللَّهُ عَلَيْهِ وَسَلَّمَ - قَالَت الفتاة من خدرها لأبويها: من خطبني إِلَيْكُمَا؟ قَالَا: رَسُول اللَّهِ، قَالَت: أفتردون على رَسُول الله - صَلَّى اللَّهُ عَلَيْهِ وَسَلَّمَ - أمره! ادفعوني إِلَى رَسُول اللَّهِ؛ فَإِنَّهُ لن يضيعني، فَذهب أَبوهَا إِلَى النَّبِي - صَلَّى اللَّهُ عَلَيْهِ وَسَلَّمَ - فَقَالَ: شَأْنك بهَا فَزَوجهَا جليبيبا.

When the father stood up to go to the Prophet ﷺ, the daughter stated to her parents from her chamber, 'Whom asked you for my hand?' They replied that it was the Messenger of Allāh, and she said, 'You reject the order of the Messenger of Allāh ﷺ? Present me to the Messenger of Allāh, for indeed he will not cause me harm.' Thus, her father went to the Prophet ﷺ and said, 'The decision is yours,' and so he married her to Julaybīb."

قَالَ إِسْحَاق بن عبد اللَّهِ بن أبي طَلْحَة لِثَابِت: أَتَدْرِي مَا دَعَا لَهَا بِهِ النَّبِي؟ قَالَ:

((اللَّهُمَّ صب عَلَيْهَا الْخَيْر صبا صبا، وَلَا تجْعَل عيشها كدا)).

Isḥāq ibn ʿAbdullāh ibn Abī Ṭalḥah said to Thābit, "Do you know what the Prophet prayed for her? He replied, 'O Allāh, pour upon her goodness time after time, and do not make her life one of difficulty.'"

قَالَ ثَابت: فَزَوجهَا إِيَّاه فَبينا رَسُول اللَّهِ فِي مغزى لَهُ قَالَ: ((هَل تَفْقِدُونَ من أحد؟)) قَالُوا: نفقد فلَانا ونفقد فلَانا، ثمَّ قَالَ: ((هَل تَفْقِدُونَ من أحد؟)) قَالُوا: نفقد فلَانا ونفقد فلَانا، ثمَّ قَالَ: ((هَل تَفْقِدُونَ من أحد؟)) قَالُوا: لَا قَالَ: ((لكني أفقد جليبيبا، فاطلبوه فِي الْقَتْلَى)) فنظروا فوجدوه إِلَى جنب سَبْعَة قد قَتلهمْ ثمَّ قَتَلُوهُ، فَقَالَ رَسُول اللَّهِ - صَلَّى اللَّهُ عَلَيْهِ وَسَلَّمَ -: ((هَذَا مني وَأَنا مِنْهُ، قتل سَبْعَة ثمَّ قَتَلُوهُ، هَذَا مني وَأَنا مِنْهُ)).

Thābit said, "So he married her to him. Then during the midst of a war, the Messenger of Allāh ﷺ said, 'Have we lost anyone?' They said, 'We are missing so-and-so and so-and-so.' Then he asked again and they said, 'We are missing so-and-so and so-and-so.' He asked again and they said, 'No.' He said, 'However, I am missing Julaybīb. Look for him amongst the dead.' They searched for him and found seven bodies surrounding him, he had killed them before he was killed.' Then the Messenger of Allāh ﷺ said, 'He is from me and I am from him. He killed seven before he was killed. He is from me and I am from him.'

فَوَضعه رَسُول اللَّهِ - صَلَّى اللَّهُ عَلَيْهِ وَسَلَّمَ - على ساعديه، ثمَّ حفروا لَهُ، مَا لَهُ سَرِير إِلَّا ساعدي رَسُول اللَّهِ - صَلَّى اللَّهُ عَلَيْهِ وَسَلَّمَ - حَتَّى وَضعه فِي قَبره.

The Messenger of Allāh ﷺ placed him between his forearms, then they dug a grave for him. His body was leaning upon the forearms of the Messenger of Allāh until he was lowered into the grave."

قَالَ ثَابت: فَمَا فِي الْأَنْصَار أيم أنْفق مِنْهَا.

Thābit continued, "There was not from the Anṣār a previously married woman who was as sought for in marriage as her."

قَالَ ابْن سعد: وَسمعت من يذكر أَن جليبيبا كَانَ رجلا من بني ثَعْلَبَة حليفا فِي الْأَنْصَار، وَالْمَرْأَة الَّتِي زَوجهَا النَّبِي إِيَّاه من بني الْحَارِث بن الْخَزْرَج.

Ibn Sa'd said, "I have heard it said that Julaybīb was a man from Banī Tha'labah, an ally of Anṣār, and that the woman whom the Prophet married him to was from Banī al-Ḥārith ibn al-Khazraj."

صَحَابِيّ حبشِي
An Abyssinian Companion

[٦٥] أَنبأَنَا مُحَمَّد بن عبد الْملك قَالَ أَنبأَنَا الْجَوْهَرِي عَن الدَّارَقُطْنِيّ عَن أبي حَاتِم التنيسِي قَالَ أَنا الْحسن بن سُفْيَان قَالَ نَا مُحَمَّد ابْن عبد اللَّهِ بن عمار قَالَ نَا عفيف بن سَالم عَن أَيُّوب عَن عتبَة عَن عَطاء عَن ابْن عَبَّاس قَالَ: جَاءَ رجل من الْحَبَشَة إِلَى النَّبِي - صَلَّى اللَّهُ عَلَيْهِ وَسَلَّمَ - فَسَأَلَهُ، فَقَالَ لَهُ النَّبِي - صَلَّى اللَّهُ عَلَيْهِ وَسَلَّمَ -: ((سل واستفهم)). فَقَالَ: يَا رَسُول اللَّهِ، فضلْتُمْ علينا بالصورة والألوان والنبوة، أَفَرَأَيْت إِن آمنت بِمثل مَا آمَنت بِهِ وعملت بِمثل مَا عملت بِهِ أَنِّي كَائِن مَعَك فِي الْجنَّة؟ قَالَ: ((نعم)) ثمَّ قَالَ النَّبِي - صَلَّى اللَّهُ عَلَيْهِ وَسَلَّمَ -: ((وَالَّذِي نَفسِي بِيَدِهِ إِنَّه ليرى بَيَاض الْأسود فِي الْجنَّة مسيرَة ألف عَام)). ثمَّ قَالَ رَسُول اللَّهِ - صَلَّى اللَّهُ عَلَيْهِ وَسَلَّمَ -: ((وَمن قَالَ: لَا إِلَه إِلَّا اللَّهِ كَانَ لَهُ بهَا عِنْد اللَّهِ عز وَجل عهد، وَمن قَالَ: سُبْحَانَ اللَّهِ وَبِحَمْدِهِ كتب لَهُ مائَة ألف حَسَنَة وَأَرْبَعَة وَعِشْرُونَ ألف حَسَنَة)).

'Aṭā' reported upon the authority of Ibn 'Abbās, "A man from the Abyssinians came to the Prophet ﷺ to pose a question to him. The Prophet

ﷺ said to him, 'Ask and inquire.' He said, 'O Messenger of Allāh, you are better than us in appearance, in colour and due to prophethood. Is it the case that if I believe in the manner that you believe, and act in the manner that you act, that I will be alongside you in Jannah?' He replied, 'Yes.' And the Prophet ﷺ continued, 'By the One who holds my soul in His hand, the whiteness (i.e. purity of colour or saturation) of the black person will be seen in Jannah from the distance of one thousand years.' Then the Messenger of Allāh ﷺ said, 'The one who says *lā ilāha illallāh* has a covenant with Allāh ﷻ. The one who says *subḥānallāh wa biḥamdihi* has written for him one hundred and twenty-four thousand good deeds.'

فَقَالَ رجل: كَيفَ نهلك بعد هَذَا يَا رَسُول اللَّهِ؟ فَقَالَ النَّبِي - صَلَّى اللَّهُ عَلَيْهِ وَسَلَّمَ - ((إِن الرجل ليَأْتِي يَوْم الْقِيَامَة بِالْعَمَلِ لَو وضع على جبل لأثقله)) قَالَ: ((فتقوم النِّعْمَة من نعم اللَّهِ عز وَجل فيكاد يستفذه ذَلِك إِلَّا أَن ينْطق اللَّهِ برحمته)).

The man said, 'What if one dies after saying this O Messenger of Allāh?' The Prophet replied ﷺ, 'A man could come on the Day of Judgement with deeds which if placed upon a mountain would overburden it, however a single blessing of Allāh ﷻ would outweigh them except through His mercy.'

قَالَ: ثمَّ نزلت هَذِه السُّورَة ﴿هَل أَتَى على الْإِنْسَان حِين من الدَّهْر﴾ إِلَى قَوْله عز وَجل: ﴿وَإِذا رَأَيْت ثمَّ رَأَيْت نعيما وملكا كَبِيرا﴾ ، قَالَ الحبشي: وَإِن عَيْنِي لترَيان مَا ترى عَيْنَاك فِي الْجنَّة؟ فَقَالَ النَّبِي - صَلَّى اللَّهُ عَلَيْهِ وَسَلَّمَ -: ((نعم)). فاستبكى الحبشي حَتَّى فاضت نَفسه، قَالَ: فَلَقَد رَأَيْت رَسُول اللَّهِ - صَلَّى اللَّهُ عَلَيْهِ وَسَلَّمَ - يدليه فِي حفرته بِيَدِهِ.

He said, "Then the following *sūrah* was revealed: **{Has there [not] come upon man a period of time ...}**[60] until Allāh's statement: **{And when you look there [in Paradise], you will see pleasure and great dominion.}**[61] The Abysinnian said, 'You mean to say that my eyes will see what yours see

60 Al-Insān: 1

61 Al-Insān: 20

in Jannah?' The Prophet ﷺ said, 'Yes.' He wept until his soul left his body.'" He continued, "I witnessed the Messenger of Allāh lowering him into his grave with his hands."[62]

❖❖❖

صَحَابِيّ أسود
A Black Companion

روى أَبُو طَاهِرِ بن العلاف فِي كِتَابِه الْمُسَمَّى بِكِتَاب [زهر] الرياض أَنَّ حَبَشِيًّا أَتَى النَّبِيَّ - صَلَّى اللَّهُ عَلَيْهِ وَسَلَّمَ - فَقَالَ: يَا رَسُولَ اللَّهِ إِنْ كنت أعمل الْفَوَاحِشَ، فَهَل لِي مِن تَوْبَةٍ؟ قَالَ: ((نعم)). فولى ثُمَّ رَجَعَ فَقَالَ: يَا رَسُولَ الله، أَكَانَ اللَّهُ يراني وَأَنا أعملها؟ قَالَ: ((نعم، يَا حبشِي)). فصاح الحبشي صَيْحَة خرجت مِنْهَا نَفسه.

Abū Ṭāhir ibn al-ʿAllāf narrated in his book *Zahr al-Riyāḍ* that an Abyssinian came to the Prophet ﷺ and said, "O Messenger of Allāh I have performed abominable sins. Will there be forgiveness for me?" He replied affirmatively. He left and then returned, saying, "O Messenger of Allāh, does Allāh see me when I am performing these sins?" He replied, "Yes, O Abyssinian." The Abyssinian then cried until his soul left.

---

62 Reported by al-Suyūṭī in *Rafʿ Shàn al-Ḥubshān* (pp. 76-77). He said in *Azhār al-ʿŪrūsh* (pp. 7-8), "It was reported by al-Ṭabarānī in *al-Awsaṭ* and Ibn Ḥibbān in *al-Ḍuʿafā*; he said: "Ayyub (one of the narrators in the chain) makes plentiful mistakes. Al-Ṭabarānī said this narration was only reported from the way of ʿAfīf." Al-Haythamī mentioned it in *al-Majmaʿ al-Zawāʾid* (10/420) on the authority of Ibn ʿUmar and he said after it, "This was reported by al-Ṭabarānī and one of its narrators is Ayūb ibn ʿUtbah who is *ḍaʿīf*." *Azhār al-ʿŪrūsh* (p. 20), and he mentioned it with this *isnād* in *Rafʿ Shàn al-Ḥubshān* (p. 80).

الْبَاب الثَّامِن عشر
Chapter Eighteen

فِي ذكر أَشْرَاف السوداوات من الصحابيات
In mention of the noble black women from the female Companions

أم أيمن مولاة رَسُول اللَّهِ صَلَّى اللَّهُ عَلَيْهِ وَسَلَّمَ وحاضنته
Umm Ayman, the *mawlāh* of the Messenger of Allāh ﷺ and his nurse.

وَاسْمهَا بركَة ورثهَا من أَبِيه، وَكَانَت سَوْدَاء فَأعْتقهَا حِين تزوج خَدِيجَة، فتزَوجهَا عبد اللَّهِ بن زيد فَولدت لَهُ أيمن، وَتزَوَّجت بعده زيد بن حَارِثَة، فَولدت لَهُ أُسَامَة.

Her name was Barakah and he inherited her from his father. She was a black woman and he manumitted her when he married Khadījah. Then she wed ʿAbdullāh ibn Zayd and bore for him a child named Ayman. After him she wed Zayd ibn Ḥārithah and bore for him a child named Usāmah.

[٦٦] أنبأنَا مُحَمَّد بن أبي طَاهِر قَالَ أَنبأَنَا أَبُو مُحَمَّد الْجَوْهَرِي قَالَ أَنا ابْن حيوية قَالَ ثَنَا أَحْمد بن مَعْرُوف قَالَ أَنا الْحُسَيْن بن الْفَهم قَالَ ثَنَا مُحَمَّد بن سعد قَالَ أَنا ابْن أُسَامَة - يَعْنِي حَمَّاد بن أُسَامَة - عَن جرير بن حَازِم قَالَ: سَمِعت عُثْمَان بن الْقَاسِم يحدث قَالَ: لما هَاجَرت أم أَيمن أمست بالمنصرف دون الروحاء، فعطشت فدلي عَلَيْهَا من السَّمَاء دلو من مَاء برشاء أَبيض، فَأَخَذته فَشَربته حَتَّى رويت، وَكَانَت تَقول: مَا أصابني بعد ذَلِك عَطش، وَلَقَد تعرضت للعطش بِالصَّوْمِ فِي الهواجر فَمَا عطشت بعد تِلْكَ الشربة.

Jarīr ibn Ḥāzim reported that he heard 'Uthmān ibn al-Qāsim narrate, "When Umm Ayman emigrated, she arrived at the Munṣaraf (i.e. a place that is close to the area of Badr) near al-Rawḥā (i.e. both locations are on the pathway between Makkah and Madina). She was extremely thirsty and then a container of water with a white rope descended to her from the sky. She took it and drank from it until her thirst was quenched. She would say, "I have not suffered thirst after that incident. I used to feel thirst whilst fasting in the midday heat, however I did not feel thirst again after that drink.'"

قَالَ المُصَنّف: وَكَانَ النَّبِي - صَلَّى اللَّهُ عَلَيْهِ وَسَلَّمَ - يكرمها ويمازحها، قَالَت لَهُ يَوْمًا: احملني، قَالَ: ((أحملك على ولد النَّاقة)). قَالَت: لَا يطيقني. قَالَ: ((لَا أحملك إِلَّا على ولد النَّاقة)). وَكَانَت تدل على رَسُول اللَّهِ - صَلَّى اللَّهُ عَلَيْهِ وَسَلَّمَ - وتخاصمه فيحتملها.

The author said: The Prophet ﷺ would honour her and jest with her. She said to him on one occasion, "Find me a ride to carry me." He replied, "I will carry you upon a child of a camel." She replied, "It will not be able to bear [the weight of] me." He said [jokingly], "No, I will not carry you except upon a child of a camel."[63] She used to gesture to the Messenger of Allāh [playfully], and dispute with him but he would be patient with her.[64]

وَكَانَ أَبُو بكر وَعمر يزورانها بعد رَسُول اللَّهِ - صَلَّى اللَّهُ عَلَيْهِ وَسَلَّمَ -، وَكَانَت تبْكي وَتقول: إِنَّمَا أبْكِي لخَبر السَّمَاء كَيفَ انْقَطع عَنَّا.

Abū Bakr and 'Umar would visit her after the Messenger of Allāh had passed away. She would weep and say, "Verily, that which I weep regarding is how the revelation from the heavens has been cut off from us."

وَحَضَرت أحدا وَكَانَت تَسْقِي المَاء وتداوي الْجَرْحى، وَشهِدت حنينا، وَتوفيت فِي

---

63 [E] The joke was that she thought it is a little child while the Prophet intended to play with words because the child of a camel is actually a camel.

64 See *al-Ṭabaqāt al-Kubrā* of Ibn Sa'd (8/179).

خلَافَة عُثْمَان، وَقيل فِي خلَافَة أبي بكر [رَضِي اللَّهِ عَنْهَا].

She was present during the Battle of Uhud. She would provide water and treat the wounded. She also witnessed the Battle of Ḥunayn. She ﷺ passed away during the Caliphate of 'Uthmān, and it was also said that she passed during the caliphate of Abū Bakr.

❁❁❁

أم زفر
Umm Zufar

[٦٧] روى البُخَارِيّ وَمُسلم فِي الصَّحِيحَيْنِ من حَدِيث عَطاء بن أبي رَبَاح قَالَ: قَالَ لي ابْن عَبَّاس: أَلا أريك امْرَأَة من أهل الْجنَّة؟ قلت: بلَى، قَالَ: هَذِه الْمَرْأَة السَّوْدَاء أَتَت النَّبِي - صَلَّى اللَّهُ عَلَيْهِ وَسَلَّمَ - فَقَالَت: إِنِّي أصرع وَإِنِّي أتكشف فَادع اللَّهِ لي قَالَ: ((إِن شِئْت صبرت وَلَك الْجنَّة، وَإِن شِئْت دَعَوْت اللَّهِ أَن يعافيك)). قَالَت: أَصْبِر، وَقَالَت: فَإِنِّي أتكشف، فَادع الله أَن لَا أنكشف. فَدَعَا لَهَا.

Al-Bukhārī and Muslim reported in the *Ṣaḥīḥayn* the following ḥadīth upon the authority of 'Aṭā ibn Abī Rabāḥ, "Ibn 'Abbās stated to me, 'Would you like me to show you a woman from the Ahl al-Jannah (people of al-Jannah)?' I replied, 'Of course.' He said, 'This black lady came to the Prophet ﷺ and said, 'I suffer from epileptic fits wherein I uncover myself, so pray to Allāh for me.' He said, 'If you wish, bear it with patience and you will have Paradise. Or if you wish I can supplicate to Allāh that he cures you.' She replied, 'I will bear it with patience, however I uncover myself, so pray to Allāh that I cease doing so.' He subsequently supplicated for her.'"

❁❁❁

جارِيَة من الصحابيات

A female slave from among the Companions

[٦٨] أخبرنا عبد الأول قَالَ أنا ابْن المظفر الدَّاوديّ قَالَ ثَنَا ابْن أعين قَالَ نَا الْفربرِي قَالَ نَا البُخَارِيّ قَالَ نَا فَرْوَة بن أبي المغراء قَالَ ثنَا عَليّ بن مسْهر عَن هِشَام عَن أَبِيه عَن عَائِشَة [رَضِي اللَّهِ عَنْهَا] قَالَت: أسلمت امْرَأَة سَوْدَاء لبَعض الْعَرَب، وَكَانَ لَهَا حفش فِي الْمَسْجِد قَالَت: فَكَانَت تَأْتِينَا فتتحدث عندنَا، فَإِذا فرغت من حَدِيثهَا قَالَت:

Hishām reported from his father upon the authority of 'Ā'ishah ﵂, "A black woman who belonged to some Arabs embraced Islām. She had a small room in the *masjid*." She continued, "She used to come and have conversations with us. When she would finish talking, she would say,

وَيَوْم الوشاح من تعاجيب رَبنَا ۞ أَلا إِنَّه من بَلْدَة الْكفْر أنجاني

On the day of the scarf I saw some wonders from my Lord,
When He saved me from the disbelievers.

فَلَمَّا أكثرت قلت لَهَا: وَمَا يَوْم الوشاح؟ قَالَت: خرجت جوَيْرِية لبَعض أَهلِي وَعَلَيْهَا وشاح من أَدَم فَيسْقط مِنْهَا، فانحطت عَلَيْهِ الحدياء وَهِي تحسبه لَحْمًا فَأَخَذته فاتهموني بِهِ فعذبوني حَتَّى بلغ من أَمْرِي أَنهم طلبوه فِي قبلي، فَبَيْنَمَا هم حَولي وَأَنا فِي كربي إِذا أَقبلت الحديا حَتَّى وازت رؤوسنا ثمَّ أَلقته فَأَخَذُوهُ، فَقلت لَهُم: هَذَا الَّذِي اتهمتموني بِهِ وَأَنا مِنْهُ بريئة.

As she would say this frequently, I asked her, 'What is this day of the scarf that you refer to?' She replied, "One day a girl from the family whom I belonged to went out with a luxurious scarf made from leather and it fell from her. A glede (a type of bird) descended and took it, as it thought that it was meat. The family accused me [of stealing it] and they dealt with me harshly, to the extent that they searched my private parts. Then, whilst they surrounded me and I was agonised by my distress, the glede returned and flew over our heads. It dropped down the scarf and they took it. I said to them, 'This is what you accused me of whilst I was innocent of it.'"

❖❖❖

ذكر صحابية سَوْدَاء
In mention of a black female Companion

[٦٩] أَنْبَأَنَا ابْنُ نَاصِرٍ قَالَ: أَنَا جَعْفَرُ بْنُ مُحَمَّدٍ قَالَ: ثَنَا عبد الْعَزِيزِ بْنُ عَلِيِّ بْنِ حمدَان أَخْبَرَهُمْ إِجَازَةً قَالَ: أَنَا أَبُو جَعْفَرٍ مُحَمَّدُ بْنُ الْحَسَنِ بْنِ هَارُونَ بْنِ بدينا قَالَ: أَمْلَى علينا مُحَمَّدُ بْنُ عبد اللَّهِ ابْنِ عمار الْمَوْصِلِي قَالَ: ثَنَا الْمُعَافَى عَنْ عبد الحميد بْنِ بَهْرَام قَالَ: ثَنَا شَهْرٌ عَنْ عبد اللَّهِ بْنِ شَدَّادٍ أَنَّ النَّبِيَّ - صَلَّى اللَّهُ عَلَيْهِ وَسَلَّمَ - خرج إِلَى بطحاء من الْمَدِينَةِ فَإِذَا النَّاسُ ينطلقون إِلَى رجلٍ من كبراء الْمَدِينَةِ يعودونه من مرضٍ، فَانْطَلَقَ وَأَصْحَابُهُ حَتَّى مروا ببطحاء، فَإِذَا هم بزنجية قد علق ولدان الْمَدِينَةِ فِي رجلها حبلًا فهم يسحبونها فَقَالَ النَّبِيُّ - صَلَّى اللَّهُ عَلَيْهِ وَسَلَّمَ - لِأَصْحَابِهِ: ((أَتَرَوْنَ هَذِهِ الزنجية؟ وَالَّذِي نفس مُحَمَّدٍ بِيَدِهِ لهي خير من ملْءِ الْأَرْضِ مثل صَاحبكُم الَّذِي تساقون إِلَيْهِ)).

Shahr reported upon the authority of 'Abdullāh ibn Shaddād, "The Prophet ﷺ went to a basin-shaped flat land in al-Madīnah, and noticed that many people were heading to the house of one of the high-esteemed people of Madīnah, visiting him due to his illness. As he went with his Companions, they reached a flat land. There they saw a black woman, some youths of Madīnah tied a rope to her foot and were dragging her. [Upon seeing this,] the Prophet ﷺ said, 'Do you see this black woman? By the One in whose hand lays Muḥammad's soul, she is better than everything within the earth, similar to the one whom you are travelling to see.'"

الْبَاب التَّاسِع عشر
Chapter Nineteen

فِي ذكر المبرزين فِي الْعلم من السودَان
In mention of the illustrious scholars from amongst the black people

فَمن أهل مَكَّة:

From amongst the people of Makkah:

عَطاء بن أبي رَبَاح
'Aṭa' ibn Abī Rabāḥ[65]

وَاسم أبي رَبَاح أسلم، أَخذ الْعلم عَن ابْن عمر وَأبي سعيد وَأبي هُرَيْرَة وَابْن عَبَّاس وَغَيرهم، وفَاق فِي الْعلم والنسك.

The name of Abī Rabāḥ was Aslam. He took knowledge from Ibn 'Umar, Abī Sa'īd, Abī Hurayrah, Ibn 'Abbās and others. He excelled in terms of knowledge and asceticism.

[٧٠] أخبرنَا إِسْمَاعِيل بن أَحْمد السَّمرقَنْدِي قَالَ: أَنا مُحَمَّد بن عبد اللَّهِ الطَّبَرِيّ قَالَ: أَنا مُحَمَّد بن الْحُسَيْن بن الْفضل قَالَ: أَنا عبد اللَّهِ ابْن جَعْفَر قَالَ: أَنا يَعْقُوب بن سُفْيَان قَالَ: نَا الْفضل بن زِيَاد قَالَ: سَمِعت أَبَا عبد اللَّهِ - يَعْنِي أَحْمد بن حَنْبَل - يَقُول: الْعلم خَزَائِن يقسم اللَّهِ [تَعَالَى] لمن أحب، كَانَ عَطاء بن أبي رَبَاح حَبَشِيًّا.

65 See *Siyar A'lām al-Nubalā* (5/78).

Al-Faḍl ibn Ziyād reported that he heard Abā 'Abdallāh—i.e. Aḥmad ibn Ḥanbal—say, "Knowledge is a treasure which Allāh ﷻ gives shares of to those whom He loves. 'Aṭā' ibn Abī Rabāḥ was an Abyssinian."

[٧١] أخبرنا عبد الْحق بن عبد الْخَالِق قَالَ: أَنا مُحَمَّد بن مَرْزُوق قَالَ: أَنا أَحْمد بن عَليّ [ثَابت] الْخَطِيب قَالَ: أَنا أَحْمد بن أبي جَعْفَر الْقطيعِي قَالَ: ثَنَا مُحَمَّد بن الْعَبَّاس الخراز قَالَ: ثَنَا أَبُو أَيُّوب سُلَيْمَان ابْن إِسْحَاق الْجلاب قَالَ: قَالَ إِبْرَاهِيم الْحَرْبِيّ: كَانَ عَطاء بن أبي رَبَاح عبدا أسود لامرأة من أهل مَكَّة، وَكَانَ أَنفه كَأَنَّهُ باقلاة، وَجَاء سُلَيْمَان بن عبد الْملك إِلَى عَطاء هُوَ وابناه فجلسوا إِلَيْهِ وَهُوَ يُصَلِّي، فَلَمَّا صلى انْفَتَلَ إِلَيْهِم، فَمَا زَالُوا يسألونه عَن مَنَاسِك الْحَج، قد حول قَفاهُ إِلَيْهِم، ثمَّ قَالَ سُلَيْمَان لابنَيْهِ: قوما، فقاما، فَقَالَ: يَا بني لَا تنيا فِي طلب الْعلم، فَإِنِّي لَا أنسى ذلنا بَين يَدي هَذَا الْعَبْد الْأسود.

Abū Ayyūb Sulaymān ibn Isḥāq al-Jallāb reported upon the authority of Ibrāhīm al-Ḥarbī, "'Aṭā' ibn Abī Rabāḥ was a black slave who belonged to a woman from the people of Makkah. His nose was like a bean. Sulaymān ibn 'Abd al-Malik and his two sons went to 'Aṭa', and they sat facing towards him whilst he was praying. When he had finished his prayer he turned to them, and whilst they were asking him a question about the rites of Hajj he turned his back to them. Sulaymān then said to his sons, 'Stand up.' They did so and he said, 'O my sons, never spare an effort in the seeking of knowledge, for indeed I will never forget how we were humiliated at the hands of this black slave.'"

[٧٢] سَمِعت مُحَمَّد بن عبد الْبَاقِي يَقُول: سَمِعت حمد بن أَحْمد يَقُول: سَمِعت أَحْمد بن عبد اللَّهِ الْحَافِظ يَقُول: سَمِعت سُلَيْمَان بن أَحْمد يَقُول: سَمِعت أَحْمد بن مُحَمَّد الشَّافِعِي يَقُول: كَانَت الْحلقَة فِي الْفتيا بِمَكَّة فِي الْمَسْجِد الْحَرَام لِابْنِ عَبَّاس، وَبعد ابْن عَبَّاس لعطاء ابْن أبي رَبَاح.

Sulaymān ibn Aḥmad reported upon the authority of Aḥmad ibn Muḥammad al-Shāfi'ī, "The circle of *fatwā* in Makkah took place in Masjid al-Ḥarām and they were given by Ibn 'Abbās, and after Ibn 'Abbās they were given by 'Aṭā' ibn Abī Rabāḥ."

[٧٣] أخبرنَا مُحَمَّد بن أبي طَاهِر قَالَ: أَنا أَبُو مُحَمَّد الْجَوْهَرِي قَالَ: نَا أَبُو عمر بن حيوية قَالَ ثنَا أَحْمد بن مَعْرُوف قَالَ: أَنا الْحُسَيْن بن الْفَهم قَالَ: ثنَا مُحَمَّد بن سعد قَالَ: أَنا الْفضل بن دُكَيْن قَالَ: نَا سُفْيَان عَن سَلمَة بن كهيل قَالَ: مَا رَأَيْت أحدا يُرِيد بِهَذَا الْعلم وَجه اللَّهِ عز وَجل غير هَؤُلَاءِ الثَّلَاثَة: عَطاء وَطَاوُس، وَمُجاهد.

Sufyān reported upon the authority of Salamah ibn Kuhayl, "I did not see anyone who sought this knowledge for the Face of Allāh ﷻ besides these three: 'Aṭā', Ṭāwūs and Mujāhid."

[٧٤] أخبرنَا إِسْمَاعِيل بن أَحْمد قَالَ: أَنا عمر بن عبيد اللَّهِ الْبَقَّال قَالَ: أَنا أَبُو الْحُسَيْن بن بَشرَان قَالَ: ثنَا عُثْمَان بن أَحْمد الدقاق قَالَ: نَا حَنْبَل قَالَ: حَدثنِي أَبُو عبد اللَّهِ قَالَ: ثنَا سُفْيَان قَالَ: قَالَ إِسْمَاعِيل بن أُميَّة: كَانَ عَطاء طَوِيل الصمت، فَإِذا تكلم يخيل إِلَيْنَا أَنه يُؤَيّد.

Sufyān reported upon the authority of Ismā'īl ibn Umayyah, "'Aṭa' was known for lengthy silences. And when he spoke it would appear to us as if he was being inspired."

[٧٥] أخبرنَا عَليّ بن مُحَمَّد بن حسنون قَالَ: أَنا أَبُو مُحَمَّد بن أبي عُثْمَان قَالَ: أَنا القَاضِي أَبُو الْقَاسِم بن الْمُنْذر قَالَ: أَنا الْحُسَيْن بن صَفْوَان قَالَ: ثنَا أَبُو بكر بن عبيد قَالَ: ثنَا إِسْحَاق بن إِبْرَاهِيم قَالَ: أَنا يعلى بن عبيد قَالَ: دَخَلنَا على مُحَمَّد بن سوقة فَقَالَ: أحدثكُم بِحَدِيث لَعَلَّ اللَّهِ [تَعَالَى] ينفعكم بِهِ؛ فَإِنَّهُ قد نَفَعَنِي ثمَّ قَالَ: قَالَ لنا عَطاء ابْن أبي رَبَاح: يَا بني أخي، إِن من كَانَ قبلكُمْ كَانُوا

يكْرهُونَ فضول الْكَلَام، وَكَانُوا يعدون فضوله مَا عدا كتاب اللَّهِ عز وَجل أَن يقرأه وَيأْمُر بِمَعْرُوف أَو يُنْهِي عَن مُنكر أَو تنطق بحاجتك فِي معيشتك الَّتِي لَا بُد لَك مِنْهَا، أتنكرون أَن عَلَيْكُم حافظين، كراما كاتبين عَن الْيَمين وَعَن الشمَال قعيد، مَا يلفظ من قَول إِلَّا لَدَيْهِ رَقِيب عتيد، أما يستحي أحدكُم أَن لَو نشرت صَحِيفَته الَّتِي أمل صدر نَهَاره، كَانَ أَكثر مَا فِيهَا لَيْسَ من أَمر دينه وَلَا دُنْيَاهُ؟!

Isḥāq ibn Ibrāhīm reported upon the authority of Ya'lā ibn 'Ubayd, "We entered into the presence of Muḥammad ibn Sawqah and he said, 'I will tell you a narration so that Allāh ﷻ might allow you to take benefit from it, as indeed I benefited from it [before you.]' He said, "Aṭa' ibn Abī Rabāḥ said to us, 'O nephews, indeed those before you used to detest needless speech. And they used to consider needless speech to be anything besides the recitation of the Book of Allāh ﷻ, enjoining the good and forbidding the evil, and speaking about matters which are necessary for one's life. Do you deny that you are with two noble preservers, the scribes sitting upon one's right and left, and that everything one says is recorded by a prepared observer? Would one not feel ashamed if his book of deeds was opened—it being an account of one's days—to find that it is replete with content not relevant to his religion or life?'"

❁❁❁

موعظة عَطاء بن أبي رَبَاح هِشَام بن عبد الْمطلب

The exhortation of 'Aṭa' ibn Abī Rabāḥ to Ḥisham ibn 'Abd al-Muṭṭalib

[٧٦] أَنبأَنَا أَبُو مَنْصُور مُحَمَّد بن عبد الْملك قَالَ أَنبأَنَا أَحْمد بن عَليّ بن ثَابت قَالَ أَخْبرنِي أَبُو الْحسن عَليّ بن أَيُّوب القمي قَالَ أَنا أَبُو عبيد مُحَمَّد بن عمر المرزباني قَالَ ثَنَا مُحَمَّد بن أَحْمد الْكَاتِب قَالَ: ثَنَا عبد الله بن أبي سعيد الْوراق قَالَ نَا عمر بن شبة قَالَ: حَدثنِي سعيد بن مَنْصُور الرقي قَالَ: حَدثنِي عُثْمَان بن

عَطاء الْخُرَاسَانِي قَالَ: انْطَلَقت مَعَ أبي وَهُوَ يُرِيد هشاما، فَلَمَّا قربنا مِنْهُ إِذا بشيخ أسود على حمَار عَلَيْهِ قَمِيص دنس، وجبة دنسة، وقلنسوة لاطية دنسة، وركاباه من خشب، فَضَحكت وَقلت لأبي: من هَذَا الْأَعرَابِي؟ قَالَ: اسْكُتْ، هَذَا سيد فُقَهَاء أهل الْحجاز، هَذَا عَطاء بن أبي رَبَاح، فَلَمَّا قرب نزل أبي عَن بغلته، وَنزل هُوَ عَن حِمَاره، فاعتنقا وتساءلا، ثمَّ عادا فركبا، وانطلقا حَتَّى وَقفا بِبَاب هِشَام.

Saʿīd ibn Manṣūr al-Raqqī reported upon the authority of ʿUthmān ibn ʿAṭāʾ al-Khurāsānī, "I set off alongside my father who wanted to visit Hishām. When we came close, an elderly black approached us whilst riding a camel. He was wearing a dirty shirt, a dirty *jubbah*, a dirty cap affixed to his head, and the stirrup of his saddle was made from wood. I began to laugh and said to my father, 'Who is this Bedouin?' He replied, 'Silence. This is the master of the jurists amongst the people of al-Ḥijāz. This is 'Atāʾ ibn Abī Rabāḥ.' When he drew close, my father descended from his mule, and he descended from his donkey. They both embraced and engaged in discussion, then they both returned and mounted their rides, riding until they reached the door of Hishām.

فَلَمَّا رَجَعَ أبي سَأَلته فَقلت: حَدثنِي مَا كَانَ مِنْكُمَا قَالَ: لما قيل لهشام: عَطاء بن أبي رَبَاح، أذن لَهُ، فوَاللَّه مَا دخلت إِلَّا لسببه، فَلَمَّا رَآهُ هِشَام قَالَ: مرْحَبًا مرْحَبًا، هَا هُنَا، فرفعه حَتَّى مست ركبته ركبته وَعِنْده أَشْرَاف النَّاس يتحدثون، فَسَكَتُوا، فَقَالَ هِشَام: مَا حَاجَتك يَا أَبَا مُحَمَّد؟

When my father returned, I asked him, 'Inform me of what took place between you.' He replied, 'When it was said to Hishām that 'Aṭāʾ ibn Abū Rabāḥ [had come to see him,] he gave him permission to enter. By Allāh, I would not have been able to enter except through [being with] him. When Hishām saw him, he said, 'Welcome, welcome, come here. He then embraced him until their knees touched. Some notable people were present with Hishām and they were speaking, then they fell silent. Hishām said, 'What do you need O Abā Muḥammad?'

قَالَ: يَا أَمِير الْمُؤمنِينَ، أهل الْحَرَمَيْنِ أهل الْحَرَمَيْنِ، أهل اللَّهِ وجيران رَسُول اللَّهِ - صَلَّى اللَّهُ عَلَيْهِ وَسَلَّمَ - يقسم فيهم أعطياتهم وأرزاقهم، قَالَ: نعم، يَا غُلَام، اكْتُبْ لأهل الْمَدِينَة وَأهل مَكَّة بعطاء أرزاقهم لسنة، ثمَّ قَالَ: هَل من حَاجَة غَيرهَا يَا أَبَا مُحَمَّد؟

He replied, 'O Commander of the Faithful, the people of the Ḥaramayn, the people of the Ḥaramayn, [they are the] people of Allāh and the neighbours of the Messenger of Allāh ﷺ. [I am asking for you to provide them with] financial aid and their provisions.' He said, 'Yes. O *ghulām* (boy), write for the people of Madīnah and the people of Makkah a financial allotment and provisions for a year.' Then he said, 'Do you have any other need, O Abā Muḥammad?'

قَالَ: نعم: يَا أَمِير الْمُؤمنِينَ، أهل الْحجاز وَأهل نجد أصل الْعَرَب، وقادة الْعَرَب ترد فيهم فضول صَدَقَاتهمْ، قَالَ: نعم، يَا غُلَام، اكْتُبْ بِأَن ترد فيهم صَدَقَاتهمْ. ثمَّ قَالَ: هَل من حَاجَة غَيرهَا يَا أَبَا مُحَمَّد؟

He said, 'Yes. O Commander of the Faithful, the people of al-Ḥijāz and the people of Najd. They are the origin of the Arabs and their leaders, let the surplus of their charity be spent on them.' Then he said, 'O *ghulām*, write for them that their benefits be given to them.' Then he said, 'Do you have any other need, O Abā Muḥammad?'

قَالَ: نعم، يَا أَمِير الْمُؤمنِينَ، أهل الثغور يرْمونَ من وَرَاء بيضتكم ويقاتلون عَدوكُم، وَقد أجريتم لَهُم أرزاقا تدرها عَلَيْهِم؛ فَإِنَّهُم إِن هَلَكُوا غزيتم، قَالَ: نعم، اكْتُبْ بِحمْل أَرْزَاقهم إِلَيْهِم يَا غُلَام، هَل من حَاجَة غَيرهَا يَا أَبَا مُحَمَّد؟

He replied, 'Yes, O Commander of the Faithful. The people of the frontier towns, they stand as a shield between the Muslims and their enemies, repelling their advances. You used to give them a stipend for their livelihood, without which they would be ruined and as a result your enemies will attack the Muslims. Indeed, if they were to be destroyed your lands would be invaded.' He said, 'Yes, write for their stipend to be given to them O *ghulām*. Do you have any other need besides this, O Abā Muḥammad?'

قَالَ: نعم، يَا أَمِيرَ الْمُؤْمِنِينَ، أَهل ذمتكم لَا تجبى صغارهم، وَلَا تتعتع كبارهم، وَلَا يكلفون مَا لَا يُطِيقُونَ فَإِن مَا تجبونه مَعُونَة لكم على عَدوكُمْ، قَالَ: نعم، اكْتُبْ يَا غُلَام، لَا يحملون مَالَا يُطِيقُونَ، هَل من حَاجَة غَيرهَا؟

He replied, 'Yes O Commander of the Faithful. In regards to the Ahl al-Dhimmah under you, do not levy the toll upon their young and do not disturb their old. Do not burden them beyond their means, for what you take from them is just used to aid you against your enemies. He replied, 'Yes, write O *ghulām*, do not burden them beyond their means. Do you have any needs besides this?'

قَالَ: نعم أَمِيرَ الْمُؤْمِنِينَ، اتَّقِ اللَّهِ [عز وَجل] فِي نَفسك فَإِنَّك خلقت وَحدك، وَتَمُوت وَحدك، وتحشر وَحدك، وتحاسب وَحدك، وَلَا وَالله مَا مَعَك مِمَّن ترى أحدا، قَالَ: فأكب هِشَام، وَقَامَ عَطَاء، فَلَمَّا كَانَ عِنْد الْبَاب إِذا رجل قد تبعه بكيس مَا أَدْرِي مَا فِيهِ أدراهم أم دَنَانِير، وَقَالَ: إِن أَمِيرَ الْمُؤْمِنِينَ أَمر لَك بِهَذَا، قَالَ: لَا أَسأَلكُم عَلَيْهِ أجرا إِن أجري إِلَّا على رب الْعَالمين، قَالَ: ثمَّ خرج عَطَاء، وَلَا وَالله مَا شرب عِنْده حسوة من مَاء فَمَا فَوْقه.

He replied, 'Yes O Commander of the Faithful. Fear Allāh ﷻ in yourself, for verily you were created alone, you will die alone, you will be resurrected alone and you will face your accounting alone. There will not—by Allāh— be any of those present with you...' Upon this Hishām looked down to the earth and so 'Atā' stood up. When we reached the door, a man followed 'Atā' [and presented him with] a pouch—within which I am not sure what was placed, dirhams or dinars. The man said, 'The Commander of the Faithful ordered these to be given to you.' He said, 'I did not ask you for any reward, as my reward is from the Lord of the worlds.' Then 'Atā' left, and by Allāh, he did not so much as drink a sip of water—let alone take for himself anything more than that.

[٧٧] أخبرنَا إِسْمَاعِيل بن أَحْمد قَالَ: أَنا عمر بن عبيد اللَّهِ الْبَقَّال قَالَ: أَنا أَبُو الْحُسَيْن بن بَشرَان قَالَ: ثَنَا عُثْمَان بن أَحْمد الدقاق قَالَ: نَا حَنْبَل بن إِسْحَاق قَالَ نَا يحيى بن معِين قَالَ: قَالَ ابْن أبي ليلى: حَنْبَل بن إِسْحَاق قَالَ نَا يحيى بن معِين قَالَ: قَالَ ابْن أبي ليلى: حج عَطاء سبعين حجَّة وعاش مائَة سنة.

Yaḥyā ibn Maʿīn reported upon the authority of Ibn Abī Laylā, "ʿAṭāʾ performed the Ḥajj seventy times, and he lived for a hundred years."

حبيب بن أبي ثَابت
Ḥabib ibn Abī Thābit[66]

وَاسم أبي ثَابت: قيس بن دِينَار، أَبُو يحيى، مولى لبني أَسد كُوفِي كَانَ عَالما كَبِيرا، سمع ابْن عَبَّاس وَابْن عمر وَسمع مِنْهُ الْأَعْمَش وَالثَّوْري، وَكَانَ كثير التَّعَبُّد كَرِيمًا، أنْفق على الْفُقَرَاء مائَة ألف، وَكَانَ أسود اللَّوْن.

His name: Qays ibn Dīnār, Abū Yaḥyā, the *mawlā* of Banī Asad Kūfī. He was a major scholar. He heard (i.e. oral transmission) from Ibn ʿAbbās and Ibn ʿUmar. Those who heard from him included al-Aʿmash and al-Thawrī. He was exceptional in his piety and generosity, and he spent one hundred thousand [dirhams] upon the poor. His skin colour was black.

يزيد بن أبي حبيب
Yazīd ibn Abī Ḥabīb[67]

66 See *Siyar al-Aʿlām al-Nubalā* (5/288), he was considered to be *thiqah* (a reliable narrator).
67 See *Siyar al-Aʿlām al-Nubalā* (6/31). He was a major *imām* and a *ḥujjah* (an au-

كَانَ عَالما كَبِيرا.

He was a major scholar.

[٧٨] أخبرنَا إِسْمَاعِيل بن أَحْمد قَالَ: أَنا مُحَمَّد بن هبة اللَّهِ الطَّبَرِيّ قَالَ: أَنا مُحَمَّد بن الْحُسَيْن بن الْفضل قَالَ: أَنا عبد اللَّهِ بن جَعْفَر قَالَ أَنا يَعْقُوب بن سُفْيَان قَالَ ثَنَا الْفضل بن زِيَاد قَالَ: سَمِعت أَحْمد بن حَنْبَل يَقُول: الْعلم خَزَائِن يقسم اللَّهِ [عز وَجل] لمن أحب، كَانَ يزِيد بن أبي حبيب نوبيا أسود.

Al-Faḍl ibn Ziyād reported upon the authority of Aḥmad ibn Ḥanbal, "Knowledge is a treasure which Allāh ﷻ gives shares of to those whom He loves. Yazīd ibn Abī Ḥabīb was a black Nubian."

مَكْحُول الشَّامي

Makḥūl al-Shāmī[68]

أَبُو عبد اللَّهِ، كَانَ عَالما فَقِيها، وَكَانَ مَمْلُوكا لعَمْرو بن سعيد بن العَاصِي، فوهبه لرجل من هُذَيْل بِمصْر، وأنعم عَلَيْهِ بهَا، قَالَ: فَمَا خرجت من مصر حَتَّى ظَنَنْت أنه لَيْسَ بهَا علم إِلَّا وَقد سمعته، ثمَّ قدمت الْمَدِينَة، فَمَا خرجت مِنْهَا حَتَّى ظَنَنْت أنه لَيْسَ بهَا علم إِلَّا وَقد سمعته.

[His *kunya* (nickname)] was Abu ʿAbdullāh. He possessed vast knowledge and was a jurist. He was in servitude to ʿAmr ibn Saʿīd ibn al-ʿĀṣ, who gifted him to a man from the tribe of Hudhayl in Egypt, which was a favour that he appreciated. Makḥūl said, "I did not leave Egypt until I was certain that there was no knowledge present therein except that I had heard it. Then I went to Madīnah, and I did not leave there until I was certain that there was no knowledge present therein except that I had heard it."

thority). He was the *mufti* of Egypt. He was *thiqah* and had many ḥadīths.
68 See *Siyar al-Aʿlām al-Nubalā* (5/155). He was a scholar of Ahl al-Shām.

وَرأى أنس بن مَالك وواثلة بن الْأَسْقَع وَأَبا أُمَامَة وَغَيرهم. وَتُوفِّي سنة سِتّ عشرَة وَمِائَة.

He saw Anas ibn Mālik, Wāthilah ibn al-Asqā', Abā 'Umāmah and others. He passed away during the year 116.

إبْرَاهِيم بن الْمهْدي بن الْمَنْصُور

Ibrāhim ibn al-Mahdī ibn al-Manṣūr[69]

يكنى أَبَا إِسْحَاق، كَانَ شَدِيد سَواد اللَّوْن، وَكَانَ فَاضلا فصيحا، مليح الشّعْر، بُويِعَ لَهُ بالخلافة؛ وَكَانَ السَّبَب أَن الْمَأْمُون بَايع لعَلي بن مُوسَى الرِّضَا بِولَايَة الْعَهْد، فَغَضب بَنو الْعَبَّاس، وَقَالُوا: لَا يخرج الْأَمر من بَين أَيْدِينَا، فَبَايعُوا إِبْرَاهِيم، فَخَطب لَهُ على المنابر، وَغلب على الْكُوفَة والسواد فتوفي عَليّ بن مُوسَى الرِّضَا، وَقدم الْمَأْمُون فضعف أَمر إِبْرَاهِيم، وتفرق النَّاس عَنهُ، فاستتر فَأَقَامَ كَذَلِك سِتّ سِنِين وَأَرْبَعَة أشهر وَعشرَة أَيَّام، فَلَمَّا ضجر من الاستتار كتب إِلَى الْمَأْمُون:

His *kunyā* was Abā Isḥāq and he was very dark in his complexion. He was virtuous and eloquent, creating beautiful poetry. He was given the *bayáa* (pledge of allegiance) of the Caliphate. The reason for this was that al-Ma'mūn appointed 'Alī ibn Mūsā al-Riḍā as the crown prince (i.e. the successor to the throne). Banū al-'Abbās were incensed by this decision, and they said, "This affair will not be taken from our hands." Thus, they gave the pledge of allegiance to Ibrāhīm, and sermons were given on his behalf from the *manābir* (pl. of *mimbar*, i.e. pulpit). He gained ascendancy over Kūfah and al-Sawād. However, when 'Alī ibn Mūsā al-Riḍā passed away, al-Ma'mūn reasserted himself and Ibrāhīm's power waned, and the people who supported him deserted him. Thus, he went into hiding for the duration of six years, four months and ten days. When he grew weary of hiding, he wrote a letter to al-Ma'mūn, saying:

69 *Siyar al-A'lām al-Nubalā* (10/557).

ولي الثأر مُحكم فِي الْقصاص، وَالْعَفو أقرب للتقوى، وَمن تنَاوله الاغترار بِمَا مد لَهُ من أَسبَاب الرَّجَاء أَمن عَادِيَة الدَّهْر، وَقد جعل اللَّهِ أَمِير الْمُؤمنِينَ فَوق كل ذِي عَفْو، كَمَا جعل كل ذِي ذَنْب دونه، فَإِن عَفا فبفضله، وَإِن عاقب فبحقه.

"There is a valid reason for punishment to be dealt to me, however to pardon is closer to *taqwā* (God-consciousness). One who allows himself to become deluded with what has been given to him which would make him wishful will not be safe from the pitfalls of time. Allāh has placed the Commander of the Faithful over those deserving of pardon, just as He has placed him over the sinful. So, if he chooses to pardon, it is from his grace and if he chooses to punish then it is within his right."

فَوَقع الْمَأْمُون على قصَّته أَمَانه، وَقَالَ فِيهَا: الْقُدْرَة تذْهب الحفيظة، وَكفى بالندم إنابة. فَدخل عَلَيْهِ إِبْرَاهِيم فَقَالَ:

Al-Ma'mūn wrote on the same letter, "Power diffuses wrath, and remorse is an adequate repentance." Then Ibrāḥīm entered his presence and said:

إِن أكن مذنبا فحظي أَخْطَأت فدع عَنْك كَثْرَة التأنيب
قل كَمَا قَالَ يُوسُف لبني يَعْقُوب لما أَتَوْهُ لَا تَثْرِيب

If I am sinful then I have procured my mistakes, so, leave off excess castigation.
State, as was stated by Yūsuf to the sons of Ya'qūb, when they came to him: there will be no castigation.

[٧٩] أخبرنَا عبد الرَّحْمَن بن مُحَمَّد قَالَ: أنا أَحْمد بن عَليّ بن ثَابت قَالَ: أنا الْجَوْهَرِي قَالَ: أنبأ مُحَمَّد بن الْعَبَّاس قَالَ: أَنْشدني عبيد اللَّهِ بن أَحْمد المروزي قَالَ: أَنْشد لإِبْرَاهِيم بن الْمهْدي:

'Ubaydallāh ibn Aḥmad al-Marūradhī reported from Ibrāhīm ibn al-Mahdī the following lines of poetry:

قد شَاب رَأْسِي وَرَأس الْحِرْص لم يشب   إِن الْحَرِيص على الدُّنْيَا لفي تَعب

قد يَنْبَغِي لي مَعَ مَا حزت من أدب   أَن لَا أخوض فِي أَمر ينقص بِي

لَو كَانَ يصدقني ذهني بفكرته   مَا اشْتَدَّ غمي على الدُّنْيَا وَلَا نصبي

أسعى فأجهد فِيمَا لست أدْركهُ   وَالْمَوْت يقْدَح فِي زندي وَفِي عصبي

بِاللَّه كم بَيت مَرَرْت بِهِ   قد كَانَ يعمر باللذات والطرب

طارت عِقَاب المنايا فِي جوانبه   فَصَارَ من بعْدهَا للويل والحزب

فامسك عنانك لَا تجمع بِهِ طلع   فَلَا وعيشك مَا الأرزاق بِالطَّلَبِ

مَعَ أنني وَاجِد فِي النَّاس وَاحِدَة   الرزق والنوك مقرونان فِي سَبَب

وخصلة لَيْسَ فِيهَا من يُنَازعنِي   الرزق أروغ شَيْء عَن ذَوي الْأَدَب

يَا ثقب الْفَهم كم أَبْصرت ذَا حمق   الرزق أعزى بِهِ من لَازم الجرب

My head has become grey but the head of greed has not, indeed, whoever is greedy for worldly things is in a perpetual toil.
It is incumbent by what I have took from knowledge, that I not take up that which degrades me.
If my mind's thoughts were truthful to me, I would have not been bothered or troubled over worldly matters.
I strive and exert for that beyond my reach, while death pierces my vigour and nerves.
By Allāh, how many are the houses which you have passed by, wherein which was pleasure and glee.
The eagle of death flew over them, thus, there became therein woe and affliction.
So, grasp hold of your reigns and do not go after it (the *dunyā*), by your life, sustenance is not attained [simply] through [man's] seeking it.
Furthermore, I note the presence within people of one trait, wealth and foolishness are connected through a rope.
And there is one trait that no one can dispute with me, wealth is far from those who possess manners.

O sharp minded, how many times have you seen the fool, wealth is stuck to him like scabies.

توفّي إِبْرَاهِيم بن الْمهْدي فِي سنة أَربع وَعشْرين وَمِائَتَيْنِ، وَصلى عَلَيْهِ المعتصم.

Ibrāhīm ibn Mahdī passed away during the year 224, and al-Muʿtaṣim led his funeral prayer.

❁❁❁

عبد اللّهِ بن حَازِم السّلمِيّ

ʿAbdullāh ibn Ḥāzim al-Sulamī

كَانَ أَمِيرا كَبِيرا على خُرَاسَان، وَجَرت لَهُ حروب كَثِيرَة، وَكَانَ ذَا علم.

He was a major *amīr* of Khurāsān, and many wars took place during his rule. He possessed knowledge.

الْبَاب الْعشْرُونَ

Chapter Twenty

فِي ذكر شعرائهم وَمن تمثل مِنْهُم بِشعر

In mention of their poets and those amongst them who recited some poetry to express a meaning

من كبار شعرائهم: عنترة بن شَدَّاد. كَانَت أمه زنجية، أسود، وَله الْأَشْعَار الفائقة من مستحسنها قَوْله فِي قصيدته الْمَشْهُورَة:

From their major poets: ʿAntarah ibn Shaddād. His mother was a Zanjī and he was black. He crafted many outstanding poems, from the most notable of them being his statement in his famous *qaṣīdah*:

هَل غادر الشُّعَرَاء من متردم   أم هَل عرفت الدَّار بعد توهم

The poets have not left any hole in a garment for me to patch,
Have you come to know the house [of your love] after doubting her?

ويروى: من مترنم، قَالَ الْأَصْمَعِي: يُقَال: ردم ثَوْبك، أَي رقعه، يَقُول: هَل ترك الشُّعَرَاء شَيْئا يرقع أَي هَل تركُوا لقَائِل شَيْئا.

It has also been narrated with the wording "*mutarannim*" (tunes) [instead of *mutaraddim*.] Al-Asmaʿī said that *radama* (the third person singular verbal root of *mutaraddim*) *thawbaka* (your garment) means it was patched. So, the meaning is: Have the poets left me anything to patch i.e. they have made poetry about everything, leaving me with no new topic to make poetry about.

[Further examples of his poetry are:]

يَا دَار عبلة بالجوى تكلمي ... وَعمي صباحا دَار عبلة واسلمي
حييت من طلل تقادم عَهده ... أقوى وأقفر بعد أم الْهَيْثَم
هلا سَأَلت الْخَيل يَا ابْنة مَالك ... إِن كنت جاهلة بِمَا لم تعلمي
يُخْبِرك من شهد الوقيعة أنني ... أغشى الوغى وأعف عِنْد الْمغنم

O House of ʿAblah at al-Jawā, tell about your dwellers, good morning O House of ʿAblah, and be safe from all harm.
Greeting is meant for you in particular from all other ruins, the house has become deserted after Umm al-Haytham left it.
Ask the horsemen about me in battles O daughter of Mālik, if you were ignorant of how I am therein.
Those who have witnessed the battles would inform that I, envelop the battlefield and do not take war booty.

وَمن شعرائهم: سحيم عبد بني الحسحاس

From among their poets: Suḥaym, a slave of Banī al-Ḥasḥās.

اشْتَرَاهُ عبد اللَّهِ بن عَامر وأهداه إِلَى عُثْمَان بن عَفَّان [رَضِي اللَّهِ عَنهُ] فَرده عَلَيْهِ، وَقَالَ: لَا حَاجَة لي فِيهِ، وَله أشعار كَثِيرَة وأخبار.

ʿAbdullāh ibn ʿĀmir purchased Suḥaym and gifted him to ʿUthmān ibn ʿAffān ﷺ, who subsequently returned him and said, "I have no need for him." He had many poems and stories.

[٨٠] أنبأنَا ابْن نَاصِر قَالَ: أنبأ أَبُو الْحُسَيْن بن عبد الْجَبَّار قَالَ: أنبأ الْجَوْهَرِي قَالَ أنبأ ابْن حيوية قَالَ نَا مُحَمَّد بن خلف قَالَ: قَالَ ابْن الْأَعرَابِي: كَانَ سحيم حَبَشِيًّا، وَقد أدْرك الْجَاهِلِيَّة.

Muḥammad ibn Khalaf reported upon the authority of Ibn al-Aʿrābī, "Sūḥaym was an Abyssinian and he was alive during the time of Jāhiliyah."

[٨١] أنبأنَا مُحَمَّد بن أبي طَاهِر الْبَزَّاز قَالَ: أنبأنَا أَبُو مُحَمَّد الْحسن بن عَليّ الْجَوْهَرِي قَالَ أنبا أَبُو عمر مُحَمَّد بن الْعَبَّاس بن مُحَمَّد قَالَ أنا أَبُو عبد اللَّهِ أَحْمد بن مُحَمَّد بن إِسْحَاق الْمَكِّيّ قَالَ: ثنَا الزبير بن بكار قَالَ: حَدثنِي عبد الْملك بن عبد الْعَزِيز عَن خَالِد بن يُوسُف بن الْمَاجشون قَالَ: اشْترى عبد اللَّهِ بن أبي عبد اللَّهِ سحيما عبد بني الحسحاس وَكتب إِلَى عُثْمَان بن عَفَّان: إِنِّي ابتعت لَك غُلَاما حَبَشِيًّا شَاعِرًا، فَكتب إِلَيْهِ عُثْمَان: لَا حَاجَة لي بِهِ فاردده، فَإِنَّمَا قصارى هَذَا العَبْد الشَّاعِر إِن شبع أَن يتشبب بنسائهم، وَإِن جَاع أَن يهجوهم، فَرده عبد اللَّهِ فَاشْتَرَاهُ رجل من بني الحسحاس من بني أَسد بن خُزَيْمَة، وَكَانَ حَبَشِيًّا مغلظا، أعجمي اللِّسَان، ينشد الشّعْر.

'Abdul Mālik ibn 'Abd al-'Azīz reported upon the authority of Khālid Yūsuf ibn al-Mājishūn, "'Abdullāh ibn 'Abdullāh purchased Suḥaym, the slave of Banī al-Ḥasḥās. Then he wrote to 'Uthmān ibn 'Affān stating, 'I have purchased for you an Abyssinian slave who is a poet.' 'Uthmān wrote back to him stating, 'I have no need for him. Take him back, for all this slave poet would do is: If he is full he will extol your women and if he is hungry he will lampoon them.' Thus, 'Abdullāh returned him and a man from Banī Asad ibn Khuzaymah purchased him from Banī al-Hasḥās. He was a robust Abyssinian; his mother tongue was not Arabic and he used to recite poetry."

قَالَ الزبير: وَحَدثنِي عمر بن أبي بكر عَن أبي صَالح الفقعسي قَالَ: كَانَ سحيم عبد بني الحسحاس، وَكَانَ حَبَشِيًّا شَاعِرًا.

Al-Zubayr said: 'Umar ibn Abū Bakr reported to me on the authority of Abī Sāliḥ al-Faq'asī, "Suḥaym was a slave of Banī al-Ḥasḥās. He was an Abyssinian poet."

قَالَ الزبير: وَحَدثنِي موهوب بن رشيد الْكلابِي عَن أبي صَالح الفقعسي قَالَ: كَانَ عبد بني الحسحاس حَبَشِيًّا شَاعِرًا وَكَانَ يهوى ابْنة مَوْلَاهُ عميرَة بنت أبي معبد

ويكنى عَن حبها إِلَى أَن خرج مَوْلَاهُ أَبُو معبد سفرا وَخرج بِهِ مَعَه، وَكَانَ أَبُو معبد يتشوق إِلَى ابْنَته يَقُول:

Al-Zubayr said: Mawhūb ibn Rashīd al-Kulābī reported to me upon the authority of Abū Ṣāliḥ al-Faqʿasī, "He was a slave of Banī al-Ḥasḥās, and he was an Abyssinian poet. He was besotted with the daughter of his master, 'Umayrah bint Abī Maʿbad, and would implicitly express his love. Then an occasion came when his master, Abū Maʿbad, set forth upon a journey and took him with him. Abū Maʿbad longed for his daughter and so he stated,

عميرَة ودع إِن تجهزت غاديا

O 'Umayrah, bid me farewell when you prepare for travel.

فردد الصَّوْت وَلَا يزِيد عَلَيْهِ

He would repeat this and not add to it.

ثمَّ قَالَ: انقذنا يَا سحيم، فهيج مِنْهُ مَا كَانَ بَاطِنا فَقَالَ:

Then he said, 'O Suḥaym, help us', which enticed his hidden emotions to arouse, and so he said,

عميرَة ودع إِن تجهزت غاديا   كفى الشيب وَالْإِسْلَام للمرء ناهيا

O 'Umayrah, bid me farewell when you prepare for travel, grey hair
and Islām are sufficient for man as prohibition.

ثمَّ بنى عَلَيْهَا فأتمها قصيدة، وانْتهى بهما فِيهَا وفحش عَلَيْهَا فَقَالَ:

Then he continued it until he made of it a complete poem, and for it he became famous. The poem includes couplets that talked about her in an inappropriate manner; he said:

وبتنا وسادانا إِلَى علجانة   وحقف تهاداه الرِّيَاح تهاديا

توسدني كفا وَتثني بمعصم عَليّ   وتحني رجلهَا من ورائيا

وهبت شمالا آخر اللَّيْل قُرَّة   وَلَا ثوب إِلَّا درعها وردائيا

فمازال ثوبي طيبا من نسيمها   إِلَى الْحول حَتَّى أنهى الثَّوْب بَالِيًا

We and her slept on two pillows next to a tree, and the wind was causing the sand to whirl strongly.
My head rested in her palms with her arms wrapped around me, and her legs enveloped me from behind.
The northerly wind brought chilliness to the late night, and there was no cover for us except her garment and mine.
My garment did not lose the fragrance of her scent, for a year, until it became worn out."

قَالَ: فَذهب بِهِ جندل أَبُو معبد إِلَى الْمَدِينَة ليَبِيعهُ بهَا فَقَالَ بعد أَن أخرجه يَوْمًا:

The reporter continued, "Then Jandal Abū Maʿbad took Suḥaym to the city so as to sell him there, and he said upon a day when he was taken out:

وَمَا كنت أخْشَى جندلا أَن يبيعني   بِشَيْء وَلَو أمست أنامله صفرا

أخوكم وَمولى مالكم وربيبكم   وَمن قد ثوى فِيكُم وعاشركم دهرا

أشوقا وَلما يمض لي غير لَيْلَة   فَكيف إِذا سَارَتْ الْمطِي بِنَا عشرا

I am not fearful of Jandal selling me, for any price, even if his hands became empty (i.e. empty of money).
[I am] your brother, your free slave, and your fosterling, the one who settled amongst you and lived with you for a long period.
I am longing already, though I have only spent away a single night, so how would it be if the steed took us away for ten nights?"

قَالَ: فرق عَلَيْهِ جندل فَرده مَخَافَة قومه فلاموه وَأَرَادُوا قتل العَبْد، وَكَانَ جندل يضن بِهِ فَخرج بِهِ إِلَى السُّلْطَان بِالْمَدِينَةِ فسجنه وضربه ثَمَانِينَ سَوْطًا ثمَّ خرج بِهِ رَاجعا إِلَى بِلَاده فتغنى بِهِ سحيم وَقَالَ:

He said, "Thus Jandal softened in his view to him and took him back. This was to the disdain of his people, who admonished him and wished that the slave be executed. However, Jandal resisted their call and went with him to the *sulṭān* of the city, and Suḥaym was subsequently jailed and flogged eighty times. Then Jandal returned with him to his land and Suḥaym recited:

أَبَا معبد بئس العريضة للفتى   ثَمَانُون لم تتْرك لحلفكم عبدا

كسوني غَدَاة الدَّار سمراء كَأَنَّهَا   شياطين لم تتْرك فؤادا وَلَا عهدا

فَمَا السجْن إِلَّا ظلّ بَيت دَخلته   وَمَا السَّوْط إِلَّا جلدَة خالطت جلدا

أَبَا معبد وَالله مَا حل حبها   ثَمَانُون سَوْطًا بل يزِيد بهَا وجدا

فَإِن تقتلوني تقتلُوا ابْن وليدة   وَإِن تتركوني تتركوا أسدا وردا

غَدا يكثر الباكون منا ومنكم   وتزداد دَاري من دِيَاركُمْ بعدا

O Abū Ma'bad, how evil are the wants of the youth, eighty [strikes] did not remove your confederate from slavery.
They draped me in brown on the morning of the infraction as if they were, devils, leaving neither spirit or a pledge.
The prison is naught but a shade of an abode under which I stayed, and the whip is naught but leather which is fused with skin.
O Abū Ma'bad, by Allāh, the love for her will not dissipate, by eighty lashes, rather the passion will increase through this.
If you kill me you would have killed a son of a female slave, and if you spare my life, you would have released a standing lion.
Tomorrow many eyes will cry from amongst my [people] and yours, and my abode will become greater in distance from yours."

قَالَ: فَأَخْبرنِي عبد الْملك بن عبد الْعَزِيز أَن هَذَا الْبَيْت الْأَخير للعرجي.

He continued: 'Abd al-Malik ibn 'Abd al-'Azīz informed me that this last couplet was composed by al-'Arajī.

قَالَ الْمُصَنّف: وَكَانَ آخر أَمر سحيم أَنه أحب امراة من أهل بَيت مَوْلَاهُ فَأَخَذُوهُ

وأحرقوه.

The author states: The end of Suḥaym's affair was that he desired after a woman from his owner's family, so they apprehended him and burned him.

❖❖❖

وَمِنْهُم نصيب بن محجن

From them was Nuṣayb ibn Miḥjan

أَبُو محجن الشَّاعِر، مولى عبد الْعَزِيز بن مَرْوَان، وَكَانَ أسود.

Abū Miḥjan the poet was the *mawlā* of ʿAbd al-ʿAzīz ibn Marwān. He was black.

[٨٦] أخبرنَا مُحَمَّد بن نَاصِر قَالَ: أنبأ الْمُبَارك بن عبد الْجَبَّار قَالَ: أَنا إِبْرَاهِيم بن عمر الْبَرْمَكِي قَالَ: أَنبأَنَا أَبُو الْحُسَيْن الزَّيْنَبِي قَالَ نَا مُحَمَّد بن خلف قَالَ: ثَنَا عبد اللَّهِ بن عَمْرو وَأحمد بن حَرْب قَالَا: نَا زبير بن أبي بكر قَالَ: حَدثنِي مُحَمَّد بن المؤمل بن طالوت قَالَ: حَدثنِي أبي عَن الضَّحَّاك ابْن عُثْمَان الْحزَامِي قَالَ: خرجت فِي آخر أَيَّام الْحَج فنزلت بالأبواء على امْرَأَة فَأَعْجَبنِي مَا رَأَيْت من حسنها وأطربني فتمثلت بقول نصيب.

Muḥammad ibn al-Mu'mmal ibn Ṭālūt's father reported upon the authority of al-Ḍaḥḥāk ibn ʿUthmān al-Ḥuzāmī, "I went out during the final days of Ḥajj and came across a woman in al-Abwā who caused me to be stunned due to her beauty, and so I mentioned the words of Nuṣayb:

بِزَيْنَب ألمم قبل أَن يرحل الركب   وَقل إِن تملينا فَمَا مل الْقلب

خليلي من كَعْب ألما هديتما بِزَيْنَب   لَا يفقد كَمَا أبدا كَعْب

وقولا لَهَا مَا فِي البعاد لذِي الْهوى   يُعَاد وَمَا فِيهِ لصدع النَّوَى شعب

فَمن شان أم الصرم أَو قَالَ ظَالِما لصَاحبه ذَنْب وَلَيْسَ لَهُ ذَنْب

If I could visit Zaynab before the caravan sets off, and say, 'If we stayed together for a long time, my heart would never grow weary.'

O my dear friends from Kaʿb, if you were to find Zaynab, may you never be lost by Kaʿb.

Then say to her that distance has no impact upon the lovers, contrary to how it causes distance between [normal] people.

So, he who wishes to stigmatise, forsake or call a wrongdoer, his companion for a fault when he was not at fault.

فَلَمَّا سمعتني أتمثل الأبيات قَالَت لي: يَا فَتى، أتعرف قَائِل هَذَا الشّعْر؟ قلت: ذَاك نصيب، قَالَت: نعم، هُوَ ذَاك. فتعرف زَيْنَب؟ قلت: لَا. قَالَت: أَنا وَالله زَيْنَب. قلت: فحياك اللَّهِ. قَالَت: أما إِن الْيَوْم موعده من عِنْد أَمِير الْمُؤمنِينَ، خرج إِلَيْهِ عَام أول، وَعَدَني هَذَا الْيَوْم، ولعلك لَا تبْرَح حَتَّى ترَاهُ. قَالَ: فَمَا برحت من مجلسي حَتَّى إِذا أَنا برَاكِب يزُول مَعَ السراب، فَقَالَت: ترى حث ذَلِك الرَّاكِب؟ إِنِّي لأحسبه إِيَّاه.

When she heard me mention these couplets, she stated to me, 'O youth, do you know the one who stated this poetry?' I replied, 'It belongs to Nuṣayb.' She said, 'Yes, it is as you stated. However, do you know who Zaynab is?' I replied, 'No.' She said, 'By Allāh, I am Zaynab.' I replied, 'May Allāh preserve you.' She said, 'Today is the day of his appointment with the Commander of the Faithful. He travelled to him during the previous year and promised to meet me today, and it is possible that you will see him before you leave.'" He said, "And so I saw a rider before I left that place approaching us from afar, [his figure was] flickering with the mirage [of the heat.] She then said, 'Do you see that incoming rider? I think that may be him.'"

قَالَ: وَأَقْبل الرَّاكِب فأمنا حَتَّى أَنَاخَ قَرِيبا من الْخَيْمَة فَإِذا هُوَ نصيب، ثمَّ ثنى رجله عَن رَاحِلَته فَنزل، ثمَّ أقبل فَسلم عَليّ وَجلسَ فِيهَا نَاحيَة، وَسلم عَلَيْهَا وسألها

وَسَأَلته فاحتفا، ثمَّ إِنَّهَا سَأَلته أَن ينشدها مَا أحدث من الشّعْر بعْدهَا، فَجعل ينشدها، فَقلت فِي نَفسِي: عاشقان أطالا التنائي لَابُد أَن يكون لأَحَدهمَا إِلَى صَاحبه حَاجَة، فَقُمْت إِلَى رَاحِلَتي أَشد عَلَيْهَا، فَقَالَ لي: على رسلك، أَنا مَعَك. فَجَلَست حَتَّى نَهَضَ، ونهضت مَعَه، فتسايرنا سَاعَة ثمَّ الْتفت فَقَالَ: فَقلت: قلت فِي نَفسك: محبان التقيا بعد طول ثَنَاء، لَا بُد أَن يكون لأَحَدهمَا إِلَى صَاحبه حَاجَة؟ قلت: نعم، قد كَانَ ذَلِك. قَالَ: لَا وَرب هَذِه البنية الَّتِي إِلَيْهَا نعمد مَا جَلَست إِلَيْهَا مَجْلِسا قطّ أقرب من مجلسي الَّذِي رَأَيْت، وَلَا كَانَ بَيْننَا مَكْرُوه قطّ.

He continued, "Then the rider approached us and set down until his camel kneeled down close to the tent, and indeed it was Nuṣayb. Then he moved his feet from his saddle and descended. Then he came and greeted me, and sat besides her, greeting her and then they inquired about each other with joy. Then she asked him to recite for her any new poetry he had composed. Thus, he began to recite and I said to myself, 'These are two lovers who have been separated for a long time and they must have a need for each other.' Upon this I stood and went to prepare my ride. He then said to me, 'Slow down, I will be with you [shortly.]' I then sat until he rose, and I rose alongside him. We walked together for a while and then he turned to me and said, 'You must have said to yourself that these are two lovers meeting after a long time of praise [without meeting], and that they must have a need for each other?' I replied, 'Yes, those were my thoughts.' He said, 'No, by the Lord of the building towards which we face [in prayer,] I have never sat with her closer than what you just saw, and no indecency has ever occurred between us.'"

قَالَ الْمُصَنّف: قلت: وَقد روى لنا أَن زَيْنَب كَانَت سَوْدَاء أَيْضا.

The author states: It has been reported to us that Zaynab was also black.

[٨٣] وأنبأنا مُحَمَّد بن أبي مَنْصُور قَالَ: أَنا الْمُبَارك بن عبد الْجَبَّار قَالَ: أَنا أَبُو

مُحَمَّد الْجَوْهَرِي قَالَ أَنا ابْن حيوية قَالَ: نَا مُحَمَّد بن خلف قَالَ: حَدثنِي مُحَمَّد بن معَاذ عَن إِسْحَاق بن إِبْرَاهِيم قَالَ: حَدثنِي رجل من قُرَيْش عَمَّن حَدثهُ قَالَ: كنت حَاجا وَمَعِي رجل من الْقَافِلَة لَا أعرفهُ وَلم أره قبل ذَلِك وَمَعَهُ هوداج وأثقال وصبية وَعبيد ومتاع فنزلنا منزلا فَإِذا فرش ممهدة وَبسط قد بسطت فَخرج من بَعْضهَا هودج امْرَأَة زنجية، فَجَلَست على تِلْكَ الْفرش الممهدة، ثمَّ جَاءَ زنجي فَجَلَسَ [إِلَى جنبها، فَبَقيت مُتَعَجِّبا مِنْهُمَا فبينا أَنا أنظر إِلَيْهَا] إِذْ مر بِنَا مار وَهُوَ يَقُود إبِلا فَجعل يتَغَنَّى وَيَقُول:

Muḥammad ibn Muʿādh reported upon the authority of Isḥāq ibn Ibrāhīm, "It was narrated to me by a man from the Quraysh upon the authority of the one whom had narrated to him: 'I was performing the Ḥajj and amongst my convoy was a man whom I did not know and had never seen before. He had with him howdahs, heavy items, young boys, slaves and luggage. We stopped at a designated place to find that a large carpet and cushions had been prepared there. A Zanjī woman subsequently exited a *hawdah* (carriages on the backs of animals) and sat upon the carpet. Then a Zanjī man came and sat to her side. I stared for a while in surprise and whilst I was staring at her, a man passed by us leading a camel whilst singing:

بِزَيْنَب ألمم قبل أَن يرحل الركب وَقل إِن تملينا فَمَا مل الْقلب

[Could I] not be with Zaynab before the caravan sets off, and tell her,
'If we stayed together for a long time, my heart would never grow
weary.'

قَالَ: فَوَثَبت الزنجية إِلَى الزنْجِي فخبطته وضربته وَهِي تَقول: شهرتني بَين النَّاس شهرك اللَّهِ. فَقلت: من هَذَا؟ فَقَالُوا لي: نصيب الشَّاعِر وَهَذِه زَيْنَب.

He continued, 'The Zanjī woman suddenly pounced upon the Zanjī man and struck him. She said, 'You have exposed me to the people, may Allāh expose you.' I then asked, 'Who is this?' They replied, 'Nuṣayb the poet and she is Zaynab.'''

[٨٤] أخبرنَا ابْن نَاصِر قَالَ: أنبأ مَحْفُوظ بن أَحْمد قَالَ: أنبأ أَبُو عَليّ مُحَمَّد ابْن الْحُسَيْن الحارذي قَالَ: ثنَا الْمعَافى بن زَكَرِيَّا قَالَ: نَا إِبْرَاهِيم ابْن مُحَمَّد بن عَرَفَة قَالَ: ثنَا أَحْمد بن يحيى قَالَ: ثنَا الزبير قَالَ: ثنَا مُحَمَّد بن أَحْمد عَن مُحَمَّد بن عبد اللَّهِ عَن معَاذ صَاحب الْهَرَوِيّ، قَالَ: دخلت مَسْجِد الْكُوفَة فَرَأَيْت رجلا لم أر قطّ أنقى ثيابًا مِنْهُ، وَلَا أَشد سوادا فَقلت لَهُ: من أَنْت؟ فَقَالَ: أَنا نصيب. فَقلت: أَخْبرنِي عَنْك وَعَن أَصْحَابك. فَقَالَ: جميل إمامنا، وَعمر أوصفنا لربات الحجال، وَكثير أبكانا على الأطلال والدمن، وَقد قلت مَا سَمِعت، قلت: فَإِن النَّاس يَزْعمُونَ أَنَّك لَا تحسن أَن تهجو. قَالَ: وأقروا لي أَنِّي أحسن أمدح؟ قلت: نعم، قَالَ: فترى لَا أحسن أَن أجعَل مَكَان عافاك اللَّهِ أخزاك اللَّهِ؟ قلت: بلَى، قَالَ: وَلَكِنِّي رَأَيْت النَّاس رجلَيْنِ: رجلا لم أسأله وَلَا يَنْبَغِي لي أَن أهجوه فأظلمه، ورجلا سَأَلته فَمَنَعَنِي، فَكَانَت نَفسِي أَحَق بالهجاء، إِذْ سَوَّلت لي أَن أطلب مِنْهُ.

Muḥammad ibn ʿAbdullāh reported upon the authority of Muʿādh the Ṣāhib of al-Harwī, "I entered the *masjid* of al-Kūfah and I saw a man of whom I have never seen anyone else with cleaner clothing than him, also I have never seen anyone with a darker complexion than him. I said to him, 'Who are you?' He replied, 'I am Nuṣayb.' I said, 'Tell me about yourself and your companions.' So, he said, 'Jamīl is our leader. And ʿUmar is the best of us at descriptive [poetry] regarding women. Kuthayr is the best of us at moving [poetry] regarding tragedies and allegory. As for me, you have heard what I recited.' I said, 'The people claim that you are not good at satire.' He replied, 'Would you agree that I am good at eulogising?' I replied, 'Yes.' 'So, do you view that I cannot utilise both 'may Allāh guard you' and 'may Allāh debase you' [in my poetry?]' I said, 'Of course [you are able to do so.]' He said, 'However, I see that men fall into two groups: (i) the man whom I ask nothing from and thus I have no need to make satire of him, and (ii) those whom I seek from and they reject me, and in this case my own self is the one deserving of satire, for it made me ask from him.'"

[٨٥] أنبأنَا أَبُو بكر بن أبي طَاهِر الْبَزَّاز قَالَ: أَنبأَنَا أَبُو إِسْحَاق الْبَرْمَكِي قَالَ: أَنبأَنَا أَبُو عَمْرو بن حيوية قَالَ: أَنا أَحْمد بن مُحَمَّد بن إِسْحَاق الْمَكِّيّ قَالَ: ثنَا الزبير بن بكار قَالَ: حَدثنِي عمي حَدثنِي أَيُّوب بن عَبَايَة قَالَ: حَدثنِي رجل من بني نَوْفَل بن عبد مناف قَالَ: لما أَصَاب نصيب من المَال مَا أَصَاب - وَكَانَت عِنْده أم محجن، وَكَانَت سَوْدَاء - تزوج امْرَأَة بَيْضَاء، فَغضِبت أم محجن وَغَارَتْ، فَقَالَ لَهَا: يَا أم محجن، وَالله مَا مثلي يغار عَلَيْهِ إِنِّي لشيخ كَبِير، وَمَا مثلك يغار، إِنَّك لعجوز كَبِيرَة، وَمَا أحد أكْرم عَليّ مِنْك وَلَا أوجب حَقًا، فحوزك هَذَا الْأَمر وَلَا تكذب بِهِ عَليّ، فرضيت وقرت، ثمَّ قَالَ لَهَا بعد ذَلِك: هَل لَك أَن أجمع إِلَيْك زَوْجَتي الجديدة، فَهُوَ أصلح لذات الْبَين وألم للشعث وَأبْعد للشماتة، فَقَالَت: افْعَل. فَأَعْطَاهَا دِينَارا وَقَالَ لَهَا: إِنِّي أكره أَن ترى بك خصَاصَة أَن تفضل عَلَيْك، فاعملي لَهَا إِذا أَصبَحت عنْدك غَدا نزلا بِهَذَا الدِّينَار، ثمَّ أَتَى زَوجته الجديدة فَقَالَ لَهَا: إِنِّي قد أردْت أَن أجمعك إِلَى أم محجن غَدا وَهِي مكرمتك، وأكره أَن تفضل عَلَيْك، فَخذي هَذَا الدِّينَار فأهدي لَهَا بِهِ إِذا أَصبَحت عِنْدهَا غَدا لِئَلَّا ترى بك خصَاصَة وَلَا تذكرين الدِّينَار لَهَا.

Ayyūb ibn 'Abāyah reported upon the authority of a man from Banī Nawfal ibn 'Abd Manāf, "When Nuṣayb gained wealth—before which he had a wife named Umm Miḥjan, a black woman—he married a white woman. Umm Miḥjan became angry and envious, so he said to her, 'O Umm Miḥjan, I am not one to be the target of jealousy, for I am an elderly man. Furthermore, the like of you should not suffer from envy, for you are an elderly woman. None is dearer to me than you and none worthier of their rights from me than you. So be easy with me and [I urge] you not to deny it from me.' Thus, she became pleased and approved. He said to her after this, 'Would you be fine with me bringing my new wife to meet you? It is better for reconciliation and a means of bringing all of us together, and to prevent people from gloating' She replied, 'That is fine.' Then he gave her a *dīnār* and stated to her, 'I would disdain that she sees in you a shortcoming that would make her feel better than you, so prepare something for her arrival tomorrow with this *dīnār*.' Then he went to his new wife and said to her, 'I would like you to meet Umm Miḥjan tomorrow, and she will bestow honour upon you, and so I would dislike her to appear more generous than you. So take this *dīnār* and gift it to her when you meet tomorrow, to prevent her seeing you as being unable [to gift money,] however do not mention to her [that I gave] the *dīnār*.'

ثمَّ أَتَى صاحبا لَهُ ليستنصحه، فَقَالَ: إنِّي أُرِيد أَن أجمع زَوْجَتي الجديدة إِلَى أم محجن غَدا فأتني مُسلما، فَإِنِّي سأستجلسك للغداء، فَإِذا تغديت فسلني عَن أحبهما إِلَيّ، فَإِنِّي سأنفر وَأعظم ذَلِك وَأبي أَن أخْبرك، فَإِذا أَبيت ذَلِك فاحلف عَليّ، فَلَمَّا كَانَ الْغَد زارت زَوجته الجديدة أم محجن وَمر بِهِ صديقه فاستجلسه فَلَمَّا تغديا أقبل الرجل عَلَيْهِ فَقَالَ: يَا أَبَا محجن، أحب أَن تُخبرنِي عَن أحب زوجتيك إِلَيْك. فَقَالَ: سُبْحَانَ اللَّهِ! أتسألني عَن هَذَا وهما يسمعان! مَا سَأَلَ عَن هَذَا أحد قبلك.

Then he went to his companion to seek his advice and said to him, 'I want to take my new wife to Umm Miḥjan tomorrow, and I would like you to pass by tomorrow and I will ask you to sit for lunch, and after you eat, ask me which of the two is more beloved to me. I will refuse to do this and will exaggerate in my refusal to do so. Upon this, you should take an oath that you must know.' During the next day his new wife met Umm Miḥjan, and his friend came and was asked to sit. After they ate, the man turned to him and said, 'O Abū Miḥjan, 'I would like to know which wife is more beloved to you.' He said, '*Subḥānallāh*! You ask me this whilst both are listening?! None have asked me this before.'

قَالَ: وَإِنِّي أقسم عَلَيْك لتخبرني، فوَاللَّه لَا أعذرك، وَلَا أقبل إِلَّا ذَاك، قَالَ: أما إِذْ فعلت فأحبهما إِلَيّ صَاحِبَة الدِّينَار، وَالله لَا أزيدك على هَذَا شَيْئا، وأعرضت كل وَاحِدَة مِنْهُمَا تضحك، ونفسها مسرورة وَهِي تظن أَنه عناها بذلك القَوْل.

Then he said, 'I ask you by Allāh to inform me, and by Allāh I will not excuse you, and I will not accept less than this.' He replied, 'If you insist, I will tell you; the one most beloved to me is the possessor of the *dīnār*. And by Allāh I will not increase upon this.' Upon this each of the wives displayed smiles, as each was pleased due to thinking that she was the one he meant."

[٨٦] أَنبأَنَا مُحَمَّد بن أبي مَنْصُور قَالَ: أَنا الْمُبَارك بن عبد الْجَبَّار قَالَ أنبأ الْحسن بن عَليّ الْجَوْهَرِي قَالَ أَنا أَبُو عمر بن حيوية قَالَ: أنبأ أَبُو بكر مُحَمَّد بن خلف قَالَ: أَخْبرنِي يزِيد بن مُحَمَّد المهلبي عَن مُحَمَّد بن سَلام قَالَ: دخل نصيب على يزِيد بن عبد الْملك فَقَالَ لَهُ: حَدثنِي بِبَعْض مَا مر عَلَيْك. فَقَالَ: يَا أَمِير الْمُؤمنِينَ علقت جَارِيَة حَمْرَاء - يَعْنِي بَيْضَاء - فَمَكثت زَمَانا تمنيني الأباطيل فَأرْسلت إِلَيْهَا بِهَذِهِ الأبيات:

Yazīd ibn Muḥammad al-Muhallabī reported upon the authority of Muḥammad ibn Sallām, "Nuṣayb entered the presence of Yazīd 'Abd al-Malik on an occasion, and 'Abd al-Malik stated to him, 'Inform me of some of your experiences.' He replied, 'O Commander of the Faithful, I fell in love with a red slavegirl (i.e. a white one). She kept me wishful for her with false promises for some time, and so I sent her these couplets:

وَإِن أك حالكا فالمسك أحوى وبالسواد جلدي من دَوَاء

ولي كرم عَن الْفَحْشَاء نائي كبعد الأَرْض من جو السَّمَاء

ومثلي فِي رجالكم قَلِيل ومثلي لَا يرد عَن النِّسَاء

فَإِن ترضي فردي قَول رَاض وَإِن تأبي فَنحْن على السوَاء

Even though I am dark-skinned, musk is darker, and there is nothing
that could change the darkness of the skin.

I have nobility that places a great distance between me and obscenity,
as the distance between the earth and sky.

The like of me amongst your men would be a rarity, and the like of

me is not a person who is kept away from women.
If you are satisfied with me then reply to confirm your approval, and
if you refuse me then we are in concurrence.

فَلَمَّا قَرَأت الأبيات، قَالَت: المَال وَالْعقل يعفيان على غيرهمَا فزوجتني نَفسهَا.

When she read these couplets she said, 'Wealth and intelligence overwhelm everything else.' She then married me.'"

[٨٧] قَالَ ابْن خلف: وحَدثني أَبُو بكر بن شَدَّاد قَالَ حَدثنِي أَبُو عبد اللَّهِ ابْن أبي بكر قَالَ: حَدثنِي إِبْرَاهِيم بن زيد بن عبد اللَّهِ السَّعْدِيّ قَالَ: حَدَّثتنِي جدتي عَن أَبِيهَا عَن جدها قَالَ: رَأَيْت رجلا أسود وَمَعَهُ امْرَأَة بَيْضَاء فَجعلت أتعجب من سَوَاده وبياضها، فدنوت مِنْهُ، فَقلت: من أَنْت؟ قَالَ: أَنا الَّذِي أَقُول:

Ibrāhīm ibn Zayd ibn ʿAbdullāh al-Saʿdī reported to me upon the authority of his great-grandfather from his grandfather, "I saw a black man with a white woman, and I became surprised at his darkness and her whiteness. I approached them and said, 'Who are you?' He replied, 'I am the one who stated:

أَلا لَيْت شعري مَا الَّذِي يحدثن لي   إِذا مَا غَدا النأي المفرق والبعد
أتصرمني عِنْد الألى فهم العدا   فتشمتهم بِي أم تدوم على الْعَهْد

O, what would happen to me, if remoteness separates and distances us.
Would you cut off from me so the enemies, gloat upon me, or would you remain faithful?'

قَالَ: فصاحت: بلَى وَالله تدوم على الْعَهْد. فَسَأَلت عَنْهَا، فَقيل: هَذَا نصيب، وَهَذِه أم بكر.

He continued, 'She cried out, 'Indeed, by Allāh I would remain faithful." I asked regarding them and it was said, 'He is Nuṣayb and she is Umm Bakr.'"

[٨٨] قَالَ [ابْن] خلف: وَأَخْبرنِي جَعْفَر بن عَليّ الْيَشْكُرِي قَالَ: حَدثنِي الرياشي قَالَ: أَخْبرنِي الْعُتْبِي قَالَ: دخل نصيب على عمر بن عبد الْعَزِيز ابْن مَرْوَان فَقَالَ لَهُ: هَل عشقت يَا نصيب؟ قَالَ: نعم، جعلني الله فدَاك. قَالَ: وَمن؟ قَالَ: جَارِيَة لبني مُدْلِج فأحدق بهَا الواشون فَكنت لَا أقدر على كَلَامهَا إِلَّا بِعَين أَو إِشَارَة، [فَكنت] أَجْلِس إِلَيْهَا على الطَّرِيق حَتَّى تمر بِي فأراها، وَفِي ذَلِك أَقُول:

Al-Riyāshī reported upon the authority of al-'Utbī, "Nuṣayb entered the presence of 'Umar ibn 'Abd al-'Azīz ibn Marwān on an occasion and he said to him, 'Have you fallen in love O Nuṣayb?' He replied, 'Yes, may Allāh make me a ransom for you.' 'Umar then asked him with whom, and he replied, 'With a slavegirl from the Banī Mudlaj. She was shielded from me constantly by informants and so I was not able to speak to her except through indicating with my eyes and gesturing. So, I would sit upon the road hoping for her to pass so that I could see her, and I wrote the following in regards to this:

جَلَست لَهَا كَيْمَا تمر لعلني   أخالسها التَّعْلِيم إِن لم تسلم
فَلَمَّا رأتني والوشاة تحدرت   مدامعها خوفًا وَلم تكلم
مَسَاكِين أهل الْعِشْق مَا كنت مُشْتَرِي   حَيَاة جَمِيع العاشقين بدرهم

I sat waiting for her, hoping for her to pass me, so that I could secretly persuade her if she does not greet me.
When she saw me whilst [enveloped by] informants, her eyes shed tears, remaining fearful and unable to speak.
Those in love are pitiful, and I would not purchase, the lives of all lovers [even] for a *dirham*.'

فَقَالَ لَهُ عبد الْعَزِيز: وَمَا فعلت المدلجية؟ قَالَ: اشْتريت وأولدت. قَالَ: فَهَل فِي قَلْبك مِنْهَا شَيْء؟ قَالَ: عقابيل أوجاع.

['Umar ibn] 'Abd al-'Azīz then asked him, 'And what happened to this girl from the Mudlaj?' He replied, 'She was purchased and bore a child.' He then asked, 'Do you still have any feeling in your heart for her?' He replied, 'Just extreme heartache.'"

أَبُو دلامة الشَّاعِر
Abū Dulāmah the Poet

واسْمه زند - بالنُّون - ابْن الجون مولى لبنى أَسد كَانَ عبدا حَبَشِيًّا لرجل من أهل الْكُوفَة من بني أَسد يُقَال لَهُ فصاص بن لَاحق فَأعْتقهُ، فصحب السفاح، ثمَّ صحب الْمَنْصُور، ثمَّ صحب الْمهْدي، وَله شعر حسن ونوادر عَجِيبَة مضحكة.

His name was Zand ibn al-Jūn, the *mawlā* of Banī Asad. He was an Abyssinian slave to a man from the people of Kūfah named Fusās ibn Lāḥiq, who was from Banī Asad. This man emancipated him. Then he became the companion of al-Saffāḥ, al-Manṣūr, and then al-Mahdī (i.e. Abbasid caliphs). He had beautiful poetry and anecdotes that were mesmerising and funny.

[٨٩] أخبرنَا عبد الرَّحْمَن بن مُحَمَّد قَالَ: أنبأ أَحْمد بن عَليّ بن ثَابت قَالَ: أنبأ الْحسن بن أبي بكر قَالَ: أنبأ أَبُو سهل أَحْمد بن مُحَمَّد بن زِيَاد قَالَ: سَمِعت ثعلبا يَقُول: لما مَاتَت حمادة بنت عِيسَى امْرَأَة الْمَنْصُور وقف الْمَنْصُور وَالنَّاس حوله على حفرتها ينتظرون مَجِيء الْجِنَازَة، وَأَبُو دلامة فيهم، فَأقبل عَلَيْهِ الْمَنْصُور فَقَالَ: يَا أَبَا دلامة، مَا أَعدَدْت لهَذَا المصرع؟ فَقَالَ: حمادة بنت عِيسَى يَا أَمِير الْمُؤمنِينَ. قَالَ: فأضحك الْقَوْم.

Abū Sahl Aḥmad ibn Muḥammad ibn Zīyād reported upon the authority of Tha'lab, "When Ḥamādah bint 'Īsā—the wife of Manṣūr—died, Manṣūr stood surrounded by the people at her grave-site, in wait of her body, and Abū Dulāmah was with them. Manṣūr then turned to Abū Dulāmah and said, 'O Abā Dulāmah, what have you prepared for this end?' He replied,

'Hamādah bint 'Īsā, O Commander of the Faithful.'" He continued, "Then the people began to laugh."

[٩٠] أخبرنَا عبد الرَّحْمَن قَالَ أنبأ أَحْمد بن عَليّ قَالَ أنبأ أَحْمد بن مُحَمَّد العتيقي قَالَ نَا مُحَمَّد بن الْعَبَّاس قَالَ نَا ابْن دُرَيْد قَالَ نَا ابْن أخي الْأَصْمَعِي قَالَ: سَمِعت الْأَصْمَعِي يَقُول: أَمر الْمَنْصُور أَبَا دلامة بِالْخرُوجِ نَحْو عبد اللَّهِ بن عَليّ، فَقَالَ لَهُ أَبُو دلامة: أنشدتك بِاللَّه يَا أَمِير الْمُؤمنِينَ أَن تحضرني شَيْئا من عساكرك، فَإِنِّي شهِدت تِسْعَة عَسَاكِر انْهَزَمت كلهَا، وأخاف أَن يكون عسكرك الْعَاشِر، فَضَحِك مِنْهُ وأعفاه.

The nephew of al-Aṣma'ī reported upon the authority of al-Aṣma'ī, "Al-Manṣūr ordered Abā Dulāmah [to lead] a military campaign against 'Abdullāh ibn 'Alī. Abū Dulāmah said to him, 'I implore you by Allāh O Commander of the Faithful, provide me with more of your soldiers, for I have bore witness to the defeat of nine military campaigns and I fear it being the tenth.' Al-Manṣūr laughed due to this and discharged him from his duty."

[٩١] أنبأنَا أَبُو بكر مُحَمَّد بن الْحُسَيْن قَالَ: أنبأ أَحْمد بن أَحْمد الوَاسِطِيّ قَالَ: أنبأ أَبُو أَحْمد الفرضي قَالَ: أنبأ أَبُو عمر مُحَمَّد بن عبد الْوَاحِد قَالَ: نَا ثَعْلَب عَن مُحَمَّد بن سَلام قَالَ: لَقِي روح بن حَاتِم بعض الحروب، فَقَالَ لأبي دلامة - وَقد دَعَا رجلا مِنْهُم إِلَى البرَاز تقوم إِلَيْهِ؟ قَالَ: لست بِصَاحِب قتال. قَالَ: لتفعلن. قَالَ: إِنِّي جَائِع فأطعمني. فَدفع إِلَيْهِ خبْزًا وَلَحْمًا، وَتقدم فهم بِهِ الرجل، فَقَالَ لَهُ أَبُو دلامة: اصبر، مَا هَذَا؟ ثمَّ قَالَ: أتعرفني؟ قَالَ: لَا. قَالَ: فَهَل أعرفك؟ قَالَ: لَا. قَالَ: فَمَا فِي الدُّنْيَا أَحمَق منا وَدعَاهُ للغداء فتغديا جَمِيعًا وافترقا. فَسَأَلَ روح عَن مَا فعل، فَحدث فَضَحِك وَدعَاهُ، فَسَأَلَهُ عَن الْقِصَّة فَقَالَ:

Tha'lab reported upon the authority of Muḥammad ibn Sallām, "Rūḥ ibn

Ḥātim was participating in a battle and he asked Abū Dulāmah to step forward, after a man from the enemy asked for an opponent in a dual. But he said, ‘I am not battle hardened.’ Rūḥ again said, ‘You must.’ He replied, ‘I am hungry so feed me.’ Then he provided him with bread and meat. [After he ate], the man then proceeded to the dual and prepared to attack Abū Dulāmah who said, ‘Be patient. Do you know me?’ He replied, ‘No.’ Abū Dulāmah then said, ‘Do I know you?’ He replied, ‘No.’ Abū Dulāmah said, ‘There is no one more foolish than us in the world,’ then he invited him for lunch, they ate together and then left. Then Rūḥ inquired from him in regards to what took place. He gave an account of what took place and he laughed and joked about it with him. He was later asked about this story and he said:

إنِّي أعوذ بِروح أَن يقدمني   إِلَى الْقِتَال فيجْرِي فيّ بَنو أَسد
آل الْمُهلب حب الْمَوْت إرثكم   إِذْ لَا أورث حب الْمَوْت عَن أحد

I besought Rūḥ that he not put me forward, to fight, so it would not start to be a custom for Banū Asad.

Ālī al-Mihlab, the love of death is your legacy, for I will not inherit from anyone the love for death.

قَالَ المُصَنّف: توفّي أَبُو دلامة سنة إِحْدَى وَسِتِّينَ وَمِائَة.

The author said: Abū Dulāmah died in the year 161.

[٩٢] أَنبأَنَا مُحَمَّد بن عبد الْبَاقِي قَالَ أنبأ جَعْفَر بن أَحْمد قَالَ أنبا أَبُو بكر مُحَمَّد بن عَليّ الدينَوَرِي قَالَ: سَمِعت أَبَا الْفضل عبد الْوَاحِد بن عبد الْعَزِيز الْوَاعِظ قَالَ: سَمِعت أَبَا الصَّقْر يَقُول: سَمِعت جمَاعَة من أَصْحَابنَا يقُولُونَ:

Abū al-Ṣaqr said that he heard a group of his companions report upon the authority Abū Zayd al-Baṣrī, “I saw a Zanjī man grasping hold of the cloth of the Kaʿbah whilst speaking something in the Zanjī language. Then I asked a Zanjī man who was fluent in the language to explain to me [what he was saying] and he translated it as,

مدامعي مِنْك قريحات   وَفِي الحشا مِنْك سريرات

طُوبَى لمن مَاتَ وأعضاؤه   من الْمعاصِي مستريحات

My eyes are wounded from excessive tears they shed for you, and due to you my inner contains that which must be hidden.

Glad tidings for one who died and his bodyparts, from sins they refrained.

[٩٣] أَنبأَنَا مُحَمَّد بن نَاصِر قَالَ: أَنا أَبُو الْحُسَيْن بن عبد الْجَبَّار قَالَ أَنبأَنَا أَبُو مُحَمَّد الْجَوْهَرِي قَالَ: أَنبأَنَا ابْن حيوية. قَالَ: نَا أَبُو بكر مُحَمَّد بن خلف قَالَ: أنبأ عبد اللَّهِ بن شبيب قَالَ: أَخْبرنِي الزبير بن بكار قَالَ: حَدثنِي مُحَمَّد ابْن الْحسن قَالَ: حَدثنِي فهَيْرَة بن مرّة قَالَ: كَانَ لي غُلَام أسود يَسُوق بِأَصْحَابِي وينطق بالزنجية بِشَيْء يشبه الشّعْر، فَمر بِنَا رجل يعرف لِسَانه، فاستمع لَهُ، ثمَّ قَالَ: يَقُول:

Muḥammad ibn al-Ḥasan reported upon the authority of Fahīrah ibn Murrah, "I had a black slave boy who was leading the ride whilst [I was] with my companions, and he would state in the Zanjī tongue some words which resembled poetry. Then we came across a man who understood the tongue. He listened to him and said that he was saying:

فَقلت لَهَا إِنِّي اهتديت لفتية   أناخوا بِي عجاج قَلَائِص سَهْما

فَقَالَت كَذَاك العاشقون وَمن يخف   عُيُون الأعادي يَجْعَل اللَّيْل سلما

I said to her that I was guided to some young men, and I made a great number of young camels kneel down easily.

She said that this is the case for the lovers, and whoever fears, the eyes of enemies, will make the night noiseless.

قَالَ ابْن خلف: وحَدثني عبد الرَّحْمَن بن سُلَيْمَان قَالَ: حَدثنِي القحطبي قَالَ:

أَخْبرنِي بعض الروَاة قَالَ: بَينا أَنا يَوْمًا على ركي قَاعِدا، وَذَلِكَ فِي أَشد مَا يكون من الْحر إِذا بِجَارِيَة سَوْدَاء تحمل جرا لَهَا، فَلَمَّا وصلت إِلَى الركي وضعت جرها، ثمَّ تنفست الصعداء وَقَالَت:

Al-Qaḥṭabī reported upon the authority of a narrator, 'One day I was sitting next to a well during scorching hot weather, when a black slave girl came whilst carrying a pot. When she reached the well, she placed her pot down, sighed deeply and said:

حر هجر وحر حب وحر   أَيْن من ذَا وَذَا وَذَاكَ المفر

The heat of farness, the heat of love, and the heat of both are mixed,
neither of which I can escape.

وملأت الجرة وانصرفت، فَلم ألبث إِلَّا يَسِيرا حَتَّى جَاءَ أسود وَمَعَهُ جر فَوَضعه بِحَيْثُ وضعت السَّوْدَاء الْجَرّ فَمر بِهِ كلب أسود فَرمى إِلَيْهِ رغيفا كَانَ مَعَه وَقَالَ:

And then her pot became filled and she left. I did not remain there long when a black man came with a pot, and he placed it where the black woman placed hers. A black dog passed by him and he threw a piece of bread to it and said,

أحب لحبها السودَان حَتَّى   أحب لحبها سود الْكلاب

I love because of her everything that is black, to the extent that I even
love black dogs due to her.

[٩٤] أَنبأَنَا مُحَمَّد بن عبد الْبَاقِي قَالَ أنبأ جَعْفَر بن أَحْمد قَالَ أنبأ أَبُو الْحسن عَليّ بن عبد الْكَرِيم الجواليقي قَالَ أنبأ مُحَمَّد بن فَارس الْحَافِظ قَالَ: نَا عبد اللَّهِ بن مُحَمَّد بن جَعْفَر قَالَ: حَدثنِي عَليّ بن حَمْزَة قَالَ: ثَنَا أَبُو العيناء قَالَ ثَنَا الْأَصْمَعِي عَن أبي عَمْرو بن الْعَلَاء عَن السّري بن جَابر قَالَ: دخلت بِلَاد الزنج فَرَأَيْت زنجية تدق الأرز وتبكي وَتقول كلَاما لم أقف عَلَيْهِ، فَسَأَلت شَيخا، فَقَالَ

تَقول:

Abī 'Amr ibn al-'Alā reported upon the authority of al-Sarrī ibn Jābir, "I entered the land of the Zanj and I saw a Zanjī woman grinding rice and crying. She was saying something which I could not comprehend, so I asked a knowledgeable man who said that she was stating:

رميت بطرفي يمنة ثمَّ يسرة فَلم أر غير اللَّهِ يألفه قلبِي

فجئتك إدلالا بِمن قد عَرفته وبالفعل وَالْإِحْسَان تغْفر لي ذَنبي

أياديك لَا تخفى وَإِن طَال عدهَا وإحسانك المبذول فِي الشرق والغرب

I cast my vision to the right and the left, but I did not find anyone besides Allāh who my heart found affability with.

I came to you in subservience with whom you already now, by your action and beneficence, you forgive my sins.

Your hands are not hidden regardless if their quantity is great, and your beneficence extends through the east and the west.

بلغنَا عَن ذِي النُّون [الْمصْرِيّ] أَنه قَالَ: كنت يَوْمًا مارا فِي تيه الشَّام فَإِذا أَنا بزنجي مفلفل الشّعْر كلما ذكر اللَّهِ [تَعَالَى] حَالَتْ لبسته وتغيرت، وَصَارَ وَجهه كدارة الْقَمَر، وَزَالَ السوَاد، فَقلت لَهُ: يَا أسود، إِنِّي أرى مِنْك عجبا، قَالَ: وَمَا الَّذِي رَأَيْت؟ قلت: أَرَاك كلما ذكرت اللَّهِ عز وَجل حَالَتْ لبستك وَتغير لونك فَقَالَ: وَمن هَذَا تعجب؟ أإنك لَو ذكرت اللَّهِ عز وَجل حَقِيقَة ذكره لحلت لبستك وَتغير لونك، ثمَّ جعل ذَلِك الزنْجِي يخطو فِي التيه وَيَقُول:

It reached us upon the authority of Dhū al-Nūn al-Miṣrī that he said, "There was a day when I was walking through a wild-land area of al-Shām when I came across a Zanjī man with pepperish hair. Whenever he would mention Allāh ﷻ his clothing would change and his [colour] would change. His face would become like the full moon, and his darkness would lighten. I said to him, 'O black man, I see something strange about you.' He replied, 'What is it that you see?' I said, 'I have seen that whenever you mention Allāh ﷻ your clothing moves and your colour changes.' He replied, 'And where is the strangeness? Are you not aware that if you mention Allāh ﷻ truly, your clothing will move and colour will change.' Then the Zanjī paced around the wilderness and said:

ذكرنَا وماكنا نَسِينَا لنذكر   وَلَكِن نسيم الْقرب يَبْدُو فيبهر

فأحيا بِهِ عني وَأَحْيَا بِهِ لَهُ   إِذْ الْحق عَنهُ مخبر ومعبر

We remembered Allāh and what we did not forget so we remember, but the breeze of being close [to Allāh] arrives and it dazzles.

I live by Allāh far from myself and I live by Allāh for Him, for He has informed us about Him and expressed it.

وبلغنا عَن بعض السّلف أَنه قَالَ: لقِيت أسود فِي الْبَرِيَّة كلما ذكر اللَّهِ [عز وَجل] ابيضّ، فَقلت لَهُ: مَا هَذَا؟ فَأَنْشد:

It reached us upon the authority of one of the Salaf that he said, "I came across a black man in the wilderness, and whenever he would mention Allāh ﷻ his complexion would turn white. I said to him, 'What is this?' And he replied by reciting,

أَمُوت إِذا ذكرتك ثمَّ أَحْيَا   فكم أَحْيَا عَلَيْك وَكم أَمُوت

شربت الْحبّ كأسا بعد كأس   فَمَا نفد الشَّرَاب وَلَا رويت

I die when I remember You and then I come back to life, how many times have I died due to You and how many times have I been brought back to life.

I have drunk love cup after cup, and the drink is never finished and neither is my thirst.

الْبَاب الْحَادِي وَالْعشْرُون

Chapter Twenty One

فِي ذكر طَائِفَة من فطناء السودَان والسوداوات وأذكيائهم وكرمائهم

In mention of a group of discerning, intelligent and generous black men and women

[٩٥] أَنبأَنَا مُحَمَّد بن نَاصِر قَالَ أَنبأَنَا جَعْفَر بن أَحْمد قَالَ أنبأ أَبُو طَاهِر مُحَمَّد بن عَليّ العلاف قَالَ أنبأ أَبُو بكر أَحْمد بن سلم فِيمَا أجَاز لنا قَالَ نَا أَبُو دلف هَاشم بن مُحَمَّد بن هَارُون الْخُزَاعِيّ قَالَ نَا مُحَمَّد بن عبد اللَّهِ عَن الْعُتْبِي عَن الْأَصْمَعِي قَالَ: بَيْنَمَا سُلَيْمَان بن عبد الْملك يسير ذَات يَوْم فِي موكبه إِذْ عرض لَهُ رجل أسود عَلَيْهِ بردَان، مؤتزر بِأَحدهمَا، مُرْتَد بِالآخِرَة، فَأخذ بلجام دَابَّة سُلَيْمَان، ثمَّ قَالَ: يَا أَمِير الْمُؤمنِينَ، اتَّقِ اللَّهِ [عز وَجل] وَاذْكُر الْأَذَان. قَالَ: وَمَا الْأَذَان؟ قَالَ الرجل: قَالَ الله تَعَالَى: ﴿فَأذن مُؤذن بَينهم أَن لعنة اللهِ على الظَّالِمين﴾.

Al-ʿUtbī reported upon the authority of al-Aṣmaʿī, "One day when Sulaymān ibn ʿAbd al-Malik was travelling with his convoy, a black man presented himself to him. He was wearing two *burdahs*, one used as an *izār* (lower garment) and one as a *ridā'* (upper garment). He took hold of the reigns of Sulaymān's animal and said, 'O Commander of the Faithful, fear Allāh ﷻ and remember the calling.' Sulaymān asked, 'And what is the calling?' The man replied, 'Allāh ﷻ stated: **{Then an announcer will announce among them, "The curse of Allāh shall be upon the wrongdoers."}**'[70]

فَبكى بكاء كثيرا، ثمَّ رفع رَأسه إِلَيْهِ فَقَالَ: وَيحك، وَمَا مظلمتك؟ قَالَ: ظَلَمَنِي

70 Al-Aʿrāf: 44

وكيلك يَا أَمِير الْمُؤمنِينَ بِالْيمن وغصبني ضيعتي وأدخلها فِي ضيعتك. قَالَ: فَدَعَا سُلَيْمَان وَهُوَ مَكَانَهُ بِدَوَاةٍ وَقِرْطَاس، وَكتب بِيَدِهِ إِلَى وَكيله بِالْيمن أَن ادْفَعْ إِلَى فلَان ضيعته الَّتِي غصبته إِيَّاهَا وَمثلهَا من ضيعتي وَلَا تظلم أحدا.

Upon this Sulaymān cried excessively, then he raised his head to him and said, 'Woe unto you, what is your complaint?' He replied, 'Your administrator in Yemen has oppressed me O Commander of the Faithful. He seized my estate and consolidated it within yours.'" He continued, "Sulaymān immediately called for ink and paper. He wrote by his own hand to his representative in Yemen, that he return the seized estate of this individual in addition to a similar sized plot from his (i.e. Sulaymān's) estate, and that he not treat anyone oppressively."

[٩٦] أنبأَنَا ابن نَاصِر قَالَ: أَنبأَنَا جَعْفَر بن أَحْمد قَالَ: أنبأ عبد الْعَزِيز ابْن الْحسن الضراب قَالَ: أنبأ أبي قَالَ: نَا أَحْمد بن مَرْوَان الدينَوري قَالَ: نَا إِبْرَاهِيم الْحَرْبِيّ قَالَ ثنَا عُثْمَان بن مُحَمَّد الْأَنمَاطِي قَالَ نَا عَمْرو بن أبي قيس قَالَ: خرج عبد اللَّهِ بن جَعْفَر إِلَى حيطان الْمَدِينَة فَبَيْنَمَا هُوَ كَذَلِك إِذْ نظر إِلَى أسود على بعض الْحِيطَان وَهُوَ يَأْكُل، وَبَين يَدَيْهِ كلب رابض، كلما أكل لقمه رمى للكلب مثلهَا، فَلم يزل كَذَلِك حَتَّى فرغ من أكله، وَعبد الله بن جَعْفَر وَاقِف على رَأسه ينظر إِلَيْهِ، فَلَمَّا فرغ دنا مِنْهُ، فَقَالَ لَهُ: يَا غُلَام، لمن أَنْت؟ قَالَ: لوَرَثَة عُثْمَان بن عَفَّان. فَقَالَ: لقد رَأَيْت مِنْك عجبا، فَقَالَ لَهُ: وَمَا الَّذِي رَأَيْت من الْعجب يَا مولَايَ؟ قَالَ: رَأَيْتُك تَأْكُل فَكلما أكلت لقْمَة رميت للكلب مثلهَا. فَقَالَ لَهُ: يَا مولَايَ، هُوَ رفيقي مُنْذُ سِنِين، وَلَا بُد أَن أجعله كأسوتي فِي الطَّعَام. فَقَالَ لَهُ: فدون هَذَا الجزيل. فَقَالَ لَهُ: يَا مولَايَ، وَالله إِنِّي لأَسْتَحي من الله [عز وَجل] أَن آكل وَعين تنظر إِلَيّ لَا تَأْكُل.

'Uthmān ibn Muḥammad al-Anmāṭī reported upon the authority of 'Amr ibn Abī Qays, "'Abdullāh ibn Ja'far went out one day to the walls of

Madīnah. Whilst he was there, he came across a black man [sitting] upon one of the walls and he was eating, and a dog was sitting in front of him. Whenever he would take a bite, he would throw the same amount to the dog, and he did not stop doing so until he finished his food. ʿAbdullāh ibn Jaʿfar stood close to him whilst watching him, and when he finished, he approached him and said, 'O *ghulām*, to whom do you belong?' He replied, 'I belong to the heirs of ʿUthmān ibn ʿAffān.' He said, 'I saw you do something strange.' 'He replied, 'What did you see as strange O sire?' He said, 'I saw you eating and whenever you ate a morsel you would throw an equal amount to the dog.' He replied, 'O sire, he has been my close companion for years and so I feel obliged to treat him as my equal in food.' ʿAbdullāh ibn Jaʿfar said to him, 'Even less than this is plenty.' He replied, 'O sire, by Allāh I would feel shame if Allāh ﷻ saw me eating whilst eyes of the hungry watched on.'

ثمَّ مضى عني، فَأتى جَعْفَر وَرَثَة عُثْمَان فنزل عِنْدهم، فَقَالَ: جِئْت فِي حَاجَة. قَالُوا: وَمَا حَاجَتك؟ قَالَ: تبيعوني الْحَائِط الْفُلَانِيّ فَقَالُوا لَهُ: قد وهبناه لَك. قَالَ: لست آخذه إِلَّا بِضعْف: فباعوه فَقَالَ لَهُم: وتبيعوني الْغُلَام الْأسود. فَقَالُوا لَهُ: إِنَّا قد ربيناه وَإنَّهُ كأحدنا، فَلم يزل بهم حَتَّى باعوه، وَانْصَرف عَنْهُم. فَلَمَّا أصبح غَدا على الْغُلَام وَهُوَ فِي الْحَائِط، فَقَالَ لَهُ: أشعرت أَنِّي قد اشتريتك واشتريت الْحَائِط من مواليك؟ فَقَالَ لَهُ: بَارك الله لَك فِيمَا اشْتريت، وَلَقَد غمني مفارقتي لموَالِي أَنهم ربوني. فَقَالَ لَهُ: وَأَنت حر، والحائط ملك لَك. قَالَ: إِن كنت يَا مولَايَ صَادِقا فاشهد عَليّ أَنِّي قد أوقفته على وَرَثَة عُثْمَان بن عَفَّان، فتعجب عبد اللَّهِ بن جَعْفَر مِنْهُ وَقَالَ: مَا رَأَيْت كَالْيَوْمِ.

Then he left, and he went to the heirs of ʿUthmān and met them. He said, 'I come with a need.' They replied, 'What is your need?' He said, 'That you sell to me a specific property.' They replied, 'We will gift it to you.' He said, 'I will not purchase it except if I pay double [its price.]' So, he brought it and said to them, 'And [I request] you to sell me the black slave boy.' They replied to him, 'Indeed we raised him and he is like one of us.' He did not leave from them until they sold him and then he left. During the next morning when he was with the slave boy in the property, he stated to him, 'Are you aware that I purchased you and this property from your masters?' He replied, 'May Allāh bless you in that which you have purchased. However, I feel dejected at being separated from my masters for they raised me.' Then it was said to him, 'You are now free and this property belongs to you.' He said, 'If you are truthful, O my master, then I testify that I endow it to the heirs of 'Uthmān ibn 'Affān.' 'Abdullāh ibn Ja'far was amazed at this and said, 'I have never seen such a thing [as I have on] this day.'"

[٩٧] أَنبأَنَا عَلِيّ بن عبد اللَّهِ عَن أبي الْحسن بن الْمُهْتَدي عَن أبي حَفْص ابْن شاهين قَالَ: ثنَا أَحْمد بن إِسْحَاق بن بهْلُول قَالَ نَا عبد اللَّهِ بن الْهَيْثَم قَالَ ثنَا الْأَصْمَعِي قَالَ: تبع رجل سَوْدَاء فَقَالَت: أما زاجر من عقل إِذا لم يكن ناه من دين. فَقَالَ: وَهل يَرَانَا إِلَّا الْكَوَاكِب؟ قَالَت: فَأَيْنَ مكوكبها؟

'Abdullāh ibn al-Haytham reported upon the authority of al-Aṣma'ī, "A man was chasing after a black woman and she said to him, "If you have no piety to refrain from that which is prohibited, do you not have an intellect sound enough to make you stop?' He said, 'Who sees us except the stars?' She replied, 'Then what about the Creator of the stars?'"

[٩٨] أَنبأَنَا مُحَمَّد بن نَاصِر قَالَ أنبأ الْمُبَارك بن عبد الْجَبَّار قَالَ: أنبأ أَبُو مُحَمَّد الْجَوْهَرِي قَالَ أنبأ أَبُو عمر بن حيوية قَالَ أنبأَنَا مُحَمَّد بن خلف قَالَ نَا أَبُو سعيد الْمَدِينِيّ قَالَ نَا بعض أَصْحَابنَا قَالَ: نزل رجل من أهل الْحجاز بِمَالك، فَسَأَلَ أبي: مَا هَذَا؟ فَقيل لَهُ: مَالك وَإِذا بَين يَدَيْهِ صبية سَوْدَاء تلتقط النَّوَى فَقَالَ: قَاتل اللَّهِ الَّذِي يَقُول:

Sa'īd al-Madīnī reported upon the authority of one of his companions, "A man from the people of al-Ḥijāz visited Mālik and stayed over at his house. My father asked, 'Who is this man?' It was said to him, 'He is Mālik.' Besides him, there was a young black girl picking up date-stones. Malik said, 'May

Allāh strike the one who stated:

احذرِ على مَاء الْعَشِيرَة والهوى   على مَالك يَا لهف نَفسِي على مَالك

Mind the love and the water of who I love, O Malik, awe to you how much in love you are.'

وَأي شَيْء كَانَ يتعشق من مَالك، إِنَّمَا هِيَ جرة سَوْدَاء، قَالَ: تَقول الصبية: أَي بِأبي إِنَّه وَالله كَانَ لَهُ بهَا شجن لم يَك لَك.

[I said,] 'I cannot see what Malik loves in her; she is just a black pot.' The young black girl replied, 'By Allāh, and truly he is in love with her, that you never experienced.'"

[١٠٠] أَنبأَنَا مُحَمَّد بن نَاصِر قَالَ أنبأ أَبُو الْحسن بن عبد الْجَبَّار قَالَ أنبأ أَبُو مُحَمَّد الْجَوْهَرِي قَالَ: أنبأ أَبُو عمر بن حيوية قَالَ ثَنَا مُحَمَّد بن خلف قَالَ: أَخْبرنِي أَبُو الْفضل الْكَاتِب عَن أبي مُحَمَّد العامري قَالَ: قَالَ إِسْمَاعِيل بن جَامع، كَانَ أبي يعظني فِي الْغناء ويضيق عَليّ، فهربت مِنْهُ إِلَى أخوالي بِالْيمن، فأنزلني خَالِي غرفَة لَهُ مشرفة على نهر فِي بُسْتَان، وَإِنِّي لمشرف مِنْهَا إِذا طلعت سَوْدَاء مَعهَا قربَة فنزلت إِلَى المشرعة فَجَلَست وَوضعت قربتها وغنت:

Abī Muḥammad al-'Āmirī reported upon the authority of Isma'īl ibn Jāmi', "My father used to admonish me for singing and he would bear down heavily upon me, and so I fled from him to my uncle in Yemen. He settled me in a room which had a balcony overlooking a river flowing through a garden. On one occasion I was on the balcony when a black woman with a water-skin appeared. She descended to the water hole, sat down, placed her water-skin down and sang:

إِلَى اللَّهِ أَشْكُو بخلها وسماحتي   لَهَا عسل مني وتبذل علقما

فردي مصاب الْقلب أَنْت قتلته   وَلَا تتركيه هائم الْقلب مغرما

To Allāh I complain about her miserliness while I am generous, I gave her honey and she retorted with wormwood.
Rectify the broken heart which you killed, and do not leave this heart to wander while being in love.

وذرفت عَيناهَا وَاسْتقر بِي مَا لَا قوام لي بِهِ، ورجوت أَن ترده، فَلم تفعل وملأت الْقرْبَة ونهضت، فَنزلت أعدُّوا وَرَاءَهَا، وَقلت: يَا جَارِيَة، بِأبي أَنْت وَأمي، ردي الصَّوْت. قَالَت: مَا أشغلني عَنْك. قلت: بِمَاذَا؟ قَالَت: عَليّ خراج كل يَوْم دِرْهَمَانِ. فأعطيتها دِرْهَمَيْنِ، وَجَلَست حَتَّى أَخَذته، وانصرفت ولهوت يومي ذَلِك، فَأَصْبَحت وَمَا أذكر مِنْهُ حرفا وَاحِدًا، وَإِذا أَنا بِالسَّوْدَاءِ قد طلعت، فَفعلت كفعلها الأول، إِلَّا أَنَّهَا غنت غير ذَلِك الصَّوْت ونهضت وعدوت فِي أَثَرهَا، فَقلت: الصَّوْت قد ذهب عَليّ مِنْهُ نَغمَة. قَالَت: مثلك لَا تذْهب عَلَيْهِ نَغمَة، فَتبين بعضه بِبَعْض. وأبت أَن تعيده إِلَّا بِدِرْهَمَيْنِ، فأعطيتها ذَلِك، فأعادته، فَذَكرته، فَقلت: حَسبك، قَالَت: كَأَنَّك تكاثر فِيهِ بِأَرْبَعَة دَرَاهِم، كَأَنِّي وَالله بك قد أصبت بِهِ أَرْبَعَة آلَاف [دِينَار] .

And then her eyes shed tears and I could not hold my feelings. I hoped that she would continue, however she did not do so. She filled her water-skin and rose, and then I went down and hurried after her. I said to her, 'O girl, I sacrifice my father and mother for you, repeat the song.' She replied, 'I have no obligation to you.' I said, 'With what [can I persuade you?]' She replied, 'There is a tax upon me, two *dirhams* for each day.' So I gave her two *dirhams* and she sat until I had memorised her words. She then left and I spent the rest of the day in leisure, and so by the next morning I could not remember a single part of it. Then the black woman appeared again and did as she had done previously, however this time she sang something else. She rose to leave and I followed after her. I said to her, 'I have forgotten a part of the rhythm [from yesterday.]' She replied, 'The like of you does not forget a rhythm, try to find it out whilst you sing the other parts.' She refused to repeat it except for two *dirhams*, and so I gave her. She then repeated it and

I remembered, so I said to her, 'That is sufficient.' She said, 'It seems that you view four *dirhams* to be excessive. By Allāh, I foresee that you will make four thousand *dīnār* from it.'"

قَالَ ابْن جَامع: فَبينا أَنا أُغني الرشيد وَبَين يَدَيْهِ أكيسة، فِي كل كيسى ألف دِينَار، إِذْ قَالَ: من أطربني فَلهُ كيس، فغن لي صَوتا. فغنيته، فَرمى إِلَيّ بكيس، ثمَّ قَالَ: أعد. فأعدته، فَرَمَانِي بكيس، وَقَالَ: أعد. فأعدته، فَرَمَانِي بكيس، فتبسمت، فَقَالَ: مِم تضحك؟ قَالَت: يَا أَمِير الْمُؤمنِينَ، [إِن] لهَذَا الصَّوْت حَدِيث أعجب مِنْهُ، فَحَدَّثته الحَدِيث فضَحِك ورمى إِلَيّ الْكيس الرَّابِع، وَقَالَ: لَا نكذب قَول السَّوْدَاء، فَرَجَعت بأَرْبعَة آلَاف.

Ibn Jāmiʿ continued, "Then on one occasion I was singing for al-Rashīd and in front of him were four sacks, and within each sack there was one thousand *dīnār*. He said, 'Whoever entertains me will have a sack, so sing a song for me.' So, I sang him a song and he threw a sack towards me, and then he asked me to repeat it. I repeated it and he threw another sack towards me. This repeated again and he threw a third sack towards me upon which I laughed. He said to me, 'Why do you laugh?' I said, 'O Commander of the Faithful, there is a strange story behind this song.' I related the incident to him and he laughed and threw a fourth sack towards me. He subsequently said, 'We will not let the black woman's words become untrue.' Thus, I left there with four thousand."

قَالَ ابْن خلف: وَذكر الْأَصْمَعِي عَن أبي عَمْرو بن الْعَلَاء قَالَ: أتيت جَرِيرًا فَقلت: أَخْبرنِي أَي بَيت هجيتم كَانَ أَشد عَلَيْكُم؟ قَالَ قَوْله:

Ibn Khalaf said: It was reported by al-Aṣmaʿī upon the authority of ʿAmr ibn al-ʿAlā', "I came to Jarīr and said to him, 'Inform me of the most offensive couplet which was composed to ridicule you.' He said that it was the statement,

أَنْت قرارة كل مدفع سوءة وَلكُل سَائِلَة يسيل قَرَار

You are the stagnant water of the source of (all) evil, as every flowing water shall eventually become stagnant.[71]

وعَلى رَأسه جَارِيَة سَوْدَاء حلوة فَقَالَت: كَذبك وَالله، أصعب مَا هجي بِهِ قَوْله:

And behind him was a pretty black girl who said, 'He has lied to you, by Allāh.' The most offensive satirical couplet to him was his statement,

لَيْسَ الْكِرَام بناحليك آبَاءَهُم　　حَتَّى يرد إِلَى عَطِيَّة نعتل

Noble men will not attribute you to their fathers, for you will always be attributed to 'Atiyyah (i.e. his father).

فَقَالَ جرير: صدقت الخبيثة.

Jarīr said, 'This mean girl has spoken the truth.'"

[١٠١] قَالَ ابْن خلف: وحَدثني حمدون بن عبد اللَّهِ قَالَ: حَدثنِي أَبُو حشيشة قَالَ: كَانَت بدل أحسن النَّاس وَجها، وَكَانَت أستاذة كل محسن ومحسنة، وَكَانَت صفراء مدينية، وَكَانَت أروى النَّاس للغناء، وَكَانَت لجَعْفَر بن مُوسَى الْهَادِي فَوضعت لمُحَمد بن زبيدة، فَبعث إِلَى جَعْفَر يسْأَله أَن يُرِيد إِيَّاهَا فأبي، فزاره مُحَمَّد فِي منزله فَسمع مَا لم يسمع مثله، قَالَ: يَا أخي، بِعني هَذِه الْجَارِيَة، فَقَالَ: يَا سَيِّدي، لَيْسَ مثلي من بَاعَ جَارِيَة. قَالَ: فهبها لي. قَالَ: هِيَ مُدبرَة. قَالَ: فاحتال لَهُ مُحَمَّد حَتَّى أسكره، فَنَامَ جَعْفَر، وَأمر مُحَمَّد بِبَدَل فَحملت مَعَه

71 [T] To translate this couplet, a different wording of the statement of al-Farazdaq to Jarīr was considered:

أنتم قرارةُ كل معدن سوءةٍ　ولكلّ سائلةٍ تسيلُ قرار

They had a famous rivalry, which was documented in the book *Naqā'iḍ Jarīr wa al-Farazdaq*. The reason for it being considered to be such a belittling form of satire is because stagnant water has seeped through the soil and gathered at the lowest part of the ground. And it is at the same time the source of evil yet stagnant i.e. useless. And Allāh knows best.

فِي حراقته، فَانْصَرَفت بهَا، فَلَمَّا انتبه جَعْفَر سَأَلَ عَن بدل، فَأخْبر خَبَرهَا فَسكت، وَبعث إِلَيْهِ مُحَمَّد من الْغد، فَجَاءَهُ وَبدل جالسة تغنيه، فلم يقل شَيْئا، فَلَمَّا أَرَادَ جَعْفَر الِانْصِرَاف قَالَ مُحَمَّد: أوقروا حراقة ابْن عمي دَرَاهِم. قَالَ: فأوقرت، فَكَانَ مبلغ ذَلِك المَال عشْرين ألف ألف، وَبقيت بدل فِي دَار مُحَمَّد بن زبيدة إِلَى أَن حدث عَلَيْهِمَا حدث.

Ibn Khalaf said: Ḥamdūn ibn ʿAbdullāh reported to me upon the authority of Abū Ḥashīshah, "Badl had the prettiest of faces, she was a teacher of the earnest, she was yellow skinned from al-Madinah, and she was the best of the people at singing. She belonged to Jaʿfar ibn Mūsā al-Hādī, and when she came to the attention of Muḥammad ibn Zubaydah he sent a message to Jaʿfar requesting to purchase her, to which he refused. Muḥammad then visited Jaʿfar at his abode and he heard [songs] the like of which he had not heard before. He said, 'O my brother, sell me this slavegirl.' He replied, 'O sire, I am not the type to sell a slave.' He said, 'Then gift her to me.' He replied, 'She is free after I die (i.e. a *mudabbirah*).' Muḥammad then duped Jaʿfar into getting drunk and Jaʿfar fell asleep. Muḥammad subsequently commanded that Badal be taken away to his ship, and then they left. When Jaʿfar became sober he asked in regards to Badal, and when he was informed of what took place, he fell silent. Muḥammad sent for him the following day, and when he went, he found Badal sitting and singing. However, he did not say anything, and when he was preparing to leave, Muḥammad said, 'Load my cousin's ship with *dirhams*.' It was loaded and the amount reached twenty million *dirhams*. Badal remained in the abode of Muḥammad ibn Zubaydah until that which took place to them occurred."

[١٠٢] قَالَ ابْن خلف: وحَدثني أَبُو عبد اللَّهِ التَّمِيمِي قَالَ: حَدثنِي أَبُو الوضاح الْبَاهِلِيّ عَن أبي مُحَمَّد الربذي قَالَ: قَالَ عبد اللَّهِ ابن عمر بن عَتيق: خرجت أَنا وَيَعْقُوب بن حمدي بن كاسب قافلين من مَكَّة، فَلَمَّا كُنَّا بودان لَقينَا جَارِيَة من أهل ودان، فَقَالَ لَهَا يَعْقُوب: يَا جَارِيَة، مَا فعلت نعم؟ فَقَالَت: سل نَصِيبا. فَقَالَ:

قَاتلك اللَّهِ، مَا رَأَيْت كَالْيَوْمِ قطّ أحد ذهنا وَلَا أحضر صَوَابا وَإِنَّمَا أَرَادَ يَعْقُوب قَول نصيب فِي نعم - وَكَانَ ينزل ودان:

Abū Muḥammad al-Rabadhī reported upon the authority of 'Abdullāh ibn 'Umar ibn 'Atīq, "I left Makkah with Ya'qūb ibn Aḥmad ibn Kāsib. When we reached Wudān we met a slave girl from the people of Wudān. Ya'qūb said to her, 'O girl, what did Nu'm do?' She replied, 'Ask Nuṣayb.' Ya'qūb said, 'May Allāh strike you, I have never seen before today one as intelligent and prepared with the correct answer as this.' Ya'qūb intended with his question the statement of Nuṣayb in regards to Nu'm, who was leaving Wudān:

أيا صَاحب الخيمات من بطن أرثد   إِلَى النّخل من ودان مَا فعلت نعم

أسائل عَنْهَا كل ركب لقيتهم   وَمَالِي بهَا من بعد مكتنا علم

O tent dweller from the heart of Irthid, travelling to the date palms of Wudān. What did Nu'm do?

I asked every rider I met in regards to her, however, I know nothing about her since she left.'"

[١٠٣] أخبرتنا شهدة بنت أَحْمد بن الْفرج قَالَ أنبأ جَعْفَر بن أَحْمد قَالَ: أنبأ القاضيان أَبُو الْحُسَيْن النوري وَأَبُو الْقَاسِم التنوخي قَالَا: أَنا أَبُو عمر بن حيوية قَالَ ثَنا مُحَمَّد بن خلف قَالَ أنبأ مُحَمَّد بن الْفضل قَالَ: أَخْبرنِي أبي قَالَ أنبأ القحدمي قَالَ: دخل ذُو الرمة الْكُوفَة، فَبَيْنَمَا هُوَ يسير فِي بعض شوارعها على نجيب لَهُ إِذْ رأى جَارِيَة سَوْدَاء واقفة على بَاب دَار فأستحسنها، وَوَقعت بِقَلْبِه فَدَنَا إِلَيْهَا فَقَالَ: يَا جَارِيَة، اسْقِنِي مَاء. فأخرجت إِلَيْهِ كوزا فَشرب، وَأَرَادَ أَن يمازحها ويستدعي كَلَامهَا، فَقَالَ لَهَا: مَا أحر ماؤك! فَقَالَت: لَو شِئْت لأقبلت على عنوت شعرك، وَتركت حر مائي وبرده. فَقَالَ لَهَا: وَأي شعري لَهُ عنت؟ فَقَالَت: أَلَسْت ذُو الرمة؟ قَالَ: بلَى: قَالَت:

Muḥammad ibn al-Faḍl reported upon the authority of his father that al-Qaḥdamī said, "Dhū al-Rummah entered al-Kūfah and whilst riding through its streets upon his high-bred camel he saw a black slave girl standing at the doorway of an abode. He became attracted to her and his heart was affected by this. He approached her and said, 'O girl, provide me with some water.' She provided him with a jug and he drank. Then he intended to jest with her in order to provoke her to enter into a conversation, thus he said to her, 'How hot is your water!' She replied, 'If you wished you would have paid heed to the defects of your poetry, instead of the temperature of my water.' He said, 'Inform me which of my poems have such defects?' She replied, 'Am I not speaking to Dhū al-Rummah?' He said, 'Indeed that is so.' She replied,

فَأَنت الَّذِي شبهت عَنْزًا بقفرة   لَهَا ذَنْب فَوق استها أم سَالم
جعلت لَهَا قرنين فَوق جبينها   وطبيين مسودين مثل المحاجم
وساقين إِن سمكًا مِنْك تبركا   فخدك يَا غيلَان مثل المياسم
أيا ظَبْيَة الوعسانين جلاجل   وَمن النقا أأَنْت أم سَالم؟

You are the one who compared your love to a goat, does your love, Umm Sālim have a tail above her behind.

You envisaged for her [with such a comparison] two horns upon her forehead, and gave her two black hoofs.

And two legs, if they can get hold of you, O Ghaylān, your cheek will be scarred like a cauterisation.

O female deer standing on the soft land with great beauty, yet you are nothing compared to Umm Salim.

قَالَ: نشدتك بِاللَّه أَلا أخذت رَاحِلَتي هَذِه وَمَا عَلَيْهَا، وَلم تظهري هَذَا وَلَا تذكري لأحد مَا جرى. [وَنزل عَن رَاحِلَته، فَدَفعهَا إِلَيْهَا، وَذهب ليمشي فدفعتها، وضمنت أَلا تذكر لأحد مَا جرى].

He replied to this, 'I beseech you by Allāh that you take my ride and everything loaded upon it, and do not expose this to anyone nor mention what took place.' He then descended from his ride and passed it to her, he left on foot but she returned his ride and promised that she will never inform anyone of what took place."

[١٠٤] أَنبأَنَا مُحَمَّد بن أبي طَاهِر قَالَ: أَنبأَنَا عَليّ بن المحسن عَن أَبِيه قَالَ: حَدثنِي أَبُو الْقَاسِم عبد اللَّهِ بن مُحَمَّد الْكَاتِب قَالَ: حَدثنِي بعض الْأَشْرَاف بِالْكُوفَةِ أَنه كَانَ بهَا رجل جني يعرف بالأدرع شَدِيد الْقلب جدا قَالَ: وَكَانَ فِي خرابات الْكُوفَة شَيْء يظْهر للمجتازين فِيهِ نَار تطول تَارَة وتقصر أُخْرَى، يَقُولُونَ: هَذَا غولة ويفزع مِنْهُ النَّاس، فَخرج الأدرع لَيْلَة رَاكِبًا فِي بعض شَأْنه، فَقَالَ لي الأدرع: فَاعْترضَ لي السوَاد وَالنَّار فطال الشَّخْص فِي وَجْهي، فأنكرته، ثمَّ رجعت إِلَى نفسِي، فَقلت: إِمَّا شَيْطَان أَو غولة فَهُوَ مين، وَلَيْسَ إِلَّا إِنْسَان، فَذكرت اللَّهِ [تَعَالَى] وَصليت على نبيه [صلى اللَّهِ عَلَيْهِ وَسلم] ، وجمعت عنان الْفرس وقنعته وطرحته على الشَّخْص فازداد طوله وَعظم الضَّوْء فِيهِ، فنفر الْفرس فمنعته، فَطرح نَفسه عَلَيْهِ، فقصر الشَّخْص حَتَّى صَار على قدر قامة، فَلَمَّا كَاد الْفرس يخالطه ولي هَارِبا فحركت خَلفه.

Abū al-Qāsim 'Abdullāh ibn Muḥammad al-Kātib reported from one of the noblemen of al-Kūfah, "There was a man within it from the descendants of al-Ḥasan, known as al-Adra', and he was known for being stout-hearted. In a dilapidated area of al-Kūfah something strange would appear to those passing within it. It gave out light and sometimes it would appear tall whilst at other times it would appear short. It was said that this was a spectre and so the people became frightened of it. One night al-Adrā' went out riding to deal with some issues. He said to me about this, 'I was confronted by something dark yet light and it appeared that a tall figure was before me. I rejected what I saw, and when I regained my senses I said, 'As for this being a devil or a spectre then this is falsehood, this is naught but a man.' I made *dhikr* of Allāh ﷻ and sent *ṣalāt* upon the Prophet ﷺ, then I gathered the reigns of my horse tightly and charged at him and hit him. The effect of this was that it increased in height and brightness of its light. My horse became frightened due to this and so I had to restrain it. The person then attempted to climb upon the horse, and his height reduced to that of a standing person. When the horse was about to trample him, he fled and I pursued him.

فَانْتهى إِلَى خربة فَدَخلَهَا، فَدخلت خَلفه، فَإِذا هُوَ قد نزل سردابا فِيهَا، فَنزلت عَن فرسي وشددته، وَنزلت وسيفي مُجَرّد، فحين حصلت فِي السرداب، أحسست بحركته يُرِيد الْفِرَار مني، فطرحت نَفسِي عَلَيْهِ، فَوَقَعت يَدي على بدن إِنْسَان، فقبضت عَلَيْهِ فَأَخْرَجته فَإِذا هُوَ جَارِيَة سَوْدَاء، فَقلت: أَي شَيْء أَنْت وَإِلَّا قتلتك السَّاعَة؟ قَالَت: قبل كل شَيْء إنسي أَنْت؟ أوجني؟ فَمَا رَأَيْت أقوى قلبا مِنْك [قطّ] فَقلت: أَي شَيْء أَنْت؟ قَالَت: أمة لآل فلَان - قوم من الْكُوفَة - أبقت مِنْهُم مُنْذُ سِنِين، فتغربت فِي هَذِه الخربة، فولد لي الْفِكر أَن أحتال بِهَذِهِ الْحَال، وأوهم النَّاس أَنِّي غولة حَتَّى لَا يقرب الْموضع أحد، وأعترضه لَيْلًا للأحداث، فيفزعونه، وَرُبمَا رمى أحدهم منديلا أَو إزارا، فَآخذهُ، وأبيعه نَهَارا، فأقتاته أَيَّامًا.

He reached a dilapidated building and entered within it, so I followed him in. He had descended within a cellar therein, I then dismounted my horse and tethered it, and descended with my sword drawn. When I reached the cellar, I anticipated that he wanted to flee from me based upon his movement, so I hurled my self on him and my hand touched the body of a human. I grasped hold of it and dragged it out. I found then that it was in fact a black woman. I said to her, 'What are you? If you do not inform me, I will strike you down this very moment.' She replied, 'Before anything, are you human or a jinn? I have never seen one as stout-hearted as you before.' I said again, 'What are you?' She replied, 'I am the slave of the people of so-and-so, a tribe from Kūfah. I fled from them many years ago and isolated myself within this dilapidated building. I had an idea that I could hide myself behind this allusion and beguile the people into thinking that I am a spectre, thus no one would approach this place. On some nights I would come out to the young people there and they would become frightened and refrain from coming here. On occasion they would throw their handkerchiefs and garments to me. I would pick them up and sell them on the next day, using the proceeds to feed myself for the following days.'

قلت: فَمَا هَذَا الشَّخْص الَّذِي يطول وَيقصر، وَالنَّار الَّتِي تظهر؟ قَالَت: كسَاء معي طَوِيل أسود فَأخْرجهُ من السرادب، وقصبات مهندمة أَدخل بَعْضهَا فِي بعض فِي الكساء وأرفعة فَيطول، فَإِذا أردْت تَقْصِيره رفعت من الأنابيب وَاحِدَة وَاحِدَة فتقصر، وَالنَّار فَتِيلَة شمع معي فِي يَدي، لَا أخرج إِلَّا رَأسهَا مِقْدَار مَا يضيء الكساء، فأرتني الشمعة والكساء والأنابيب ثمَّ قَالَت: قد وَالله جَازَت هَذِه الْحِيلَة نيفا وَعشْرين سنة، واعترضت فرسَان الْكُوفَة وشجعانها، فَمَا أقدم عَليّ أحد غَيْرك، وَلَا رَأَيْت أَشد قلبا مِنْك. فحملها الأدرع إِلَى الْكُوفَة فردهَا على مواليها، وَكَانَت تحدث بِهَذَا الحَدِيث، وَلم ير بعد ذَلِك أثر غولة، فَعلم أَن الحَدِيث حق.

I said, 'Then what was this presence which would sometimes appear tall and sometimes short, and the light that could be seen?' She replied, 'I have a long, black garment which I took from the cellar and also a number of solid tubes. I joined the tubes together in the garment and when I would raise it, it would appear tall. When I wanted it to appear shorter, I would remove the tubes one by one so as to make it shorter. As for the light, I would hold the thread of a candle in my hand, and I would only show the tip of the candle, enough to illuminate the garment.' She then showed me the candle, garment and the tubes. She then said, 'By Allāh, this illusion has worked for twenty odd years. I have rebuffed the horsemen of Kūfah and the valiant people therein. None came forward to me except you. I have not witnessed one more stout-hearted than you." Al-Adra' took her to Kūfah and returned her to her masters. She used to mention this story, and none saw a sign of this spectre after this, so it seems that it is true."

الْبَاب الثَّانِي وَالْعشْرُونَ

Chapter Twenty Two

فِي ذكر المتعبدين مِنْهُم والزهاد

In mention of the worshippers and ascetics amongst the black people

فَمن المعروفين الْأَسْمَاء مِنْهُم غير من سبق ذكره من الصَّحَابَة [وَالتَّابِعِينَ].

From those whose names are known, besides those mentioned previously from the Companions and the Tābiʿīn, are:

أَبُو مُعَاوِيَة الْأسود

Abū Muʿāwiyah al-Aswād[72]

واسْمه الْيَمَان، نزل طرسوس.

His name is al-Yamān, and he resided in Ṭarsūs.

[١٠٥] أَنبأَنَا عَليّ بن عبيد اللَّهِ عَن الْحُسَيْن بن الْمُهْتَدي عَن أبي حَفْص ابْن شاهين قَالَ: سَمِعت عبد اللَّهِ بن سُلَيْمَان بن الْأَشْعَث يَقُول: سَمِعت أَبَا حَمْزَة - يَعْنِي ابْن الْفرج الْأَسْلَمِيّ وَكَانَ خَادِم أبي مُعَاوِيَة الْأسود - قَالَ: كَانَ أَبُو مُعَاوِيَة مولى أبي جَعْفَر أَمِير الْمُؤمنِينَ وَكَانَ يَقُول للنَّاس: استخدموني أنا عبدكم، إِنَّمَا اشْتريت من الْفَيْء، وَكَانَ لَهُ فرس رائع يَغْزُو عَلَيْهِ، قد أعطي بِهِ سبعين دِينَارا فَرَأى

72 His biography is in *Siyar Aʿlām al-Nubalā* (9/78). Al-Dhahabī said, 'He is amongst the major *awliyā* of Allāh. He was the companion of Sufyān al-Thawrī, Ibrāhīm al-Adham and others. He would give exhortations and wise adages.

شَابًّا فِي الدَّار نزل لَيْلَة فاغتسل، ثمَّ أُخْرَى فاغتسل ثمَّ نزل فاغتسل، فَلَمَّا أصبح أَبُو مُعَاوِيَة جَاءَ فَحل فرسه وَأَعْطَاهُ الْفَتى، وَقَالَ: هاك يَا فَتى، اشْترِ بِهِ جَارِيَة.

'Abdullāh ibn Sulaymān ibn al-Ash'ath reported upon the authority of Abā Ḥamzah—i.e. Ibn al-Faraj al-Aslamī the servant of Abū Mu'āwiyyah al-Aswad—, "Abū Mu'āwiyyah, the *mawlā* of Abū Ja'far the Commander of the Faithful, would state to the people, 'Make use of me for I am your slave. For indeed I was purchased with the spoils of war.' He had in his possession a pure-bred horse upon which he had rode during incursions. He was offered seventy *dinārs* for it. He saw a young man in the house go out to perform *ghusl*; he did it three times during the same night. The following morning Abū Mu'āwiyyah took his horse and gave it to the youth. He said to him, 'This is yours O youth, use it to attain a bondmaiden.'"

قَالَ: وَكَانَ قد دَعَا اللَّهِ عز وَجل أَن يطيب فِي فَمه جَمِيع مَا يَأْكُلهُ، فَكَانَ يخرج إِلَى الْبَرِيَّة، فيجتني من بقولِهَا ويجففه فِي بَيته، وَيَطوف على الْمَزَابِل فينتقي مِنْهَا الْعِظَام الَّتِي عرق مِنْهَا اللَّحْم وطرحت، فيلطخها بذلك البقل.

He continued, "He would supplicate to Allāh ﷻ to make tasty anything he put in his mouth. He would go out to the wilderness and gather herbs, drying them within his abode. He would circulate the *mazābil* (dumps) and pick out bones from which the meat had been boiled off or removed, and he would mix them with the herbs.

[١٠٦] أَنبأَنَا ابْن نَاصِر قَالَ: انبأنا جَعْفَر بن أَحْمد قَالَ: أنبأ أَبُو مُحَمَّد الْخلال قَالَ: نَا عبد الْوَاحِد بن عَليّ الفامي قَالَ: نَا عبد اللَّهِ بن سُلَيْمَان بن عِيسَى قَالَ ثَنَا مُحَمَّد بن أبي هَارُون الوارق قَالَ ثَنَا أَحْمد بن إِبْرَاهِيم قَالَ حَدثنِي عَبدة الْخُرَاسَانِي قَالَ: كَانَ أَبُو مُعَاوِيَة الْأسود إِذا مرض يعمد إِلَى قَصْعَة، فَيجْعَل فِي جَانب مِنْهَا عسلا، فَإِذا دخل عَلَيْهِ رجل يسْأَل عَنهُ يَقُول: يَا أَبَا مُعَاوِيَة، تشْتَهي شَيْئا؟ فَيَقُول: رجل لَا يقدر يَأْكُل هَذَا، أَي شَيْء يشتهى يحتجز بِهِ عَن النَّاس.

Aḥmad ibn Ibrāhīm reported upon the authority of ʿAbdah al-Khurāsānī, "When Abū Muʿāwiyyah al-Aswād fell ill he would place down a bowl and put honey to its side. If someone came to visit him, he would be asked, 'O Abā Muʿāwiyyah, do you not desire to eat?' And he would reply:, 'I am too full to eat the little honey left in the pot. There is nothing else I desire to eat that would keep me away from people.'"

[١٠٧] أخبرنَا مُحَمَّد بن عبد الْبَاقِي قَالَ: أنبأ حمد بن أَحْمد قَالَ أنبأ أَحْمد بن عبد اللَّهِ قَالَ نَا أَبُو مُحَمَّد بن حَيَّان قَالَ: نَا إِبْرَاهِيم بن مُحَمَّد بن الْحُسَيْن قَالَ ثنَا مُحَمَّد بن إِسْحَاق قَالَ ثنَا أَحْمد بن أبي الْحوَارِي قَالَ: سَمِعت أَحْمد بن وديع يَقُول: قَالَ أَبُو مُعَاوِيَة الْأسود: إِخْوَانِي كلهم خير مني. قيل لَهُ: وَكَيف ذَاك يَا أَبَا مُعَاوِيَة؟ قَالَ: كلهم رأى الْفضل لي على نَفسه وَمن فضلني على نَفسه فَهُوَ خير مني.

Aḥmad ibn Abī al-Hawārī reported upon the authority of Aḥmad ibn Wadīʿ, "Abū Muʿāwiyah al-Aswād said, 'My brothers are all better than me.' It was subsequently said to him, 'How is that O Abā Muʿāwiyah?' He replied, 'All of them view me as superior to them, and he who views me as superior to himself is actually better than me.'"

[١٠٨] أخبرنَا أَبُو بكر بن حبيب قَالَ أنبأ عَليّ بن أبي صَادِق قَالَ أنبأ ابْن باكويه قَالَ نَا عَليّ بن الْحسن الأرجاني قَالَ ثنَا جَعْفَر بن مُحَمَّد بن الْحسن الرامَهُرْمُزِي قَالَ: سَمِعت أبي يَقُول: سَمِعت أَبَا مُعَاوِيَة الْأسود وَهُوَ على سور طرسوس من جَوف اللَّيْل يبكي وَيَقُول: أَلا من كَانَت الدُّنْيَا من أكبر همه طَال فِي الْقيام غَدا همه، وَمن خَافَ مَا بَين يَدَيْهِ ضَاقَ فِي الدُّنْيَا ذرعه، وَمن خَافَ الْوَعيد أبى من الدُّنْيَا عَن مَا يُرِيد. يَا مِسْكين، إِن كنت تُرِيدُ لنَفسك الجزيل، فاقلل نومك بِاللَّيْلِ إِلَّا الْقَلِيل، اقبل من اللبيب الناصح إِذا أَتَاك بِأَمْر وَاضح. لَا تهتمن بأرزاق من تخلف، فلست بأرزاقهم تكلّف. نظف طريقك للمقال، إِذا وقفت بَين يَدي رب

الْعِزَّة للسؤال. قدم صَالح الْأَعْمَال، ودع عَنْك كَثْرَة الأشغال. بَادر ثمَّ بَادر قبل نزُول مَا تحاذر. إِذا بلغ روحك التراقي، انْقَطع عَنْك من أَحْبَبْت أَن تلاقي، كَأَنِّي بهَا وَقد بلغت الْحُلْقُوم، وَأَنت فِي سَكَرَات الْمَوْت مغموم، وَقد انْقَطَعت حَاجَتك إِلَى أهلك، وَأَنت تراهم حولك، وَبقيت مرتهنا بعملك. الصَّبْر ملاك الْأَمر، وَفِيه أعظم الْأجر، فَاجْعَلْ ذكر اللَّهِ [عز وَجل] من جلّ شَأْنك، واملك فِيمَا سوى ذَلِك لسَانك.

Muḥammad ibn al-Ḥasan al-Rāmahurmuzī reported upon the authority of his father, "I heard Abū Muʿāwiyah al-Aswād—whilst he was upon the border of Ṭarsūs deep within the night—crying, whilst saying, 'Indeed, he who places this worldly life as his main concern will face a lengthy standing [on the Day of Judgement] due to this. He whom fears that which awaits him will not be able to find a way out, and he whom fears the recompense will abstain from that which he desires from this worldly life. O destitute, if you desire abundant reward, reduce your sleep in the night to the minimum and accept the intelligent counsellor when he provides you with clear advice. Do not concern yourself with the livelihood of those who you will leave behind, as you are not burdened with this. Be prepared to present answers for when you stand before the Majesty of your Lord. Do good deeds and leave alone the many distractions, hasten in doing so before that which is warned about takes place. [This is] when your soul will reach your throat, and that which you love will be cut off from you. I am envisaging the soul reaching up to the throat and you are in the throes of dead and in distress, your need for your family then ceases whilst you see them around you. Your final destiny there depends upon your deeds. Patience is the most enveloping of deeds, and it has a lofty reward. Make the remembrance of Allāh the predominant part of your deeds, and withhold your tongue from anything else.'"

ثمَّ بَكَى أَبُو مُعَاوِيَة بكاء شَدِيدا ثمَّ قَالَ: أوه، من يَوْم يتَغَيَّر فِيهِ لوني، ويتلجلج فِيهِ لساني، ويجف فِيهِ ريقي، ويقل فِيهِ زادي.

Then Abū Muʿāwiyah cried heavily and said, 'Woe [to me] for the day upon which my colour will change, my tongue will stammer, my saliva will dry and my provisions will be minute.'"

[١٠٩] أخبرنَا أَحْمد بن ظفر قَالَ: أنبأ الْحسن بن أَحْمد بن الْبَنَّا قَالَ أنبا هِلَال بن مُحَمَّد قَالَ أَنا عَليّ بن أَحْمد الْمصْرِيّ قَالَ: سَمِعت عُثْمَان بن السكن قَالَ: سَمِعت مُؤذن غَزَّة قَالَ: حدثت عَن أبي الزهراء أَنه قَالَ: قدمت طرسوس فَدخلت على أبي مُعَاوِيَة، وَهُوَ مكفوف الْبَصَر، وَفِي منزله مصحف مُعَلّق، فَقلت: رَحِمك اللَّهِ، مصحف وَأَنت لَا تبصر! قَالَ: تكْتم عَليّ يَا أخي حَتَّى أَمُوت؟ قلت: نعم، قَالَ: إِنِّي إِذا أردْت أَن أَقرَأ الْقُرْآن فتح لي بَصرِي.

'Uthmān ibn al-Sakan heard from the *mu'adhin* of Gaza on the authority of Abū al-Zahrā', "I arrived at Tursūs and entered the presence of Abī Mu'āwiyah. He had become blind and in his house was a hanging *muṣḥaf* (copy of the Qur'ān). I said to him, 'May Allāh have mercy upon you, [you have] a *muṣḥaf* though you are blind?' He replied, 'My brother, will you keep what you have witnessed a secret until I die?' I replied, 'Yes.' He said, 'Verily, when I desire to recite the Qur'ān my vision becomes restored.'"

[١١٠] أخبرنَا مُحَمَّد بن نَاصِر [الْحَافِظ] قَالَ أَنبأَنَا الْحسن بن أَحْمد قَالَ: ثَنَا ابْن أبي القواس قَالَ أَنا إِبْرَاهِيم بن مُحَمَّد الْمُزَكي قَالَ نَا مُحَمَّد بن الْمسيب قَالَ: سَمِعت عبد اللَّهِ بن خبيق يَقُول: حَدثنِي عبد الرَّحْمَن بن عبد اللَّهِ قَالَ: استطال رجل على أبي مُعَاوِيَة الْأسود، فَقَالَ لَهُ رجل: مَه. فَقَالَ لَهُ أَبُو مُعَاوِيَة: دَعه يشتفي، ثمَّ قَالَ: اللَّهُمَّ اغْفِر الذَّنب الَّذِي سلطت عَليّ بِهِ هَذَا.

'Abdullāh ibn Khubayq reported upon the authority of 'Abd al-Raḥmān ibn 'Abdullāh, "A man transgressed against Abū Mu'āwiyah al-Aswad. A man said to him, 'Cease this.' Abū Mu'āwiyah then said, 'Let him take it all out on me until he is satisfied.' Then he said, 'O Allāh, forgive the sin which caused You to impose this man upon me.'"

[١١١] أخبرنَا ابْن نَاصِر قَالَ أَنبأَنَا عَليّ بن مُحَمَّد العلاف قَالَ أنبأ عَليّ بن أَحْمد الحماس قَالَ أَنا إِسْمَاعِيل بن عَليّ الحطبي قَالَ نَا الْحُسَيْن بن مُحَمَّد بن الْفَهم قَالَ: سَمِعت يحيى بن معِين قَالَ: رَأَيْت أَبَا مُعَاوِيَة الْأسود وَهُوَ يلتقط الْخرق من الْمَزَابِل، فيلفقها ثمَّ يغسلهَا، فَقيل لَهُ: يَا أَبَا مُعَاوِيَة، إِنَّك تُكْسَى. فَقَالَ: مَا ضرهم مَا أَصَابَهُم فِي الدُّنْيَا، جبر اللَّهِ [عز وَجل] لَهُم بِالْجنَّةِ كل مُصِيبَة.

Al-Ḥusayn ibn Muḥammad ibn al-Fahm reported upon the authority of Yaḥyā ibn Maʿīn, "I witnessed Abū Muʿāwiyah al-Aswad collecting torn clothes from a dumping ground and he would sew them and wash them. It was said to him, 'O Abū Muʿāwiyah, why do you dress so?' He replied, 'What befalls a person in this life is not of consequence, for Allāh ﷻ will compensate the unfortunate with Jannah.'"

ذُو النُّون [ثَوْبَان] بن إِبْرَاهِيم أَبُو الْفَيْض الْمصْرِيّ
Dhū al-Nūn Thawbān ibn Ibrāhīm Abū al-Fayḍ al-Maṣrī

أَصله من النّوبَة.

He was of Nubian origin.

قَالَ أَبُو عمر فِي كتاب (أَعْيَان الموَالِي) : وَمِنْهُم ذُو النُّون بن إِبْرَاهِيم الأخميمي، كَانَ أَبوهُ إِبْرَاهِيم نوبيا.

Abū 'Umar stated in the book *A'yān al-Mawālī* (*The Elite of the Mawālī*), "Amongst them was Dhū al-Nūn ibn Ibrāhīm al-Ikhmīmī. His father was a Nubian named Ibrāhīm."

قَالَ الْمُصَنّف: قلت: كَانَ لِإِبْرَاهِيم بنُون: ذُو النُّون، وَذُو الكفل وَعبد الْهَادِي والهميسع، وَكَانَ ذُو النُّون قد حبس، فجيء بِطَعَام، فَنَاوَلَهُ إِيَّاه السجان، فَلم

يَأْكُلهُ، وَقَالَ: إِنَّه مر على يَد ظَالِم.

The author says: Ibrāhīm had a number of sons: Dhū al-Nūn, Dhū al-Kifl, ʿAbd al-Hādī and al-Humaysaʿ. Dhū al-Nūn was once incarcerated, then food was brought to him and it was given to him by his jailer. He refused to eat it, and said, 'Verily it has passed through the hand of an oppressor.'"

قَالَ ابْن الْجلاء: لقِيت سِتّمائَة شيخ، مَا لقِيت فيهم مثل أَرْبَعَة، أحدهم ذُو النُّون.

Ibn Jallāʾ said, "I met six hundred *shaykhs*, four amongst them were unparalleled. Dhū al-Nūn was one of them."

[١١٢] أخبرنَا المحمدان: ابْن نَاصِر وَابْن عبد الْبَاقِي قَالَ: أَنا حمد ابْن أَحْمد قَالَ أَنا أَبُو نعيم الْأَصْفَهَانِي قَالَ ثَنَا عُثْمَان بن مُحَمَّد العثماني قَالَ قرئَ على أبي الْحُسَيْن أَحْمد بن مُحَمَّد بن عِيسَى الرَّازِيّ سَمِعت يُوسُف بن الْحُسَيْن يَقُول: سَمِعت ذَا النُّون يَقُول: بِصُحْبَة الصَّالِحين تطيب الْحَيَاة، وَالْخَيْر مَجْمُوع فِي القرين الصَّالح؛ إِن نسيت ذكرك، وَإِن ذكرت أعانك.

Abū al-Ḥusayn Aḥmad ibn Muḥammad ibn ʿIsā al-Rāzī reported upon the authority of Yūsuf ibn al-Ḥusayn, "I heard Dhū al-Nūn say, 'Accompanying the pious beautifies one's life. One will find the entirety of good in a pious companion; for if you forget, they will remind you, and if you remember, they will aid you.'"

[١١٣] أخبرنَا أَبُو بكر بن حبيب قَالَ أنبأ ابْن أبي صَادِق قَالَ أَنا ابْن باكويه قَالَ: سَمِعت فَارِسًا الْبَغْدَادِيّ يَقُول: سَمِعت يُوسُف ابْن الْحُسَيْن يَقُول: قلت لذِي النُّون وَقت مفارقتي لَهُ: من أجالس؟ قَالَ: عَلَيْك بِصُحْبَة من يذكرك اللَّهِ عز وَجل رُؤْيَته، وَتَقَع هيبته على باطنك، وَيزِيد فِي علمك مَنْطِقه، ويزهدك فِي الدُّنْيَا عمله، وَلَا تَعْصِي اللَّهِ [عز وَجل] مَا دمت فِي قربه، يعظك بِلِسَان فعله، وَلَا يعظك بِلِسَان قَوْله.

Fāris al-Baghdādī reported upon the authority of Yūsuf ibn al-Ḥusayn, "I said to Dhū al-Nūn as I left him, 'Whom should I frequent?' He replied, 'It is upon you to make as your companion the one who will remind you of Allāh ﷻ just through looking at him. The one whose religiosity moves you from deep within, conversations with him increase you in knowledge, his deeds make you tread through this earth as an ascetic, and you will not infringe against Allāh ﷻ whilst you are in his proximity. He is the one who exhorts you through his actions and not through his words.'

وَسمعت ذَا النُّون يَقُول: سقم الْجَسَد فِي الأوجاع، وسقم الْقُلُوب فِي الذُّنُوب، فَكَمَا لَا يجد الْجَسَد لَذَّة الطَّعَام عِنْد سقم، كَذَلِك لَا يجد الْقلب حلاوة الْعِبَادَة مَعَ الذُّنُوب.

I also heard Dhū al-Nūn saying, 'The body ails with pain and the heart ails through sin. So just as the body does not attain the pleasure of food during an ailment, the heart does not attain the sweetness of worship in the presence of sin.'

وسمعته يَقُول: من لم يعرف قدر النعم سلبها من حَيْثُ لَا يعلم.

I also heard him saying, 'The one who does not comprehend the true extent of Allāh's blessings will have it taken away in a manner which he cannot foresee.'"

[١١٤] قَالَ ابْن باكويه: وَسمعت بكران بن أَحْمد يَقُول: سَمِعت يُوسُف بن الْحُسَيْن يَقُول: سَمِعت ذَا النُّون يَقُول: مَا خلع اللَّهِ عز وَجل على عبد من عبيده خلعة أحسن من الْعقل، وَلَا قَلّدهُ قلادة أجمل من الْعلم، وَلَا زينه بزينة أفضل من الْحلم وَكَمَال ذَلِك كُله: التَّقْوَى.

Bakrān ibn Aḥmad reported upon the authority of Yūsuf ibn al-Ḥusayn, 'I heard Dhū al-Nūn say, 'Allāh ﷻ has not rewarded his slaves with a robe greater than the intellect, a necklace more beautiful than knowledge, nor an ornament superior to prudence. The perfect result of their combination is *taqwā* (God-consciousness).'"

[١١٥] أخبرنَا المحمدان ابْن نَاصِر وَابْن عبد الْبَاقِي قَالَ: أَنا حمد بن أَحْمد قَالَ ثَنَا أَبُو نعيم الْحَافِظ قَالَ ثَنَا أبي قَالَ ثَنَا أَحْمد بن مُحَمَّد بن مصقلة قَالَ ثَنَا سعيد بن عُثْمَان قَالَ: سَمِعت ذان النُّون يَقُول: من ذبح حنجرة الطمع بِسيف الْيَأْس، وردم خَنْدَق الْحِرْص ظفر بكيمياء الْخدمَة، وَمن استقى بِحَبل الزّهْد على دلو الْعُرُوق استقى من جب الْحِكْمَة، وَمن سلك أَودِيَة الكمد جنى حَيَاة الْأَبَد، وَمن حصد عشب الذُّنُوب بمنجل الْوَرع، أَضَاءَت لَهُ رَوْضَة الاسْتقَامَة، وَمن قطع لِسَانه بشفرة الصمت، وجد عذوبة الرَّاحَة، وَمن تدرع درع الصدْق، قوي على مجاهدة عَسْكَر الْبَاطِل، وَمن فَرح بمدحة الْجَاهِل ألبسهُ الشَّيْطَان ثوب الحماقة.

Aḥmad ibn Muḥammad ibn Maṣqalah reported upon the authority of Saʿīd ibn ʿUthmān, "I heard Dhū al-Nūn say, 'Whomsoever slits the throat of avarice with the sword of abstinence and fills with [soil] the trench of attachment [to the worldly,] he will gain the pleasure of servitude. He who seeks water with the rope of asceticism attached to the pail of good deeds will drink from the well of wisdom. He whom treads through the valleys of despondency will surely gain the everlasting life. The one who cuts down the grass of sins with the sickle of devoutness will have the gardens of uprightness illuminated for him. He who cuts his tongue with the blade of silence will gain the pleasantness of bliss. He who armours himself with truthfulness will find strength when combating the army of falsehood. However, he who becomes happy due to the praise of the ignorant will be clothed by the Devil in the garment of the fool.'"

[١١٦] أخبرنَا عمر بن ظفر قَالَ أنبأ جَعْفَر بن أَحْمد السراج قَالَ: أنبأ عبد الْعَزِيز بن عَليّ الْأَزجيّ قَالَ أَنا ابْن جَهْضَم قَالَ ثَنَا أَحْمد بن مُحَمَّد بن عِيسَى قَالَ حَدثنِي يُوسُف بن الْحُسَيْن قَالَ: قَالَ الْفَتْح بن شحرف: دخلت على ذِي النُّون عِنْد مَوته فَقلت لَهُ: كَيفَ تجدك؟ فَقَالَ:

Yūsuf ibn al-Ḥusayn reported that al-Fatḥ ibn Shaḥraf said, "I entered the presence of Dhū al-Nūn whilst he was in the throes of death, and I said to him, 'How do you feel?' He replied by saying:

أَمُوت وَمَا مَاتَت إِلَيْك صبابتي   وَلَا رويت من صدق حبك أوطاري
مناي المنى كل المنى أَنْت لي منى   رَأَيْت الْغنى كل الْغنى عِنْد إقتاري
وَأَنت مدى سؤلي وَغَايَة رغبتي   وَمَوْضِع آمالي ومكنون إضماري
تضمن قلبِي مِنْك مَالك قد بدا   وَإِن طَال سري فِيك أَو طَال إظهاري
وَبَين ضلوعي مِنْك مَا لَا أبثه   وَلم أَبد بادية لأهل وَلَا جَار
سرائر لَا يخفى عَلَيْك خفيها   وَإِن لم أبح حَتَّى التنادي بأسراري
فَهَب لي نسيما مِنْك أحيى بِقُرْبِهِ   وجد لي بيسر مِنْك يطرد إعساري
أنرت الْهدى للمهتدين وَلم يكن   من الْعلم فِي أَيْديهم عشر معشار
وعلمتهم علما فبانوا بنوره   وَبَانَتْ لَهُم مِنْهُ معالم أسرار
مُعَاينَة للغيب حَتَّى كَأَنَّهَا لما   غَابَ عَنْهَا مِنْهُ حَاضِرَة الدَّار
وأخبارهم محجوبة وَقُلُوبهمْ تراك   بأوهام حديدات أبصار
جمعت لَهَا الْهم المفرق والتقى   وعَلى قدر والهم يجْرِي بِمِقْدَار
أَلَسْت دَلِيل الركب إِن هم تحيروا   وعصمة من أَمْسَى على جرف هار

I am dying but my intense love for you (referring to Allāh) will not pass away, and my thirst for truthful love for you will not be quenched nor will my hastiness.

Towards indulging in my desires, all of which [revolve around] you, I experienced sufficiency in all aspects when I was in need.

You are the utmost that I seek and the end point of my desires, and the focus of my hope, the protector of my secrets.

My heart is certain of you, what you have manifested.

Between my ribs there are [feelings] for You which I do not reveal, and of which I never showed a hint, even to my family and neighbours.

My secrets are not hidden to you, though I do not make these known, let alone announce them.

So bestow upon me your breeze which breathes life into me when it draws close, and provide me with ease from you to repulse my hardships.

You have illuminated [the path to] guidance for the guided though they, did not possess from knowledge even one hundredth of it.

You provided them with knowledge and they were directed by its light, and through this they became aware of deep, intricate matters.

[They pierced] the meanings of the unknown to the extent that it was as if, the unknown was something present in a house.

Their information was limited but their hearts saw you, mentally yet like [they saw you through] ironclad vision.

And You gathered within it scattered grief,

According to decree and grief is in accordance to that which is decreed.

Are you not the guide of the riders when they are confused and lost? And the safeguard of whoever is standing on the edge of a bank."

قَالَ الْفَتْح بن شحرف: فَلَمَّا ثقل قلت لَهُ: كَيفَ تجدك؟ فَقَالَ:

Al-Fatḥ ibn Shaḥraf continued, "And when it became heavy upon him, I asked him, 'How are you finding it?' He replied,

وَمَا لي سوى الإطراق والصمت حِيلَة　　　ووضعي على خدي يَدي عِنْد تذكاري

وَإِن طرقتني عِبْرَة بعد عِبْرَة تجرعتها　　　حَتَّى إِذا عيل تصباري

أفضت دموعا جمة مستهلة أطفي　　　بهَا حرا تضمن أسراري

فيا مُنْتَهى سؤل المحبين كلهم　　　أبحني مَحل الْأنس مَعَ كل زوار

وَلست أُبَالِي فائتا بعد فَائت   إِذا كنت فِي الدَّارِيْنِ يَا واحدي جَار

There is nothing I can do except to hold my tongue and fall in silence, and place my cheek on my hand when I remember You.

If a tear rushed into my eyes, one after another I would withhold, until I could no longer hold them back.

My tears then flood out with which I cool down, the heat of the hidden feelings I have.

O You who is the ultimate hope of all devotees, grant me the joy of Your company with all visitors.

I then would never care about anything, if you will be my Lord, my neighbour in this life and next.

قَالَ المُصَنّف: أَسْند ذُو النُّون أَحَادِيث كَثِيرَة عَن مَالك وَاللَّيْث بن سعد وسُفْيَان بن عُيَيْنَة والفضيل بن عِيَاض وَغيرهم وَتُوفِّي بالجيزة، وَحمل فِي مركب إِلَى الْفسْطَاط خوفًا من زحمة النَّاس على الجسر، وَدفن فِي مَقَابِر أهل المعافر فِي ذِي الْقعدَة من سنة سِتّ وَأَرْبَعين وَمِائَتَيْنِ.

The author says: Dhū al-Nūn reported many *aḥādīth* upon the authority of Mālik, Layth ibn Sa'd, Sufyān ibn 'Uyaynah, al-Fuḍayl ibn 'Iyāḍ and others. He passed away in Giza, and he was transported upon a ride to a large canopy in fear of the extent of crowding by the people upon the bridge. He was buried within the graveyard of the people of Ma'āfir in Dhū al-Qi'dah of the year 146.

أَبُو الْخَيْر التيناتي

Abū al-Khayr al-Tīnātī[73]

سكن التينات وَهِي قَرْيَة من قرى أنطاكية، وَيُقَال لَهُ: الأقطع لِأَنَّهُ كَانَ مَقْطُوع الْيَد، وَكَانَ سَبَب ذَلِك أَنه كَانَ فِي جبال أنطاكية يطْلب الْمُبَاح وينام فِي الْجبَال،

73 His biography is in *Siyar al-A'lām al-Nubalā* (16/22).

وَأَنه عَاهَدَ اللَّهِ أَن لَا يَأْكُل من ثَمَر الْجبَال شَيْئا، إِلَّا مَا طرحته الرّيح، فَبَقِيَ أَيَّامًا لم تطرح الرّيح إِلَيْهِ شَيْئا، فَرَأى يَوْمًا شَجَرَة كمثرى، فاشتهى مِنْهَا، فَلم يفعل، فأمالتها الرّيح إِلَيْهِ، فَأخذ وَاحِدَة وَاتفقَ أَن لصوصا قطعُوا هُنَالك الطَّرِيق، وجلسوا يقتسمون، فَوَقع عَلَيْهِم السُّلْطَان فَأَخذهُم وَأخذ مَعَهم فَقطعت أَيْديهم وأرجلهم، وَقطعت يَده فَلَمَّا هموا بِقطع رجله عرفه رجل فَقَالَ للأمير: أهلكت نَفسك، هَذَا أَبُو الْخَيْر، فَبكى الْأَمِير، وَسَأَلَهُ أَن يَجعله فِي حل فَفعل، وَقَالَ: أَنا أعرف ذَنبي.

He resided in al-Taynāt, a village in Antioch. He was nicknamed as al-Aqtaʿ due to him having a severed hand. The reason for this was that he was in a mountainous region of Antioch seeking permissible [sustenance,] and he was sleeping there. He took an oath by Allāh that he would not eat any of the fruits of the mountain except that which fell due to the wind. He remained there for days without the wind blowing to him anything at all. Then a day came where he saw a pear tree from which he craved to eat, but he did not act upon this craving. The wind then blew it towards him, and he picked one of the pears. It so happened that a group of thieves had crossed this route and were sitting and dividing [their spoils.] The Sultān caught up to them and apprehended them, taking Abū al-Khayr with them. A hand and foot from each of them was amputated. Abū al-Khayr's hand was amputated, and when his foot was about to be amputated a man recognised him and said to the leader, 'Do you wish to ruin yourself? This is Abū al-Khayr.' The leader wept at hearing this, and he asked for his forgiveness and so he forgave him, and then he said, 'I am cognisant of my sin [which led to the amputation.]'"

[١١٧] أخبرنَا ابْن نَاصِر قَالَ أنبأنَا أَبُو بكر بن خلف قَالَ أنبأ أَبُو عبد الرَّحْمَن السّلمِيّ قَالَ: سَمِعت مَنْصُور بن عبد اللَّهِ يَقُول: قَالَ أَبُو الْخَيْر: الدَّعْوَى رعونة لَا يحْتَمل الْقلب إمْسَاكهَا فيلقها إِلَى اللِّسَان، فتَنْطِق بهَا أَلْسِنَة الحمقى.

Abū ʿAbd al-Raḥmān al-Sulamī reported upon the authority of Manṣūr ibn ʿAbdullāh, "Abū al-Khayr said, 'Frivolous words are too much for the heart to hold so it moves them to the tongue, and then they are expressed by the tongues of the fools.'"

قَالَ: وسمعته يَقُول: دخلت مَدِينَة الرَّسُول [- صَلَّى اللَّهُ عَلَيْهِ وَسَلَّمَ -] وَأَنا بفاقة فأقمت خَمْسَة أَيَّام مَا ذقت ذواقا، فتقدمت إِلَى الْقَبْر، فَسلمت على النَّبِي - صَلَّى اللَّهُ عَلَيْهِ وَسَلَّمَ - وَعَلى أبي بكر وَعمر، وَقلت: أَنا ضيفك اللَّيْلَة يَا رَسُول اللَّهِ، وتنحيت فَنمت خلف الْمِنْبَر، فَرَأَيْت فِي الْمَنَام النَّبِي - صَلَّى اللَّهُ عَلَيْهِ وَسَلَّمَ - وَأَبُو بكر عَن يَمِينه وَعمر عَن شِمَاله، وَعلي بن أبي طَالب بَين يَدَيْهِ، فحركني عَليّ، وَقَالَ: قُم، قد جَاءَ رَسُول الله [- صَلَّى اللَّهُ عَلَيْهِ وَسَلَّمَ -] فَقُمْت إِلَيْهِ وَقبلت بَين عَيْنَيْهِ، فَدفع إِلَيّ رغيفان فَأكلت نصفه، وانتبهت، وَإِذا فِي يَدي نصف رغيف.

He said, "I also heard him say, 'I entered Madīnat al-Rasūl ﷺ (Madīnah) and I was destitute. I resided there for five days without tasting any food. I went to the grave and greeted the Prophet ﷺ and Abī Bakr and 'Umar. I then said, 'I am your guest tonight, O Messenger of Allāh.' So, I lay upon a side and slept behind the *minbar*. Whilst sleeping I saw the Prophet ﷺ in a dream; Abū Bakr was to his right, 'Umar was to his left and 'Alī ibn Abī Ṭālib was at his front. 'Alī ibn Abī Ṭālib moved me and said, 'Stand, for the Messenger of Allāh ﷺ has come.' So, I stood and went to him, and I kissed him [on the forehead] between his eyes. He provided me with a loaf, I ate half and then awoke, finding within my hand half a loaf.'"

[١١٨] أخبرنَا أَبُو بكر العامري قَالَ أنبأ ابْن أبي صَادِق قَالَ ثَنَا ابْن باكويه قَالَ: سَمِعت إِبْرَاهِيم بن مُحَمَّد المراغي يَقُول: سَمِعت أَبَا الْخَيْر التيناتي يَقُول: بقيت بِمَكَّة سنة فَأَصَابَنِي ضرّ وفاقة فَكلما أردْت أَن أخرج إِلَى الْمَسْأَلَة هتف بِي هَاتِف يَقُول: الْوَجْه الَّذِي تسْجد لي بِهِ تبذله لغيري؟

Ibn Bākawayh reported upon the authority of Ibrāhīm ibn Muḥammad al-Marāghī, "I heard Abū al-Khayr al-Tīnātī saying, 'I resided in Makkah for a year and endured therein hardship and poverty. And whenever I wished to leave to deal with my issue, I would hear a voice stating, 'Would you turn the forehead with which you prostrate to Me towards another besides me?'"

[١١٩] أخبرنَا المحمدان ابْن نَاصِر وَابْن عبد الْبَاقِي قَالَا أنبأ أَحْمد بن الْحسن بن خيرون قَالَ: قَرَأت على أبي الْحُسَيْن عَليّ بن مَحْمُود الصُّوفِي أخْبركُم عَليّ بن الْمثنى قَالَ: سَمِعت أَبَا الْخَيْر يَقُول: مَا بلغ أحد إِلَى حَالَة شريفة إِلَّا بملازمة الْمُوَافقَة، ومعانقة الْأَدَب وَأَدَاء الْفَرَائِض، وصحبة الصَّالِحين، وخدمة الْفُقَرَاء الصَّالِحين.

Abū al-Ḥusayn 'Alī ibn Maḥmūd al-Ṣūfī reported upon the authority of 'Alī ibn Muthannā, "I heard Abū al-Khayr say, 'One does not attain the station of nobility except through compliance [with the Sunnah,] observing the religious mandates, accompanying the pious and serving the needy and the righteous.'"

[١٢٠] أخبرنَا ابْن حبيب قَالَ أنبأ ابْن أبي صَادِق قَالَ أنبأ أَبُو عبد الله الشِّيرَازِيّ قَالَ: سَمِعت عبد الْوَاحِد بن بكر يَقُول: سَمِعت مُحَمَّد بن الْفضل يَقُول: خرجت من أنطاكية، وَدخلت تينات، وَدخلت على أبي الْخَيْر الأقطع على غَفلَة مِنْهُ بِغَيْر إذن، فَإِذا هُوَ ينسج ربيلا بيدَيْهِ، فتعجبت، فَنظر إِلَيّ وَقَالَ: يَا عَدو نَفسه، مَا الَّذِي حملك على هَذَا؟ فَقلت: هيجان الوجد لما بِي من الشوق إِلَيْك، فَضَحِك، ثمَّ قَالَ لي: اقعد، لَا تعد فِي شَيْء من هَذَا بعد الْيَوْم، ثمَّ قَالَ: اسْتُرْ عَليّ فِي حَيَاتِي. فَفعلت.

'Abd al-Wāḥid ibn Bakr reported upon the authority of Muḥammad ibn al-Faḍl, "I left Antioch and entered Taynāt. I entered the presence of Abū al-Khayr al-Aqtā' unexpectedly, and without his permission. I saw him sewing with his hands, and I became surprised at this. He saw me and said, 'O enemy of your self, what made you do this?' I replied, 'I was moved to do so by the affection I have for you.' He laughed and said to me, 'Sit, but do not do such a thing after today.' Then he said, 'Conceal what you have seen for as long as I am alive.' And so I obliged.'"

قَالَ الشِّيرَازِيّ: وَسمعت إِبْرَاهِيم بن مُحَمَّد السباك يَقُول: كُنَّا نطلع على أبي الْخَيْر التيناتي من الخوخة وَهُوَ يشق الخوص بِيَدِهِ فَإِذا خرج رَأَيْنَاهُ أقطع.

Al-Shīrāzī reported upon the authority of Ibrāhīm ibn Muḥammad al-Sabbāk, "We used to watch Abū al-Khayr al-Tīnātī through a small opening and he would be sewing with his hand but when he would come out we would see it still amputated."

[١٢١] أخبرنَا أَبُو الْقَاسِم الْجريرِي قَالَ أنبأ أَبُو طَالب العشاري قَالَ ثَنَا مبادر بن عبد اللَّهِ الرقي قَالَ: سَمِعت أَبَا بكر الْمصْرِيّ يَقُول: سَمِعت فَقِيرا من أَصْحَابنَا يعرف بِالْأَنْصَارِيِّ يَقُول: دخلت على أبي الْخَيْر فناولني تفاحتين فجعلتها فِي جيبي، وَقلت: لَا أتناولهما وأتبرك بهما لموْضِع الشَّيْخ عِنْدِي، فَكَانَت تجْرِي عَليّ فاقات لَا أتناولهما، فأجهدتني الْفَاقَة، فأخرجت وَاحِدَة فَأَكَلتهَا، وأدخلت يَدي لأخرج الثَّانِيَة، فَإِذا التفاحتان مكانهما فَمَا زلت آكل مِنْهُمَا حَتَّى دخلت الْموصل، فجزت على خراب، فَإِذا بعليل يُنَادي من الخراب: يَا نَاس، أشتهي تفاحة، وَلم يكن وَقت التفاح، فأخرجت التفاحتين، فناولتهما إِيَّاه فَأكل، وَخرجت روحه، فَعلمت أَن الشَّيْخ أَعْطَانِي من أجل ذَلِك العليل.

Abū Bakr al-Miṣrī said, "I heard a poor man from amongst us known as al-Anṣārī saying, 'I entered the presence of Abū al-Khayr and he gave me two apples, placing them in my pocket. I said, 'I will not eat them, rather I will keep them and enjoy the blessings of his apples as I hold him in high esteem. I suffered greatly from poverty at the time but I endeavoured not to eat them. I placed great exertion into this until I finally capitulated and took one out to eat. I then put my hand in to take the second one and found two apples there. I remained eating them until I reached Mosul. I passed by a ruined building from which an ill man called, 'O people, I desire apples and it is not the season for apples.' I took out the two apples and gave them to him.

He ate them and his soul left him thereafter. I thus came to the realisation that the *shaykh* gave me them due to this ill individual.'"

[١٢٢] أَنبأَنَا ابْن نَاصِر قَالَ أَنبأَنَا جَعْفَر بن أَحْمد قَالَ أنبأ عبد الْعَزِيز بن عَليّ قَالَ أَنا ابْن جَهْضَم قَالَ: ثَنَا بكير بن مُحَمَّد قَالَ: كنت عِنْد أبي الْخَيْر فِي جمَاعَة فتذاكروا الكرامات، فَقَالَ: كم تَقولُونَ فلَان مَشى إِلَى مَكَّة فِي لَيْلَة، أَنا أعرف عبدا حَبَشِيًّا كَانَ جَالِسا فِي جَامع أطرابلس وَرَأسه فِي جنب مرقعته فخطر لَهُ ظَبْيَة الْحرم، فَقَالَ فِي سره: يَا لَيْتَني كنت بِالْحرم، ثمَّ أمسك، فتغامز الْجَمَاعَة، وَأَجْمعُوا على أَنه ذَلِك الرجل.

Ibn Jahḍam reported upon the authority of Bukayr ibn Muḥammad, "I was with Abū al-Khayr amongst a group, and they were making mention of miracles. He said, 'Many have made mention of so-and-so walking to Makkah in a night. [However,] I know of an Abyssinian slave who was sitting within the *Jāmiʿ Masjid* of Aṭarāblūs. His head was lying upon his rags and the goats of the Ḥaram (i.e. the holy sanctuary of Makkah) crossed his mind, so he said in his heart, 'I wish I was at the Ḥaram.' At this point he stopped narrating the story. The congregation indicated to each other with their eyes and concurred that he (Abū al-Khayr) was that man."

توفّي أَبُو الْخَيْر بعد الْأَرْبَعين وثلاثمائة.

Abū al-Khayr passed away after [the year] 340.

مقبل الأسود
Muqbil al-Aswad

أَنبأَنَا يحيى بن الْحسن بن الْبَنَّا قَالَ أَنبأَنَا القَاضِي أَبُو يعلى مُحَمَّد بن الْحُسَيْن قَالَ: حكى لنا أَبُو بكر أَحْمد بن إِسْحَاق بن سكينَة الْأَزجيّ عَن أبي الْحسن

بن خيرون صَاحب أبي بكر عبد الْعَزِيز قَالَ: قَالَ لي أَبُو بكر عبد الْعَزِيز: كنت مَعَ أستاذي يَعْنِي أَبَا بكر الْخلال وَأَنا غُلَام مشتد فَاجْتمع جمَاعَة يتذاكرون بعد عشاء الْآخِرَة، فَقَالَ بَعضهم لبَعض: أَلَيْسَ مقبل - يعنون رجلا أسود كَانَ ناظورا بِبَاب حَرْب - لنا مُدَّة مَا رَأَيْنَاهُ؟ فَقَامُوا يقصدونه، وَقَالَ لي أستاذي - يَعْنِي الْخلال -: لَا تَبْرَح، احفظ الْبَاب. فتركتهم حَتَّى مضوا وأغلقت الْبَاب وتبعتهم. فَلَمَّا بلغنَا بعض الطَّرِيق، قَالَ: هُوَ ذَا أرى وَرَاءَنَا شخصا، فوقفوا، فَقَالُوا لي: من أَنْت؟ فَأَمْسَكت فَزعًا من أستاذي، فَقَالَ أحدهم لأستاذي: بِاللَّه عَلَيْك إِلَّا تركته فتركني ومضيت مَعَهم.

Abū Bakr Aḥmad ibn Isḥāq ibn Sakīnah al-Azajī reported upon the authority of Abū al-Ḥasan ibn Khayrūn, the companion of Abū Bakr 'Abd al-'Azīz, "Abū Bakr 'Abd al-'Azīz stated to me, 'I was with my teacher—i.e. Abū Bakr al-Khallāl—whilst I was a growing youth. A group gathered after *'ishā* to talk about the Hereafter. Then they said to each other, 'We have not seen Muqbil, i.e. the black man who works as a guard, for a lengthy period.' They then stood and sought after him, and my teacher—i.e. al-Khallāl—said to me, 'Do not leave, rather guard the door.' I waited until they had traversed a fair distance and then I locked the door and followed them. When we reached a certain pathway, he said, 'He is there... I can see an individual behind us.' They came to a halt and said to me, 'Who are you?' I remained quiet due to fear of my teacher. One of them said to him, 'By Allāh, can you leave him?' So, he let me be, and I went with them.

فَدَخَلْنَا إِلَى قراح فِيهِ باذنجان، وَالْأسود قَائِم يُصَلِّي، فَسَلمُوا وجلسوا إِلَى أَن سلم، وَأخرج كيسا فِيهِ كسر يابسة وملح جريش، وَقَالَ: كلوا، فَأَكَلُوا وتحدثوا وَأخذُوا يذكرُونَ كرامات الْأَوْلِيَاء وَهُوَ سَاكِت، فَقَالَ وَاحِد من الْجَمَاعَة: يَا مقبل، قد زرناك فَمَا حَدَّثتنَا بِشَيْء فَقَالَ: أَي شَيْء أَنا، وَأي شَيْء عِنْدِي أحدثك، أَنا أعرف رجلا لَو سَأَلَ اللَّهِ تَعَالَى أَن يَجْعَل هَذَا القراح الباذنجان ذَهَبا لفعل، فَوَاللَّه مَا

استتم الْكَلَام حَتَّى رَأَيْت القراح يتقد ذَهبا، فَقَالَ لَهُ أستاذي - يَعْنِي الْخلال -: يَا مقبل: [هَل] لأحد سَبِيل أَن يَأْخُذ من هَذَا القراح أصلا وَاحِدًا؟ فَقَالَ: خُذ، وَكَانَ القراح مستنبتا، فَأخذ أستاذي الأَصْل فقلعه بعروقه وَجَمِيع مَا فِيهِ ذهب فَوَقَعت من الأَصْل باذنجانة صَغِيرَة وَشَيْء من الْوَرق فَأَخَذته، وبقاياه معي إِلَى يومي. قَالَ: ثمَّ صلى رَكْعَتَيْنِ وَسَأَلَ اللَّهِ تَعَالَى فَعَاد القراح كَمَا كَانَ، وَعَاد مَكَانَهُ ذَلِك الأَصْل أصل باذنجان آخر.

We then entered a plantation within which were aubergines, and a black man was therein standing in prayer. They gave the *salām* and then sat until he completed the prayer. [After he finished,] he brought out a bag within which was dry pieces of bread and ground salt, and then he stated, 'Eat.' They thus ate and recounted the miracles of the *Awliyā*, and the man remained silent. One individual from the group said, 'O Muqbil, we came to visit you yet you have not said anything to us.' He replied, 'Whom am I [to speak,] and I do not have anything to mention except that I know of a man who if he would ask Allāh ﷻ to turn this plantation of aubergine into gold, it would happen.' By Allāh, he had barely finished speaking when I saw the aubergine turning into gold. My teacher—i.e. al-Khallāl—said to him, 'O Muqbil, is there permission for one to take from it?' He replied, 'Take [from it.]' The aubergine was still in the soil and so my teacher pulled it out of the soil with all of its roots, and found that everything within it was gold. A small aubergine and some leaves fell off it, which I picked up and some of which remain with me today.' He continued, 'He then prayed two units and asked Allāh to return the plantation to its original state. Then the place of that root reverted to that of an aubergine.'"

حامد الأسود

Ḥāmid al-Aswad

كَانَ زوج أُخْت إِبْرَاهِيم الْخَواص، وَكَانَ صَالحا، وَكَانَ سَافر مَعَ الْخَواص على

التَّوَكُّل.

He was married to the sister of Ibrāhīm al-Khawāṣ. He was a pious man and would travel with al-Khawāṣ whilst relying upon Allāh (i.e. for provisions etc.).

أَبُو حَمَّاد الْأسود
Abū Ḥammād al-Aswad

[١٢٤] أنبأَنَا مُحَمَّد بن نَاصِر قَالَ أَنبأَنَا جَعْفَر بن أَحْمد السراج قَالَ أَبُو حَمَّاد الْأسود وَيعرف بالزنجي من أستاذي أبي الْحُسَيْن الرُّوذَبَارِي ذكر عَنهُ عَليّ بن مُحَمَّد المزين أَنه جلس فِي الْمَسْجِد الْحَرَام بحذاء الْكَعْبَة ثَلَاثِينَ سنة لَا يخرج إِلَّا لطهارة الصَّلَاة وَمَا رُؤِيَ أكل وَلَا شرب.

Muḥammad ibn Nāsīr reported upon the authority of Ja'far ibn Aḥmad al-Sarrāj that 'Alī ibn Muḥammad al-Muzayyin said regarding Abū Ḥammād al-Aswad—known as al-Zanjī,— "He spent thirty years in front of the Ka'bah at Masjid al-Ḥarām. He would not leave there except to purify himself for the prayer and he was not seen eating or drinking."

وَقَالَ أَبُو الْحسن المزين: كَانَ أَبُو حَمَّاد إِذا تُوجد يبيض، وَإِذا ذهب، وَجهه يسود.

It was also said by Abū al-Ḥasan al-Muzayyin, 'Abū Ḥammād would turn white when he attained *wajd* (spiritual ecstasy) and when it would subside, he would return to his original colour.'"

صُهَيْب الْأسود
Ṣuhayb al-Aswad

[١٢٥] أَنبأَنَا عَليّ بن عبيد اللَّهِ عَن أبي الْحُسَيْن بن الْمُهْتَدي عَن أبي حَفْص ابْن شاهين قَالَ: نَا عمر بن الْحسن قَالَ ثَنَا عبد اللَّهِ بن سيف قَالَ حَدثنِي مُحَمَّد بن الْحُسَيْن قَالَ حَدثنِي ابْن أبي بكر الْمقدمِي قَالَ نَا جَعْفَر الضبعِي عتن مَالك بن دِينَار قَالَ: كَانَ بِمَكَّة عبد أسود يُقَال لَهُ صُهَيْب فَكَانَت مولاته تقول لَهُ: يَا صُهَيْب قد أفسدت نَفسك عَليّ؛ أما النَّهَار فصائم، وَأما اللَّيْل فَأَنت قَائِم. قَالَ: يَقُول: يَا مولاتي إِذا ذكرت النَّار طَار نومي، وَإِذا ذكرت الْجنَّة اشْتَدَّ شوقي.

Jaʿfar al-Dubaʿī reported upon the authority of Mālik ibn Dīnār, "There was a black man within Makkah who was called Ṣuhayb. His mistress would say to him, 'O Ṣuhayb you have made yourself of no use for me, as during the day you fast and you spend your nights standing in prayer.'" He continued, "He would reply to her, 'When I remember the Fire my sleep flutters away and when I remember the Paradise my motivation for it intensifies.'"

فصل
Section

فَأَما من لم نَعْرِف اسْمه من عباد الْقَوْم وزهادهم
The worshippers and ascetics from amongst them whose names are not known

فَمنهمْ:

From them:

عابِد من أهل الْمَدِينَة
A worshipper from the people of Madīnah

[١٢٦] أَنبأَنَا أَبُو الْقَاسِم هبة اللَّهِ بن أَحْمد الحريري قَالَ أَنبأَنَا أَبُو طَالب مُحَمَّد

بن عَليّ العشاري قَالَ أنبأَنَا يُوسُف بن عمر القواس إجَازَة قَالَ أنبأ أَبُو الْفضل الْخُرَاسَانِي قَالَ نَا سعيد بن عُثْمَان قَالَ نَا مُحَمَّد بن يحيى الْكِنْدِيّ قَالَ نَا الْحُسَيْن بن مُحَمَّد الْمروزِي عَن أبي عبد ربه عَن مُوسَى بن حابَان عَن أنس ابْن مَالك قَالَ: شهِدت عمر بن الْخطاب وجاءه مَمْلُوك أسود فَقَالَ: يَا أَمِير الْمُؤمنِينَ، أَلَيْسَ اللَّهِ عز وَجل يَقُول: ﴿**إِنَّمَا الْمُؤْمِنُونَ إِخْوَة**﴾ ، قَالَ: بلَى. قَالَ: فَإِنِّي أَخُوك، فَقُمْ معي لحَاجَة لتعينني عَلَيْهَا، فَوَثَبَ عمر فَوضع يَده فِي يَد الْأسود، فَانْطَلق بِهِ إِلَى خص لَهُ بِالبَقِيعِ، فَقَالَ: يَا أَمِير الْمُؤمنِينَ، أما خشيت اللَّهِ عز وَجل أَن تأوي إِلَى ظلّ، وَأَنا فِي سملة بالية قذرة أتزر بِبَعْضِهَا وأفترش بَعْضهَا، وَالَّذِي بعث مُحَمَّدًا بِالْحَقِّ لَا أحللتك حَتَّى أتعلق بك يَوْم الْقِيَامَة، فَيَأْخُذ لي مِنْك الْحق بِمَا أغفلتني.

Mūsā ibn Ḥābān reported upon the authority of Anas ibn Mālik, "I saw 'Umar ibn al-Khaṭṭāb on an occasion when a black slave came to him and said, 'O Commander of the Faithful, did not Allāh ﷻ state: **{The believers are naught but brothers.}**'[74] He replied, 'Certainly, yes.' The man said, 'As I am your brother, come with me and help me with a need of mine.' 'Umar sprung up, placed his hand within the hand of the black man and went to a hut he had in al-Baqīʿ. The man said, 'O Commander of the Faithful, are you not fearful of Allāh that your abode is sheltered whilst I am here in a damp, dilapidated and filthy condition, [using some of the rags] to cover myself and some to sleep upon. By the One who sent Muḥammad with the truth, I will not exonerate you from this until the Day of Judgement unless I receive from you my rights which have been denied to me.'

فَصَرَخَ عمر، وَوضع التُّرَاب على رَأسه، وَجعل يَقُول: واعمراه، ثكلت عمر أمه، يَا أسود الْعَفو. فَبكى الْأسود وَقَالَ: قد غفرت لَك فَأمر لَهُ عمر بكسوة وَنَفَقَة، فَقَالَ: أما الْكسْوَة فأقبلها مِنْك، وَأما النَّفَقَة فَلَا حَاجَة لي فِيهَا، فَقَالَ لَهُ عمر: وَلم؟ قَالَ:

74 Al-Ḥujarāt: 10

أَخَاف إِن أَمْسَكت الدَّرَاهِم أَن أفتتن بحبها، فودعه عمر، ثمَّ جهد بعد ذَلِك فِي طلبه وَسَأَلَ عَنهُ، فَلم يدر أَيْن سلك.

'Umar cried out at this, placed earth upon his head and lamented, "May the mother of 'Umar be deprived of him, O black man please forgive me.' The black man then wept and said, 'I have forgiven you.' 'Umar then ordered him to be given clothing and money. At this the man said, 'As for the clothing you offer, I accept it from you, however I have no need for the money.' 'Umar replied, 'Why so?' He said, 'I fear that if I take these *dirhams*, I will be tested by infatuation with them.' 'Umar left him after this. He later sought to find him and enquired regarding him, however he was not able to ascertain where he had gone."

عَابِد آخر مدنِي
Another worshipper from Madīnah

[١٢٧] أخبرنَا مُحَمَّد بن نَاصِر الْحَافِظ قَالَ أنبأنَا جَعْفَر بن أَحْمد بن السراج قَالَ أنبأ أَبُو الْقَاسِم عبيد اللَّهِ بن عمر بن شاهين قَالَ نَا أبي قَالَ ثَنَا أَحْمد بن سعد بن إِبْرَاهِيم الزُّهْرِيّ قَالَ نَا عبيد اللَّهِ بن عمر قَالَ نَا صَالح بن سُلَيْمَان عَن مُحَمَّد بن الْمُنْكَدر قَالَ: كَانَت لي سَارِيَة فِي مَسْجِد رَسُول اللَّهِ - صَلَّى اللَّهُ عَلَيْهِ وَسَلَّمَ -، ثمَّ جِئْت فتساندت إِلَى ساريتي فجَاء رجل أسود تعلوه صفرَة متزر بكساء وعَلى رقبته كسَاء أَصْغَر مِنْهُ، فتقدم إِلَى السارية الَّتِي بَين يَدي. فكنت خَلفه، فَقَامَ فصلى رَكْعَتَيْنِ، ثمَّ جلس فَقَالَ: أَي رب خرج أهل حرم بَيْتك يستسقون فَلم تسقهم، فَأَنا أقسم عَلَيْك لما سقيتهم. قَالَ ابْن الْمُنْكَدر: فَمَا وضع يَده حَتَّى سَمِعت الرَّعْد، ثمَّ جَاءَت السَّمَاء بِشَيْء من الْمَطَر أهمني الرُّجُوع إِلَى أَهلِي، فَلَمَّا سمع الْمَطَر حمد اللَّهِ محامدا لم أسمع بِمِثْلِهَا قطّ.

Ṣāliḥ ibn Sulaymān reported upon the authority of Muḥammad ibn al-Munkadir, "I had a pillar of my own in the *masjid* of the Messenger of Allāh ﷺ. I leant upon it on one occasion when a black man came, he had yellowness in his skin tone, and was wearing a garment as an *izār* (lower garment) with another smaller garment around his neck. He moved towards the pillar which was in front of him, and I was subsequently situated behind him. He stood to pray two units of prayer and then he sat and said, 'O my Lord, the people of Your sacred house came out to seek rain and You did not give them it. I implore You to provide them with rain.'" Ibn al-Munkadir said, "He had not yet lowered his hands when I heard the sound of thunder. Thereafter some rain fell from the sky and it delayed my return to my family. When the man heard the rain, he praised Allāh in a manner which I have never seen the like of."

قَالَ: ثمَّ قَالَ: وَمن أَنا؟ وَمَا أَنا حَيْثُ اسْتُجِيبَ لي، وَلَكِن عذت بحَمْدك وعذت بطولك، ثمَّ قَامَ فتوشح بكسائه الَّذِي كَانَ متزرا بِهِ، وَألقى الكساء الآخر الَّذِي كَانَ على ظَهره فِي رجلَيْهِ، ثمَّ قَامَ فَلم يزل قَائِما يُصَلِّي حَتَّى إِذا أحس الصُّبْح سجد وأوتر، وَصلى رَكْعَتي الصُّبْح، ثمَّ أُقِيمَت صَلَاة الصُّبْح، فَدخل مَعَ النَّاس فِي الصَّلَاة وَدخلت مَعَه، فَلَمَّا سلم الإِمَام قَامَ فَخرج، وَخرجت خَلفه حَتَّى انْتهى إِلَى بَاب الْمَسْجِد، فَخرج يرفع ثَوْبه يَخُوض المَاء، فَخرجت خَلفه رَافعا ثوبي أخوض المَاء، فَلم أدر أَيْن ذهب.

He continued, "He then said, 'Who am I to receive an answer from Allāh, except that I sought refuge in Your praise and Your generosity.' Then he stood and covered his upper-body with the garment he had used as an *izār*, and he covered his legs with the garment which was previously upon his back. He then prayed continuously until he sensed that the time of the *fajr* prayer was about to enter, whereupon he performed the prostration and the *witr* (ending the night prayer upon an odd unit). Then he prayed the two [Sunnah] units of the morning prayer, after which the *iqāmah* (the second call to the prayer) for the morning prayer was given and he entered the prayer with the people and I did so as well. When the *imām* performed the *taslīm* he stood and left, I followed behind to the *masjid* door and he exited it whilst lifting his garment so as to wade through the water. I followed him in doing the same action and then I lost track of him.

فَلَمَّا كَانت اللَّيْلَة الثَّانِيَة صليت الْعشَاء فِي مَسْجِد رَسُول الله - صَلَّى اللَّهُ عَلَيْهِ وَسَلَّمَ - وَجئْت إِلَى ساريتي فتوسدت إِلَيْهَا، وَجَاء فَقَامَ فتوشح بكسائه وَألقى الكساء الآخر الَّذِي كَانَ على ظَهره فِي رجلَيْهِ وَقَامَ يُصَلِّي، فَلم يزل قَائِما حَتَّى إِذا خشِي الصُّبْح، سجد، ثمَّ أوتر، ثمَّ صلى رَكْعَتي الْفجْر، وأقيمت الصَّلَاة، فَدخل مَعَ النَّاس فِي الصَّلَاة فَدخلت مَعَه، فَلَمَّا سلم الإِمَام خرج من الْمَسْجِد، وَخرجت خَلفه، فَجعل يمشي، وَأتبعهُ حَتَّى دخل دَارا قد عرفتها من دور الْمَدِينَة، وَرجعت إِلَى الْمَسْجِد، فَلَمَّا طلعت الشَّمْس وَصليت خرجت حَتَّى أتيت الدَّار فَإِذا أَنا بِهِ قَاعد يخرز، وَإِذا هُوَ أسكاف، فَلَمَّا رَآنِي عرفني وَقَالَ: أَبَا عبد اللَّهِ، مرْحَبًا، لَك حَاجَة؟ تُرِيدُ أَن أعمل لَك خفا؟ فَجَلَست فَقلت: أَلَسْت صَاحِبي بارحة الأولى؟ فاسود وَجهه وَصَاح وَقَالَ: يَا ابْن الْمُنْكَدر، مَا أَنْت وَذَاكَ، وَغَضب ففَزِعت وَالله مِنْهُ، وَقلت: أخرج من عِنْده الْآن. فَلَمَّا كَانَ فِي اللَّيْلَة الثَّالِثَة صليت الْعشَاء الْآخِرَة فِي مَسْجِد رَسُول اللَّهِ.

On the following night I prayed *ʿishā* in the *masjid* of the Messenger of Allāh and then proceeded to my pillar and leant upon it. The man came again and covered his upper body with a garment and wore the garment he had previously covered his back with to cover his legs. He then stood and prayed, continuing in this until he felt the morning was arriving, and then he prostrated and performed the *witr*. He prayed the two [Sunnah] units of *fajr* and then the *iqāmah* was called for the prayer. He joined the people in the prayer and I did also. When the *imām* performed the *taslīm* the man exited the *masjid*. I exited behind him and followed him until he entered a property, and it was one of the buildings of Madīnah which I knew of. I returned to the *masjid*, and when the sun rose and I had prayed, I went to that property and found a man sitting there and crafting, it was a shoe maker.

When he saw me, he recognised me and stated, 'O Abā 'Abdullāh, welcome. Are you in need of anything? Do you need my service for footwear?' I sat and said, 'Are you not my companion from the previous night?' His face darkened at this and he yelled at me, 'O Ibn al-Munkadir, what is it to you?' By Allāh, his fury caused me to become scared, and I said to myself that I should leave his presence immediately.

فَلَمَّا كَانَ فِي اللَّيْلَةِ الثَّالِثَةِ صليت الْعِشَاءَ الْآخِرَةَ فِي مَسْجِدِ رَسُولِ اللَّهِ - صَلَّى اللَّهُ عَلَيْهِ وَسَلَّمَ -، ثُمَّ أتيت ساريتي فتساندت إِلَيْهَا فَلم يَجِيء. قَالَ: قلت: إِنَّا لله، مَا صنعت؟ فَقَالَ: فَلَمَّا أَصْبَحت جَلَست فِي الْمَسْجِدِ حَتَّى طلعت الشَّمْسُ، ثُمَّ خرجت حَتَّى أتيت الدَّارَ الَّتِي كَانَ فِيهَا فَإِذا بَاب الدَّار مَفْتُوح وَإِذا لَيْسَ فِي الْبَيْتِ شَيْء، فَقَالَ لِي أهل الدَّار: يَا أَبَا عبد اللَّهِ، مَا كَانَ بَيْنك وَبَين هَذَا أمس؟ قلت: مَا لَهُ؟ قَالُوا: لما خرجت من عِنْده أمس بسط كساءه فِي وسط الْبَيْتِ، ثُمَّ لم يدع فِي بَيته جلدا وَلَا قالبا إِلَّا وَضعه فِي كسائه، ثُمَّ حمله، فَلم ندر أَيْنَ ذهب؟ قَالَ ابْن الْمُنْكَدِرِ: فَمَا تركت فِي الْمَدِينَةِ دَارا أعلمها إِلَّا وَقد طلبته فِيهَا فَلم أجده.

On the third night I prayed the *'ishā* prayer within the *masjid* of the Messenger of Allāh ﷺ, and then I went to my pillar and leant upon it. The man did not come. I said to myself, 'By Allāh, what have you done?' When the morning came, I sat in the *masjid* until the sun rose. I left there and when I reached the property wherein the man had been, I found the door open and the inside of it completely empty. The people there said to me, 'O Abā 'Abdullāh, what happened between you and the man yesterday?' I replied, 'What did he do?' They said, 'When you left him yesterday, he spread his garment in the middle of his abode and did not leave any of his materials except that he placed them within it. Then he carried it off, and none knows where he went.'" Ibn al-Munkadir said, "I did not leave any of the houses of Madīnah I was aware of except that I sought for him there, and I did not find him."

❋❋❋

عَابِد آخر
Another worshipper

[١٢٨] أنبأَنَا مُحَمَّد بن نَاصِر قَالَ أَنبأَنَا جَعْفَر بن أَحْمد قَالَ أنبأ أَبُو طَالب مُحَمَّد بن عَليّ بن يُوسُف الْوَاعِظ قَالَ أنبأ أَبُو الْحسن عبد السَّلَام بن عبد الْملك بن حبيب قَالَ ثَنَا جَعْفَر بن أَحْمد بن سِنَان قَالَ نَاصِر بن عَليّ قَالَ حَدثنِي الْأَصْمَعِي عَن أبي مودود عَن مُحَمَّد بن الْمُنْكَدر قَالَ: أَبْطَأَ الْمَطَر سنة فَجئْت إِلَى الْمَسْجِد فَإِذا رجل أسود عِنْد الْمِنبَر وَهُوَ يَقُول: اللَّهُمَّ اسقنا السَّاعَة، فَرعدَت وأبرقت، فَقَالَ: يَا رب لَيْسَ هَذَا أُرِيد، ثمَّ مطرَت، فَقَامَ: واتبعته حَتَّى أَتَى دَار آل حزم، فَأَتَيْته فعرضت عَلَيْهِ دَرَاهِم فأبي، فَقلت: هَذَا أَوَان الْحَج فتخرج معي؟ فَقَالَ: هَذَا من الْخَيْر، وَلَك فِيهِ أجر، فَخرج معي.

Abū Mawdūd reported upon the authority of Muḥammad ibn al-Munkadir, "Rain had been held back from us for a year. I went to the *masjid* and found therein a black man sitting at the *mimbar* whilst saying, 'O Allāh, provide us with rain immediately.' Subsequently there came thunder and lightning, and he said, 'O my Lord, this is not what I desired,' and then rain began to fall. He then stood and I followed him to the house of Āli Ḥazm. I went to him and presented him with *dirhams*, to which he refused. I said to him, 'This is the season of Ḥajj so will you go with me?' He replied, 'This is better and for you therein will be reward.' And so, he went with me."

عَابِد أسود من أهل مَكَّة
A Black Worshipper from Makkah

[١٢٩] أخبرنَا مُحَمَّد بن نَاصِر قَالَ ثَنَا جَعْفَر بن أَحْمد بن السراج قَالَ أنبأ عبد الْعَزِيز بن الْحسن بن إِسْمَاعِيل الضراب قَالَ ثَنَا أبي قَالَ ثَنَا أَحْمد ابْن مَرْوَان

الْمَالِكِي قَالَ نَا سُلَيْمَان بن الْحسن قَالَ ثنَا أبي قَالَ: قَالَ ابْن الْمُبَارك: قدمت مَكَّة فَإِذا النَّاس قد قحطوا من الْمَطَر وهم يستسقون فِي الْمَسْجِد الْحَرَام، فَكنت فِي النَّاس مِمَّا يَلِي بَاب بني شيبَة، إِذْ أقبل غُلَام أسود عَلَيْهِ قطعتا خيش قد ائتزر بِإِحْدَاهُمَا، وَألقى الْأُخْرَى على عَاتِقه، فَصَارَ فِي مَوضِع خَفِي إِلَى جَانِبي فَسَمعته يَقُول: إلهي، أخلقت الْوُجُوه كَثْرَة الذُّنُوب ومساوئ الْأَعْمَال، وَقد منتعنا غيث السَّمَاء لتؤدب الخليقة بذلك، فأسألك يَا حَلِيمًا ذَا أَنَاة، يَا من لَا يعرف عباده مِنْهُ إِلَّا الْجَمِيل، اِسْقِهِمْ السَّاعَة السَّاعَة. قَالَ: فَلم يزل يَقُول: السَّاعَة السَّاعَة حَتَّى اسْتَوَت بالغمام وَأَقْبل الْمَطَر من كل مَكَان، وَجلسَ مَكَانَهُ يسبح، وَأخذت أبْكِي، فَقَامَ فتبعته حَتَّى عرفت مَوْضِعه.

Sulaymān ibn al-Ḥasan reported from his father upon the authority of Ibn al-Mubārak, "I entered Makkah during a time when its inhabitants were suffering drought. The people were praying for rain within al-Masjid al-Ḥarām. I was amongst the people next to the door of Banī Shaybah when a black boy entered. He was wearing two pieces of cloth, one as an *izār* and the other covering his upper body. He went to a concealed area which was to my side, and I heard him saying, 'My Deity, the faces are ashamed of their numerous sins and vile deeds. You have prevented the downpour of the sky as a means of punishing the creation. I implore you, O Ḥalīm—the possessor of patience, O Who forbearance is one of His attributes—the One whom does not let His slaves perceive except beauty, provide them with water immediately.'" He said, "He did not stop saying '*al-sāʿah, al-sāʿah*' until clouds had formed in the sky and rainfall became widespread. He then sat there making *tasbīḥ* and I began to cry. He stood up and I followed him until I saw where he [lived.]

فَجئْت إِلَى الفضيل بن عِيَاض فَقَالَ لي: مَا لي أَرَاك باكيا؟ فَقلت: سبقنَا إِلَيْهِ غيرنَا، فتولاه دُوننَا. قَالَ: وَمَا ذَاك؟ فقصصت عَلَيْهِ الْقِصَّة، فصاح وَسقط، وَقَالَ: وَيحك يَا ابْن الْمُبَارك، خذني إِلَيْهِ. قلت: قد ضَاقَ الْوَقْت وسأبحث عَن شَأْنه.

I then went to al-Fuḍayl ibn 'Iyād and he asked me, 'What causes you to cry?' I said, 'One has preceded us to Allāh and He has favoured him over us.' He replied, 'What is this?' I then recounted the story to him and he fell to the ground whilst crying out, he said, 'Woe to you O Ibn al-Mubārak, take me to him.' I replied, 'Time is short [today,] but we will seek him out later.'

فَلَمَّا كَانَ من الْغد صليت الْغدَاة، وَخرجت أُرِيد الْموضع فَإِذا شيخ على الْبَاب قد بسط لَهُ وَهُوَ جَالس فَلَمَّا رَآنِي عرفني، فَقَالَ: مرْحَبًا بك يَا أَبَا عبد الرَّحْمَن، حَاجَتك. فَقلت لَهُ: احتجت إِلَى غُلَام أسود، فَقَالَ: نعم، عِنْدِي عدَّة فاختر أَيهمْ شِئْت، فصاح: يَا غُلَام. فَخرج غُلَام جلد، فَقَالَ: هَذَا مَحْمُود الْعَاقِبَة أرضاه لَك. فَقلت: لَيْسَ هَذَا حَاجَتي، فَمَا زَالَ يخرج وَاحِدًا وَاحِدًا حَتَّى أخرج إِلَيّ الْغُلَام، فَلَمَّا بصرت بِهِ بدرت عَيْنَايَ، فَقَالَ: هَذَا؟ قلت: نعم، فَقَالَ: لَيْسَ إِلَيّ بَيْعه سَبِيل، قلت: وَلم؟ قَالَ: قد تبركت بموضعه فِي الدَّار، وَذَلِك أَنه لَا يرزؤني شَيْئا، قلت: وَمن أَيْن طَعَامه؟ قَالَ: يكْسب من فتل الشريط نصف دانق وَأَقل وَأكْثر فَهُوَ قوته، فَإِن بَاعه فِي يَوْمه وَإِلَّا طوى ذَلِك الْيَوْم. وَأَخْبرنِي الغلمان عَنهُ: أَنه لَا ينَام هَذَا اللَّيْل الطَّوِيل، وَلَا يخْتَلط بِأحد مِنْهُم، مهتم بِنَفسِهِ، وَقد أحبه قلبِي، فَقلت لَهُ: انْصَرف إِلَى سُفْيَان الثَّوْريّ والفضيل بَين عِيَاض بِغَيْر قَضَاء حَاجَة؟ فَقَالَ: إِن ممشاك عِنْدِي كَبِير، خُذْهُ بِمَا شِئْت.

On the next day, I performed the *fajr* prayer and then went towards his place where I came across an elderly man at the door sitting upon a mat which was being spread out for him. When he saw me, he recognised me and said, 'Welcome O Abā 'Abd al-Raḥmān, what can I do for you?' I replied to him, 'I am in need of a black slave.' He said, 'Indeed, I have many of them so choose which one you prefer.' He then shouted, 'O *ghulām*,' and a strong black youth came. The man said, 'He would be good for you, I will give him to you.' I replied, 'I do not require him.' They continued to be presented to me, one by one, until the last one came. When I saw him, my eyes widened and the man said, 'Is he the one?' I replied affirmatively and he said, 'There is no possibility of me selling him.' I asked, 'Why is that?' He said, 'His presence in the house is a blessing, for he does not cause me any expense.' I said, 'Where does he feed himself from?' He replied, 'He earns a living of half a *dāniq*—more or less—through working with ribbons, and if he does not sell anything, he refrains from eating during that day. And I was informed by my other slaves that he does not sleep during the night, neither does he mix with them—rather he remains preoccupied with himself. I love him from the depths of my heart.' I said to him, '[So do I] go back to Sufyān al-Thawrī and al-Fuḍayl ibn 'Iyāḍ without my need being fulfilled?' He replied, 'Coming here to my place in person is of great weight to me, so take him for what you need.'

قَالَ: فاشتريته، فَأَخَذته نَحْو دَار الفضيل بن عِيَاض، فمشيت سَاعَة فَقَالَ لي: يَا مولَايَ، قلت: لبيْك. قَالَ: لَا تقل لي لبيْك، فَإِنَّهُ العَبْد أولى بِأَن يُلَبِّي من الْمولى. قلت: حَاجَتك يَا حَبِيبِي؟ قَالَ: أَنا ضَعِيف الْبدن لَا أُطِيق الْخدمَة، وَقد كَانَ لَك فِي غَيْرِي سَعَة، قد أخرج إِلَيْك من هُوَ أجلد مني. فَقلت: لَا يراني اللَّهِ وَأَنا استخدمك، وَلَكِن أَشْتَرِي لَك منزلا وأزوجك وأخدمك أَنا بنفسي. قَالَ: فَبكى. فَقلت لَهُ: مَا يبكيك؟ قَالَ: أَنْت لم تفعل بِي هَذَا إِلَّا وَقد رَأَيْت بعض متصلاتي بِاللَّه عز وَجل، وَإِلَّا فَلم اخترتني من بَين أُولَئِكَ الغلمان؟ فَقلت لَهُ: لَيْسَ بك حَاجَة إِلَى هَذَا. فَقَالَ: سَأَلتك بِاللَّه إِلَّا اخترتني فَقلت: بإجابة دعوتك. فَقَالَ: إِنِّي أحسبك إِن شَاءَ اللَّهِ [تَعَالَى] رجلا صَالحا. إِن لله عز وَجل خيرة من خلقه لَا يكْشف شَأْنهمْ إِلَّا لمن أحب من عباده، وَلَا يظْهر عَلَيْهِم إِلَّا من ارتضى.

Thus, I purchased him and took him to the abode of al-Fuḍayl ibn 'Iyāḍ. As we were going, he said to me, 'O master.' I said to him, 'I am at your service.' He replied, 'Do not say that you are at my service, for indeed this statement is more appropriate to emanate from the slave rather than the master.' Then I said, 'What is your need my beloved?' He replied, 'I am physically weak and so I cannot bear service to you. You had the choice of selecting other than me, and you were presented with those who were physically stronger than me.' I said, 'I would not want Allāh to see me bearing you with servitude, rather I will buy you a property, marry you off and serve you myself.' He wept and so I asked him what caused him to cry. He replied, 'You would not have done this unless you witnessed one of my unisons with Allāh ﷻ. If not for this, why did you choose me over the other slaves? I said, 'This is of no concern to you.' He urged me, 'I ask you by Allāh, why did you choose me.' I said, 'Due to your *du'ā* being answered.' He replied, 'Indeed I view you—by the will of Allāh—to be a righteous man. Indeed, Allāh has a certain elite group amongst His creation whom He does not reveal their identities to except to the beloved from His slaves, and he does not display this group except to the ones He is pleased with.'

ثمَّ قَالَ لي: ترى أَن تقف عَليّ قَلِيلا، فَإِنَّهُ قد بقيت عَليّ رَكْعَات من البارحة. قلت: هَذَا منزل فضيل قريب. قَالَ: لَا، هَاهُنَا أحب إِلَيّ، أَمر اللَّهِ [عز وَجل] لَا يُؤخر. فَدخل من بَاب الباعة إِلَى الْمَسْجِد فَمَا زَالَ يُصَلِّي حَتَّى إِذا أَتَى عَليّ مَا أَرَادَ الْتفت إِلَيّ وَقَالَ: يَا أَبَا عبد الرَّحْمَن، هَل من حَاجَة؟ قلت: وَلم؟ قَالَ: لِأَنِّي أُرِيد الإنصراف. قلت إِلَى أَيْن؟ قَالَ: إِلَى الْآخِرَة. قلت: لَا تفعل، دَعْنِي أسر بك. فَقَالَ لي: إِنَّمَا كَانَت تطيب الْحَيَاة حَيْثُ كَانَت الْمُعَامَلَة بيني وَبَينه تَعَالَى، فَأَما إِذا اطَّلَعت عَلَيْهَا أَنْت فسيطلع عَلَيْهَا غَيْرك فَلَا حَاجَة لي فِي ذَلِك. ثمَّ خر لوجهه فَجعل يَقُول: إلهي، اقبضني السَّاعَة السَّاعَة. فدنوت مِنْهُ فَإِذا هُوَ قد مَاتَ. فوَاللَّه مَا ذكرته [قطّ] إِلَّا طَال حزني [عَلَيْهِ] ، وصغرت الدُّنْيَا فِي عَيْني.

Then he said to me, 'Is it possible that we could stop for a short while as I have some units of prayer from the previous night still to pray.' I said, 'Fuḍayl's abode is close.' He said, 'No, this location is better for me. The command of Allāh should not be delayed ﷻ.' He then entered the *masjid* through the entrance of the traders and he did not cease praying until he prayed the units which he missed from the night. He said, 'O Abā 'Abd al-Raḥmān, do you have any need from me?' I said, 'Why?' He replied, 'Because I wish to depart?' I said, 'To where?' He replied, 'To the Hereafter.' I said, 'Do not depart, I will tell you something that will please you.' He said to me, 'Indeed this life was beautiful when the transaction was between me and Him ﷻ. As for the current juncture, you have come to know of it and subsequently others will also. I have no need for this.' Then he lowered his forehead to the floor and began to say, 'My Deity, take me immediately.' I went towards him and found him to have died. By Allāh, never do I remember him except that I feel deep sadness in regards to him, and the worldly life diminishes within my eyes."

عَابِدٍ أسود بغدادي

A black worshipper from Baghdād

[١٣٠] أخبرنَا مُحَمَّد بن أبي مَنْصُور الْحَافِظ قَالَ أَنبأَنَا أَبُو الْقَاسِم عَليّ بن أَحْمد قَالَ أَنبأَنَا أَبُو عبد اللَّهِ بن بطة العكبري قَالَ: حَدثنِي أَبُو بكر مُحَمَّد بن الْحُسَيْن قَالَ: حَدثنِي أَبُو الْقَاسِم عبد اللَّهِ بن مُحَمَّد الطشي قَالَ: حَدثنِي أَبُو جَعْفَر السقا قَالَ: خرجت يَوْمًا من بَيْتِي فِي وَقت مطير فَإِذا أسود مطروح على مزبلة مَرِيض فجررته فأدخلته إِلَى بَيْتِي، فَلَمَّا أمسينا دَعَانِي، فَقَالَ: يَا أَبَا جَعْفَر، لَا تفْسد مَا صنعت، اقعد عِنْدِي، وفاح الْبَيْت بريح الْمسك وَصَارَ ريح جبتي وكسائي وجرتي وكوزي وكل شَيْء فِي الْبَيْت ريح الْمسك. قَالَ: فَقَالَ: اقعد عِنْدِي، ثمَّ قَالَ بِيَدِهِ: هَكَذَا لَا تضيق عَليّ جلسائي. قَالَ: فَسَمعته يَقُول: أيدك اللَّهِ أيدك اللَّهِ ارْفُقْ بِي يَا مولَايَ قَالَ: ثمَّ خرجت نَفسه. قَالَ: قلت: أبيع كسائي، أبيع جبتي، وأشتري لَهُ كفنا. قَالَ: فطرق بَابي قريب من سبعين إنْسَانا كل يَقُول: يَا أَبَا جَعْفَر: مَاتَ عنْدك إنْسَان يحْتَاج إِلَى كفن.

Abū al-Qāsim 'Abdullāh ibn Muḥammad al-Ṭashī reported upon the authority of Abū Ja'far al-Saqqā', "I left my house on an occasion when it was raining. I saw a black man who was lying ill in a rubbish dump. I moved him and took him to my house. When evening fell, he called me and said,

'O Abā Ja'far, do not spoil what you have done. Sit with me.' At this the house began to exude the smell of musk. The scent covered my clothing, utensils and everything else within my house. He again said, 'Sit with me.' Then he spoke whilst expressing with his hand, 'This way you do not make those who are sitting with me now annoyed.' I heard him saying, 'My Lord, be gentle with me. My Lord, be gentle with me.' Then his soul departed from him and I said to myself, 'I will sell my garments and my *jubbahs* and through this I will buy him a shroud.' Around seventy people then knocked upon my door, each of them saying, 'O Abā Ja'far, a man has died with you and he will be in need of a shroud.'"

عَابِد أسود بَصرِي

A black worshipper from Baṣrah

[١٣١] أخبرنَا مُحَمَّد بن عبد الْبَاقِي قَالَ أنبأ حمد بن أَحْمد قَالَ أنبأ أَبُو نعيم أَحْمد بن عبد اللَّهِ قَالَ أَنا أَبُو الْأَزْهَر ضَمرَة بن حَمْزَة الْمَقْدِسِي فِي كِتَابه. وحَدثنِي عَنهُ مُحَمَّد بن إِبْرَاهِيم بن أَحْمد قَالَ: حَدثنِي أبي قَالَ: ثَنَا عبد الله بن سعيد الْهَاشِمِي قَالَ نَا أبي قَالَ نَا عبد اللَّهِ بن إِدْرِيس عَن مَالك بن دِينَار قَالَ: احْتبسَ علينا الْمَطَر بِالْبَصْرَةِ فخرجنا يَوْمًا بعد يَوْم نستسقي فَلم نر أثر الْإِجَابَة، فَخرجت أَنا وَعَطَاء السّلمِيّ وثابت الْبنانِيّ وَمُحَمّد بن وَاسع وحبِيب الْفَارِسِي وَصَالح المري فِي آخَرين حَتَّى صرنا إِلَى الْمصلى بِالْبَصْرَةِ فاستسقينا، فَلم نر أثر الْإِجَابَة، وَانْصَرف النَّاس، وَبقيت أَنا وثابت [الْبنانِيّ] فِي الْمصلى، فَلَمَّا أظلم اللَّيْل بِالسَّوَادِ إِذا أَنا بأسود دَقِيق السَّاقَيْن، عَظِيم الْبَطن عَلَيْهِ مئزران من صوف، فجَاء إِلَى مَاء، فتمسح ثمَّ صلى رَكْعَتَيْنِ خفيفتين، ثمَّ رفع طرفه إِلَى السَّمَاء فَقَالَ: سَيِّدي، إِلَيّ كم تردد عِبَادك فِيمَا لَا ينْقصك، أنفد مَا عنْدك؟ أَقْسَمت عَلَيْك بحبك لي إِلَّا مَا سقيتهم غيثك السَّاعَة السَّاعَة. فَمَا أتم الْكَلَام حَتَّى

تغيمت السَّمَاء، وأخذتنا كأفواه الْقرب.

'Abdullāh ibn Idrīs reported upon the authority of Mālik ibn Dīnār, "Rain was held back from us in Baṣrah, so we went out day after day to pray for rain, however we did not see any sign of an answer to our prayers. I went out with 'Aṭā' al-Sulamī, Thābit al-Bunānī, Muḥammad ibn Wāsi', Ḥabīb al-Fārisī, Sāliḥ al-Murrī amongst others, until we arrived at the *muṣallā* in Baṣrah and prayed *al-istisqā* (the prayer for rain). We did not see a sign that our prayer had been answered and so the people departed. I remained therein with Thābit al-Bunānī, and when the night became enveloped in darkness, I saw a black man with thin legs. He had a large belly and was wearing two garments made of wool. He went to the water and touched it, then he performed two short units of prayer and raised his face to the heavens and said, 'My Master, for how long will you rebuff your slaves from that which does not decrease from You? Nothing with you will ever diminish. I swear to you by Your love for me, provide them with rain immediately.' He had barely finished speaking when the sky became cloudy and it started to rain heavily.

فَمَا خرجنَا حَتَّى خضنا المَاء، فتعجبنا من الْأسود فتعرضت لَهُ فَقلت: أما تَسْتَحي مِمَّا قلت؟ قَالَ: وَمَا قلت؟ فَقلت: قَوْلك بحبك لي، وَمَا يدْريك أَنه يحبك. فَقَالَ: تَنَح عَن همتي يَا من اشْتغل عَنهُ بِنَفسِهِ، أَيْن كنت أَنا حِين خصني بتوحيده ومعرفته؟ أَتَرَى خصني بذلك إِلَّا لمحبته. ثمَّ بَادر يسْعَى، فَقلت: ارْفُق بنَا فَقَالَ: أَنا مَمْلُوك عَليّ فرض من طَاعَة مالكي الصَّغِير فَدخل دَار نخاس.

We found as we left the *muṣallā* that we were having to wade through the water. We were amazed by this black man, and I presented myself to him and said, 'Do you not feel shame for what you stated?' He replied, 'What did I say?' I said, 'I am referring to your statement 'by Your love for me,' how do you know that He loves you?' He replied, 'Do not concern yourself with my affairs, O you who concerns himself with his own self over Him . Where were you when He chose me to believe in *tawḥīd* (Oneness of Allāh) and to know Him? Do you not see that Him choosing me for this was due to His love?' Then he rushed away and I said, 'Remain with us.' He replied, 'I am a slave, and it is incumbent upon me to be dutiful to my lesser master.' Then he entered the property of a slave-trader.

فَلَمَّا أَصْبَحْنَا أتيت على النخاس فَقلت لَهُ: عنْدك غُلَام تبيعنيه للْخدمَة؟ قَالَ: نعم، عِنْدِي مائَة غُلَام، فَجعل يخرج إِلَيّ وَاحِدًا بعد وَاحِد، وَأَنا أَقُول: غير هَذَا. إِلَى أَن قَالَ: مَا بَقِي عِنْدِي أحد فَلَمَّا خرجنَا إِذا بالأسود قَائِم فِي حجرَة خربة فَقلت: بِعني هَذَا. فَقَالَ: هَذَا غُلَام مُشَوه لَا همة لَهُ إِلَّا الْبكاء. فَقلت: وَذَلِكَ أريده، فَدَعَاهُ وَقَالَ لي: خُذْهُ بِمَا شِئْت بعد أَن تبرئني من عيوبه. فاشتريته بِعشْرين دِينَارا.

On the next morning I went to this slave-trader and said to him, 'Do you have any slaves to sell for service?' He replied, 'Yes, I have a hundred slaves.' He brought them out for me, one by one, to each of which I would reply, 'Not this one.' This continued until he said, 'There are no more with me.' When we left, we came across the black man standing in a dilapidated room. I said, 'Sell me this one.' He replied, 'This slave is an invalid, he serves no purpose except to cry.' I said, 'That is why I want him.' He called for him and said to me, 'Take him for however much you wish, however, after you agree to acquit me from whatever defects you may find in him.' I subsequently purchased him for twenty *dīnārs*.

فَلَمَّا خرجنَا قَالَ: يَا مولَايَ، لم اشتريتني؟ قلت: لنخدمك نَحن. قَالَ: وَلم ذَاك؟ قلت: أَلَيْسَ أَنْت صاحبنا البارحة فِي الْمصلى؟ قَالَ: وَقد اطَّلَعت على ذَلِك؟ فَجعل يمشي حَتَّى دخل مَسْجِدا فصلى رَكْعَتَيْنِ، ثمَّ قَالَ: إلهي وسيدي سر كَانَ بيني وَبَيْنك أظهرته للمخلوقين، أَقْسَمت عَلَيْك إِلَّا قبضت روحي السَّاعَة. فَإِذا هُوَ ميت، فبقبره نستسقي ونطلب الْحَوَائِج إِلَى يَوْمنَا هَذَا.

When we exited that place, he said to me, 'O master, why did you purchase me?' I replied, 'So that we can serve you.' He said, 'And why is that?' I replied, 'Are you not our companion from the previous night at the *muṣallā*?' He said, 'You are aware of that?' He carried on walking until he entered a *masjid*. There he prayed two units and said, 'My Deity and Master, the secret between me and You has been displayed to the creation. I swear by You that you take my soul immediately.' Upon this he passed away, and we seek rain and aid for our needs from his grave to this day (i.e. as an intermediary)."[75]

عابِد آخر أسود بصري

Another black worshipper from Baṣrah

[١٣٢] أخبرنَا مُحَمَّد بن أبي مَنْصُور قَالَ أنبأ أَبُو الْحُسَيْن بن عبد الْجَبَّار قَالَ أنبأ مُحَمَّد بن عَليّ بن الْفَتْح قَالَ أنبأ مُحَمَّد بن عبد اللَّهِ الدقاق قَالَ نَا الْحُسَيْن بن صَفْوَان قَالَ نَا أَبُو بكر الْقرشِي قَالَ حَدثنَا جدي أَبُو السكن الطَّائِي قَالَ: حَدثنِي مُحَمَّد بن هَارُون بن مُسلم. قَالَ: وحَدثنِي عبد الْوَاحِد ابْن زيد قَالَ: خرجت إِلَى نَاحيَة الخريبة فَإِذا إِنْسَان أسود مجذوم قد تقطعت كل جارحة لَهُ بالجذام وَعمي وأقعد، وَإِذا صبيان يرمونه بِالْحِجَارَةِ قد دموا وَجهه، فرأيته يُحَرك شفتين، فدنوت مِنْهُ لأسْمع مَا يَقُول: فَإِذا هُوَ يَقُول: يَا سَيِّدي، إِنَّك لتعلم أَنَّك إِن قرضت لحمي بِالْمَقَارِيضِ ونشرت عِظَامِي بالمناشير مَا ازددت لَك إِلَّا حبا، فَاصْنَعْ بِي مَا شِئْت.

Muḥammad ibn Hārūn ibn Muslim reported upon the authority of 'Abd al-Wāḥid ibn Zayd, "I was going towards the direction of al-Khuraybah when I came across a black leper. All of his limbs had come off due to the

75 It is not permissible to seek help from the dead in this manner, as has been mentioned by the scholars. During the time of the Companions they would seek rain through al-'Abbās (the uncle of the Messenger), and this was after the death of the Prophet ﷺ. During the time of Muā'wiyah they would seek rain through Yazīd al-Jurshī. Both of these individuals were from the best of people and the most pious. They were known for their *taqwā*, devoutness and that their supplications were answered.

leprosy and he was also blind. He was sitting down and I noticed some boys throwing stones at him, causing his face to bleed. I saw his lips were moving and so I approached him to hear what he was saying. I heard him say, 'O Master, You know that if You sheared away my flesh and sawed off by bones, I will only love You more and more. So, do with me as You please.'"

عَابِد أسود من عبادان

A black worshipper from ʿAbādān

[١٣٣] أخبرنَا أَبُو بكر بن حبيب قَالَ أنبأ أَبُو سعد بن أبي صَادِق قَالَ أنا ابْن باكويه قَالَ: أَخْبرنِي أَبُو عبد اللَّهِ الشِّيرَازِيّ قَالَ: أَخْبرنِي أَبُو الْخيرَات الْمَعْرُوف بالعسقلاني قَالَ: كَانَ بعبادان رجل زنجي مفلفل الشّعْر يأوي الخرابات، فَحملت معي شَيْئا وطلبته، فَلَمَّا وَقع بَصَره عَليّ تَبَسم، وَأَشَارَ بِيَدِهِ إِلَى الأَرْض، فَرَأَيْت حوالي إِلَى حَيْثُ أرى دَرَاهِم ودنانير تلمع، ثمَّ قَالَ لي: هَات مَا مَعَك. فناولته، وهربت وهالني أمره.

Abū ʿAbdullāh al-Shīrāzī reported upon the authority of Abū al-Khayrāt, famously referred to as al-ʿAsqalānī, 'In ʿAbādān there was a Zanjī man with peppery hair who was taking shelter within ruins. I took some things with me and sought after him. When he saw me, he smiled and pointed with his hand to the ground. I saw that spread widely around me were shining *dirhams* and *dīnārs*. Then he said to me, 'Give me what you have.' I gave him and fled from there, as I was overwhelmed by what I saw from him."

عَابِد آخر لَقِي بطرِيق مَكَّة

Another worshipper, who was seen en route to Makkah

[١٣٤] أخبرنَا أَبُو مَنْصُور الْقَزاز قَالَ أنبأ أَحْمد بن عَليّ بن ثَابت قَالَ: أنا مُحَمَّد

بن أَحْمد بن رزق قَالَ أنبأ أَحْمد بن سلمَان الْفَقِيه قَالَ ثنَا ابْن أبي الدُّنْيَا قَالَ حَدثنِي مشرف بن أبان قَالَ: سَمِعت صَالح بن عبد الْكَرِيم قَالَ: رَأَيْت غُلَاما أسود فِي طَرِيق مَكَّة عِنْد ميل يُصَلِّي، فَقلت لَهُ: عبد أَنْت؟ قَالَ: نعم. قلت: فَعَلَيْك ضريبة؟ قَالَ: نعم. قلت: أَفلا أكلم مَوْلَاك أَن يضع عَنْك. قَالَ: وَمَا الدُّنْيَا كلهَا فأجزع من ذلها. قَالَ: فاشتريته فأعتقته فَقعدَ يبكي، وَقَالَ لي: أعتقتني؟ قلت: نعم. قَالَ: أعتقك الله يَوْم الْقِيَامَة، وَقعد يبكي وَيَقُول: اشْتَدَّ عَليّ الْأَمر، فناولته دَنَانِير فَأبى أَن يَأْخُذهَا، قَالَ: فحججت بعد ذَلِك بِأَرْبَع سِنِين. فَسَأَلت عَنهُ، فَقَالُوا: غَابَ عَنَّا، فمذ غَابَ قحطنا، وَصَارَ إِلَى جدة.

Musharraf ibn Abān reported upon the authority of Sāliḥ ibn 'Abd al-Karīm, "I saw a black slave on the route to Makkah, next to the milepost and he was praying. I said to him, 'Are you a slave?' He replied affirmatively, then I asked, 'Are you burdened with a tax?' He replied, 'Yes.' I said, 'Should I speak to your master to see if he will lift this?' He said, 'This worldly life in its entirety is naught but abasement.' Thus, I brought him and emancipated him. After this he sat and cried, and said to me, 'You have emancipated me?' I replied, 'Yes,' and he then said to me, 'Allāh will emancipate you on the Day of Judgement.' He again sat down and cried whilst saying, 'Matters are burdensome upon me.' I took out some *dinars* to give him but he refused to take them. I performed Ḥajj four years later and asked regarding him. The people said that he had disappeared, and that since he had left they had been suffering from drought, and he moved to Jeddah.

عابِد آخر

Another worshipper

[١٣٥] أخبرنَا أَحْمد بن أَحْمد المتوكلي قَالَ أنبأ أَحْمد بن عَليّ بن ثَابت قَالَ أنبأ عَليّ بن مُحَمَّد بن عِيسَى الْبَزَّاز قَالَ أنبأ أَبُو الْحسن عَليّ بن مُحَمَّد الْمصْرِيّ قَالَ

نَا أَحْمد بن مُحَمَّد الطوسي قَالَ نَا دَاوُد بن رشيد قَالَ: حَدثنِي الصبيح والمليح شابان كَانَا يتعبدان بِالشَّام سميا: الصبيح والمليح لحسن عبادتهما - قَالَ: جعنا يَوْمًا فَقلت لصاحبي أَو قَالَ لي: اخْرُج بِنَا إِلَى الصَّحرَاء الْعليا نرى رجلا نعلمهُ بعض دينه لَعَلَّ اللَّهِ أَن ينفعنا بِهِ، فَلَمَّا ضجرنا استقبلنا أسود على رَأسه حزمة حطب، فدَنَوْنَا مِنْهُ، فَقلت لَهُ: يَا هَذَا، من رَبك؟ فرمى بالحزمة عَن رَأسه وَجلسَ عَلَيْهَا، وَقَالَ: لَا تقولا لي من رَبك؟ - وَلَكِن قولا لي: أَيْن مَحل الْإِيمَان من قَلْبك؟ فنَظَرت إِلَى صَاحِبي وَنظر إِلَيّ صَاحِبي، ثمَّ قَالَ: سلا، سلا؛ فَإِن المريد لَا تَنْقَطِع مسَائِله. فَلَمَّا رَآنا لَا نجيز جَوَابا قَالَ: اللَّهُمَّ إِن كنت تعلم أَن لَك عبادا كلما سألوك أَعطيتهم فحول حزمتي هَذِه ذَهَبا. فرأيناها قضبان ذهب يلتمع، ثمَّ قَالَ: اللَّهُمَّ إِن كنت تعلم أَن لَك عبادا الخمول أحب إِلَيْهِم من الشُّهْرَة فَردهَا حطبا. فَرَجَعت وَالله حطبا. ثمَّ حملهَا على رَأسه وَمضى، فَلم نجسر أَن نمنعه.

Dāwūd ibn Rashīd reported, "It was narrated to me by al-Ṣubayḥ and Maliḥ—who were two pious youths from al-Shām, and they were nicknamed al-Ṣubayh and Maliḥ due to their proficient worship—, one of them said, 'One day we were hungry so I said to my companion, or he said to me, 'Let us go deep into the desert, for we may see a man whom we can teach him his religion and for this Allāh may reward us.' When we grew weary [from walking in the desert,] we came across a black man who was carrying a load of firewood upon his head. We approached him and I said, 'O man, who is your lord?' He then threw the firewood which was upon his head to the ground, and then he sat upon it. He said, 'Do not ask me who my lord is, rather ask me where the position of *īmān* is in my heart.' I glanced at my companion after this, and he glanced at me. Then he said, 'Ask away, for verily the *murīd* does not run out of questions.' When he saw that there would be no response from us, he said, 'O Allāh, if you know that You have slaves whom You give whenever they ask, then turn this bundle [of firewood] into gold.' We then saw them change into shining bars of gold. The man then said, 'O Allāh, if You know that You have slaves to whom anonymity is more beloved than fame, then return this gold to firewood.' Thus Allāh returned it, and he placed it upon his head and went off, and we did not dare to follow him.'"

عابِد آخر
Another worshipper

[١٣٦] أخبرنَا عبد الْوَهَّاب بن الْمُبَارك قَالَ أنبأ أَبُو الْحسن بن عبد الْجَبَّار قَالَ أنبأ أَبُو بكر مُحَمَّد بن عَليّ الْخياط قَالَ نَا أَحْمد بن مُحَمَّد بن يُوسُف قَالَ أنبا ابْن صَفْوَان قَالَ: ثَنَا أَبُو بكر الْقرشِي قَالَ نَا مُحَمَّد بن الْحُسَيْن قَالَ: حَدثنِي رجل من آل أبي بكرَة عَن مَيْمُون بن سياه قَالَ: كنت أَنا وخَالِد الربعِي وَنَفر من أَصْحَابنَا نذْكر اللَّهِ [عز وَجل] ، فَوقف علينا رجل أسود فَقَالَ: هَل ذكرْتُمْ الْمَوْت فِيمَا كُنْتُم فِيهِ؟ قَالَ: قُلْنَا: إِنَّا لنذكره كثيرا، وَمَا ذكرْنَاهُ يَوْمنَا هَذَا. قَالَ: فَبكى، وَقَالَ: لقد غفلتم مَا لَا يغفلكم، ونسيتم مَا يحصي عَلَيْكُم الأنفاس لقدومه عَلَيْكُم. قَالَ: ثمَّ مَال ليسقط، وسانده رجل من الْقَوْم فَخرجت نَفسه، وَأَنا أنظر إِلَيْهِ. قَالَ: فنظَرْنَا فَلم نجد أحدا نعرفه، فغسلناه وحنطناه وكفناه ودفناه.

A man from Āli Abī Bakrah reported upon the authority of Maymūn ibn Siyāh, "I was with Khālid al-Raba'ī and a group of our companions, and we were making *dhikr* (remembrance) of Allāh ﷻ. A black man came to us and said, 'Have you mentioned death during this [gathering] of yours?" We said, 'Indeed we make mention of it frequently but we have not done so today.' The man cried and said, 'You have overlooked that which will never overlook you, and you have forgotten that which counts down your breaths until it arrives.' Then his legs gave way and he was about to fall, a man from the people gave him support and then his soul exited him. I was looking at him as he passed away. We looked [for someone who knew him] but none had any knowledge of him. We then washed, embalmed, shrouded and buried him."

عَابِد من عباد السواحل
One of the worshippers of al-Sawāḥil

[١٣٧] أنبأنَا مُحَمَّد بن نَاصِر قَالَ أَنبأنَا جَعْفَر بن أَحْمد قَالَ نَا عبد الْعَزِيز بن الْحُسَيْن بن إِسْمَاعِيل الضراب قَالَ: حَدثنِي أبي قَالَ نَا أَحْمد ابْن مَرْوَان الْمَالِكِي قَالَ ثَنَا مُحَمَّد بن عبد الْعَزِيز قَالَ: سَمِعت أَحْمد بن مَحْبُوب يَقُول: حَدثنِي جدي قَالَ: سَمِعت إِبْرَاهِيم بن أدهم يَقُول: دخلت حصنا من حصون السَّاحِل وَأَنا مجتاز، وَقد أخذتني السَّمَاء فَدخلت إِلَى أتون وَقلت: أقعد سَاعَة حَتَّى يهدأ الْمَطَر فَإِذا أسود يُوقد فِيهِ فَسلمت وَقلت لَهُ: تَأذن لي إِلَى أَن يسكن الْمَطَر؟ فَأَوْمأ إِلَيّ أَن ادخل، فَدخلت فَجَلَست حذاءه، فَجعلت أنظر إِلَيْهِ وَلَا أُكَلِّمهُ، وَهُوَ يُوقد وَلَا يكلمني، ويحرك شَفَتَيْه ويلتفت يَمِينا وَشمَالًا لَا يفتر، فَلَمَّا أصبح أقبل عَليّ فَقَالَ: لَا تلمني إِن لم أحسن ضيافتك وَأَقْبل عَلَيْك؛ إِنِّي عبد مَمْلُوك، وَقد وكلت بِمَا ترى، فَكرِهت أَن أشتغل عَن مَا وكلت بِهِ. قلت: فَمَا كَانَ التفاتك يَمِينا وَشمَالًا لَا تفتر؟

Aḥmad ibn Maḥbūb reported from his grandfather upon the authority of Ibrāhīm ibn Adham, "I entered one of the fortresses of al-Sāḥil as I was passing by and had been overpowered by the sky (i.e. due to rain), so I sheltered myself in a furnace room. I thought to myself that I would sit here until the rain eased. A black man was there, attending to a fire. I greeted him and said to him, 'Do you permit me to [stay] until the rain abates?' He nodded to indicate that I should enter. I thus entered, sitting close to him. I was looking at him but did not say a word, watching him attend to the fire silently. He was moving his lips and turning right to left without a sign of fatigue. When the next day arrived, he came to me and addressed me, saying, 'Do not hold it against me that I did not host you well or welcome you. I am a slave, and I have been charged with what you see. I hate to turn my focus away from that which I have been charged with.' I said, 'Why do you turn to the right and the left in that tireless manner?'

قَالَ: خوفًا من الْمَوْت، وَقد علمت أَنه نَازل بِي، وَلَكِن لم أعلم من أَيْن يأتيني؟ وَلَا مَتى يأتيني؟ فَقلت: فَمَا تحرّك شفتيك؟ قَالَ: أَحْمد اللَّهِ وأهلله وأسبحه لِأَنَّهُ بَلغنِي عَن النَّبِي - صَلَّى اللَّهُ عَلَيْهِ وَسَلَّمَ - أَنه قَالَ لبَعض أَصْحَابه: اعْمَلْ، لَا يَأْتِيك الْمَوْت إِلَّا وَلِسَانك رطب من ذكر اللَّهِ عز وَجل. قَالَ إِبْرَاهِيم: فَبَكَيْت وَصحت صَيْحَة، وَقلت: برز عَلَيْك الْأسود يَا إِبْرَاهِيم.

He replied, 'It is due to the fear of death. I am certain that it will descend upon me, however I do not know from where (i.e. which side) it will come and when it will come.' I then asked, 'Why do you move your lips in that manner?' He replied, 'I say *alḥamdulillāh, lā ilāha illallāh* and *subḥanallāh*. This is because it reached me that the Prophet said to some of his Companions, 'Perform good deeds, do not allow death to descend upon you except that your tongue is moist with the *dhikr* of Allāh ﷻ.'' I wept at this and cried out. I said, 'This black man has excelled you, O Ibrāhīm.''

الْبَاب الثَّالِث وَالْعشْرُونَ
Chapter Twenty Three

فِي ذكر المتعبدات من السوداوات فَمن المعروفات الْأَسْمَاء
In mention of the worshippers from amongst the women of the black people

فَمن المعروفات الْأَسْمَاء

Amongst those whose names are known is:

مَيْمُونَة السَّوْدَاء
Maymūnah al-Sawdā

[١٣٨] أخبرنَا مُحَمَّد بن عبد الْبَاقِي بن أَحْمد قَالَ نَا حمد بن أَحْمد الْحداد قَالَ نَا أَحْمد بن عبد اللَّهِ الْحَافِظ قَالَ نَا عُثْمَان بن مُحَمَّد العثماني قَالَ نَا أَبُو الْحسن مُحَمَّد بن أَحْمد قَالَ ثَنَا عمر بن مُحَمَّد بن يُوسُف قَالَ: سَمِعت أَبَا جَعْفَر الصفار يَقُول: سَمِعت الْفَيْض بن إِسْحَاق الرقي يَقُول: سَمِعت الفضيل بن عِيَاض يَقُول: قَالَ عبد الْوَاحِد بن زيد: سَأَلت اللَّهِ عز وَجل ثَلَاث لَيَال أَن يريني رفيقي فِي الْجنَّة، فَرَأَيْت كَأَن قَائِلا يَقُول: يَا عبد الْوَاحِد رفيقك فِي الْجنَّة مَيْمُونَة السَّوْدَاء، فَقلت: وَأَيْنَ هِيَ؟ فَقَالَ: فِي آل بني فلَان بِالْكُوفَةِ قَالَ: فَخرجت إِلَى الْكُوفَة، وَسَأَلت عَنْهَا، فَقيل: هِيَ مجنونة بَين ظهرانينا ترعى غنيمات لنا - فَقلت: أُرِيد أَن أَرَاهَا. قَالُوا: خرجت إِلَى الجبان. فَخرجت فَإِذا بهَا قَائِمَة تصلي، وَإِذا بَين يَديهَا عكاز لَهَا، وَعَلَيْهَا جُبَّة من صوف عَلَيْهَا مَكْتُوب: لَا تبَاع وَلَا تشترى،

وَإِذا الْغنم مَعَ الذئاب، فَلَا الذئاب تَأْكُل الْغنم، وَلَا الْغنم تخَاف الذئاب، فَلَمَّا رأتني أوجزت فِي صلَاتهَا، ثمَّ قَالَت: ارْجع يَا ابْن زيد، لَيْسَ الْموعد هَاهُنَا، إِنَّمَا الْموعد ثمَّ. فَقلت: رَحِمك اللَّهِ، وَمن أعلمك أَنِّي ابْن زيد؟ فَقَالَت: أما علمت أَن الْأَرْوَاح جنود مجندة، فَمَا تعارف مِنْهَا ائتلف، وَمَا تناكرمنها اخْتلف. فَقلت لَهَا: عظيني؟ فَقَالَت: وَاعجَبا لواعظ يوعظ! ثمَّ قَالَت: يَا ابْن زيد، إِنَّك لَو وضعت معايير الْقسْط على جوارحك لخبرتك بمكتوم مَكْنُون مَا فِيهَا، يَا ابْن زيد، إِنَّه بَلغنِي أَنه مَا من عبد أعطي من الدُّنْيَا شَيْئا فابتغي إِلَيْهِ ثَانِيًا إِلَّا سلبه اللَّهِ [تَعَالَى] حب الْخلْوَة مَعَه، وبدله بعد الْقرب الْبعد، وَبعد الْأنس الوحشة، ثمَّ أنشأت تَقول:

Al-Fuḍayl ibn 'Iyāḍ reported upon the authority of 'Abd al-Wāḥid ibn Zayd, "I sought from Allāh ﷻ over three nights to show me my companion in Jannah. It seemed to me as if someone was saying, 'O 'Abd al-Wāḥid, your companion in Jannah will be Maymūnah al-Sawdā.' I asked, 'Where is she?' The reply was, 'Amongst the people of so-and-so in Kūfah.' I then went out to Kūfah and asked about her. It was said to me that she was a crazy woman living among them and she herded sheep for them. I said that I wished to see her. They said, 'She went to al-Jubbān.' I went there and found her standing in prayer. There was a cane in front of her and there was a wool *jubbah* upon it which had written on it, 'Not for sale and not for purchase.' The sheep were mingling with wolves, neither did the wolves attempt to eat the sheep nor were the sheep scared of the wolves. When she saw me she curtailed her prayer and said to me, 'Return O Ibn Zayd, the rendezvous is not here, rather it is promised for the future.' I said, 'May Allāh have mercy upon you, from where did you ascertain that I am Ibn Zayd?' She replied, 'Do you not know that the souls are like conscripted soldiers, those whom they recognise, they get along with, and those whom they do not recognise, they will not get along with.' I said, 'Can you provide me with an exhortation?' She said, 'I am amazed to see a preacher [desiring to] be exhorted!' She continued, 'O Ibn Zayd, when you let your limbs judge others with justice, they will reveal to you that which they conceal. O Ibn Zayd, it has reached me that if a slave is given something in this worldly life and covets it greedily again, Allāh will take away his love of being in solitude with Him, and substitute His closeness with distance, and intimacy with estrangement.' Then she recited the following:

يَا واعظا قَامَ لاحتساب　　　يزْجر قوما عَن الذُّنُوب

تنْهى وَأَنت السقيم حَقًّا　　　هَذَا من الْمُنكر العجيب

لَو كنت أصلحت قبل هَذَا　　　عيبك أوتبت من قريب

كَانَ لما قلت يَا حَبِيبِي　　　موقع صدق من الْقُلُوب

تنْهى عَن الغي والتمادي　　　وَأَنت فِي النَّهْي كالمريب

O preacher, who stood seeking the reward for, reprimanding the people against sin.

You prohibit while you are corrupt in truth, this is both abominable and astonishing.

If you had reformed before this, your faults, or quickly asked for forgiveness,

Whenever you addressed Him with "my love", it would land as truthful in the hearts.

You forbid aggression and corruption, whilst you seem in your forbidding somewhat doubtful.

فَقلت لَهَا: إِنِّي أرى هَذِه الذئاب مَعَ الْغنم، فَلَا الْغنم تفزع من الذئاب وَلَا تَأْكُل الذئاب الْغنم، فَأَي شَيْء هَذَا؟ فَقَالَت: إِلَيْك، فَإِنِّي أصلحت مَا بيني وَبَينه، فَأصْلح مَا بَين الذئاب وَالْغنم.

I said to her, 'I saw wolves amongst the sheep, however the sheep were not afraid of the wolves, nor did the wolves attempt to eat the sheep. How is this so?' She replied, 'Off with you, I have rectified that which is between me and Him, so He rectified that which is between these wolves and sheep.'"

شعوانة من أهل الأبلة

Sha'wānah from the People of al-Ubullah

[١٣٩] أخبرنَا المحمدان ابْن نَاصِر وَابْن عبد الْبَاقِي قَالَا أَنبأَنَا جَعْفَر ابْن أَحْمد قَالَ أنبأ أَحْمد بن عَليّ النوري قَالَ أنبأ مُحَمَّد بن عبد اللَّهِ الدقاق قَالَ نَا أَبُو عَليّ بن صَفْوَان قَالَ نَا أَبُو بكر بن عبيد قَالَ: حَدثنِي مُحَمَّد بن الْحُسَيْن قَالَ: نَا معَاذ بن الْفضل قَالَ: بَكت شعوانة حَتَّى خفنا عَلَيْهَا الْعَمى، فَقُلْنَا لَهَا فِي ذَلِك، فَقَالَت: أعمى وَالله فِي الدُّنْيَا من الْبكاء، أحب إِلَيّ من أَن أعمى فِي الْآخِرَة من النَّار.

Muḥammad ibn al-Ḥusayn reported upon the authority of Mu'ādh ibn al-'Aqīl, "Sha'wānah cried to the extent that we feared blindness would take her. We mentioned our concern to her to which she replied, 'By Allāh, blindness in this world due to crying is beloved to me in comparison to blindness in the hereafter due to the fire.'"

قَالَ مُحَمَّد بن الْحُسَيْن: وحَدثنِي مَالك بن ضيغم قَالَ: كَانَ رجل من أهل الأبلة يَأْتِي أبي كثيرا وَيذكر لَهُ شعوانة وَكَثْرَة بكائها فَقَالَ لَهُ أبي يَوْمًا: صف بكاءها. فَقَالَ: مَا أصف لَك! هِيَ وَالله تبْكي اللَّيْل وَالنَّهَار لَا تكَاد تفتر. قَالَ مَالك: وَقَالَ لي أبي: انْطلق حَتَّى تَأتي هَذِه الْمَرْأَة الصَّالِحَة فتنظر إِلَيْهَا، فَانْطَلَقت مَعَ رجل فَقَالَ لَهَا: هَذَا ابْن أَخِيك ضيغم، فرحبت بِي، وَقَالَت: مرْحَبًا يَا ابْن من لم نره، وَنحن نحبه، أما وَالله يَا بني إِنِّي لمشتاقة إِلَى أَبِيك، وَمَا يَمْنعنِي من إِتْيَانه، إِلَّا أَنِّي أَخَاف أَن أشغله عَن خدمَة سَيّده، وخدمة سَيّده، أولى من محادثة شعوانة، ثمَّ قَالَت: وَمن شعوانة؟ وَمَا شعوانة؟ أمة سَوْدَاء عاصية. قَالَ: ثمَّ أخذت فِي الْبكاء، فَلم تزل تبْكي حَتَّى خرجنَا وتركناها.

Muḥammad ibn al-Ḥusayn said that Mālik ibn Ḍaygham reported to him, "A man from the people of al-Ubullah used to frequent my father often. He would dictate to him in regards to Shaʿwānah and her constant crying. My father said to him one day, 'Describe to me her crying.' He replied, 'How can I describe it to you! She cries day and night without end.'" Mālik said, "My father said to me, 'Leave until you come across this pious woman and then observe her.' Thus, I left with a man who said to her, 'This is the son of your brother Ḍaygham.' She welcomed me and said, 'Welcome O son of whom we have not laid eyes upon but still we love. By Allāh my dear son, I seek longingly to meet your father and nothing bars me from coming to him except my fear of distracting him from service to his master. And indeed, service to his master is more important than conversing with Shaʿwānah.' Then she said, 'Who is Shaʿwānah and what is Shaʿwānah? [She is merely] a sinful black bondmaiden.'" He continued, "Then she took to crying, and she did not cease in this whilst we exited and left her."

قَالَ مُحَمَّد بن الْحُسَيْن: وحَدثني يحيى بن بسطَام قَالَ: استأذنا على شعوانة فَأَذنت، فَإِذا منزل رث الْهَيْئَة، أثر الخرب عَلَيْهِ بَين، فَقَالَ لَهَا صَاحب لي: لَو رفقت بِنَفْسِك فقصرت من هَذَا الْبكاء شَيْئا كَانَ أقوى لَك على مَا تريدين. ثمَّ قَالَت: وَالله لَوَدِدْت أَنِّي أبْكِي حَتَّى تنفد دموعي، ثمَّ أبْكِي الدِّمَاء حَتَّى لَا تبقى فِي جَسَدِي جارحة فِيهَا قَطْرَة من دم، وأنى لي بالبكاء.

Muḥammad ibn al-Ḥusayn said that Yaḥyā ibn Busṭām reported to him, "We called at the door of Shaʿwānah and she permitted us to enter. Her abode was decrepit and had clear signs of ruin. One of my companions said to her, 'If you were easier on yourself and stopped crying so much then you would be more able to achieve what you desire.' She replied, 'By Allāh, I wish that I could cry until my tears are exhausted, and then cry [tears of] blood until there no longer remains within my body a single organ which contains a drop of it. But then how far for me will be the shed of tears.'"

قَالَ مُحَمَّد: وحَدثني روح بن سَلمَة قَالَ: قَالَ لي مُضر: مَا رَأَيْت أحدا أقوى على

كَثْرَة الْبكاء من شعوانة، وَلَا سَمِعت صَوتا قطّ أحرق لقلوب الْخَائِفِينَ من صَوتهَا إِذا هِيَ نشجت، ثمَّ تَقول: يَا موتى وَبني الْمَوْتَى وإخوة الْمَوْتَى.

Muḥammad reported upon the authority Muḍar, "I have never seen anyone who cried more excessively than Sha'wānah, and I have never heard a voice more inciting to the hearts of the pious than hers, when she would whimper and say, 'O deceased ones, O son of the deceased, O brothers of the deceased.'"

قَالَ مُحَمَّد: وَقلت لأبي عمر الضَّرِير: أتيت شعوانة؟ قَالَ: قد شهِدت مجلسها مرَارًا، مَا كنت أفهم مَا تَقول من كَثْرَة بكائها. وَسمعتهَا تَقول: من اسْتَطَاعَ مِنْكُم أَن يبكي فليبك، وَإِلَّا فَارْحَمْ الباكي، فَإِن الباكي إِنَّمَا يبكي لمعرفته بِمَا أَتَى إِلَى نَفسه.

Muḥammad said, "I stated to Abū 'Umar al-Ḍarīr, 'Have you seen Sha'wānah?' He replied, 'I have frequented her assemblies on a number of occasions, however I could not decipher [much of] her words due to her excessive crying. I heard her say once, 'Whomever amongst you is able to weep then he should do so. If you are not capable of this then you should display compassion to those who do so. Indeed, the one who weeps does so because he is aware of that which made him cry.'"

[١٤٠] قَالَ أَبُو بكر الْقرشِي: وحَدثني الْحَارِث بن مُحَمَّد التَّمِيمِي قَالَ: حَدثنِي مُحَمَّد بن سُهَيْل عَن الْحَارِث بن الْمُغيرَة قَالَ: كَانَت شعوانة تنوح بِهَذَيْنِ الْبَيْتَيْنِ:

Al-Ḥārith ibn al-Mughīrah reported that Sha'wānah used to lament whilst reciting these two couplets:

يؤمل دنيا لتبقى لَهُ فَوَافى الْمنية قبل الأمل

حينا يروي أصُول الفسيل فَعَاشَ الفسيل وَمَات الرجل

He lays hope in this world that some of it remain for him, but the

end descended before the hope [came to fruition.]
The living is expeditious in irrigating the roots of the sapling, however, the sapling [grew and] lived whilst the man perished.

[١٤١] أخبرتنا شهدة بنت أَحْمد قَالَت أنبأ جَعْفَر بن أَحْمد السراج قَالَ أنبأ أَحْمد بن عَليّ بن الْحُسَيْن قَالَ نَا مُحَمَّد بن عبيد اللَّهِ الْقطيعِي قَالَ نَا الْحُسَيْن بن صَفْوَان قَالَ نَا عبد اللَّهِ بن مُحَمَّد الْقرظِيّ قَالَ: حَدثنِي إِبْرَاهِيم بن عبد الْملك قَالَ: قدمت شعوانة وَزوجهَا مَكَّة فَجعلَا يطوفان ويصليان، فَإِذا كل وأعيا جلس وَجَلَست خلفه، فَيَقُول هُوَ فِي جُلُوسه: أَنا العطشان من حبك لَا أروى، وَهِي تَقول بِالْفَارِسِيَّةِ: أنبت لكل دَاء دَوَاء فِي الْجبَال، ودواء المحبين فِي الْجبَال لم ينْبت.

'Abdullāh ibn Muḥammad al-Qurḍī reported upon the authority of Ibrāhīm ibn 'Abd al-Malik, "Sha'wānah and her husband entered Makkah. They would perform *ṭawāf* and pray, and when they grew weary, he would sit and she would sit behind him. He would say whilst sitting, 'I am thirsty for Your love and nothing can quench it.' And she would say in Persian, 'You have cultivated in the mountains a remedy for every disease, however the cure for lovers does not grow in the mountains.'"

تَحِيَّة النوبية
Taḥiyyah al-Nūbiyyah

[١٤٢] أخبرنَا مُحَمَّد بن عبد الْبَاقِي قَالَ أَنبأَنَا رزق اللَّهِ بن عبد الْوَهَّاب عَن أبي عبد الرَّحْمَن السّلمِيّ قَالَ: سَمِعت الْمَالِينِي الصُّوفِي يَقُول: دخلت [على] تَحِيَّة زَائِرًا فسمعتها من دَاخل الْبَيْت تَقول فِي مناجاتها: يَا من يحبني وأحبه. فَقلت: يَا تَحِيَّة، من أَيْن تعلمين أَنه يحبك؟ فَقَالَت: كنت فِي بلد النّوبَة، وأبواي كَانَا

نَصْرَانِيين، وَكَانَت أُمِّي تحملنِي إِلَى الْكَنِيسَة وتجيء بِي إِلَى الصَّلِيب، وَتقول: قبلي الصَّلِيب فَإِذا هَمَمْت بذلك أرى كفا تخرج فَترد وَجْهي حَتَّى لَا أقبله، فَعلمت أَن عنايته بِي قديمَة.

'Abd al-Wahhāb reported upon the authority of his father 'Abd al-Raḥmān al-Sulamī, "I heard al-Mālīnī al-Ṣūfī say, 'Tuḥiyyah visited me on one occasion, and I heard her invoking Allāh quietly from within the house, 'O the one who loves me and whom I love.' I said, 'O Tuḥiyyah, from where do you ascertain that He loves you?' She replied, 'I am from the land of al-Nūbiyyah, and my parents were Christians. My mother used to bring me to the church and take me to the cross. She would instruct me to kiss it, and whenever I would try to comply, I would see a hand protrude and push me away so that I would not kiss it. Thus, I have come to know that He has cared for me for a long time.'''

فصل
Section

فَأَما المجهولات الْأَسْمَاء من متعبداتهن فمنهن
From the Female Worshippers Amongst Them Whose Names Are Not Known

أم مُحَمَّد بن الْحَنَفِيَّة
Umm Muḥammad ibn al-Ḥanafiyyah

كَانَت جَارِيَة سندية سَوْدَاء من سبي الْيَمَامَة، فَصَارَت إِلَى عَليّ بن أبي طَالب رَضِي اللَّهِ عَنهُ.

She was a Sindī girl with black skin who was from the captives of al-Yamāmah. She came into the possession of 'Alī ibn Abī Ṭālib ﵁.

[١٤٣] أَنبأَنَا مُحَمَّد بن نَاصِر قَالَ أنبأ الْمُبَارك بن عبد الْجَبَّار قَالَ أَنبأَنَا أَبُو مُحَمَّد الْجَوْهَرِي قَالَ أَنبأَنَا أَبُو عمر بن حيويه قَالَ ثَنَا مُحَمَّد بن خلف قَالَ أنبأ أَبُو مُحَمَّد التَّمِيمِي عَن مُحَمَّد بن سعد قَالَ: أَخْبرنِي مُحَمَّد بن عمر قَالَ أنبأ عبد الرَّحْمَن بن أبي الزِّنَاد عَن هِشَام بن عُرْوَة عَن فَاطِمَة بنت الْمُنْذر عَن أَسمَاء بنت أبي بكر قَالَت: رَأَيْت أم مُحَمَّد بن الْحَنَفِيَّة سندية سَوْدَاء، وَكَانَت أمة لبني حنفية، وَلم تكن مِنْهُم، فَإِنَّمَا صَالحهمْ خَالِد بن الْوَلِيد على الرَّقِيق، وَلم يصالحهم على أنفسهم.

Fāṭimah bint al-Mundhir reported upon the authority of Asmā bint Abī Bakr, "I saw Umm Mūhammad ibn al-Ḥanafiyyah the black Sindī. She was a bondmaiden of Banī Ḥanafiyyah, and she was not from their tribe. This is because Khālid ibn Wālīd made a treaty with them to take their slaves as captives, instead of their free people.

عابدة مَكِّيَّة

A Female Worshipper from Makkah

[١٤٤] أخبرنَا أَبُو بكر مُحَمَّد بن عبد اللَّهِ بن حبيب قَالَ أنبأ أَبُو سعد ابْن أبي صَادِق قَالَ نَا مُحَمَّد بن عبد اللَّهِ بن باكويه قَالَ نَا بشر بن أَحْمد قَالَ نَا جَعْفَر بن مُحَمَّد قَالَ أنبأ إِسْحَاق بن بشر الرَّازِيّ قَالَ: نَا الصَّبَّاح بن محَارب قَالَ نَا الْمثنى بن الصَّبَّاح قَالَ: كَانَ عَطاء وَمُجاهد يَخْتَلِفَانِ إِلَى جَارِيَة سَوْدَاء إِلَى نَاحيَة مَكَّة تبكيهما، ثمَّ يرجعان.

Al-Ṣabāḥ ibn Muhārib reported upon the authority of al-Muthanā ibn al-Sabbāḥ, "'Atā and Mujāhid used to visit a black woman in one of the areas of Makkah, and she would make them cry [due to her piety and words.] Then they would return."

عابدة كوفية
A Female Worshipper from Kūfah

[١٤٥] أخبرنَا المحمدان ابْن أبي مَنْصُور وَابْن عبد الْبَاقِي قَالَا أنبأَنَا جَعْفَر بن أَحْمد السراج قَالَ أنبأ أَبُو التوزي قَالَ أنبأ مُحَمَّد بن عبد اللَّهِ الدقاق قَالَ أنبأ الْحُسَيْن بن صَفْوَان قَالَ نَا عبد اللَّهِ بن [مُحَمَّد الْقرشِي قَالَ حَدثنِي مُحَمَّد بن مُوسَى الصايغ قَالَ حَدثنَا عبد اللَّهِ بن نَافِع قَالَ: أُتِي الرّبيع بن خثيم فِي مَنامه فَقيل لَهُ: إِن فُلَانَة السَّوْدَاء زَوجتك فِي الْجنَّة، فَلَمَّا أصبح سَأَلَ عَنْهَا فدلَّ عَلَيْهَا، فَإِذا هِيَ ترعى أَعْنُزًا، فَقَالَ: لأقيمن عِنْدهَا فَأنْظر مَا عَملهَا؟ فَأَقَامَ عِنْدهَا ثَلَاثًا لَا يَرَاهَا تزيد على الْفَرِيضَة، فَإِذا أمست جَاءَت إِلَى عنز لَهَا فحلبت ثمَّ شربت ثمَّ حلبت فسقته، فَقَالَ هلا فِي الْيَوْم الثَّالِث: يَا هَذِه، أَلا تَسْقِنِي من هَذِه العنز. قَالَت: يَا عبد اللَّهِ، إِنَّهَا لَيست لي قَالَ: فَلم تَسْقِنِي من هَذِه؟ قَالَت: إِن هَذِه منحتها أشْرب من لبنهَا، وأسقي من شِئْت، فَقَالَ: يَا هَذِه، فَلَيْسَ لَك من الْعَمَل أَكثر مِمَّا أرى؟ قَالَت لَهُ: لَا إِلَّا أَنِّي مَا أَصبَحت على حَال قطّ فتمنيت أَنِّي على حَال سواهَا، وَلَا أمسيت على حَال قطّ فتمنيت أَنِّي على حَال سواهَا رِضَاء بِمَا قسمه اللَّهِ [عز وَجل] لي، فَقَالَ: يَا هَذِه، علمت أَنِّي رَأَيْت فِي الْمَنَام أَنَّك زَوْجَتي فِي الْجنَّة؟ قَالَت لَهُ: فَأَنت الرّبيع بن خَيْثَم. فَقلت لعبد الله بن نَافِع: كَيفَ علمت هَذَا؟ قَالَ: لَعَلَّهَا أَن تكون رَأَتْ فِي منامها مثل مَا رأى.

ʿAbd Allāh ibn Nāfīʿ reported that Rabīʿ ibn Khaytham had a dream wherein someone said to him, "*Fulānah* (i.e. so and so), a black woman, will be your wife in Jannah." When morning came, he enquired about her and was told where to find her. He found her tending to goats, and he said, "I will stay with her to see what she does (i.e. good deeds to earn Paradise)." He spent three days observing her and did not see her increase upon the compulsory acts. During the evenings she would go to her goat, milk it and drink it, then milk it again to give him a drink. On the third day he asked her, "O lady, why do you not give me milk to drink from this goat?" She replied, "O ʿAbdullāh, this one does not belong to me." He said, "So why do you give me milk to drink from this other one?" She replied, "I have been permitted to drink from this one, and also to give its milk to anyone I want." He then said, "O lady, so do you perform other than that which I have seen?" She replied, "No, however there is never a morning wherein I wish my condition is other than what it is, and neither is there an evening where I wish so. Rather I am pleased with what Allāh the Most High has commissioned for me." He then said, "O lady, do you know that I saw you in a dream wherein it was said that you will be my wife in Jannah?" She replied, "So you are al-Rabīʿ ibn Khaytham." The narrator asked ʿAbdullāh ibn Nāfiʿ, "How did she know this?" He said, "It is possible that she saw a dream similar to his."

عابدة بصرية

A Female Worshipper from Baṣrah

[١٤٦] وَبِالْإِسْنَادِ قَالَ الْقرشِي: وحَدثنِي أَبُو عبد اللَّهِ أَحْمد بن بجير عَن صَالح بن عبد الْكَرِيم قَالَ: رَأَيْت امْرَأَة سَوْدَاء بِالْبَصْرَةِ، وَالنَّاس مجتمعون عَلَيْهَا، ثمَّ قَامَت فَدخلت دَارا فَدَخلُوا مَعهَا وَأَحْدَقُوا بهَا، فدنوت مِنْهَا فَقلت: يَا هَذِه، أما تَخَافِينَ الْعجب؟ فَرفعت رَأسهَا وَنظرت [لي ثمَّ قَالَت: كَيفَ يعجب بِعَمَلِهِ من لَا يدْرِي لَعَلَّه قد رد عَلَيْهِ؟ !

Abū ʿAbdullāh ibn Bujayr reported upon the authority of Ṣāliḥ ibn ʿAbd al-Karīm, "I saw a black woman in al-Bāsrah. The people were gathered around her and she then stood and entered a house, being subsequently followed by the people. They surrounded her but I was able to approach her and say, 'O lady, are you not moved by this astonishing situation?' She raised her head to look at me, and she replied, 'How can a person be astonished at his own good deed if one does not know whether his deed has been rejected (i.e. by Allāh)?'"

❁❁❁

عابدة لقيت في [تيه] بني إسرائيل

A Female Worshipper Who Was Found in the Lands in Which Banī Isrā'īl Were Lost

[١٤٧] أخبرنَا أَبُو بكر بن حبيب قَالَ أنبأ أَبُو سعد بن أبي صَادِق قَالَ نَا أَبُو عبد الله بن باكويه قَالَ ثَنَا عَليّ بن حَفْص قَالَ حَدثنِي مُحَمَّد بن زَنْجوَيْه قَالَ نَا أَبُو بكر مُحَمَّد بن هَارُون الصُّوفِي قَالَ نَا مُحَمَّد بن الْحسن الْمصْرِيّ قَالَ: سَمِعت ذَا النُّون الْمصْرِيّ يَقُول: بَيْنَمَا أَنا أَسِير فِي تيه بني إِسْرَائِيل إِذا أَنا بِجَارِيَة سَوْدَاء قد استلبها الوله من حب الرَّحْمَن شاخصة ببصرها نَحْو السَّمَاء، فَقلت: السَّلَام عَلَيْك يَا أختاه، فَقَالَت: وَعَلَيْكُم السَّلَام يَا ذَا النُّون، فَقلت لَهَا: من أَيْن عَرفتنِي يَا جَارِيَة؟ فَقَالَت: إِن اللَّهِ عز وَجل خلق الْأَرْوَاح قبل الأجساد بألفي عَام، ثمَّ أدارها حول الْعَرْش فَمَا تعارف مِنْهَا ائتلف، وَمَا تناكر مِنْهَا اخْتلف، فَعرفت روحي روحك فِي ذَلِك الجولان. قلت: إِنِّي لأَرَاك حكيمة، علميني شَيْئا مِمَّا علمك اللَّهِ. فَقَالَت: يَا أَبَا الْفَيْض، ضع على جوارحك ميزَان الْقسْط حَتَّى يذوب كل مَا كَانَ لغير اللَّهِ [عز وَجل]، وَيبقى الْقلب مصفى لَيْسَ فِيهِ غير الرب جلّ وَعز فَعِنْدَ ذَلِك يقيمك على الْبَاب ويوليك وَلَايَة جَدِيدَة، وَيَأْمُر الْخيرَات لَك [بِالطَّاعَةِ، فَقلت: يَا أختاه زيديني] فَقَالَت: يَا أَبَا الْفَيْض خُذ من نَفسك لنَفسك، وأطع رَبك إِذا خلوت، يجيبك إِذا دَعَوْت.

Muḥammad ibn al-Ḥasan al-Maṣrī reported upon the authority of Dhū al-Nūn al-Maṣrī, "While I was walking in the barren land of Banī Isrā'īl in which they were lost, I met a black slave girl who was consumed with devotion and love for al-Raḥmān. Her vision was fixed to the sky, and I said to her, '*Assalāmu 'alayk* O sister.' She replied, '*Wa 'alaykum al-salām*, O Dhā al-Nūn.' I said to her, 'Where do you know me from O girl?' She replied, 'Indeed Allāh the Mighty and Majestic created the souls two thousand years before the bodies. Then he circulated them around His throne; those favourable to each other formed an accord and those antagonistic to each other differed. During that period our souls became acquainted.' I said, 'Indeed I can see wisdom in you, teach me something from which Allāh has taught you.' She said, 'O Abā al-Fayḍ, fashion your body parts on the scales of justice, until all that which goes against Allāh dissolves and the heart becomes filtered pure, so that nothing remains within it except your love for the Lord. Upon this, He will place you at His doorstep and elevate you to a new rank. Good things will be presented to you with obedience.' I said, 'O sister, tell me more.' She replied, 'O Abā al-Fayḍ, exercise discipline so that you benefit [later,] practice obedience to your Lord when you are in solitude and He will answer you when you supplicate.'"

عابدة أُخْرَى

Another Female Worshipper

[١٤٨] أَنبأَنَا مُحَمَّد بن نَاصِر قَالَ أنبأ جَعْفَر بن أَحْمد قَالَ أنبأ مُحَمَّد بن عبد الْملك بن بَشرَان قَالَ أَنا أَبُو طَالب مُحَمَّد بن عَليّ بن عَطِيَّة قَالَ ثَنَا عبد اللَّهِ بن مُحَمَّد قَالَ نَا عبد اللَّهِ بن جَعْفَر بن فَارس قَالَ: حَدثنِي أبي قَالَ نَا إِبْرَاهِيم بن الْجُنَيْد قَالَ نَا أَحْمد بن المؤمل قَالَ: نَا زَكَرِيَّا بن يحيى الطَّائِي قَالَ: أرِي إِبْرَاهِيم فِي مَنَامه كَأَنَّهُ يُقَال لَهُ: زَوجتك فِي الْجنَّة فُلَانَة السَّوْدَاء جَارِيَة بني فلَان من الْموصل راعية معزاهم فَمضى إِبْرَاهِيم نَحْو الْموصل، فَسَأَلَ عَن الْقَوْم فَدلَّ عَلَيْهِم، فَسَأَلَهُمْ عَن الْجَارِيَة، فَقَالُوا: هِيَ فِي المعزى ترعاها، فَخرج إِلَيْهَا فِي الصَّحرَاء وَإِذا حبشية ولهى، فَقَالَ لَهَا: السَّلَام عَلَيْك يَا هَذِه، فَقَالَت: وَعَلَيْك

السَّلَام [وَرَحْمَة اللَّهِ وَبَرَكَاته] من أَنْت؟ قَالَ لَهَا: زَوجك فِي الْجنَّة، قَالَت: إِن كنت صَادِقا، فَأَنت إِبْرَاهِيم بن أدهم.

Zakariyyā ibn Yaḥyā al-Ṭā'ī reported, "Ibrāhīm saw in a dream that someone said to him, 'Your wife in Jannah will be *Fulānah* (i.e. so and so), the black slave of a certain tribe from Mosul who tends to their goats.' Ibrāhīm subsequently embarked towards Mosul and asked in regards to that tribe. He was directed to them and he then asked them in regards to this slave. They said that she was with the goats, tending to them. He thus departed to the desert seeking for her until he came to her, she was an Abyssinian who was devoted [to Allāh.] He said to her, '*Assalāmu 'alayk*, O lady.' She replied, '*Wa 'alayk al-salām wa raḥmatullāhī wa barakātuh*. Who are you?' He replied, 'I am your husband in Jannah.' She said, 'If you are truthful, then you must be Ibrāhīm ibn Adham.'"

الْبَاب الرَّابِع وَالْعشْرُونَ

Chapter Twenty Four

فِي ذكر من كَانَ يُؤثر الْجَوَارِي السود على الْبيض وَمن كَانَ يعشقهن وَمن مَاتَ من عشقهن

In mention of those who preferred black bondmaidens to white ones, those who loved them, and those who died due to their love

[١٤٩] أنبأَنَا مُحَمَّد بن نَاصِر قَالَ: أنبأ عبد الْقَادِر بن مُحَمَّد قَالَ أَنا أَبُو مُحَمَّد الْجَوْهَرِي قَالَ: أَنا أَبُو عمر بن حيويه قَالَ أنبأ أَبُو بكر مُحَمَّد بن خلف الْمَرْزُبَان [قَالَ] ثنَا عبد اللَّهِ بن عَمْرو الْبَلْخِي قَالَ نَا الزبير بن بكار قَالَ: حَدثنِي عمي مُصعب بن عبد اللَّهِ قَالَ: كَانَ عبد اللَّهِ بن أبي بكر الصّديق [رَضِي اللَّهِ عَنهُ] يحب جَارِيَة لَهُ سَوْدَاء، وَكَانَت قد شغلت قلبه فَنَهَاهُ أَبُو بكر [رَضِي اللَّهِ عَنهُ] عَنْهَا فتجافي لَهَا، فِي قلبه مِنْهَا شَيْء وَقَالَ:

Zubayr ibn Bakkār reported upon the authority of his uncle Muṣʿab ibn ʿAbdullāh, "ʿAbdullāh ibn Abī Bakr al-Siddīq ﷺ was in love with a black bondmaiden. His heart was preoccupied with her but his father Abū Bakr ﷺ kept them apart. Despite this he still felt something in his heart for her. He said,

أحب لحبها السودَان حَتَّى ... أحب لحبها سود الْكلاب

Due to my love for her I love black, to the extent that I love black dogs due to my love for her.[76]

---

76 This narration is not established. See the biography of ʿAbdullāh ibn Abī Bakr ﷺ in *al-Ṭārīkh al-Awsaṭ* of al-Bukhārī (1/115-116), *al-Iṣābah* (2/283-284) and in other

[١٥٠] [قَالَ ابْن الْمَرْزُبَان: وَأَخبرنِي مُحَمَّد بن إِسْحَاق قَالَ أَخْبرنِي مُحَمَّد بن حبيب قَالَ: أَخْبرنِي هِشَام بن مُحَمَّد بن السَّائِب قَالَ: كَانَ ابْن عَبَّاس يعْزل عَن جَارِيَة لَهُ سَوْدَاء].

Ibn al-Marzubān said [...]: Hishām ibn Muḥammad ibn al-Sāʾib reported, "Ibn ʿAbbās practiced coitus interruptus (*ʿazl*) with one of his bondmaidens who was black."

قَالَ ابْن الْمَرْزُبَان: وَأَخبرنِي أَحْمد بن زُهَيْر قَالَ: أَخْبرنِي مُصعب بن عبد اللَّهِ الزبيرِي قَالَ: أَخْبرنِي عبد اللَّهِ بن رَبَاح الْعجْلَاني قَالَ: إِنِّي لفي مَسْجِد منى إِذْ أَبْصرت بِأبي الجليد الْفَزارِيّ وَاقِفًا على جَارِيَة سَوْدَاء كَأَنَّهَا صنم، فملت إِلَيْهِ، فَقلت: مَا لي أَرَاك هَاهُنَا. قَالَ: أصوب بَصرِي وأصاعده فِي هَذِه الْجَارِيَة وأتمناها على اللَّهِ [عز وَجل] وَأَنْشَأَ يَقُول:

Ibn al-Marzubān reported upon the authority of ʿAbdullāh ibn Rabāḥ al-ʿAjalānī, "I was in the *masjid* on one occasion when I saw Abī al-Jalīd al-Fazārī standing by a black slave, and it was as if she was a statue. I went to him and said, 'What is this that I see you doing here?' He replied, 'I am fixing my gaze upon this bondmaiden placing hope in Allāh that he allows me to have her.' Then he recited,

أَلا يُصِبْنِي أَجلي فأحترم　　أشتر من مَالِي ضناكا كالصنم

عريضة المعطس خشناء الْقَدَم　　تكون أم وَلَدي وتختدم

If death does not afflict me then I swear, to buy with my wealth this poor one who is like a statue.

With a flat nose and rough feet, to bear me a son and to serve."

قَالَ مُصعب: وَكَانَ أَبُو الجليد أَعْرَابِيًا بدويا عَلامَة، فَرَأَيْت الضَّحَّاك بن عُثْمَان

sources.

يروي مِنْهُ وَيَأْخُذ عَنهُ.

Muṣʿab said, "Abū al-Jalīd was a Bedouin and a well-learned individual. I saw al-Ḍaḥḥāk ibn ʿUthmān narrating from him and taking knowledge from him."

[١٥١] قَالَ ابْن الْمَرْزُبَان: وَأَخْبرنِي عبد اللَّهِ بن شبيب قَالَ حَدثنِي مُحَمَّد بن إِسْمَاعِيل الْجَعْفَرِي قَالَ حَدثنِي حَكِيم بن طَلْحَة الْفَزارِيّ قَالَ حَدثنِي سيار بن نجيح قَالَ: طلبت ابْن ميادة فَقيل لي: خرج أمس فَعرفت أَنه ذهب فِي اتِّبَاع أمة بني سهل، فغبت فِي بغائه، فَوَقَعت عَلَيْهِ فِي قرارة بَيْضَاء قد حفت بحرة سَوْدَاء، وَإِذا غنم، وَإِذا حمَار ابْن ميادة مُقيّد، وَهُوَ مَعهَا تَحت سَمُرَة وَكَانَت الْأمة سَوْدَاء فَسلمت وَجَلَست، فَأقبل ابْن ميادة على الْأمة فَقَالَ لَهَا: أنشديهم مَا قلت فِيك فأنشدتنا:

Ibn al-Marzubān said: Hakīm ibn Ṭalḥah al-Fazārī reported upon the authority of Sayyār ibn Najīḥ, "I was seeking Ibn Mayyādah and it was said to me that he left on the previous day. I came to know that he had left to go after a bondmaiden of Banī Sahl. So, I sought after him, finding him in a low ground which was surrounded by a dark stony area. I saw sheep there and Ibn Mayyādah's donkey was bound there also. He was there with it under a tree and so was the black bondmaiden, so I greeted them and sat. Ibn Mayyādah turned to her and said recite to them the poem I made for you, so she recited,

تمنونني مِنْك اللِّقَاء وإنني لأعْلم ... لَا أَلْقَاك من دون بابل

إِلَى ذَاك مَا جَاءَت أُمُور وَمَا انْقَضتْ ... غيابة حبيك أنجاد المخايل

وحالت شهور الْحَج بيني وَبَينهَا ... وَرفع الأعادي كل حق وباطل

أَقُول لعذالي لما تقابلا عَليّ ... بلوم مثل طعن المعايل

فَلَا تكثرن فِيهَا الهجا فَإِنَّهَا مصلصلة من بعض تِلْكَ الصلاصل

من الصفر لأورها سمح دلالها وَلَيْسَت من الْبيض الْقصار الحوائل

وَلكنهَا رَيْحَانَة طَابَ نشرها بأجرح تندي بالضحى والأصايل

They promised me that I will meet you whilst I knew, that I would not meet you except in Babylon.

And in regards to it the matters have not passed me nor has ceased, the depth of my love [and the] intense fantasy.

The months of Ḥajj have passed to separate between me and her, and my enemies have raised many true and false [contentions.]

I say to those criticising me when they face me, with criticism like the stabbing of a sharp knife,

Do not be excessive in lampooning her, for she is a dove from those doves,

Which are yellow, unrefined and direct in affection, and she is not from the white, uncoloured and fickle.

Rather, she is like sweet basil in emission of pleasant scent, which is found upon her both in the morning day and the evening."[77]

قَالَ سيار: فَقلت: مَالك لَا تشتربها؟ فَقَالَ: إِذا يقتل حبها.

Sayyār said, "I said to him, 'Why do you not purchase her?' To which he replied, 'Doing so will put her love in my heart to an end (i.e. having her will make her within my reach and so my passion will fade away).'"

[١٥٢] قَالَ ابْن الْمَرْزُبَان: وحَدثني إِسْحَاق بن أبان قَالَ، حَدثنِي مُحَمَّد بن

---

77 [T] The translation of the last three couplets is based upon the wording found in *Tārīkh Dimishq* by Ibn 'Asākir (18/207), with the wording:

فلا تكثرا فيها الهجاء فإنها مصلصلة من بعض تلك الصلاصل

من الصفر لا ورهاء سمج دلالها وليست من البيض القصار الحوائل

ولكنها ريحانة طاب شمها وردت عليها بالضحى والأصائل

سَلام قَالَ: عرض إِنْسَان أسود لامْرَأَة كَانَ لَهَا ابْن عَم يعشقها فأجابت الْأسود، فَقَالَ ابْن عَمها:

Ibn al-Marzubān reported upon the authority of Muḥammad ibn Sallām, "A black man was presented (i.e. for marriage) to a woman who had a cousin deeply in love with her. However, she chose the black man. Her cousin thus said,

شابت أعالي قروني وانجلى بَصرِي فَمَا أحدث عَن قمرية الْوَادي

نبئت أَن غرابا ظلّ محتضا قمرية فَوق أَغْصَان وأعواد

The crown of my hair has turned grey and my eyesight faded, as I talk about the *qumriyyah* (a form of dove) of the valley.

I was told a crow embraced the *qumriyyah*, over branches and sticks."

قَالَ: وأنشدني بَعضهم:

Ibn al-Marzubān said that some of them recited:

قَالُوا تعشقها سمراء قلت لَهُم لون الغوالي ولون الْمسك وَالْعود

إِنِّي امْرُؤ لَيْسَ شَأْن الْبيض مرتفعا عِنْدِي وَلَو خلت الدُّنْيَا من السود

They said that I love the brown skinned women and I replied, [yes,] the colour of *ghawālī* and of musk and *al-ʿūd*.

I am a man to whom whiteness has no special rank, and this would be the case for me even if the world became bereft of darkness.

قَالَ: وأنشدت لأبي الشيص فِي جَارِيَة كَانَت لَهُ سَوْدَاء وَكَانَ اسْمهَا تبر:

He said that the following was composed for Abī al-Shīṣ's black bondmaiden named Tibr (the word *tibr* refers to small pieces of gold):

لم تنصفي يَا سميَّة الذَّهَب تتْلف نَفسِي وَأَنت فِي لعب

يَا بنت عَم الْمسك الذكي وَمن لولاه لم يجتني وَلم يطب
ناسبك الْمسك فِي السوَاد وَفِي الرّيح فَأكْرم بِذَاكَ من نسب

You are not being fair with me O you, who is named after gold, my soul is being destroyed whilst you remain in jest.

O cousin of the fragrant musk, if not for him we would not be able to gather it nor perfume.

Musk befits you in being black, and in scent. So what lofty attributes are shared in this *nasab* (i.e. relationship/ancestry).

قَالَ: وأنشدني أَبُو مُحَمَّد العباسي لبَعْضهم:

He said that Abū Muḥammad al-ʿAbbāsī recited the following to him from some people:

أَقُول لمن عَابَ السوَاد سفاهة وللسود قوم عائبون وحسد
وعيب سَواد اللَّوْن إِن قيل حالك وَهَذَا سَواد الْمسك وَالْعود أسود
وَهَذَا سَواد الرُّكْن يشفى بلمسه ويهوى إِلَيْهِ بِالرُّكُوعِ وَيسْجد
وَلَوْلَا سَواد الْعين لم يكن طرفها صَحِيحا وذمت طرفها حِين ترقد
وَلَو علم الْمهْدي لونا يفوق لألوى بِهِ راياته حِين تعقد

I say to the one who finds fault in blackness with foolishness, and in blackness there are certainly those who find fault in it and those who begrudge it.

If the fault you find is the blackness itself, then know that musk and *al-ʿūd* are black too.

And there is the black corner [of the Kaʿbah) of which people touch to attain *shifā*, and towards which people fall in *rukūʿ* and *sujūd*.

And if not for the blackness of the eye, its sight, would not be correct, and it would not sit right while it sleeps.

And if al-Mahdī knew of a colour better than it, he would utilise another colour for his banners when his affair arises.

[١٥٣] قَالَ ابْن الْمَرْزُبَان: وَأَخبرنِي مُحَمَّد بن الْعَبَّاس بن أبي حَاتِم قَالَ قَالَ لي أبي: كَانَ عندنَا بِالْبَصْرَةِ رجل من المهالبة يعشق زنجية كَانَت لبَعض جيراننا، فَلم يزل يدس إِلَى مولاتها حَتَّى اشْتَرَاهَا، وَكَانَت قد شغلت قلبه عَن أَهله فَعَاتَبَهُ فِي أمرهَا جمَاعَة من أَهله وإخوانه فَلم يلْتَفت إِلَى قَوْلهم.

Muḥammad ibn al-ʿAbbās ibn Abī Ḥātim reported upon the authority of his father, "In Baṣrah there was a man with us from al-Mahālabah who was deeply in love with a Zanjī woman who belonged to one of his neighbours. He did not stop pressing her owner until he allowed him to purchase her. She consumed his heart over his family. He was admonished due to this matter by a group from his family and brothers, however he did not pay heed to their words.

[١٥٤] قَالَ ابْن الْمَرْزُبَان: وَأَخْبرنِي إِسْحَاق بن أبان عَن الْعُتْبِي أَنه قَالَ فِي جَارِيَة سَوْدَاء كَانَت لَهُ:

Ibn al-Marzubān reported that al-ʿUtbī composed the following for a black bondmaiden of his,

ثكلتها أَن لم يكن وَجههَا   أحسن عِنْدِي من رُجُوع الشَّبَاب

May I be deprived of her if her face, is not more favourable to me
than the return of youth.

قَالَ ابْن الْمَرْزُبَان: وَأنْشد لأبي عَليّ الْبَصِير:

Ibn al-Marzubān said that the following was recited from Abī ʿAlī al-Baṣīr:

أسكرتني سكرا بِغَيْر شراب   وَأَتَتْ إِذْ أَتَت بِأَمْر عُجاب

لم ترجع بِآيَة من كتاب اللَّهِ   حَتَّى نسيت أم الْكتاب

لم يعبها اسْتِحَالَة اللَّوْن عِنْدِي   إِنَّهَا صبغة كلون الشَّبَاب

She intoxicated me without any drink, [as] she did something that was awe-inspiring.

As she recited a single *āyah* from the Book of Allāh, her voice made me forget Umm al-Kitāb (i.e. al-Fātiḥah).

I never minded her different colour, for she is tanned in the colour of youth.

قَالَ: وأنشدني بعض أهل الْأَدَب:

He said that one of the scholars of literature recited the following to him:

أَهْدَت لقلبك صبوة وَفَسَادًا ولجفن عَيْنك عِبْرَة وسهادا

من كَانَ يرغب فِي الْبيَاض لحسنه فَأَنا الْمعَارض بالبياض سوادا

لَا ينفذ القرطاس فِي حاجاته حَتَّى تنمق ساحتيه مدادا

نَفسِي الْفِدَاء لَك خود طفلة سَوْدَاء أقربت الْفُؤَاد بعادا

She bestowed your heart with desires and immorality, and your eyelid with a tear and sleeplessness.

The one who craves whiteness, due to its beauty, I can challenge whiteness [with the beauty] of blackness.

For the parchment cannot serve its purpose, until both sides have been written on with [black] ink.

My life is sacrificed to you, O black girl that brought my heart closer.

[١٥٥] قَالَ ابْن الْمَرْزُبَان: وَأَخْبرنِي الْحَارِث قَالَ: قَالَ الْمَدَائِنِي: اتخذ الفرزدق على النوار جَارِيَة زنجية فأحبها فَولدت لَهُ جَارِيَة، وَكَانَ يُحِبهَا ويمدح الزنج.

Ibn al-Marzubān reported upon the authority of al-Madā'inī, "Al-Farazdaq took a Zanjī as a slave girl besides his wife, al-Nawwār. He loved her and she bore him a girl. He adored her and would praise the Zanjī people."

[١٥٦] قَالَ ابْن الْمَرْزُبَان: وحَدثنِي مُحَمَّد بن جَعْفَر قَالَ حَدثنِي بعض الشاميين

عَن أبي زيد الدِّمَشْقِي قَالَ: حَدثنِي جَعْفَر بن زِيَاد الشَّامي قَالَ: هوى رجل منا جَارِيَة سَوْدَاء فلامه أَهله على ذَلِك، وَقَالُوا: عشقت سَوْدَاء! فَأَنْشَأَ يَقُول:

Ibn al-Marzubān reported upon the authority of Ja'far ibn Ziyād al-Shāmī, "A man from amongst us desired a black slave girl, however his family chastised him for this. They said to him, 'You desire after a black woman!?" So, he recited the following:

يكون الْخَال فِي خد قَبِيح　　فيكسره الملاحة والجمالا

فَكيف يلام إِنْسَان على من يرَاهُ　　كُله فِي الْعين خالا

A beauty spot upon an ugly cheek, will clothe it with allure and beauty.

Thus, how can one be chastised over the one he sees, all of her in essence to be like a beauty spot.

[١٥٧] قَالَ ابْن الْمَرْزُبَان: وأنشدني أَحْمد بن حبيب [لأبي حَفْص] الشطرنجي فِي دَنَانِير جَارِيَة يحيى بن خَالِد الْبَرْمَكِي وَكَانَت سَوْدَاء:

Ibn al-Marzubān said that Aḥmad ibn Ḥabīb recited to him couplets from the poetry of Abī Ḥafṣ about the bondmaiden of Yahyā ibn Khālid al-Barmakī, who was black:

أشبهك الْمسك وأشبهته　　قَائِمَة فِي لَونه قَاعِدَة

لاشك إِذْ لونكما وَاحِد　　أنكما من طِينَة وَاحِدَة

Musk resembles you and you resemble it, in colour, whether you are standing or sitting.

There is no doubt—as your colours are one—, that you are both created from the same clay.

[١٥٨] قَالَ ابْن الْمَرْزُبَان: وَحدثنَا مُحَمَّد التَّمِيمِي عَن أبي الْحسن الْمَدِينِيّ قَالَ:

كَانَ ليزِيد بن مُعَاوِيَة جَارِيَة سَوْدَاء وَكَانَ يُحِبهَا، فَخَلا بهَا يَوْمًا وَعلمت امْرَأَته، فَأَتَت الْموضع فَمَال إِلَيْهَا وَترك السَّوْدَاء واستحى مِنْهَا.

Ibn al-Marzubān reported upon the authority of Abī al-Ḥasan al-Madanī, "Yazīd ibn Mu'āwiyah had a black bondmaiden whom he loved dearly. One day, he was with her alone but his wife came to know about it and walked in on them. He then went with his wife, leaving the black bondmaiden and feeling embarrassment from her."

قَالَ ابْن الْمَرْزُبَان: وَسمعت بعض أهل الْأَدَب يَقُول: بَلغنِي أَن رجلا عوتب فِي سَوْدَاء كَانَ يُحِبهَا فَقَالَ: وَالله مَا صلحت إِلَّا أَن تقطع خيلانا فِي خدود القيان.

Ibn al-Marzubān said that he heard one of the scholars of literature say, "It reached me that a man was blamed for falling in love with a black woman. He responded by saying, 'By Allāh, she befits to be a beauty spot upon the cheeks of young females.'"

[١٥٩] قَالَ ابْن الْمَرْزُبَان: وَأخبرنَا حَمَّاد بن إِسْحَاق بن إِبْرَاهِيم الْموصِلِي عَن أَبِيه قَالَ: اعْترض الْفضل بن الرّبيع جواري، وَكَانَ فِيهِنَّ جَارِيَة سَوْدَاء، وَكَانَ لَهَا لِسَان وبنان وحلاوة وشكل، فَوَقعت بِقَلْبِه فكلمها، فَرَأى سرعَة جوابها، فَزَاد إعجابا، فاشتراها.

Ibn al-Marzubān reported upon the authority of Ḥammād ibn Isḥāq ibn Ibrāhīm al-Mūṣalī from his father, "Al-Faḍl ibn al-Rabī' stood in the way of some slavegirls, and in the group was a black girl. She possessed a good tongue, sweetness and looks. She struck his heart and he spoke to her. When he saw her quick-witted response, it increased his amazement with her. Thus, he purchased her."

قَالَ ابْن الْمَرْزُبَان: وأنشدني أَحْمد بن جَعْفَر الْكَاتِب لبَعْضهِم:

Ibn al-Marzubānd said that Aḥmad ibn Ja'far recited:

أحب الْجَوَارِي الْأدم من أجل تكْتم وَمن أجلهَا أَحْبَبْت من كَانَ أسودا

فجئني بِمثل الْمسك أطيب رَاحَة وجئني بِمثل اللَّيْل أطيب مرقدا

I like black slavegirls only because of *Takttum*, for her I also loved whoever is black.

There is nothing better than musk as a fragrance, And there is nothing like a black night to sleep well.

قَالَ: وأنشدني أَبُو عبد الله الأسباطي:

And he said that Abū ʿAbdullāh al-Asbāṭī recited,

ألم تَرَ أَن الْمسك مِنْهُ حصية بِمَال وَأَن الْملح وقر بدرهم

وَأَن سَواد الْعين فِي الْعين نورها وَمَا لبياض الْعين نور فيفهم

Don't you see that a little of musk is worthy of wealth (i.e. expensive), whereas a bulk-load of salt only costs a dirham.

And that the blackness of the eye is its light, whereas the whiteness of the eye gives no light.

قَالَ: وأنشدت لإسماعيل بن أبي هَاشم مولى آل الزبير:

He said that he recited for Ismāʿīl ibn Abī Hāshim, the *mawlā* of Āl al-Zubayr:

جَارِيَة مجدولة من الْحَبَش فِي وَجههَا آثَار كي ونمش

كَأَنَّهَا غُصْن تثنى يَوْم طش

A slavegirl with a tuned body from Abyssinia, in her face are signs of burns and freckles,

She is like a twig that has bent in a rainy day.

وَله أَيْضا:

And also:

نوبية طيبَة الأردان   تخطر فِي حلَّة أرجوان

كَأَنَّهَا غُصْن من الأغصان

A Nubian girl with a good spun, walking in a purple garment,
As if she is a twig.

قَالَ: وأنشدت لِابْنِ الجهم حب أَدَم النِّسَاء من سنة الظّرْف على أَنه جمال الْقُلُوب:

And he said that he recited poetry to Ibn al-Jahm regarding loving black women being a habit of jolly men; due to it being an indication of beauty in the heart:

كَيفَ يهوى الْفَتى الظريف   وصال الْبيض شُبُهَات المشيب

وأصل الْأدم مشبهات سَواد الْعين   والمسك فِي نعيم وَطيب

مشبهات السوَاد والمسك تفديكن   نَفسِي من نائبات الخطوب

How could an amusing youth desire, the love of white women whose whiteness resembles grey hair?

While black women resemble the blackness of the eyes, and musk which is dipped in fragrance and goodness.

Those who resemble musk and blackness of the eye I sacrifice, myself to save you from the hardships of time.

[١٦٠] قَالَ ابْن الْمَرْزُبَان: وَأَخْبرنِي الْقَاسِم بن عبد الرَّحْمَن قَالَ: كَانَ لمُحَمد بن عبد الْملك الْأَسدي جَارِيَة سَوْدَاء فأحبها وَولدت لَهُ.

Ibn al-Marzubānd reported upon the authority of Qāsim ibn 'Abd al-Raḥmān, "Muḥammad ibn 'Abd al-Malik al-Asadī had a black slave girl whom he loved, and she bore him a child."

قَالَ: وَأخْبرنَا أَبُو الْفضل الأيادي قَالَ: وحَدثنِي الْحُسَيْن بن إِسْمَاعِيل الْعَتكِي قَالَ أنبأ الصَّقْر بن عبد اللَّهِ الْمَكِّيّ قَالَ: كَانَ عندنَا بِمَكَّة رجل يُقَال لَهُ: الحسام بن قدامَة مشتهرا بحب السود، وَكَانَ إخوانه يلومونه على ذَلِك وَلَا يرجع، وَكَانَت لَهُ فِيهِنَّ أشعار كَثِيرَة فَمِنْهَا:

He reported upon the authority of al-Ṣaqar ibn ʿAbdullāh al-Makkī, "In Makkah there was a man with us who was known as al-Ḥusām ibn Qudāmah, famous for his love of black women. His brothers would criticise him for this but he did not change. He composed many poems in regards to them, from them is:

لَا تلوما فلات حِين ملامة　　أزهق الْحبّ نَفسه والمستهامة

فتنته بشكلهن الْجَوَارِي　　والجواري فِي شكلهن غَرَامَة

يَا جواري حَدثنِي بحياتي　　هَل عليكن فِي هلاكي قسَامَة

صَاح إِن القيان غير امتراء　　سَوف يقتلني وَرب الْقِيَامَة

فَإِذا مت فاجمعوا الحرميات　　وصفراء مولدات الْيَمَامَة

والثقال الحقائب الْمَدَنِيَّات　　ذَوَات المضاحك البسامة

ثمَّ قومُوا على الْحجُون فصيحوا　　يَا قَتِيل القيان يَا بن قدامَة

[١٦١] قَالَ ابْن الْمَرْزُبَان: وَأَخْبرنِي أَبُو الْفضل الأيادي عَن أبي دَاوُد المصاحفي قَالَ: كَانَت للنضر بن شُمَيْل جَارِيَة سَوْدَاء قد أدبها وخرجها وفرحها، وَكَانَت فصيحة، وَكَانَ يمِيل إِلَيْهَا ويحبها، قَالَ: فَقَالَت لي يَوْمًا - وَقد ذاكرتها بالشعر -: الغ عَن هَذَا، فَإِنَّهُ حرفه كُله، وَالله مَا زَالَ بيتنا قفرا مَا كَانَ فِيهِ:

Ibn al-Marzubānd reported upon the authority of Abī Dāwūd al-Maṣāḥifī, "Al-Naḍr ibn Shamīl had a bondmaiden who he cultivated, took out and gave joy to. She was very eloquent, and he was enamoured with her and loved her dearly. She said to him one time—whilst they were talking about poetry, 'Refrain from such poetry, for it is in vain and by Allāh our house will remain poor so long as we recite:

عفت الديار محلهَا فمقامها   وآذنتنا بَينهَا أَسمَاء

The abodes have been deserted, and Asmā has notified me that she will be departing.

وأشباههما حَتَّى أبدلنا اللَّهِ [عز وَجل] بذلك فخصبت رحلنا وَأمن بيتنا فَجعلت أعجب من تَخْلِيصهَا وجودة تمييزها.

And the like of this couplet. [Refrain from this,] and then [you will see] Allāh will give us in exchange an increase in our belongings and security in our abode.' Her words caused me to become amazed at her refinement and level of discernment."

[١٦٢] أخبرنَا مُحَمَّد بن نَاصِر قَالَ أنبأ الْمُبَارك بن عبد الْجَبَّار قَالَ أنبأ أَبُو مُحَمَّد الْجَوْهَرِي قَالَ أنبأ ابْن حيويه قَالَ أنبأ مُحَمَّد بن خلف قَالَ: أَخْبرنِي أَبُو بكر الْقرشِي قَالَ: حَدثنِي مُحَمَّد بن بكير عَن الْأَصْمَعِي قَالَ: كَانَ أَبُو حَازِم سَلمَة بن دِينَار الْأَعْرَج يتَمَثَّل بِهَذَا الْبَيْت:

Muḥammad ibn Nāṣir reported upon the authority of al-Aṣmaʿī, "Abū Ḥāzim Salamah ibn Dīnār al-Aʿraj cited the following couplet,

فَمن يَك معجبا بينات كسْرَى   فَإِنِّي معجب بَنَات حام

One may be enamoured with Persian women, I am like so but with the women of Ḥām."

قَالَ مُحَمَّد بن خلف: وَأَخْبرنِي بعض أهل الْأَدَب قَالَ: كَانَ إِسْمَاعِيل بن جَامع قد تزوج بالحجاز جَارِيَة سَوْدَاء مولاة لقوم يُقَال لَهَا مَرْيَم، فَلَمَّا صَار من الرشيد

بالموضع الَّذِي صَار بِهِ اشتاق إِلَى السَّوْدَاء، فَقَالَ يذكرهَا، وَيذكر الْموضع الَّذِي كَانَ يألفها بِهِ، ويجتمعان فِيهِ -:

Muḥammad ibn Khalf reported upon the authority of one of the scholars of literature, "Ismāʿīl ibn Jāmiʿ married a black woman named Maryam—who was the freedwomen (*mawlāt*) of a people—in al-Ḥijāz. When he became from the close people to al-Rashīd, he grew to miss her deeply, and he said that he was remembering her, the places they would frequent together and the places they would have relations:

هَل لَيْلَتي بفضاء الحصحاص عايدة فِي قبَّة ذَات أشراج وأزرار

تسمو مجامرهما بالمندلي كَمَا تسمو بجنابه أَفْوَاج إعصار

الْمسك يَبْدُو إِلَيْنَا من غلائلها والعنبر الْورْد تذكيه على النَّار

وَمَرْيَم بَين أتراب منعمة طورا وطورا تغنيني بأوتار

Will the nights I spent [with her] at al-Ḥis-ḥas return, in the tent of knots and adornments.

The fragrance of their fumigator pierces through the perfume, like an arrow flies through a windy storm.

The smell of her musk travels to me through her garments, and the rosy umber smells stronger with fire.

All the while Maryam wears soft clothes and sings for me beautiful tones.

فَقَالَ لَهُ الرشيد - وَقد سمع شعره -: وَيلك، من مريمك هَذِه الَّتِي قد وصفتها صفة الْحور الْعين؟ قَالَ: زَوْجَتي، فوصفها كلَاما أَضْعَاف مَا وصفهَا شعرًا. فَأرْسل الرشيد إِلَى الْحجاز فَإِذا هِيَ سَوْدَاء طمطانية ذَات مشافر فَقَالَ لَهُ: وَيلك، هَذِه مَرْيَم الَّتِي مَلَأت الدُّنْيَا بذكرها؟ قَالَ: يَا سَيِّدي، إِن عمر بن عبد اللَّهِ ابْن أبي

ربيعة يَقُول:

Al-Rashīd said to him after hearing his poetry, 'Woe to you, who is this Maryam that you attributed with the characteristics of al-Ḥūr al-'Īn (the women of Paradise)?' He replied, 'She is my wife, and I can describe her with traits which are double what I mentioned in the poetry.' So, al-Rashīd sent a detachment to al-Ḥijāz and he then saw a black Ṭamaṭanī woman who had large lips. He then said to him, 'Woe to you, this is the Maryam of which you fill the whole world with her praise?' He replied, 'O sire, indeed 'Umar ibn 'Abdullāh ibn Abī Rabī'ah said,

فتضاحكن وَقد قُلْنَ لَهَا   حسن فِي كل عين من تود

They laughed and then said to her, beauty is in the eye of the beholder.

[١٦٣] أَنبأَنَا مُحَمَّد بن نَاصِر قَالَ أنبأ أَبُو الْحُسَيْن بن عبد الْجَبَّار قَالَ أنبأَنَا الْحسن بن عَليّ قَالَ أنبأ مُحَمَّد بن الْعَبَّاس قَالَ أنبأ مُحَمَّد بن خلف قَالَ: حَدثنِي إِسْحَاق بن مُحَمَّد الْكُوفِي قَالَ أنبأ مُحَمَّد بن سَلام الجُمَحِي قَالَ: قَالَ أَبُو السَّائِب الْمدنِي: كَانَت بِالْمَدِينَةِ قينة، وَكَانَت من أَجود النَّاس غناء، فاشتراها رجل من بني هَاشم، وَكَانَت تهوى غُلَاما أسود من أهل الْمَدِينَة، فَقَالَ لَهَا مَوْلَاهَا يَوْمًا: غَنِي، فأنشأت تَقول:

Al-Ḥasan ibn 'Alī reported upon the authority of Abū al-Sā'ib al-Madanī, "In Madīnah there was a girl singer, and she was from the best of people at singing. A man from Banī Hāshim purchased her. She was in love with a black youth from the people of Madīnah. Her master said to her to sing for him on one occasion, so she recited,

إِذا شَاب الغرب نسيت ليلِي   وهيهات المشيب من الْغُرَاب

أحب لحبها السودَان حَتَّى   أحب لحبها سود الْكلاب

If the black hair became grey, I would forget my night, and how is it possible for the grey to become black.
I love due to this love the colour black, to the extent I love dogs that are black in colour.

فقَالَ الْمولى: وَالله مَا أَنا بأسود، فَمن عنيت؟ قَالَت: فلَانا قَالَ: أتحبيه؟ فَقَالَت: إي وَالله، قَالَ: فلَا عذر فِي حَبسك عَنهُ، وهيئت أحسن تهيئة، ثمَّ بعث بهَا إِلَيْهِ.

Her master said, 'By Allāh, I am not black. Who are you referring to?' She replied, 'So and so.' He said, 'Do you love him?' She replied, 'Yes, by Allāh.' He said, 'There is no excuse for me to prevent you from him then. So, he prepared her in the best manner and then sent her to him."

[١٦٤] قَالَ ابْن خلف: وَأخْبرنَا أَبُو حَاتِم السجسْتانِي قَالَ أنبأ أَبُو عُبَيْدَة معمر بن الْمثنى قَالَ: كَانَ ابْن الدمينة يتتبع أمة سَوْدَاء لبَعض الْحَيّ، فعذله أَهله وعشيرته على ذَلِك، فَأَبت نَفسه إِلَّا اتباعها فشكوا ذَلِك مِنْهُ إِلَى أَمِير الْمُؤمنِينَ فحبسه، فَأَقَامَ فِي الْحَبْس شهرا.

Ibn Khalf reported upon the authority of Abū 'Ubaydah Ma'mar ibn al-Muthanā, "Ibn al-Damīnah would follow after a black bondmaiden in a certain neighbourhood. His family and clan rebuked him for this, but he refused to abandon this practice and they complained to the Commander of the Faithful regarding this. He was thus imprisoned for a month."

[١٦٥] قَالَ ابْن خلف: وأنشدني أَبُو عبد اللَّهِ بن أبي مُحَمَّد لبَعض شعراء أهل الْبَصْرَة.

Ibn Khalf said, "Abu 'Abdullāh ibn Abī Muḥammad cited some poetry to me which was composed by some poets from Basrah.

قَالُوا الْبيَاض على علاته حسن   كَمَا السوَاد على علاته سمج
هَل تُوصَف الْعين فِي تغير لحظتها   إِن لم تحسنها الأجفان والدعج

أَو يشرق الدّرّ فِي الأجياد مبسما   حَتَّى يكون مدَار اللبة السبج

يَا نفس صبرا على حر الْهوى أبدا   مَا بعد ذَا الْحبّ إِلَّا الْمَوْت والفرج

They said that white possesses beauty despite all its defects, just like how black is boring due its defects.

But would an eye be described as beautiful without its eyelids and strong black and white area?

Or would gems glow on horses if there was no necklace with black gems around it?

O my self, be patient with the troubles of love, for there is nothing after such love except death and ease.

[١٦٦] قَالَ ابْن خلف: وَحدثنَا عبد الرَّحْمَن بن بشير قَالَ: أنبأ مُحَمَّد بن إِسْحَاق المسيني قَالَ نَا الْفَروِي عَن الْمَاجشون قَالَ: كَانَت جليدة السَّوْدَاء صَبِيحَة مُتَقَدّمَة فِي الصباحة حلوة فرآها مُحَمَّد بن عبد اللَّهِ بن عَمْرو بن عُثْمَان فَوَقَعت فِي نَفسه، فَأرْسل يخطبها سرا، فَأَبت إِلَّا النِّكَاح الظَّاهِر، وَقَالَت: لَا أكون إِلَّا عارا على السودَان. فتسلى عَنْهَا.

Ibn Khalf reported upon the authority of al-Mājishūn, "Jalīdah was a black woman who was known for her beauty. One day, Muḥammad ibn 'Abdullāh ibn 'Amr ibn 'Uthmān saw her and he fell in love with her. He proposed to her in secret but she refused and insisted that such a marriage be known and not in secret, and said, 'If I agree to be married in secret, I will be putting all black people to shame.' Then, he forgot about her."

[١٦٧] قَالَ ابْن خلف: وَأَخْبرنِي عبد الرَّحْمَن بن سُلَيْمَان قَالَ حَدثنِي مُحَمَّد بن جَعْفَر قَالَ حَدثنِي أَحْمد بن مُوسَى قَالَ: دخلت على مُحَمَّد بن عبد اللَّهِ بن الْمهْدي - وَقد قعد مَعَ جواريه فاحتشمت، فَقَالَ لي: لَا تحتشم، ثمَّ قَالَ لي: بِاللَّه من ترى أعشق من هَؤُلَاءِ؟ فَنَظَرت إِلَى سَوْدَاء كَانَت فِيهِنَّ فَقلت: هَذِه. فَتقدم فَقعدَ إِلَى جنبها. فَوَاللَّه مَا بَرحت حَتَّى بَكَى من عَشِقهَا.

Ibn Khalf reported upon the authority of Aḥmad ibn Mūsā, "I entered into the presence of 'Abdullāh ibn al-Mahdī and he was sitting with his bond-maidens and I became shy. He said to me, 'Do not be shy. By Allāh, tell me which one from these are you most fond of?' I looked at a black one from the group of women and stated that she was the one. She came forward and he sat next to her. By Allāh it was not long before he wept due to his love for her."

[١٦٨] أخبرنَا ابْن نَاصِر قَالَ: أَنا أَبُو الْحسن بن عبد الْجَبَّار قَالَ أنبأ الْحسن بن عَليّ الْجَوْهَرِي قَالَ أنبأ مُحَمَّد بن الْعَبَّاس قَالَ أنبأ مُحَمَّد بن خلف قَالَ: ذكر بعض الروَاة عَن الْعمريّ قَالَ: كَانَ أَبُو عبد اللَّهِ الحبشاني يعشق صفراء العلاقمية - وَكَانَت سَوْدَاء - فاشتكى من حبها وضني حَتَّى صَار إِلَى حد الْمَوْت، فَقَالَ بعض أَهلهَا لمولاتها: لَو وجهت صفراء إِلَى أبي عبد اللَّهِ الحبشاني، فَلَعَلَّهُ أَن يعقل إِذا رَآهَا، ففعلت، فَلَمَّا دخلت عَلَيْهِ قَالَت: كَيفَ أَصبَحت يَا أَبَا عبد اللَّهِ؟ قَالَ: بِخَير مالم تبرحي. قَالَت: مَا تشْتَهي؟ قَالَ: قربك. قَالَت: فَمَا تَشْتَكِي؟ قَالَ: حبك، قَالَت: فتوصي بِشَيْء؟ قَالَ: أوصِي بك إِن قبلوا مني فَقَالَت: إِنِّي أُرِيد الِانْصِرَاف. قَالَ: فتعجلي ثَوَاب الصَّلَاة عَليّ. فَقَامَتْ فَانْصَرفت، فَلَمَّا رَآهَا مولية تنفس الصعداء، وَمَات من سَاعَته.

Ibn Nāṣir reported upon the authority of al-'Umrī, "Abū 'Abdullāh al-Ḥūb-shānī was deeply in love with a woman named Ṣafrā al-'Alāqimiyyah, who was black. He grieved due to his love for her to such an extent that he neared death. So, some of his family members said to her master, 'If you send Ṣafrā to Abū 'Abdullāh al-Ḥubshānī he may regain his senses due to seeing her.' Her master ceded to this. When she entered his presence, she said to him, 'How are you this morning O Abā 'Abdullāh?' He replied, 'I am fine so long as you do not leave me.' She said, 'What is it that you desire?' He replied, 'Being close to you.' She said, 'What is it that causes you grief from me?' He replied, 'Your love.' She said, 'Do you wish to make a bequest?' He replied, 'I bequeath to you if they accept it from me.' She said, 'I wish to leave.' He replied, 'You wish to hasten in the reward of praying upon me (i.e. the funeral prayer)?' She stood and left. When he saw her leaving, he let out a sigh and subsequently died.

الْبَاب الْخَامِس وَالْعشْرُونَ
Chapter Twenty Five

فِي ذكر أَبنَاء الحبشيات من قُرَيْش
In Mention of the Sons of Ḥabashī Women from Quraysh

[They are:]

نَضْلَة بن هَاشم بن عبد منَاف بن قصي، نفَيْل بن عبد الْعُزَّى الْعَدوي، عَمْرو بن ربيعَة بن حبيب، الْخطاب بن نفَيْل الْعَدوي، الْحَارِث بن أبي ربيعَة المَخْزُومِي، عُثْمَان بن الْحُوَيْرِث بن أَسد بن عبد الْعُزَّى، صَفْوَان بن أُميَّة بن خلف الجُمَحِي، هِشَام بن عقبَة بن أبي معيط، مَالك بن عبد اللَّهِ بن جدعَان، عبيد اللَّهِ بن عبد اللَّهِ بن أبي ملكية، المُهَاجر بن قنفذ بن عَمْرو، مسافع بن عِيَاض بن صَخْر التَّيْمِيّ، عَمْرو بن الْعَاصِ بن وَائِل [السَّهْمِي] قرظة بن عبد، عَمْرو بن نَوْفَل بن عبد منَاف، مَالك بن حسن بن عَامر بن لؤَي، عبد اللَّهِ بن قيس بن عبد اللَّهِ بن الزبير، سَمُرَة بن حبيب بن عبد شمس، عبد اللَّهِ بن زَمعَة من بني عَامر بن لؤَي، عَمْرو بن هصيص بن كَعْب بن لؤَي، يعلى بن الْوَلِيد بن عقبَة بن أبي معيط، عبد اللَّهِ بن عبد اللَّهِ بن عَامر بن كريز، مُحَمَّد بن عَليّ بن مُوسَى بن جَعْفَر بن مُحَمَّد بن عَليّ بن الْحُسَيْن، جَعْفَر بن إِسْمَاعِيل بن مُوسَى بن جَعْفَر، عبيد اللَّهِ بن حَمْزَة بن مُوسَى بن جَعْفَر، مُحَمَّد وجعفر ابْنا إِبْرَاهِيم بن حسن بن حسن وأبوهما سُلَيْمَان بن حسن من بني عقيل بن أبي طَالب، مُحَمَّد بن دَاوُد بن مُحَمَّد من بني الْحسن بن عَليّ، أَحْمد بن عبد الْملك من ولد عُثْمَان بن

عَفَّان، أَحْمد بن مُحَمَّد بن صَالح المَخْزُومِي، الْعَبَّاس بن المعتصم، هبة اللَّهِ بن إِبْرَاهِيم بن الْمهْدي، مُحَمَّد بن عبد اللَّهِ بن إِسْحَاق الْمهْدي، عِيسَى وجعفر ابْنا أبي جَعْفَر الْمَنْصُور، الْعَبَّاس بن مُحَمَّد بن عَليّ بن عبد اللَّهِ بن الْعَبَّاس، عبد الْوَهَّاب بن إِبْرَاهِيم بن مُحَمَّد.

Naḍlah ibn Hāshim ibn 'Abd Manāf ibn Quṣay, Nufayl ibn 'Abd al-'Uzzā al-'Adawī, 'Amr ibn Rabī'ah ibn Ḥabīb, al-Khaṭṭāb ibn Nufayl al-'Adawī, al-Hārith ibn Abī Rabī'ah al-Makhzūmī, 'Uthmān ibn al-Ḥuwayrith ibn Asad ibn 'Abd al-'Uzzā, Ṣafwān ibn Umayyah ibn Khalf al-Jumaḥī, Hishām ibn 'Uqbah ibn Abī Mua'yṭ, Mālik ibn 'Abdullāh ibn Jad'ān, 'Ubaydullāh ibn 'Abdullāh ibn Abī Mulakīah, al-Muhājir ibn Qunfudh ibn 'Amr, Musāfi' ibn 'Iyāḍ ibn Ṣakhr al-Taymī, 'Amr ibn al-'Āṣ ibn Wā'il al-Suhamī, Furẓat ibn 'Abd, 'Amr ibn Nawfal ibn 'Abd Manāf, Mālik ibn Ḥasan ibn 'Āmir ibn L'uay, 'Abdullāh ibn Qays ibn 'Abdullāh ibn al-Zubayr, Sumrah ibn Ḥabīb ibn 'Abd Shams, 'Abdullāh ibn Zam'ah from Banī 'Āmir ibn L'uay, 'Amr ibn Haṣīṣ ibn K'ab ibn L'uay, Ya'lā ibn al-Walīd ibn 'Uqbah ibn Abī Mua'īṭ, 'Abdullāh ibn 'Abdullāh ibn 'Āmir ibn Kurayz, Muḥammad ibn 'Alī ibn Mūsā ibn Ja'far ibn Muḥammad ibn 'Alī ibn al-Ḥusayn, Ja'far ibn Ismā'īl ibn Mūsā ibn Ja'far, 'Ubaydullāh ibn Ḥamzah ibn Mūsā ibn Ja'far, Muḥammad and Ja'far the sons of Ibrāhīm ibn Ḥasan ibn Ḥasan whose father was Sulaymān ibn Ḥasan from Banī 'Aqīl ibn Abī Ṭālib, Muḥammad ibn Dāwūd ibn Muḥammad from Banī al-Ḥasan ibn 'Alī, Aḥmad ibn 'Abd al-Malik from the sons of 'Uthmān ibn 'Affān, Aḥmad ibn Muḥammad ibn Ṣāliḥ al-Makhzūmī, al-'Abbās ibn al-Mu'taṣim, Hibbatullāh ibn Ibrāhīm ibn al-Mahdī, Muḥammad ibn 'Abdullāh ibn Isḥāq al-Mahdī, 'Īsā and Ja'far the sons of Abī Ja'far al-Manṣūr, al-'Abbās ibn Muḥammad ibn 'Alī ibn 'Abdullāh ibn al-'Abbās, and 'Abd al-Wahhāb ibn Ibrāhīm ibn Muḥammad.

وَمن أَبناء السنديات

From the sons of Sindī women were:

مُحَمَّد بن الْحَنَفِيَّة، وَعلي بن الْحُسَيْن بن عَليّ بن أبي طَالب، وَسَعِيد بن هِشَام بن عبد الْملك بن مَرْوَان.

Muḥammad ibn al-Ḥanafiyyah, ʿAlī ibn al-Ḥusayn ibn ʿAlī ibn Abī Ṭālib, and Saʿīd ibn Hishām ibn ʿAbd al-Malik ibn Marwān.

وَمن أَوْلَاد الْجَوَارِي الصفر

Amongst the children of the yellow bondmaidens was:

شهريار

Shahrayār.

[١٦٩] أَنبأَنَا ابْن نَاصِر قَالَ أنبأ الْمُبَارك بن عبد الْجَبَّار قَالَ أنبأ الْجَوْهَرِي قَالَ حَدثنِي ابْن حيوية قَالَ: ثَنَا ابْن خلف قَالَ حَدثنِي أَحْمد بن الْهَيْثَم ابْن فراس عَن عمرَان الْكَلْبِيّ قَالَ: كَانَت مُلُوك الْأَعَاجِم إِنَّمَا تحجمهم النِّسَاء، فَأَرَادَ كسْرَى أَن يحتجم فَأَتَتْهُ الْحجامَة، وَكَانَت صفراء طَوِيلَة ضخمة جميلَة، فَأَلْقت ثِيَابهَا - وَكَذَا كَانُوا يصنعون - ثمَّ أدخلت كسْرَى بَين فخذيها فاشتهاها كسْرَى فَوَقعت بِقَلْبِه، فَوَقع عَلَيْهَا فَولدت شهريار.

Ibn Nāṣir reported to us upon the authority of ʿImrān ibn al-Kalbī, "The kings of the non-Arabs would receive cupping from the women. When the Kisrā (the Persian ruler) would wish to be cupped, his cupper would come. She was a tall, large, beautiful yellow woman. She would take off her clothes—as was their practice—and then sit the Kisrā between her thighs. The Kisrā desired her and fell in love with her. And due to this relationship Shahrayār was born."

الْبَاب السَّادِس وَالْعشْرُونَ
Chapter Twenty Six

فِي مواعظ ووصايا
In exhortation and counsel

قَالَ الْمُصَنّف: لما سطرت فِيمَا وضعت لَهُ هَذَا الْكتاب مَا يَكْفِي من ذكر أكَابِر هَذَا الْجِنْس آثرت أَن أختمه بمواعظ ووصايا وأذكار وأدعية ينظر فِيهَا من وضعت هَذَا الْكتاب لأَجله.

The author said: As I have written enough to satisfy the purpose of this book, i.e. in mention of the great people of this race, I deem it appropriate to end it with exhortation, counsel, *dhikr* and supplications that the one whom the book is addressed to will benefit from.

أما المواعظ والوصايا المنقولة فقد سَمِعت، وَمن الْعَادة حب المستطرف وَاخْتِيَار المتجدد، فقد جعلت هَذَا الْبَاب مُشْتَمِلًا على كَلَامي وَحده.

In terms of the exhortations and counsels which have been transmitted (i.e. from scholars of the past) then these have already been heard, however it is the nature [of humans] to desire novelties and to prefer fresh material. And it is due to these reasons that I have crafted this chapter based upon my words alone.

فصل
Section

إن المواعظ قد أفصحت وأعربت، غير أَن الزخارف للاحظ قد أدهشت وأعجبت، وَإِنَّمَا تقطع مراحل الْجد بالعزم وَالصَّبْر، وَنظر اللبيب الْمجد إِلَى آخر الْأَمر.

Exhortations have been explicit and expressive but decorations and adornments have amused and attracted whoever noticed them. Hardship is overcome with determination and patience, and the hard-working who is wise always focusses on the final destination.

يَا من سينأى عَنهُ بنيه　　كَمَا نأى عَنهُ أَبوهُ

مثل لنَفسك قَوْلهم　　جَاءَ الْيَقِين فوجهوه

وتحللوا من ظلمه　　قبل الْممَات وحللوه

O the one who is to be distanced from his children, just as his father was distanced from him.

Keep in mind the statement, certainty has come and they put him in the right direction.

They cleared themselves from his oppression, before death, and they cleared him too.

يَا مجموعا سيبدد عَن قريب، لَا تبدد الْأَوَامِر، فتندم يَوْم جمع مبددك. جبال الدُّنْيَا خيال يغر الغر، المتمسك بهَا يلْعَب بلعاب الشَّمْس.

O you who will shortly decompose, do not neglect the religious orders so you do not regret this dearly on the day your decomposed parts will rejoin. The mountains of this world are merely a delusion that would bait only the inexperienced; the example of the one who is attached to it is like a person playing with the rays of sun.

وَالله لَو كَانَت الدُّنْيَا بأجمعها　　تبقى علينا وَيَأْتِي رزقها غَدا

مَا كَانَ من حق حر أَن يذل لَهَا　　فَكيف وَهِي مَتَاع يضمحل غَدا

By Allāh, if this worldly life is ours, and its provisions come for us tomorrow,

No free person should exert effort for it, so what is the case when it is destined to expire and vanish!

يَا هَذَا، حَاكم نَفسك عِنْد حَاكم عقلك، لَا عِنْد قَاضِي هَوَاك، فحاكم الْعقل دين، وقاضي الْهوى يجور.

O reader, control your soul by judging with your intelligence and abstain from making your desires as the adjudicator [for your actions.] Indeed, the one who judges with his intelligence will be pious, and the one whose judge is his desires will be a wrongdoer.

من قبل مشورة الْعقل لم يتجرع: لَو، وليت.

And from the aspect of advice regarding the mind: do not let it indulge in thoughts of "if" or "would that".

فصل
Section

وَمِمَّا أوصِي بِهِ أَن أَقُول: يَنْبَغِي لمن رزق الذِّهْن أَن لَا يتْرك الْفِكر فِيمَا بَين يَدَيْهِ، وَفِيمَا خلق لَهُ، وليعلم أَنه فِي مجَاز إِلَى دَار مجازاة، وَفِي كل لَحْظَة للمنايا رَسُول، وبقرب الرحيل نَذِير، وَكم بَغت مطمئن، ومهاد الْحَسْرَة فِي الْقَبْر مستخشن رعب للغب، فِيمَا يحلو عواقبه مستحسن، فَيَنْبَغِي للْعَبد المتيقظ أَن لَا يخلي نفسا من أنفاسه عَن فعل خير، فَإِن كل نفس خزانَة، وليعد لكل عمل جَوَابا، فَإِن السُّؤَال عَنهُ لَا بُد مِنْهُ، وليتأهب للرحلة الَّتِي لَا يدْرِي مَتى تقع، وليراقب من يرَاهُ سرا وَعَلَانِيَة، فَإِنَّهُ إِن تكلم سمع، وَإِن نظر رأى، وَإِن تفكر علم، وَالْجنَّة الْيَوْم فِي السَّمَاء تزخرف، وَالنَّار تَحت الأَرْض توقد.

That which I advise is as follows: It is necessary for the one given intelligence that he does not neglect thought in that which is before him and that which has been created for him. However, he should know that the world he finds himself in is merely a passageway to the terminal abode, and that within every moment is a messenger for death, for merely the journey drawing close serves as adequate alarm. How many an unprepared have been unexpectedly overcome? And there is a resting place encumbered with horror in the grave, it is coarse and terrible. The vigilant slave should seek to do good with every breath he inhales, for each breath inhaled is the likeness of a chamber. One must prepare himself with an answer for each deed, for there will certainly be questions posed regarding them. Likewise, he must be ready for the journey upon which he does not know when he will embark. He must pay heed to the One observing his actions—the silent and the open, for what one speaks He hears, what one sees He witnesses and what one thinks He comprehends. Paradise is decorated in the heavens whilst the Fire is kindled under the earth.

والقبر عَن قَلِيل يحْفر، والملكان عَن يَمِين وشمال، والصحائف تملأ بِالْخَيرِ أَو الشَّرّ، فاغتنم يَا هَذَا صحتك فِي هَذَا الزَّمن قبل وجود الزَّمن، واعمر دَار الْبَقَاء بإنقاص من دَار الفناء، وَإِيَّاك أَن تغفل عَن نَفسك، فَإِن الْمُؤمن أَسِير فِي الدُّنْيَا يسْعَى فِي فكاك رقبته، وَلَا تذْهب لَحْظَة إِلَّا فِي فعل خير، وَأَقل مَرَاتِب الْأَفْعَال الْإِبَاحَة، واستوثق من قفل الْبَصَر وغلق اللِّسَان، فَإِنَّهُ إِن فتحهما الْهوى نهب مَا فِي الْقلب من الْخَيْر. وزاحم الْفُضَلَاء فِي أَعْمَالهم، وَقد أجمع الْحُكَمَاء أَنه لَا تنَال رَاحَة براحة، وَمثل لنَفسك عَاقِبَة الطَّاعَة ومغبة الْمعْصِيَة، فَكَأَنَّهُ مَا شبع من شبع، وَلَا التذ من عصى، وَلَا تألم من صَبر، وَأَيْنَ لَذَّة [لقْمَة] آدم؟ وَأَيْنَ مشقة صَبر يُوسُف؟ وَاحْذَرْ من مُخَالطَة أهل هَذَا الزَّمَان، فَإِن الطَّبْع يسرق عادات المعاشرين، ولتكن مخالطتك للسلف بالاطلاع على أَحْوَالهم. وحادث الْقُرْآن بالفكر فِيهِ فِي الخلوات، وتصفح جهاز الرحيل قبل أَن تفاجأ بَغْتَة، فَلَا ترى عندك غير النَّدَم.

One's grave is soon to be dug and [he should bear in mind,] the two angels of the left and right and the parchments within which is recorded the good deeds and the bad. So take advantage, O reader, of your health in your lifespan before it elapses. Construct for yourself the everlasting abode through the means of this transient one. Be heedful, for the faithful are prisoners in this world, constantly striving to free themselves (i.e. from the punishment in the hereafter). Do not let a moment pass except in the performance of good deeds, and do not overindulge in that which is permissible (*mubāḥ*). Be sure to control your eyes and fasten your tongue, for indeed if they are opened by lust then the goodness within the heart will be spoiled. Compete with the deeds of the pious. All sages agree that comfort is not attained through comfort, and take as motivation the consequence of obedience and the fruit of sinfulness. Then, it will be as if the one who satiates himself has never done so before, the sinner has never enjoyed his sin, and as if the patient has never suffered before. Where is the delight of Ādam's bite and where is the hardship of Yūsuf's patience? Be weary of your mixing with people of this time for indeed it is in man's nature to adopt the practices of his contemporaries, rather mix with the Salaf by acquainting yourself with their conditions and lifestyle. Study the Qur'ān by contemplating it during your times of solitude. Make sure of the provisions you have—which you will need for the coming journey—before death takes you by surprise and leaves you with naught but regret.

الْبَاب السَّابِع وَالْعشْرُون
Chapter Twenty Seven

فِيهِ أذكار وتسبيحات
Words of Remembrance and Glorification of Allāh

قَالَ الْمُصَنّف: كثير من النَّاس قد أولعوا بأذكار وتسبيحات لَا تثبت عَن رَسُول اللَّهِ - صَلَّى اللَّهُ عَلَيْهِ وَسَلَّمَ - وَلَا لَهَا أصل، فآثرت أَن أذكر من الصِّحَاح مَا يكون عَلَيْهِ الِاعْتِمَاد.

The author said: Many people are infatuated with certain *adhkār* (words of remembrance) and *tasbīḥāt* (words of glorification) which are not established from the Messenger of Allāh ﷺ and which do not have any basis. Thus, I deemed it appropriate to mention some of the authentic forms of *dhikr* and *tasbīḥ* which can be relied upon.

أفضل الْأَذْكَار تِلَاوَة الْقُرْآن:

The best form of *dhikr* is recitation of the Qur'ān:

[١٧٠] فقد روى عبد اللَّهِ بن عَمْرو عَن النَّبِي - صَلَّى اللَّهُ عَلَيْهِ وَسَلَّمَ - أَنه قَالَ: ((يُقَال لصَاحب الْقُرْآن اقْرَأ وارق، ورتل كَمَا كنت ترتل فِي الدُّنْيَا، فَإِن منزلتك عِنْد آخر آيَة تقرؤها)).

'Abdullāh ibn 'Amr reported from the Prophet ﷺ, "The companion of the Qur'ān will be told [on the Day of Judgement,] 'Recite and ascend, as you would do so in the *dunyā*, for your station will be correspondent to the last *āyah* you recite.'"[78]

وَأَما غَيرهُ مِنَ الْأَذْكَارِ:

As for other forms of *adhkār*:

[١٧١] فَفِي الصَّحِيحَيْنِ مِن حَدِيثِ أَبِي هُرَيْرَةَ عَنِ النَّبِي - صَلَّى اللَّهُ عَلَيْهِ وَسَلَّمَ - أَنَّهُ قَالَ: ((كلمتان خفيفتان على اللِّسَان، ثقيلتان فِي الْمِيزَان، حبيبتان إِلَى الرَّحْمَن: سُبْحَانَ اللَّهِ وَبِحَمْدِهِ، سُبْحَانَ اللَّهِ الْعَظِيمِ)).

In the two *Ṣaḥīḥs* (i.e. the books of al-Bukhārī and Muslim) there is the ḥadīth of Abī Hurayrah wherein the Prophet ﷺ said, "Two words are light upon the tongue yet heavy upon the scale and beloved to al-Raḥmān: *subḥānallāhi wa biḥamdihi, subḥānallāhi al-ʿaẓīm*."

[١٧٢] وَفِي صَحِيحِ الْبُخَارِيّ مِن حَدِيثِ أَبِي هُرَيْرَةَ عَنِ النَّبِي - صَلَّى اللَّهُ عَلَيْهِ وَسَلَّمَ - أَنَّهُ قَالَ: ((من قَالَ: سُبْحَانَ اللَّهِ وَبِحَمْدِهِ فِي يَوْمٍ مِائَةَ مرَّةٍ حطت خطاياه وَإِن كَانَت مثل زبد الْبَحْر)).

In *Ṣaḥīḥ al-Bukhārī* there is the ḥadīth of Abī Hurayrah from the Prophet ﷺ, "Whomsoever states '*subḥānallāhi wa biḥamdihi*' one hundred times within a day, his sins will be forgiven even if they are as much as the foam of the sea."

[١٧٣] وَفِي أَفْرَادِ مُسلِم مِن حَدِيثِ أَبِي ذَرٍ قَالَ: سُئِلَ رَسُول الله أَي الْكَلَام أفضل؟ فَقَالَ: ((سُبْحَانَ الله وَبِحَمْدِهِ)).

There is another narration which was only reported by Muslim, that being the ḥadīth of Abī Dhar, "The Messenger of Allāh ﷺ was asked, 'Which speech is the most meritorious?' He replied, '*Subḥānallāhi wa biḥamdihi*.'"

---

78 Reported by Imām Aḥmad in *al-Musnad* (2/192), al-Tirmidhī in his *Sunan* (8/117)—who graded it as *ḥasan ṣaḥīḥ*, al-Nasā'ī in *Faḍā'il al-Qur'ān* (97), and al-Ḥākim in *al-Mustadrak* (1/552)—which al-Dhahabī graded as *ṣaḥīḥ*.

[١٧٤] وَفِي أَفْرَاده من حَدِيث جوَيْرِية قَالَت: أَتى عَليّ رَسُول اللَّهِ - صَلَّى اللَّهُ عَلَيْهِ وَسَلَّمَ - غدْوَة وَأنا أسبح، ثمَّ انْطلق لِحَاجَتِهِ، ثمَّ رَجَعَ قَرِيبا من نصف النَّهَار، فَقَالَ: أما زلت قَاعِدَة؟ قلت: نعم فَقَالَ: أَلا أعلمك كَلِمَات لَو عدلن بِهن عدلتهن، أَو وزن بِهن وزنتهن - يَعْنِي جَمِيع مَا سبحت -: سُبْحَانَ اللَّهِ عدد خلقه (ثَلَاث مَرَّات) سُبْحَانَ اللَّهِ زنة عَرْشه (ثَلَاث مَرَّات) ، سُبْحَانَ اللَّهِ رضَا نَفسه (ثَلَاث مَرَّات)، سُبْحَانَ اللَّهِ مداد كَلِمَاته (ثَلَاث مَرَّات) .

In another ḥadīth collected only by Muslim, Juwayriyyah said, 'The Messenger of Allāh ﷺ came to me one morning whilst I was engaged in *tasbīḥ*. Then he left due to a need of his and returned at approximately the middle of the day. He said to me, 'Are you still engaged in *tasbīḥ*?' I replied affirmatively, so he said, 'Should I not teach some words which if placed against yours (i.e. the words of *tasbīḥ* she made) would outweigh them? (i) *Subḥānallāhi 'adada khalqihi* thrice, (ii) *subḥānallāhi zinata 'arshihi* thrice, (iii) *subḥānallāhi riḍā nafsihi* thrice, and (iv) *subḥānallāhi midāda kalimātihi* thrice.'"

الْبَاب الثَّامِن وَالْعشْرُونَ

Chapter Twenty Eight

فِي الْأَدْعِيَة

Supplications

[قَالَ المُصَنّف] : كثير من النَّاس يدعونَ من كتب لَا يوثق بهَا، وَلَا يَنْبَغِي أَن يتَخَيَّر إِلَّا الصَّحِيح.

The author said: Many of the people use supplications from unreliable books, and it is not correct to do so except from authentic sources.

فَأَما أَوْقَات الدُّعَاء:

As for the timings of *du'ā'*:

[١٧٥] فروى مُسلم فِي صَحِيحه من حَدِيث أبي هُرَيْرَة عَن النَّبِي - صَلَّى اللَّهُ عَلَيْهِ وَسَلَّمَ - أَنه قَالَ: ((أقرب مَا يكون العَبْد من ربه وَهُوَ ساجد؛ فَأَكْثرُوا الدُّعَاء)). وَمن أَوْقَات الدُّعَاء: عِنْد الْأَذَان، وَالْإِقَامَة، ونزول الْغَيْث، وَعند الْفَرَاغ من الختمة، وَإِذا وجد الْإِنْسَان خشوعا.

Muslim reported in his *Ṣaḥīḥ* on the authority of Abī Hurayrah that the Prophet ﷺ said, "The closest position the slave gets to his Lord is during the prostration, so be excessive in your *du'ā'* [whilst in prostration.]"

قَالَت أم الدَّرْدَاء: إِذا وجدت قشعريرة من الوجل فادع؛ فَإِن الدُّعَاء يُسْتَجَاب عِنْد ذَلِك.

And from the other times in which the *du'ā'* is preferred and accepted is between the *adhān* and *iqāmah*, during rainfall, upon finishing the Qur'ān, and whenever one finds *khushū'* (when one feels spiritual humility).

فصل

Section

فَأَما مَا يَبْتَدِئ بِهِ قبل الدُّعَاء، فقد قَالَ عمر: الدُّعَاء مَوْقُوف لَا يصعد مِنْهُ شَيْء حَتَّى تصلي على نبيك - صَلَّى اللَّهُ عَلَيْهِ وَسَلَّمَ -.

As for that which should precede the *du'ā'*, 'Umar said, "The *du'ā'* is suspended and will not rise from the individual until he sends *ṣalāh* upon the Prophet ﷺ."

وَمن آدَاب الدُّعَاء: تَقْدِيم التَّوْبَة، والتنزه من أكل الْحَرَام:

And from the etiquettes of *du'ā'* is that one precedes with seeking forgiveness and refrains from consuming the unlawful:

[١٧٦] فَفِي أَفْرَاد مُسلم من حَدِيث أبي هُرَيْرَة عَن النَّبِي - صَلَّى اللَّهُ عَلَيْهِ وَسَلَّمَ -: أَنه ذكر الرجل يُطِيل السّفر أَشْعَث أغبر ثمَّ يمد يَده إِلَى السَّمَاء: يَا رب، مطعمه حرَام ومشربه حرَام وملبسه حرَام وغذي بالحرام فَأنى يُسْتَجَاب لذَلِك.

Muslim reported the ḥadīth of Abī Hurayrah that the Prophet ﷺ recounted the case of a man who had journeyed far and was dishevelled and covered in dust. He then stretched out his hands to the sky and said, "O Lord," whilst his food was unlawful, his drink was unlawful, his clothing was unlawful and he had been sustained by the unlawful, so how could his call be answered?

وَمن آدابه: حسن الظَّن بالإجابة.

And from amongst the etiquettes of *du'ā'* is to think positively in regards to it being answered:

[١٧٧] فقد جَاءَ فِي الحَدِيث: ((ادعوا اللَّهِ وَأَنْتُم موقنون بالإجابة)).

It is mentioned in a ḥadīth, "Supplicate to Allāh whilst being certain of a response."

وَمن آدابه: حُضُور الْقلب:

And from amongst the etiquettes of *du'ā'* is for one's heart to be present:

[١٧٨] فقد قَالَ النَّبِي - صَلَّى اللَّهُ عَلَيْهِ وَسَلَّمَ -: ((لَا يقبل اللَّهِ الدُّعَاء من قلب غافل لاه)).

The Prophet ﷺ said, "Allāh does not accept the *du'ā'* from one whose heart is inattentive and heedless."[79]

❖❖❖

ذكر الدُّعَاء [عِنْد الكرب]

In mention of *du'ā's* during times of distress

[١٧٩] فَفِي الصَّحِيحَيْنِ من حَدِيث ابْن عَبَّاس عَن النَّبِي - صَلَّى اللَّهُ عَلَيْهِ وَسَلَّمَ - أَنه كَانَ يَقُول عِنْد الكرب: ((لَا إِلَه إِلَّا اللَّهِ الْعَظِيم الْحَلِيم، لَا إِلَه إِلَّا اللَّهِ رب الْعَرْش الْعَظِيم، لَا إِلَه إِلَّا اللَّهِ رب السَّمَاوَات وَالْأَرْض رب الْعَرْش الْكَرِيم)).

In the two *Ṣaḥīḥs* there is a ḥadīth on the authority of Ibn 'Abbās that the Prophet ﷺ would say during times of distress: "*Lā ilāha illallāhul 'aẓīmul ḥalīm* (No deity is worthy of worship except Allāh, the Most Great and the Most Forbearing), *lā ilāha illallāhu rabul 'arshil 'aẓīm* (No deity is worthy

---

79 This ḥadīth and the one before it are one. Both are found in *al-Musnad* of Imām Aḥmad, and the *Sunan* of al-Tirmidhī. Al-Tirmidhī said, "This ḥadīth is *gharīb* and we do not know of it except from this way."

of worship except Allāh, Lord of the great throne), *lā ilāha illallāhu rubbus samāwāti wa rabbul arḍi wa rabbul ʿarshil karīm* (No deity is worthy of worship except Allāh, Lord of the heavens, Lord of the earth, and Lord of the honourable throne)."

ذكر الدُّعَاء عِنْد الْهم والحزن

In mention of *duʿā's* during times of grief and sadness

[١٨٠] روى ابْن مَسْعُود عَن النَّبِي - صَلَّى اللَّهُ عَلَيْهِ وَسَلَّمَ - أَنه قَالَ: ((مَا أصَاب أحد هم قطّ وَلَا حزن فَقَالَ: اللَّهُمَّ إِنِّي عَبدك وَابْن عَبدك وَابْن أمتك، ناصيتي بِيَدِك مَاض فِي حكمك، عدل فِي قضاؤك، أسأَلك بِكُل اسْم هُوَ لَك سميت بِهِ نَفسك، أَو عَلمته أحدا من خلقك، أَو أنزلته فِي كتابك، أَو استأثرت بِهِ فِي علم الْغَيْب عنْدك أَن تجْعَل الْقُرْآن ربيع قلبِي وَنور صَدْرِي وجلاء حزني وَذَهَاب همي، إِلَّا أذهب اللَّهِ عز وَجل همه وحزنه، وأبدل مَكَانَهُ فرحا)).

Ibn Masʿūd reported that the Prophet ﷺ said, "If one of you is stricken with grief or sorrow and he says, '*Allāhumma innī ʿabduka wa ibn ʿabdika wa ibn amatika* (O Allāh, I am your slave, the son of your male and female slaves), *nāṣiyatī biyadika māḍin fī hukmuka* (my forelock is in Your hand, subject to your command), *ʿadlun fī qaḍāuka* (You are just in Your decree), *as'aluka bi kullismin huwa laka sammayta bihi nafsaka* (I implore you through every name of Yours, that which You named Yourself), *aw ʿallamtahu aḥadan min khalqika* (Or taught it to one of Your creation), *aw anzaltahu fī kitābika* (or revealed it in Your book), *aw istảtharta bihi fī ʿilmil ghaybi ʿindaka* (Or that You kept unseen from us), *an tajʿalal qur'ān rabīʿa qalbī wa nūr ṣadrī wa jakāʾa ḥuznī wa dhahāba hammī* (that You make the Qur'ān a solace for my heart, a light for my chest and the clearance of my sadness and grief)', except that Allāh ﷻ will remove his grief and sadness—replacing it with happiness."

ذكر الدُّعَاء عِنْد الْخَوْف من السُّلْطَان

In mention of *du'ā'* when one is fearful of the ruler

[١٨١] قَالَ ابْن مَسْعُود: ((إِذا كَانَ على أحدكُم سُلْطَان يخافه فَلْيقل: اللَّهِ رب السَّمَاوَات السَّبع وَرب الْعَرْش الْعَظِيم كن لي جارا من فلَان بن فلَان وأحزابه من خلقك أَن يفرط عَليّ أحد مِنْهُم أَو أَن يطغى، عز جَارك وَجل ثناؤك، وَلَا إِلَه إِلَّا أَنْت)).

Ibn Mas'ūd said, "If one of you is under a ruler whom instils fear within him, then say, '*Allāhumma rabbas samāwātis sab'i wa rabbal 'arshil 'aẓīm* (O Allāh, Lord of the seven heavens and the great throne), *kun lī jāran min fulān ibni fulānin wa aḥzābihi min khalqika* (Be my protector from so and so and his supporters from Your creation), *an yafruṭa 'alayya aḥadun min-hum aw yaṭghā* (Lest they exceed the limits with me or oppress me), *'azza jāruka wa jalla thanā'ukka, walā ilāha illa anta* (Mighty is Your protection and glorified is Your praise, and there is no deity worthy of being worshipped besides you).'"

❁❁❁

أدعية مأثورة

Authentic *du'ā's*

[١٨٢] روى البُخَارِيّ وَمُسلم فِي الصَّحِيحَيْنِ عَن عَائِشَة [رَضِي اللَّهِ عَنْهَا] أَن رَسُول اللَّهِ - صَلَّى اللَّهُ عَلَيْهِ وَسَلَّمَ - كَانَ يَدْعُو بهؤلاء الدَّعْوَات:

Al-Bukhārī and Muslim reported in their *Ṣaḥīḥs* on the authority of 'Ā'ishah ﵂ that the Messenger of Allāh ﷺ would supplicate with the following *du'ā's*:

((اللَّهُمَّ إِنِّي أعوذ بك من فتْنَة النَّار وَعَذَاب النَّار وفتنة الْقَبْر وَعَذَاب الْقَبْر وَمن شَرّ فتْنَة الْغنى وَمن شَرّ فتْنَة الْفقر وَأَعُوذ بك من فتْنَة الْمَسِيح الدَّجَّال. اللَّهُمَّ اغسل

خطاياي بِمَاء الثَّلج وَالْبرد، ونق قلبِي من الْخَطَايَا كَمَا نقيت الثَّوْب الْأَبْيَض من الدنس، وباعد بيني وَبَين خطاياي كَمَا باعدت بَين الْمشرق وَالْمغرب، اللَّهُمَّ إِنِّي أعوذ بك من الكسل والهرم والمأثم والمغرم)).

"*Allāhumma innī a'ūdhu bika min fitnatin nāri wa min 'adhābin nāri wa fitnatil qabr wa 'adhābil qabr* (O Allāh, I seek refuge in You from the trials of the Fire and its torment, and the trials of the grave and its torment), *wa min sharri fitnatil ghinā wa min sharri fitnatil faqri* (And from the evil of being tested with wealth and from the evils of being tested with poverty), *wa a'ūdhu bika min sharri fitnatil masīḥid dajjāli* (And I seek refuge in you from the trials of al-Masīh al-Dajjāl). *Allāhumma-ghsil qalbī khatāyāyī bimā'i al-thalji wal baradi* (O Allāh, cleanse my heart of sin with water of snow and hail), *wa naqqi qalbī min al-khatāyā kamā naqqayta al-thawba al-abyaḍ min al-danasi,* (and purify my heart from sin as You purify a white garment from filth) *wa bā'id baynī wa bayna khaṭāyā kamā bā'dta bayna al-mashriqi wal maghribi* (And distance me from my mistakes as you have distanced the east from the west), *allāhumma innī a'ūdhu bika min al-kasli wal harami wal-maghrimi wal math'ami wal maghrami* (O Allāh, I seek your refuge from laziness, senility, sin and being burdened with debt.)"

[١٨٣] وَفِي الصَّحِيحَيْنِ من حَدِيث أبي مُوسَى عَن النَّبِي - صَلَّى اللَّهُ عَلَيْهِ وَسَلَّمَ - أَنه كَانَ يَدْعُو بِهَذَا الدُّعَاء: ((اللَّهُمَّ اغْفِر لي جدي، وهزلي وخطئي، وعمدي، وكل ذَلِك عِنْدِي، اللَّهُمَّ اغْفِر لي مَا قدمت، وَمَا أخرت، وَمَا أسررت، وَمَا أعلنت، وَمَا أَنْت أعلم بِهِ مني، أَنْت الْمُقدم وَأَنت الْمُؤخر، وَأَنت على كل شَيْء قدير)).

In the *Ṣaḥiḥayn*, there is the ḥadīth on the authority of Abī Mūsā that the Prophet ﷺ would supplicate with the following *du'ā'*: *Allāhumma-ghfir lī jiddi wa hazli* (O Allāh, forgive me for what I have done in seriousness and in jest), *wa khaṭā'ī wa 'amdī* (My deliberated mistakes and the inadvertent), *wa kullu dhalika 'indī* (all of this emanated from myself). *Allāhumma-ghfir lī mā qaddamtu wa ma aḥzartu, wa mā asrartu, wa mā a'lantu, wa ma anta a'lamu bihi minni* (O Allāh forgive me for that which has been done and that which will occur in the future, that which I concealed and that which I did openly, and that which You are better aware of than me). *Anta-l-muqaddimu, wa anta-l-mu'akhkhiru; wa anta 'alā kulli shay'in qadīr* (You are the one who advances and the one who holds back, and You are over all things able)."

[١٨٤] وَفِي أَفْرَاد مُسلم من حَدِيث زيد بن أَرقم عَن النَّبِي - صَلَّى اللَّهُ عَلَيْهِ وَسَلَّمَ - أَنه كَانَ يَقُول: ((اللَّهُمَّ إِنِّي أعوذ بك من الْعَجز والكسل والجبن وَالْبخل والهرم وَعَذَاب الْقَبْر، اللَّهُمَّ آتِ نَفسِي تقواها، وزكها أَنْت خير من زكاها، أَنْت وَليهَا ومولاها، اللَّهُمَّ إِنِّي أعوذ بك من علم لَا ينفع وَمن قلب لَا يخشع وَمن دَعْوَة لَا يُسْتَجَاب لَهَا)).

Muslim reported the ḥadīth on the authority of Zayd ibn 'Arqam that the Prophet ﷺ would say: "*Allāhumma innī a'ūdhu bika minal 'ajzi wal-kasali, wal-jubni wal-bukhli, wal-harami wa 'adhābil qabri* (O Allāh I seek refuge in You from inability, laziness, cowardice, miserliness, senility, and the torment of the grave), *allāhumma āti nafsī taqwāhā, wa zakkihā, anta khayru man zakkāhā* (O Allāh grant my soul *taqwā* and purify it, for You are the greatest purifier), *anta waliyyuhā wa mawlāhā* (You are its guardian and its master), *allāhumma innī a'ūdhu bika min 'ilmin lā yanfa'u, wa min qalbin lā yakhsha'a, wa min da'watin lā yustajābu lahā* (O Allāh, I seek refuge in You from un-beneficial knowledge, a heart with no *khushū'* and from an unanswered prayer)."

[١٨٥] وَفِي أَفْرَاده من حَدِيث أبي هُرَيْرَة قَالَ: كَانَ رَسُول اللَّهِ - صَلَّى اللَّهُ عَلَيْهِ وَسَلَّمَ - يَقُول: ((اللَّهُمَّ أصلح لي ديني الَّذِي هُوَ عصمَة أَمْرِي، وَأَصْلح لي دنياي الَّتِي فِيهَا معاشي، وَأَصْلح لي آخرتي الَّتِي فِيهَا معادي، وَاجعَل الْحَيَاة زِيَادَة لي فِي كل خير وَاجعَل الْمَوْت رَاحَة لي من كل شَرّ)).

Muslim reported a ḥadīth upon the authority of Abī Hurayrah that the Messenger of Allāh ﷺ would say: "*Allāhumma aṣliḥ lī dīnī alladhī huwa 'iṣmatu amrī* (O Allāh, rectify my religious affairs in which my protection lies). *Wa aṣliḥ lī dunyā allatī fīhā ma'āshī* (And rectify my worldly life in which my livelihood lies). *Wa aṣliḥ lī ākhiratī allatī fīhā ma'ādī* (Rectify my hereafter in which my return lies). *Waj'ali l-ḥayāta ziyādatan lī fī kulli khayrin waj'ali l-mawta rāḥatan lī min kulli sharrin* (Make this life a means of increase for me in goodness, and make death a rest for me from every evil)."

[١٨٦] وَفِي أَفْرَاده من حَدِيث ابْن عَبَّاس قَالَ: كَانَ رَسُول الله - صَلَّى اللَّهُ عَلَيْهِ وَسَلَّم - يَدْعُو يَقُول: ((رب أعني وَلَا تعن عَليّ، وَانْصُرْنِي على من بغى عَليّ، رب اجْعَلنِي لَك شكارا، لَك ذكارا، لَك رهابا، لَك مطواعا، لَك مخبتا، إِلَيْك أواها منيبا، رب تقبل تَوْبَتِي، واغسل حوبتي، وأجب دَعْوَتِي، وَثَبت حجتي، وسدد لساني، وأهد قلبِي، واسلل سخيمة صَدْرِي)).

Muslim reported a ḥadīth upon the authority of Ibn 'Abbās that the Messenger of Allāh ﷺ would supplicate with: "*Rabbi a'innī wa lā tu'in 'alayya* (My Lord, help me and do not give help against me). *Wanṣurnī 'alā man baghā 'alayya* (Give me victory over those who vie against me). *Rabbi-j'alnī laka shakkāran, laka dhakkāran, laka rahhāban, laka miṭwā'an, laka mukhbitan, ilayka awwāhan munība* (My Lord, make me thankful to You, mindful of You, fearful of You, obedient to You, humble to You and penitent). *Rabbi taqabbal tawbatī, wa-ghsil ḥawbatī, wa ajib da'watī, wa thabbit ḥujjatī, wa saddid lisānī, wahdi qalbī, waslul sakhīmata ṣadrī* (My Lord, accept my repentance, wash away my misdeeds, answer my supplications, clearly establish my evidence, set right my tongue, guide my heart, and remove the malice from my chest)."

[١٨٧] وروى بُرَيْدَة قَالَ: سمع رَسُول اللَّهِ - صَلَّى اللَّهُ عَلَيْهِ وَسَلَّمَ - رجلا يَقُول: اللَّهُمَّ إِنِّي أَسأَلك بِأَنِّي أشهد أَنَّك اللَّهِ الَّذِي لَا إِلَه إِلَّا أَنْت الْأَحَد الصَّمد الَّذِي لم يلد وَلم يُولد وَلم يكن لَهُ كفوا أحد فَقَالَ: ((قد سَأَلَ باسم اللَّهِ الْأَعْظَم الَّذِي إِذا سُئِلَ بِهِ أعْطى، وَإِذا دعِي بِهِ أجَاب)).

Buraydah reported that the Prophet ﷺ heard a man saying, "*Allāhumma innī asaluka biannī ashhadu annaka aladhī lā ilāha illā anta, al-aḥadu al-ṣamadu aladhī lam yalid wa lam yūlad wa lam yakun lahu kufuwan aḥad* (O Allāh, I ask You by my testification that you are Allāh, there is no deity worthy of being worshipped besides You, You are the One, the Eternal, the One whom does not beget nor is begotten and to whom there is none comparable)." The Prophet said to this, "He has asked by the great name of Allāh, the one which when it is asked alongside, what is sought is given, and when it is supplicated alongside, the supplication is answered."

[١٨٨] وروى شَدَّاد بن أَوْس عَن النَّبِي - صَلَّى اللَّهُ عَلَيْهِ وَسَلَّمَ - قَالَ: ((إِذا أكثر النَّاس الذَّهَب وَالْفِضَّة، فَأَكْثرُوا هَؤُلَاءِ الْكَلِمَات: اللَّهُمَّ إِنِّي أسأَلك الثَّبَات فِي الْأَمر والعزيمة على الرشد، وَأَسأَلك شكر نِعْمَتك، وَأَسأَلك حسن عبادتك، وَأَسأَلك قلبا سليما، وَأَسأَلك لِسَانا صَادِقا، وَأَسأَلك من خير مَا تعلم، وَأَعُوذ بك من شَرّ مَا تعلم، وأستغفرك لما تعلم، إِنَّك أَنْت علام الغيوب)).

Shadād ibn Aws reported that the Prophet ﷺ said, "If [you see] the people amassing gold and silver, then greater a gathering is that of the words, "*Allāhumma innī as'aluka-thabāta fil-amri, wal 'azīmatu 'alā l-rushdi, wa as'aluka shukra ni'matika, wa as'aluka ḥusna 'ibādatika, wa as'aluka qalban salīman wa as'aluka lisānan ṣādiqan, wa as'aluka min khayri mā ta'lamu wa a'ūdhu bika min sharri mā ta'lamu, wa astaghfiruka limā ta'lamu, innaka anta 'allāmul-ghuyūb* (O Allāh, I ask you for firmness in all matters and resolution to remain upon the right way. I ask You to make me grateful for Your blessings. I ask You to perfect me in worshipping to You. I ask You for a sound heart and a truthful tongue. I ask you the good from what You know, seek refuge from the evil from what You know, and I seek forgiveness for what You know. Indeed, You have knowledge of the unseen)."

[١٨٩] وروى الْبَراء عَن النَّبِي - صَلَّى اللَّهُ عَلَيْهِ وَسَلَّم - أَنه قَالَ: ((إِذا أَرَادَ اللَّهِ بِعَبْد خيرا علمه هَؤُلَاءِ الكمات ثمَّ لم ينسهن: اللَّهم إِنِّي ضَعِيف فقوني فِي

رضاك، وَخذ إِلَى الْخَيْر بناصيتي، وَاجعَل الْإِسْلَام مُنْتَهى رضاي، اللَّهُمَّ إِنِّي ضَعِيف فقوني وَإِنِّي ذليل فأعزني، وَإِنِّي فَقير فأغنني)).

Al-Barā' reported that the Prophet ﷺ said, "If Allāh wishes good for His slave, he teaches him these words and then ensures that he will not forget them, '*Allāhumma innī ḍa'īf faqūnī fī riḍāka, wa khudh ilā l-khayri bināṣītī, waj'ali l-islāma muntahā riḍā'ī, allāhumma innī ḍa'īfun fa qawwinī, wa innī dhalīlun fa a'izzanī, wa innī faqīrun fa aghninī* (O Allāh, I am weak; strengthen me with the deeds that assure Your pleasure, and direct me towards the good. Make Islam be the utmost of my pleasure. O Allāh, I am weak so strengthen me, I am lowly so increase me in status. I am poor so enrich me).'"

نجز الْكتاب بِحَمْد اللَّهِ وعونه.

We have concluded the book, with the praise of Allāh and His aid.

وَالْحَمْد لله أَولا وَآخرا وَصلَاته على سيدنَا مُحَمَّد وَآله وَسَلَامه.

All praise be to Allāh, the first and the last, and may His *ṣalāt* and *salām* be upon our leader Muḥammad and his family.

Tanwīru 'l-Ghabashi fī Faḍli 's-Sūdāni wa 'l-Ḥabashi